Revolution from
Within

Also by Gloria Steinem

Outrageous Acts and Everyday Rebellions
Marilyn: Norma Jeane

Gloria Steinem

Revolution from Within

A Book of Self-Esteem

Little, Brown and Company

Boston Toronto London

First Paperback Edition

The author is grateful for permission to reprint the following copyrighted material:

Excerpt from "Time-Travel" from *Satan Says* by Sharon Olds. Copyright © 1980 by Sharon Olds. Used by permission of University of Pittsburgh Press.

Excerpt from "The Network of the Mother" from *Upstairs in the Garden, Poems Selected and New, 1968–1988*, by Robin Morgan. Copyright © 1990 by Robin Morgan. Used by permission of W. W. Norton & Company, Inc.

Excerpt from "An Ordinary Woman" from *Good Woman: Poems and a Memoir 1969–1980* by Lucille Clifton. Copyright © 1987 by BOA Editions Ltd. Used by permission of the publisher.

Excerpt from *Work Addiction* by Bryan Robinson, Ph.D. Copyright © 1989. Used by permission of the publisher, Health Communications, Inc., Deerfield Beach, Florida.

"Motheroot" from *Abiding Appalachia: Where Mountain and Atom Meet* by Marilou Awiakta. Copyright © 1978. Used by permission of St. Luke's Press.

"The low road" from *The Moon Is Always Female* by Marge Piercy. Copyright © 1980 by Marge Piercy. Reprinted by permission of Alfred A. Knopf, Inc.

Library of Congress Cataloging-in-Publication Data
Steinem, Gloria.
Revolution from within: a book of self-esteem
   / Gloria Steinem. — 1st ed.
       p.   cm.
   Includes bibliographical references and index.
   ISBN 0-316-81240-4 (hc)
   ISBN 0-316-81247-1 (pb)
   1. Self-respect.   I. Title.
BF697.5.S46S74   1991
155.2 — dc20   91-11356

10 9 8 7 6

MV-NY

Designed by Barbara Werden

Published simultaneously in Canada by Little, Brown & Company (Canada) Limited

Printed in the United States of America

*This book is intended for everyone — women, men,
children, and even nations — whose power has been
limited by a lack of self-esteem.*

*It is dedicated to anyone who respects
the unique self inside a child,*

*and inspired by women, whose
self-esteem is making the
deepest revolution.*

"You have come here to find what you already have."

BUDDHIST APHORISM

Contents

Revolution from Within

A Personal Preface

"The last thing we find in making
a book is to know what we must
put first."

BLAISE PASCAL

The idea for this book began a decade ago when even I, who had spent the previous dozen years working on external barriers to women's equality, had to admit there were internal ones, too. Wherever I traveled, I saw women who were smart, courageous, and valuable, who didn't *think* they were smart, courageous, or valuable — and this was true not only for women who were poor or otherwise doubly discriminated against, but for supposedly privileged and powerful women, too. It was as if the female spirit were a garden that had grown beneath the shadows of barriers for so long that it kept growing in the same pattern, even after some of the barriers were gone.

Yet when I looked for books on self-esteem to recommend, I found that, though many offered helpful advice, they focused on either the "inner" or the "outer" part of change: The "inner" books were the more spiritual and New Age ones, with an important message about the worth of each human being, but with little mention

3

of the external structures that undermine this worth in order to assure their own authority. The "outer" books told women how to look better, deal with stress better, and succeed in our many roles, but rarely mentioned that women's self-esteem might be damaged by the very expectation of filling all those roles; or that, if success alone could create self-esteem, there wouldn't be so many powerful men out there whose appetite for ever more success is insatiable, precisely because they feel an inner void that can't be filled.

Finally, with important exceptions (see the appendix on Bibliotherapy), a lot of self-help books put even more of a burden on the individual. I couldn't tell whether they were protecting the status quo or just had no faith in anyone's ability to change it, but they promised readers an internal power that would, in the words of one of them, "bind up mental and physical wounds, proclaim liberty to the fear-ridden mind, and liberate you completely from the limitations of poverty, failure, misery, lack, and frustration."[1] Somehow, that hadn't been my experience.

So I set out to research current thinking on the factors that affect self-esteem, and to combine this research with the experience of individual women. There were new studies on the long-lasting effects of alcoholism in our families, and a new willingness to believe in the frequency with which sexual abuse occurs in childhood. In many fields, the idea that hallmarks of low self-esteem weren't "normal" female characteristics was just beginning to be absorbed, and was producing some basic rethinking about such things as education for women and girls. I combined this research with women's personal stories, which are, like all personal accounts of any group that has been marginalized, our best textbooks: the only way to make our experience central.

But right away, this book had a mind of its own. It decided it had to be for men, too. After all, it's men with low self-esteem who give women (and other men) the most problems, from subtle condescension to grandiosity and outright violence; yet they are neglected as readers when they do look for help. I found many books directed at women's disease of empathy sickness (knowing what other people are feeling better than we know what *we* are feeling) but few for men with an empathy deficiency (an inability to know what other people are feeling, which causes men to get blindsided by emotions — sometimes even their own). There were books about low expectations for women in the public sphere, but almost none about low expectations for men in the private one; many books to comfort women trying to play a double role at home and on the job, but few for men whose work was killing them because they had no lives outside it. Even the welcome new books about men's regret at not having had nurturing fathers, and their resulting need to bond with other men, included no corresponding sentiment of regret for the inequality of their mothers, and men's resulting inability to bond with women as equals.

The more I talked to men as well as women, the more it seemed that inner feelings of incompleteness, emptiness, self-doubt, and self-hatred were the same, no matter who experienced them, and even if they were expressed in culturally opposite ways. I don't mean to gloss over the difficulties of equalizing power, even when there is the will to do so: to the overvalued and defensive, the urge to control and dominate others may be as organic as a mollusk's shell; and to the undervalued and resentful, the power to destroy the self (and others who resemble the self) may be the only power there is. But at both extremes — as well as in the more subtle areas between, where most of us struggle every day — people seemed to stop punishing others or themselves only when they gained some faith in their own unique, intrinsic worth. Making male readers feel welcome, this book decided, was the least it could do.

With this in mind — and with time newly freed by the fact that Australian feminists had taken on the responsibility for *Ms.*, the magazine that had been my major commitment for seventeen years — I spent months researching and interviewing, and more months writing 250 pages of psychological research, anecdotal examples, and philosophical prose. It was a peaceful time of sitting at my computer with my cat on my lap, traveling and *tummeling* less than I had at any time since I was in college, and finally having time to write something longer than an article.

Too peaceful. When Carmen Robinson, a friend from Montreal who is a family therapist, read that labored-over manuscript, she said, "I don't know how to tell you this — but I think you have a self-esteem problem. You forgot to put yourself in."

And it was true. I had lost my "voice," as writers say. It was as if I had been walking on a plate of glass just above the real world, able to see but not touch it. I began to understand with a terrible sureness that we teach what we need to learn and write what we need to know. I had felt drawn to the subject of self-esteem not only because other people needed it, but because I did. I had come to the burnt-out end of my ability to travel one kind of feverish, productive, but entirely externalized road — and I had no idea why.

But at the time Carmen identified this underlying problem for me, I also had a more immediate crisis. If you want to imagine what might be called a "situational" or perhaps a "traumatic" self-esteem problem, try thinking about a writer who has spent years with no time to write, feels she has an unwritten book in every toe and elbow and tooth, finally achieves the enormous luxury of enough solitude in which to begin, and then blows it on 250 of the wrong pages. Just at that moment, I also got a letter from something called *The Keri Report: Confidence and the American Woman,* a nationwide survey of 6,000 men and women sponsored by a hand-cream company, informing me that I had been named one of the ten most confident women in the United States.[2] It made me realize all over again what deep shit women were really in. Worst of all, I happened to open a paperback from college and discovered a note I had scribbled there: "Most writers write to say something about other people — and it doesn't last. Good writers write to find out about themselves — and it lasts forever." It was humbling — even depressing — to discover that I knew more in college than I did so many years later.

In the empty months that followed, I gave up those elaborate and intellectualized pages, but it took much longer for me to give up my image of myself as someone who helped other people through crises and never had any of my own. I began to realize that this writing crisis had been one of an underground series of them, some past and unsuccessfully buried, some present and denied — all of which were trying to tell me something. I had felt burnt out many times in the past twenty years, like so many people in social-justice movements — especially in the feminist movement, to which women bring the very training in selflessness we are trying to change — yet unlike other women with more self-vision, I believed so little in my own inner world that I couldn't stop to replenish it. Like a soldier who is wounded but won't lie down for fear of dying, I just kept marching. Why? Well, if I stopped, I would have given up the way I made myself "real" — that is, by being useful to people in the outside world — just as I had made myself "real" as a child by keeping so busy that I numbed the sad unreality at home where I looked after my mother.

And with that realization, emotions from the past began to flood into the present, often with a familiar feeling of hopelessness in the pit of my stomach, a feeling I thought I had left behind in childhood; sometimes with even more despair because this *was* my life, I was no longer at its beginning when I could look to the escape of growing up. I finally began to admit that I, too, was more aware of other people's feelings than my own; that I had been repeating the patterns of my childhood without recognizing them; that I had no idea why certain landscapes or sounds could make me ineffably sad; that my image of myself was very distant from other people's image of me; and that, in short, my childhood years — a part of my life I thought I had walled off — were still shaping the present as surely as a concealed magnet shapes metal dust. And as I acknowledged those effects of the distant past, I also uncovered anger about more recent events. After all the energy and years that I and many other women had poured into *Ms.*, the sheer injustice of being unable to scrape up the money needed to keep it going — despite the fact that we had lost less in nearly two decades than other serious magazines lose in a single year — had resulted in a profound feeling of depression that I was only now beginning to recognize.* It was partly the covering over of that emotion that had led to my calm, intellectualized, impersonal writing.

---

*Since that time, *Ms.* has changed hands again: in spite of investment from their home company, Fairfax, Australian feminists Anne Summers and Sandra Yates couldn't get enough advertising to keep *Ms.* going either. Now, though it is no longer woman-owned, its new owner, Lang Communications, agreed to let us try an experiment we had longed for: publishing an advertising-free *Ms.* that is entirely reader supported. I'm happy to say that with Robin Morgan as editor and with generous readers, *Ms.* is doing better than ever before. As consulting editor, I can now spend all my *Ms.* time on editorial content — and I never have to beg for another ad as long as I live. (For my exposé of advertising and women's media, see "Sex, Lies, and Advertising," *Ms.*, July/August 1990. To contact us, write *Ms.*, 230 Park Avenue, New York, New York 10169.)

Most of all, I began to understand there was a reason why, as a friend of mine put it, I was "co-dependent with the world." It was also why I was so moved by anyone whose plight seemed invisible. Carried over from my own childhood — and redoubled by growing up with the invisibility of a female in a male-run society — my sympathy reflected my own feelings of nonexistence. I had retreated to researching and reporting because I doubted the reality of my inner voice.

So I started over again in a very different way. For the next three years, I worked on this book — and it worked on me. I didn't end by writing an autobiography — I'm a long way from that, with many stored-up books to do first — but I did write much more personally. My hope is that each time you come upon a story of mine, you will turn inward and listen to a story told by your own inner voice. These last three years have taught me that, like the spider spinning her web, we create much of the outer world from within ourselves. "The universe as we know it," as Teilhard de Chardin said and as the new physics confirms, "is a joint product of the observer and the observed." We make progress by a constant spiraling back and forth between the inner world and the outer one, the personal and the political, the self and the circumstance. Nature doesn't move in a straight line, and as part of nature, neither do we.

I know, however, that each of us enters the spiral at a different place and should progress along its circles in the direction we have not been. For me, as Carmen said, this meant traveling inward, but for others, it may mean the reverse. Trying to approach self-esteem from many different vantage points on the spiral in the hope that this book will be useful to as many people as possible, I've included theory as well as practical exercises, scientific studies as well as a wide variety of stories and experiences that people have entrusted to me. To enable you to enter the spiral at whatever point is most useful to you, I've made each chapter, and each section within a chapter, a complete essay in itself. You may read everything in order, which will take you in concentric circles that move from the center (the self) to the cosmos (or at least as much of it as I've been able to comprehend), or you may pick out the headings that interest you — or proceed in any other way that suits you. To make this approach work, I've restated some themes and premises from chapter to chapter, but in forms different enough so I hope they will resonate, not repeat. I've also tried to explain concepts as I go and keep scholarly references to a minimum, so that no reader is made to feel she or he should have read eighty-nine other things *first*. My sixteen-year-old self in Toledo certainly needed this book: I didn't want to write anything that would make her feel excluded.

Throughout the text, there are also what I think of as modern parables — stories of people's growth that convey the process of change, mini-novels that are themselves self-contained. In reading the parables, I hope that, as with those of earlier times, you'll look beyond the specifics of the situation to the heart of the experience, and thus take from stories told by people of a different gender, sexuality, or ethnicity what is universal and true for you. I especially hope that men who read these pages will identify with women's parables, as we so often have empathized with theirs. As for their literal truth, when I use both first and last name, the story is real. When I use no name or only a first name, I'm either disguising someone who requested anonymity or creating one story from the similar experiences of more than one person, so that the result is, as a poet friend of mine used to say, "true, but only basically."

During the course of writing this book, I've not only looked inward, but I've gained a new prism through which to look outward. The past couple of years have been momentous ones for everyone on this earth: the long-overdue release of Nelson Mandela in South Africa, followed by the first steps away from apartheid and toward self-determination; the joyful destruction of the Berlin Wall and the disintegration of the Iron Curtain as a democratic spirit swept through Eastern Europe and the Soviet Union; a Gulf War in which the Iraqi people, with no opportunity to freely elect their leader, were bombed "into the Stone Age," and then left to the mercies of the dictator who had inspired the attack; and the thwarting of a Communist coup in the Soviet Union by ordinary citizens who took to the streets of Moscow to change the course of tanks — and of history. I've learned from these events that self-esteem plays as much a part in the destiny of nations as it does in the lives of individuals; that self-hatred leads to the need either to dominate or to be dominated; that citizens who refuse to obey anything but their own conscience can transform their countries; in short, that self-esteem is the basis of any real democracy.

It's clear, for instance, that the disproportionate number of writers and other artists among democratic movements is no accident. Because their work demands that they see with their own eyes and listen to an inner voice, they are more resistant to political indoctrination, and more trusted as spokespeople than those in other fields. It's a trust for which many pay a high price during authoritarian regimes — just as the curious or truthful child in a family of secrets and denial pays a high price — but they help others to trust their own eyes and instincts, too. In a Soviet press digest in the fall of 1989, for example, I read a speech by M. Antonov, himself a sociologist and scholar, in which he told the Writers Union of the U.S.S.R., "It was not from scholars or social scientists, but from writers, that we learned the very essence of what happened in the era of stagnation." He warned against losing self-authority once again if poverty were to make their country "a colony of the transnational corporations." In response, a speaker who identified himself as "from a peasant family" said of Marxism, "There is no human being in that doctrine, and that is why it leads us up blind alleys. . . . The only thing present in it is wages." In its presumption of speaking "for the human soul," he compared it to the hierarchy of the church.[3]

On New Year's Day 1990, when the playwright Václav Havel found himself addressing the people of Czechoslovakia as their president — a position he had not expected or sought, yet had earned by speaking his mind — he pled for an end to the national and personal insecurity that leads to repression. "Only a person or a nation self-confident in the best sense of the word," he said, "is capable of listening to the voice of others and accepting them as equal to oneself. Let us try to introduce self-confidence into the life of our community and into the conduct of nations."

When Estonia, a Soviet republic smaller than West Virginia, defied Moscow and demanded self-government, its strategy seemed fueled entirely by self-esteem. In what Estonians called "The Singing Revolution," 300,000 people, a fifth of the nation's population, turned out for a peaceful, joyous, but rebellious rally in the capital, singing, "Estonian, I am . . . free . . ." Dr. Maurji Lauristin, a tough-minded Estonian political leader, seemed amused at the surprise of a U.S. television commentator. "The strength of small people isn't in guns," she explained, "it is in intellect, it is in culture and traditions and in self-belief."[4]

In Romania, where the Communist government had outlawed abortion and contraception in its effort to force women to bear children, "Liberty, Democracy, and Abortion" was the official motto of the revolution, and the banner behind which both men and women marched through the streets. President Ceausescu had inspired this rebellion by declaring, "The fetus is the socialist property of the whole society," a conviction shared by anti-abortion movements in other countries, and he had required all employed women up to age forty-five to submit to regular fertility exams or be punished like military "deserters." As we saw so poignantly on television after he was overthrown, the result was nurseries full of malnourished, unheld, unloved children, many of whose mothers had died or been imprisoned because of illegal abortions, thus leaving their other children uncared for. "The state tried to own women, invade their bodies, compel their motherhood, kill their souls," said Gabriela Bocec, head of the Romanian Nurses' Association, who had seen the dimensions of suffering among women and children with her own eyes. "We marched out of self-respect."[5] So it was that a nurse, as unlikely a candidate for political leadership as a playwright, became one of this country's new democratic voices.

Here at home in the streets of New York City, I watched huge crowds cheering Nelson Mandela during his visit in the summer of 1990. There are almost no words to express the poignancy of seeing him honored as a world leader just a few blocks from the wharves where African women and men had once arrived and then been sold at auction; in the same city where Southern slaves had later fled via the Underground Railroad, only to be relegated first to Sugar Hill and then Harlem; and just a few miles from the place where only the summer before, a young African-American man, answering an ad to buy a car, had been killed for entering a white neighborhood. "When I was in school, we were taught to be ashamed of being African," said a woman standing next to me in the crowd. "They called us 'jungle bunnies' and names a lot worse — and now here's

Mandela. I can't tell you what a difference seeing him would have made to me when I was a kid." Later as I stood backstage in a Brooklyn theater watching schoolchildren file in to hear Winnie Mandela, who had carried on the fight outside prison walls, a six-year-old boy pointed at her with pride: "She looks like my mom!"

In that summer, I was not the only one to begin seeing self-esteem as the prerequisite for democracy — and for equal power within a democracy. Some of the California activists about whom I write in the first chapter met in Oslo with educators, psychologists, and health-care providers from eleven countries, including the U.S.S.R., Poland, and other nations of Eastern Europe. Topics of concern included how to decrease child abuse, alcoholism, prejudice, and other destructive behavior. Since studies show that low self-esteem correlates with both prejudice and violence — that people who have a negative view of themselves also tend to view other people and the world negatively[6] — representatives were interested in introducing self-esteem programs in schools. For the six Soviet delegates, the commitment to finding methods of developing self-esteem was even more basic, for they recognized that in Russia, where individual will had for so long been subordinated to the group, self-esteem was the most effective guarantor of the democratic freedoms they had just won. Other Eastern European countries had had some experience with democracy before Communism, but Russia was having its first open election in a thousand years.

Privately, the Soviet representatives told Robert Reasoner, a California educator and co-chair of that International Council for Self-Esteem formed in Oslo, that they had about three years of grace in which to put forward the central concept of self-esteem — the belief that each person counts and can make a difference — before there would be a right-wing coup against *glasnost*.

As it turned out, they were overly optimistic. In only one year, not three, a military coup was attempted by an authoritarian group within the Supreme Soviet. But those antidemocratic officials had themselves underestimated how contagious the idea of dignity and democracy could be. In late August of 1991, just as I was completing this book — and just as a First National Council for Self-Esteem was scheduled to meet near Moscow — Soviet citizens took their national future into their own hands by flooding into the streets in defiance of martial law, forming barricades to protect Boris Yeltsin and other elected leaders in their headquarters. As one old woman yelled up to the very young driver of a Soviet tank, "You can't do this, we were the ones who fed you when you were little — just leave." And he did.

It was an object lesson in ordinary people making a difference that Soviet citizens, and the world, would not soon forget. Listening to the reports of Boris Yeltsin's words as he called for people to resist the coup — on radio and television stations that Mikhail Gorbachev had set free, conscious that no democracy could survive unless people could hear each other's voices — I thought of all the studies I had been reading on the power of expectation. When teachers of randomly selected students are told their students are slow, they become slower; when teachers believe their students are gifted, they become more gifted. Yeltsin and other popular leaders expected people to take control of their own fate, and people did just that — an example of a leader's ability to free the powers of self-esteem.

Later, when I phoned Moscow on the assumption that tanks in the streets must have delayed that meeting of the First National Council for Self-Esteem, I was told no, it had gone right on. The Minister of Education had been there, and they were planning self-esteem programs for the schools.

I've noticed, too, that economists have begun to speak in terms of self-esteem. Development experts more comfortable with citing natural resources, capital, markets, and other "hard" quantifiable elements have begun to talk about such "soft" factors as "national inferiority complex," "national will," "basic worldview," "equality," and "belief in reward for work." In a deep sense, economic development without self-esteem is only another form of colonialism: an economic development ruled from the top, in which, whatever is being developed, it is not what people have decided for themselves, and thus it may develop products, but not people.

Consider the examples of Barbados and Haiti. Both are small island countries with similar crops and climate, a population mainly from West Africa, and a history of slavery and colonialism. Yet Barbados has had a representative system of government longer than the United States (indeed, it was part of the inspiration for our Constitution); its crime rate is lower, its life expectancy and literacy rates are just as high (or higher, if one takes as a measure the "functional illiteracy" of a third of all United States residents, not the official figure of 99 percent). When people from Barbados migrate to the U.S., they do better than the average African American whose family has been here for generations, and they earn about the same as the average European American (though if this were not a racist society, they probably would earn more, since immigrants from Barbados are often better educated than their white counterparts). On the other hand, Haiti is one of the world's poorest, most divided, least literate countries, with a history of cruel and corrupt dictatorships, a small middle class and a few wealthy in the midst of great poverty, and until very recently, a sadistic secret police who ruled by terror. Instead of an adult literacy rate of 99 percent, as in Barbados, it is 23 percent in Haiti; and though Haitian immigrants to the United States are often political refugees who are activist and educated, they don't yet occupy the leadership positions in the African-American and larger community that those from Barbados do.

The differences between the cultures of these two small nations have complex and deep roots: the British versus the French as colonial powers; an individualized Protestantism versus a hierarchical Catholicism as very different overlays on African spiritual traditions; and perhaps most important, the self-fulfilling prophecy of any system once it is entrenched. Because we tend to treat others as we have been treated, a trustworthy system leads to more trust, corruption leads to more corruption, violence to more violence. But all these factors can be summed up in the frequent cynicism among the poor of Haiti and the obsessive need for display among its rich rulers, contrasted with the sense of personal efficacy, irreverence, and pride among the people of Barbados: in other words, the marks of low and high self-esteem. As Dantes Bellegards, a Haitian writer early in this century, wrote about his country: "Everyone has two faces — one for those above him and one for those below" — a classic description of the character type created when self-authority is taken away, whether in a family or in a nation.

If such a clear contrast seems to be an idiosyncracy of two small agricultural countries, consider two industrialized nations among the ten largest in the world: Argentina and Australia. Both have great natural wealth, a large population of European immigrants, sad histories of brutality toward indigenous people (as does, of course, the United States), and large, rich, underpopulated areas. But Argentina's efforts at democracy have often fallen victim to cultlike military dictatorships; its society is divided into extremes of rich and poor, urban and rural; and its role as a refuge for Nazis and other escapees from democracy has become legendary. Australia, however, has a stable democracy, a per capita income almost three times higher than that in Argentina, far less violence and corruption, and a much smaller military. Even Australia's cult of masculinity is not as aggressive as that of Argentina. Since more immigrants went out of free will to Argentina than to Australia, which was largely a dumping ground for Britain's overcrowded prisons, one might think the difference in self-esteem would be reversed. But a fatalistic and sin-focused religion, economic extremes, generations of military regimes, and a tradition of political torture have plagued Argentineans, who are, of course, not intrinsically different from Australians.

Looking at Barbados and Australia as relatively positive examples, one societal hallmark of self-esteem seems to be an ability to both give and demand fairness, an expectation that extends from the personal to the political. There is at least a belief that the law, an institution before which all should be equal, has a duty to play no favorites; yet in Argentina and Haiti, there is rarely even this expectation. "People could make it against flood and pestilence," Brazilian novelist Jorge Amado wrote about similar problems in his own country, "but not against the laws; they went under."

When I was in college and my government professor said, "The family is the basic unit of the state," he described a paternalistic, hierarchical kind of family; yet somehow, he expected a perfect democracy to emerge from this model of inequality in which one parent lived "through" others, the other parent had authority "over" others, and the children were possessions with few personal rights, even under the law. Feminism is just beginning to change this earliest hierarchical paradigm, and to create a microcosm of democracy inside this group from which we acquire our deepest sense of self and human possibilities; yet we haven't begun to change even in our minds our image of nationalism. It remains insular and territorial, a dangerous anachronism on this fragile and shrinking planet where neither war nor environmental dangers can be contained by national boundaries anymore. Even those of us most skeptical about nationalism have drifted into considering it a necessary evil. How can we ask any group to go without it in the aftermath of classical colonialism, and the presence of racial, economic, and corporate colonialisms that often go just as deep?

But we can't afford old either/or prisons. We need to take a leap of the imagination and envision nations as the best kinds of families: the democratic ones we are trying to create in our own lives. A hierarchical family must be changed anyway if we are to stop producing leaders whose unexamined early lives are then played out on a national and international stage. Think of such current examples as Saddam Hussein, a boy beaten and tortured daily by his stepfather, who grew up to enjoy the close-up torture of others; or President Ceausescu, whose police state normalized his own earliest years of living in one room with nine siblings and an alcoholic, sadistic father. Think also of Ronald Reagan, who seems to have learned endless cheerful denial as the child of an alcoholic father; or George Bush, whose biographers describe a well-to-do childhood with an aristocratic, religious father who used a belt for discipline, controlled every aspect of family life, and insisted his sons compete, win, and become leaders, whether they wanted to or not. This is not to take free will away from them (or from us), or to excuse destructive behavior in them (or in us); for if anyone is willing or able to go back and confront those earliest years, feelings can be directed at their real sources instead of being expressed in bigger and bigger ways. But changing the way we raise children is the only long-term path to peace or arms control, and neither has ever been more crucial. As the feminist adage says, *The personal is political.*

When we imagine nation states, however, we could envision families that nurture self-esteem and unique talents in each person; that create independence, not dependence; and that produce people secure enough to take pleasure in empowering others. Even now, if we listen to a dictator or a humane revolutionary, we sense the difference in their motives: one wants to impose a vision, the other to help discover a shared vision; one promises benefits to some and punishment to others, the other knows that nothing benefits those who haven't participated in it, and that violence only produces violent people. In other words, one of the crucial differences between the despot and the creative leader is low self-esteem versus high self-esteem. And just as the point of a truly nurturing family is not to keep its members at home forever, the point of a nation is not to draw a line in the sand and keep its members behind it, but to create world citizens who are secure enough to treat others equally: not *worse than* in the "masculine" and colonial style, or *better than* in the colonized and "feminine" one, but *as well as*.

It's time to turn the feminist adage around. *The political is personal.*

A friend asked my hopes for this book. I began by quoting Thomas Carlyle: "The best effect of any book is that it excites the reader to self-activity." But then I remembered the message of chapter 3, perhaps best summed up in Vita Sackville-West's smart couplet:

> I worshipped dead men for their strength,
> Forgetting I was strong.

In the course of rewriting this book, I was able to uncover some of those forgotten strengths. If you learn a tenth as much from this book as I have, I'll be a happy writer.

One

What Is Self-Esteem?

"The notion of giving something a *name* is the vastest generative idea that was ever conceived."

SUZANNE K. LANGER

I The Plaza Parable

"The mind is its own place, and in itself
Can make a Heav'n of Hell, a Hell of Heav'n."
JOHN MILTON

As I write this, I'm still the same person who grew up mostly in a Midwestern, factory-working neighborhood where talk about "self-esteem" would have seemed like a luxury. In my memory of those times and that place, men were valued by what they did, women by how they looked and then by what their husbands did, and all of life was arranged (or so we thought) from the outside in.

This experience of living among good people who were made to feel *un*good by an economic class system imposed from above — people who often blamed themselves for hard times they had done nothing to deserve — left me with a permanent resistance to any self-help book or religion or psychological theory that tells us we can solve all our problems on our own. So did a later realization that sexual and racial caste systems are even deeper and less in our control than class is. After all, we know that if children are treated badly enough for long enough, they come to believe they are bad people. As adults, we often try to rationalize the world by asking what we did to deserve some instance of bad luck, violence, humiliation, or even illness.

As Susan Sontag wrote in *Illness as Metaphor,* many theories of disease "assign to the luckless ill the ultimate responsibility both for falling ill and for getting well." And we often accept this, for it gives us an illusion of control. As Princeton mayor Barbara Boggs Sigmund protested in the *New York Times* shortly before she died of the cancer that she had been courageously battling for years, "We humans would rather accept culpability than chaos. . . ."

That's why to this day, if I were forced to choose between "Bread and Roses" — the dual demands of nineteenth-century women millworkers who organized one of this country's first

21

strikes — I still would start with "bread" (and warmth and physical safety and a roof over everyone's head) before moving on to self-knowledge, self-expression, and other "roses." I still would balk at phrases like "She [or he] just has a self-esteem problem," as if this were something an individual *chose* to have.

But not until sometime in my thirties did I begin to suspect that there might be an internal center of power I was neglecting. Though the way I'd grown up had encouraged me to locate power almost anywhere but within myself, I began to be increasingly aware of its pinpoint of beginning within — my gender and neighborhood training notwithstanding.

And with this awareness, I gradually began to notice that many of the people I had been brought up to envy and see as powerful — mostly men from groups who were supposed to be the givers of approval — actually had the other half of the same problem I was experiencing. I had been raised to assume all power was outside myself, but they had been raised to place power almost nowhere but within themselves. Often, they were suffering, too. Just as the fantasy of no control was the enemy of my self-esteem, the fantasy of total control was the enemy of theirs. For both of us, the goal should have been a point of balance in between: a back-and-forth between the self and others, uniqueness and unity, the planned and the accidental, our internal selves and the universe. As wise women and men in every culture tell us: The art of life is not controlling what happens to us, but *using* what happens to us.

Like all great oaks, this understanding began with a very small acorn.

It was the late sixties, those days that were still pre-feminist for me. I didn't question the fact that male journalists with less experience than I were getting the political assignments that were my real interest. Instead, I was grateful to be writing profiles of visiting celebrities — a departure from the fashion and family subjects that female reporters were usually given — and this included an interview that was to take place over tea in the Palm Court of the Plaza Hotel.

Because the actor was very late, I waited while the assistant manager circled disapprovingly and finally approached. "Unescorted ladies," he announced loudly, were "absolutely not allowed" in the lobby. I told him I was a reporter waiting for an arriving guest who couldn't be contacted any other way — an explanation that sounded lame even to me. The manager escorted me firmly past curious by-standers and out the lobby door.

I was humiliated: Did I look like a prostitute? Was my trench coat too battered — or not battered enough? I was anxious: How was I going to find my subject and do my work? I decided to wait outside the revolving door in the hope of spotting the famous actor through its glass, but an hour passed with no success.

Later, I learned that he had arrived, failed to see me, and left. His press agent called my editor to complain that I had "stood up" his client. The actor missed his publicity, the editor missed a dead-line, and I missed a check that I needed to pay the rent. I also blamed myself for not figuring out how to "get the story" and worried about being demoted permanently back to the ghetto of "women's inter-est" articles I was trying to escape.

By coincidence a month or so later, I was assigned to interview another celebrity who was also staying at the Plaza. To avoid a sim-ilar fiasco, I had arranged to meet this one in his suite, but on my way through the lobby, I noticed my former nemesis standing guard. Somehow, I found myself lingering, as if rooted to the spot — and sure enough, the manager approached me with his same officious speech. But this time I was amazed to hear myself saying some very different things. I told him this was a public place where I had every legal right to be, and asked why he hadn't banished the several "unescorted men" in the lobby who might be male prostitutes. I also pointed out that since hotel staffs were well known to supply call girls in return for a percentage of their pay, perhaps he was just worried about losing a commission.

He looked quite startled — and let me stay. I called my subject and suggested we have tea downstairs after all. It turned out to be a newsworthy interview, and I remember writing it up with more ease than usual and delivering it with an odd sense of well-being.

What was the lesson of these two incidents? Clearly, the assis-tant manager and I were unchanged. I was even wearing the same trench coat and freelancing for the same publication. Only one thing was different: my self-esteem. It had been raised almost against my will — by contagion.

Between those two interviews, a woman doctor had made a reservation for herself and a party of friends at the Plaza's Oak Room, a public restaurant that was maintained as a male-only bastion at lunchtime on the grounds that female voices might disturb men's business meetings. When this woman was stopped at the Oak Room door for being the wrong gender of "Dr.," as she knew she would be, her lunch group of distinguished feminists turned into a spirited sidewalk picket line and held a press conference they had called in advance.

Now, I also had been invited to join this protest — and refused. In New York as in most cities, there were many public restaurants and bars that either excluded women altogether or wouldn't serve "unescorted ladies" (that is, any woman or group of women without the magical presence of one man). Certainly, I resented this, but protesting it in the Oak Room, a restaurant too expensive for most people, male or female, seemed a mistake. The only remedy was a city council ordinance banning discrimination in public places, and that would require democratic support. Besides, feminists were already being misrepresented in the media as white, middle class, and frivolous, a caricature that even then I knew was wrong: the first feminists I had heard of in the sixties were working-class women who broke the sex barrier in factory assembly lines, and the first I actually met were black women on welfare who compared that demeaning system to a gigantic husband who demanded sexual faithfulness (the no-man-in-the-house rule) in return for subsistence payments. If groups like those were not publicized — and if well-to-do women who lunched at the Plaza were — I feared this new movement's image would become even more distorted.

As it turned out, I was right about tactics and the media's continuing image of feminism: "whitemiddleclass" did become like one key on the typewriter of many journalists (though polls showed that black women were almost twice as likely to support feminist changes as white women were[1]). But I was very wrong about women's responses — including my own. For instance: By the time of that demonstration at the Plaza, I already had picketed for civil rights, against U.S. involvement in Vietnam, and with migrant farm workers, often in demonstrations that were far from tactically perfect; so why was I suddenly demanding perfection of women? When blacks or Jews had been kept out of restaurants and bars, expensive or not, I felt fine about protesting; so why couldn't I take my own half of the human race (which, after all, included half of all blacks and half of all Jews) just as seriously?

The truth was that I had internalized society's *un*serious estimate of all that was female — including myself. This was low self-esteem, not logic. Should a black woman demonstrate for the right to eat at dimestore lunch counters in the South, where she was barred by race, and then quietly leave when refused service at an expensive New York restaurant on account of sex? Of course not. The principle — and, more important, the result for one real woman — was the same. But I had been raised to consider any judgment based on sex alone less important than any judgment based on race, class, or anything else alone. In fact, if you counted up all groups in the world other than white women, I was valuing just about everybody more than I valued myself.

Nonetheless, all the excuses of my conscious mind couldn't keep my unconscious self from catching the contagious spirit of those women who picketed the Oak Room. When I faced the hotel manager again, I had glimpsed the world *as if women mattered.* By seeing through their eyes, I had begun to see through my own.

It still would be years before I understood the seriousness of my change of view. Much later, I recognized it in "Revolution," the essay of Polish journalist Ryszard Kapuscinski, who describes the moment when a man on the edge of a crowd looks back defiantly at a policeman — and when that policeman senses a sudden refusal to accept his defining gaze — as the imperceptible moment in which rebellion is born. "All books about all revolutions begin with a chapter that describes the decay of tottering authority or the misery and sufferings of the people," Kapuscinski writes. "They should begin with a psychological chapter — one that shows how a harassed, terrified man suddenly breaks his terror, stops being afraid. This unusual process — sometimes accomplished in an instant, like a shock — demands to be illustrated. Man gets rid of fear and feels free. Without that, there would be no revolution."[2]

But even then, this moment in a hotel lobby was my first inkling that there is a healthier self within each of us, just waiting for encouragement. It's such a common experience of unexpected strength that we have ordinary phrases for it: "I surprised myself," or "In spite of myself." In *The Red and the Black,* Stendhal called this inner self "a little friend." In Alice Walker's *The Color Purple,* Celie writes letters to a strong friend called God, but she is also writing to the strength within herself. Children create imaginary playmates, and athletes, musicians, and painters strive to free this true and spontaneous self in their work. Meditation, prayer, creativity — all these are ordinary ways of freeing an inner voice. It's a feeling of "clicking in" when that self is recognized, valued, discovered, *esteemed* — as if we literally plug into an inner energy that is ours alone, yet connects us to everything else.

To put it another way: I began to understand that self-esteem isn't everything; it's just that there's nothing without it.

II   *Modern Ideas and Ancient Wisdom*

"Happiness is self-contentedness."
ARISTOTLE, C. 300 B.C.

"Oft-times nothing profits more
Than self-esteem, grounded on just and right
Well manag'd."
JOHN MILTON, 1667

"Appreciating my own worth and importance
and having the character to be accountable for
myself and to act responsibly toward others."
OFFICIAL DEFINITION OF THE CALIFORNIA
TASK FORCE TO PROMOTE SELF-ESTEEM AND
PERSONAL AND SOCIAL RESPONSIBILITY, 1990

Several years ago, I opened a newspaper to discover that California's legislature had created a statewide Task Force to Promote Self-Esteem. In the phrase of Assemblyman John Vasconcellos, the legislator most responsible for its formation, self-esteem is a "social vaccine" against an epidemic of school dropouts, teenage pregnancy, domestic violence, drug and alcohol addiction, child abuse, and other destructions of the self and others. As chair of the Ways and Means Committee, he had convinced his pragmatic colleagues that a little money spent on prevention could reduce the skyrocketing billions being spent on welfare, illiteracy, drug programs, crowded prisons, overburdened courts, academic underachievement, and other public penalties of self-destructive behavior.

Finally, I thought, self-esteem is being presented with such pragmatism that even an outer-directed society like ours will take it seriously. Right?

Wrong. The Task Force captured our national imagination — but in quite a different way. "Hold on to your hot tubs," began one typical newspaper report. Other articles ridiculed this government interest in self-esteem as soft-headed California-think at best, and as a ridiculous misuse of public funds at worst.

Soon, self-esteem jokes were turning up in the monologues of television talk-show hosts. Garry Trudeau, creator of the literate, loony, delightful comic strip "Doonesbury," began to immortalize the Task Force's meetings in a nationally syndicated story about a fictional Task Force member, Barbara Ann ("Boopsie") Boopstein, an actress and mystic who was already well known to "Doonesbury" fans for her suspiciously Shirley MacLaine–like adventures. Since her qualifications included "twenty years of feeling good about myself" and "a history of out-of-body experiences," other Task Force members were not surprised when she turned out to be the channel for "a really good-looking 21,355-year-old warrior named Hunk-Ra," though they did question mildly whether Hunk-Ra should be allowed to vote. The "Doonesbury" series ended only after this ancient cynic had disrupted so many meetings with his un-Californian skepticism that both he and Boopsie were asked to move on.

I don't know whether popular misconceptions about self-esteem created this media ridicule, or vice versa, but in the case of the Task Force, it stuck. My picture of this group's work would have been very unserious, too, if I hadn't kept track of its proceedings over the three years of its legislative life. What I discovered was a very different story.

For instance: There had been more applications to serve on this Task Force than on any other body in state history — and this was true in spite of its heavy part-time work with no pay. The twenty-five members finally chosen were a very un-Boopsie-like group of ten women and fifteen men, a rainbow of European-American, African-American, Latin, and Asian-American leaders in education, small business, psychology, criminal justice, civil rights, sex discrimination, domestic violence, welfare, drug and alcohol abuse, religion, gay and lesbian rights, and the delivery of social services.

In the first stage of their work, they assembled and commissioned expert studies and scheduled ambitious, statewide public hearings to discover whether self-esteem was a root cause in any of seven major areas: "crime and violence, alcohol abuse, drug abuse, teenage pregnancy, child and spousal abuse, chronic welfare dependency, and failure to achieve in school." The outpouring of public interest and the unprecedented number of people asking to testify were the first clue that the Task Force had struck a populist nerve. These hearings turned out to be more like the civil rights meetings of the sixties and the feminist speak-outs of the seventies than the usual dry, government-run proceedings. Though national media had lost interest once the Task Force was under way, local reporters were so impressed that they began to temper their past ridicule.

When all the results of both the expert studies and the public hearings were in, low self-esteem had been documented as "a primary causal factor" in each of the seven areas of targeted social problems. News of these results created requests for information from experts and ordinary citizens in all fifty states, as well as in many foreign countries.

In its second stage, the Task Force looked for effective programs in elementary schools and prisons, drug-treatment centers and battered women's shelters — all the settings where problems in the seven target areas were being addressed — and put out a report on those, plus their own hearings and studies. In the third and final stage, model programs and policies were recommended for replication.

Even such simple and short-term efforts as holding classroom discussions on the importance of self-esteem, or asking students to keep daily notebooks on what made them feel either empowered or powerless, were found to create a practical, measurable, positive difference. In one school district that addressed self-esteem among teachers, for instance, those who said they planned to retire dropped from 45 percent to 5 percent in one year. In a high school that explored connections between self-esteem and unwanted teenage pregnancy, the number of such pregnancies fell over three years from 147 to 20. In a mostly Hispanic school district that was also the poorest per capita in the state, student discipline problems fell by 75 percent after self-esteem became a subject of discussion.

In the Task Force offices, positive letters about its work began to outweigh negative ones by a ratio of ten to one. State legislators and officials from Maryland, Michigan, Florida, New Mexico, Virginia, Arkansas, Hawaii, Louisiana, and Missouri were impressed enough to consider using the California model for legislation and programs of their own. So were several members of the U.S. Congress.

Many of California's own lawmakers had been skeptical in the beginning — "self-esteem" had sounded so suspect in the title of a government commission that they had agreed to it only after Vasconcellos added "and Personal and Social Responsibility" — but now, their main concern was how to continue the Task Force work. By enacting new legislation, they empowered each of California's fifty-eight counties to create a local Self-Esteem Task Force of its own.

The cost of this entire three-year effort? Exactly $735,000: less than the price of keeping one twenty-year-old in prison for a life sentence. Even Assemblyman Vasconcellos was surprised by the high return on such a small investment. What splitting the atom had been to the 1940s and exploring outer space had been to the 1960s, he predicted, exploring "the reaches and mysteries of inner space" would become to the 1990s — and beyond.

Given the effect of Task Force work on the very problems that polls show Americans fear most — violent crime, drug addiction, and declining standards in schools — one would think so. In fact, however, to this day, few people have heard about its practical successes. Its final report was met with more media coverage of seven dissenting members who criticized its philosophy (mainly for failing to "recognize the eternal God as the origin of all human worth") than with reporting of its programs. As a result, the California experience is known to those who have read its published summary, or who have heard of the private foundation to whom the Task Force passed its work after its mandate expired.³ But for the majority of us who depend on public sources for information and ideas, its lessons are largely lost.

Indeed, at the national level, the wheel seems to be in the process of reinvention at best and rejection at worst. When U.S. Senator Claiborne Pell of Rhode Island was impressed enough with results of the California Task Force to introduce a similar bill to create a National Commission on Human Resource Development, for instance, it was defeated by a campaign of pressure from the religious right wing. Even though "Self-Esteem" was nowhere in the title and "Human Resource Development" seemed to safely distance the center of power from the individual and put it in the hands of authorities — and even though. Pell and co-sponsor Senator Nancy Kassebaum of Kansas had asked for no public funds at all — it was condemned as "godless," "dangerous." Senate offices were deluged by well-orchestrated phone calls and letters, and the bill was indefinitely withdrawn. By 1991, Pell so despaired of it ever receiving government support that he began his own Human Potential Foundation in the hope of attracting private funds. Meanwhile, the Bush administration had announced a plan to improve the public schools by subjecting teachers to more paper tests.

Why is there such a split between grass-roots interest in self-esteem and support from much of the government, religious, or even media establishments? I think the idea of an inner authority is upsetting to those accustomed to looking outside for orders — and certainly to those accustomed to giving them. Moreover, if only outside authority is serious, then any inner experience becomes a frivolous concern.

Perhaps we would feel more comfortable with the concept of self-esteem if we knew that it was neither new nor frivolous. Far from being a product of California-think or of a selfish Me Generation, it goes beyond the West and modern individualism. It is as old and universal as humanity itself.

Everyone has a word for it. Indeed, there has always been a way of saying it.

In France and French-speaking parts of the world, self-esteem is *amour-propre,* "love of self," in Italian it's *autostima,* in Danish *selvvaerd,* and Spanish speakers everywhere call it *autoestima.* To the Germans it's *selbstachtung,* to the Dutch, *zelfwaardering.* Arabic speakers say *al-jtibar al-dhati.* In Hebrew it's *haaracha atzmit;* and in Yiddish, *zelbst gloibn.*

Samouvazhenie is the single word in Russian; *kujistahi* in Swahili; and *swavhimani* in Hindi. The Chinese combine the pictogram for self (pronounced *zi*) with the one for esteem or respect (pronounced *zun*) and say *zizun.* The Japanese say *ji son shin.*

But however different the words, their meaning is the same. *The Oxford English Dictionary* gives the primary definition as a "favourable appreciation or opinion of oneself," and cites uses of "selfe-esteem" from the 1600s. North American dictionaries shorten its meaning to "belief in oneself" or "self-respect." Thesaurus synonyms are "self-reliance," "self-consequence," "poise," "confidence," "assurance," "pride," or "self-sufficiency." Antonyms run the negative gamut from "self-doubt" and "self-effacement" to "self-hatred" and "shame."

Tracing the English word even further back, we find unfamiliar spellings: *silfe, soelf, suelf;* and *extyme, aesteam, extseme.* By 1657, when Augustine Baker, a mystical theologian and Benedictine monk, declared "Selfe-esteem, Selfe-judgment, & selfe-will" to be the three requisites of independence, the term had been used by scholars in Latin and by common people in English for centuries, with origins in the Western world dating back at least to the ancient Greeks. *Allotriosis,* "self-alienation," for instance, was the greatest evil in Greek philosophy, and *oikeiosis* ("self-love," "self-acceptance," or "self-contentedness") was the greatest goal. Plato called "rational self-love" crucial to progress because it alone "requires a man [*sic*] to be concerned for his own future condition." Aristotle equated self-contentedness with happiness. For him, the full realization of one's own specific nature was the ultimate good. Indeed, in that

Golden Age of Greece more than three centuries before the birth of Christ, *oikeiosis* was seen as the root of almost everything positive. From this center radiated successive circles of love: first for oneself, then for one's children, then for one's family, and finally for the whole human species.

The Stoics added another circle to this progression: love of nature. Thus, self-love became the keystone of their belief that unity with nature was a greater good than obedience to social convention. Self-alienation was seen as destructive far beyond the boundaries of the individual self: it prevented one from honoring the natural world.

But even this thinking came relatively late in written history. Some 2,500 years before the birth of Christ in what is believed to be the first formal book, a priest named Ptahhotep, a sage and prime minister of Egypt, recorded wisdom gathered during his 110 years of life, and its core was: "Follow your heart."

In the same era, Asian religions were exploring an outer circle that extended even beyond nature in radiating out from the self: the universe, the cosmos, the mind of God. The idea that self-knowledge was God-knowledge — that the self was a microcosm of the universe, and that knowing the self was our individual way of knowing the mind of God — was central to the origins of Hinduism, and thus to Buddhism, Sufism, and the many other religions that sprang from it. Self-realization became a goal placed over caste duties, external rules, obedience — everything.

In the Upanishads, dialogues that codified the wisdom of the Vedic period in India from 2500 to 600 B.C., there is one central text from which all else derives: *Tat tvam asi,* "That art Thou," a circular statement that is often translated, "Truth is within us." Instead of creating a hierarchy in which humans were placed above nature, and kinds of knowledge were ranked, Vedic teaching described a circle: starting at any point could complete the whole. Thus, *Brahman* (the truth discovered objectively through observation) and *Atman* (the truth discovered subjectively through introspection) could become one and the same. As scholar Sarvepalli Radhakrishnan summed up the belief at the core of these ancient commentaries: "The real which is at the heart of the universe is reflected in the infinite depths of the self."

This quest for universal understanding through self-understanding has been misused to create the uncaring, navel-contemplating stereotype of Eastern philosophies. In fact, their turn toward passivity had more to do with the politics of poverty and despair superimposed upon them. Even in rich countries, religion, psychoanalysis, and self-help theories have been used to justify passivity and enshrine external injustices. In many ways, Freud's biological determinism is a simpler and more passivity-producing theory than Eastern ideas of a present life set in the context of past lives and the forces of the universe.

It seems that the older the teaching, the more it presents self-wisdom and self-honor as a source of strength, rebellion, and a kind of meta-democracy — a oneness with all living things and with the universe itself. Returning to this concept of circularity and oneness that preceded patriarchy, racism, class systems, and other hierarchies that ration self-esteem — and that create obedience to external authority by weakening belief in our natural and internal wisdom — is truly a revolution from within.

"When we realize the universal Self in us," ask the Upanishads defiantly, "when and what may anybody fear or worship?"[4]

III   *Premises and Parables*

"The universe is made of stories, not of atoms."
MURIEL RUKEYSER

"Tell me, and I'll forget. Show me, and I may
not remember. Involve me, and I'll understand."
NATIVE AMERICAN SAYING

It's comforting to find that, in the five millennia that have passed between the writing of the Upanishads and the formation of the California Task Force, there is a core of wisdom that hasn't changed. Hierarchies try to convince us that all power and well-being come from the outside, that our self-esteem depends on obedience and measuring up to their requirements, but it's interesting that even the most totalitarian cultures have never been able to convince everyone. There have always been rebels and visionaries who persisted in believing that each person has a center of power and wisdom within, whether it's called the soul or the authentic self, Atman or the spirit. We don't have to reinvent the wheel, just rediscover it.

But old or new, this wisdom too often remains in our heads. Only experience can make it a visceral part of our daily lives by bridging the distance from head to heart. That's why a storyteller is magic, but a teller of facts is not. There is a reason why parables are the oldest form of teaching: they work.

The following are lived experiences of self-esteem — some my own, some observed, some recounted to me. In the context of this book, each one is the harbinger of a chapter to come. Perhaps we share stories in much the same spirit that explorers share maps, hoping to speed each other's journey, but knowing that the journey we make will be our own.

Self-Esteem Is Personal: An Inner Child of the Past

Until recently, I thought I had built a brick wall between myself and my childhood. I valued those early years for making me an optimist (nothing could ever be that bad again) and a survivor (learning how to cope has its advantages). Then I put their memories and feelings behind me.

Of course, I did notice that small things made me feel irrationally sad or depressed — for instance, any story about a mother and daughter on their own, certain landscapes, or the sound of a radio in an empty room — but I just avoided them. When bigger things made me feel self-pitying but defiant — feeling rootless and proud of it, for example, or giving money away but then feeling deprived — I assumed they were the inevitable results of my conscious, rational decisions to remain free, unencumbered, with no possessions to possess me.

I continued in this way for decades while pressures grew. I worked for a magazine I loved and a movement that had given me life. I organized and traveled and lectured; I campaigned and raised contributions and solicited ads to keep the magazine going; I turned my apartment into a closet where I changed clothes and dumped papers into cardboard boxes; and I only once in twenty years spent an entire week without getting on a plane. But at home or away, I often woke up with sweaty palms and pounding heart, worried that I was going to mess up some public event, fail to find enough money to pay the printer and meet the payroll, or otherwise let down this movement that meant as much to me as it did to millions of other women.

After the first five or six years, I had become aware that I was usually doing over again things I already knew how to do and often saying things I'd said before — that I was *re*acting more than acting — but I also knew that no matter what happened, I could always keep on functioning. It was part of my survivor's skills, my childhood defiance. If there had been an Olympic team for just *functioning,* I would have been on it. Later, as economic times got tougher for magazines in general and ours in particular, and inevitable backlashes greeted women's advances, I felt pressure to do more and more. When my friends asked about my state of mind or emotions, I made them laugh — and despair — by turning Plato on his head. "The examined life," I explained, "is not worth living."

Then one evening after a lecture on the road, a woman in the audience recommended a book, *Your Inner Child of the Past.* She described it with such conviction that I went out and bought it.

Of course, I wasn't interested in self-knowledge, just research — or so I thought. In this case, I needed insight for a book of essays I was writing about Marilyn Monroe, especially about her childhood as Norma Jeane Baker.[5] The author, Hugh Missildine, a child psychiatrist, had identified the most common sins and excesses of childrearing — overindulgence, neglect, perfectionism, sexual abuse, and so on — and then described each one as it manifested itself in later life. Because Marilyn's story of being sexually abused as a little girl had been disbelieved by other biographers, I was looking to Missildine for confirmation of my belief that Marilyn's lifelong inability to value herself as anything other than a sexual being was a classic result of sexual abuse in childhood.

Even more than obvious abuse, however, the hallmark of Marilyn's earliest years had been neglect. Boarded out as a baby by a mother with severe emotional problems of her own, Marilyn had been so neglected that as a little girl, she believed she was invisible. When her mother was committed to a state mental institution, Marilyn was sent to an orphanage. Only the early maturing of her body and the attention it attracted made her feel "visible" and convinced her that she did indeed exist. It was this division between an internal, worthless self and an external, sexually valuable self that would haunt her for the rest of her short life. Missildine's text described some of the typical results of the kind of neglect Marilyn had experienced: a lifelong search for nurturing, wanting to belong yet feeling a perpetual outsider, trying to make fathers out of husbands and lovers, using sex to get childlike warmth and approval, and neglecting one's own welfare because neglect feels familiar, *like home*. These were all problems Marilyn herself described. As Missildine wrote: "Many such people, particularly women, are drawn into theatrical and movie work because . . . 'When you're a nobody, the only way to be anybody is to be somebody else.' " It was almost as if he had met Marilyn Monroe; certainly, she had said almost exactly those words.

Such extremes of childhood neglect — and of response in adulthood to that neglect — were clearly Marilyn's, not my own. I read them feeling interested and safe. But soon, this slender, simple little book was describing more ordinary results of neglect — among those with alcoholic, ill, or absent parents, for example — that gave me a jolt of recognition. "The childhood of persons who suffered from neglect," wrote Missildine in his matter-of-fact way, "usually reveals a father who somehow wasn't a father and a mother who somehow wasn't a mother."[6]

Well, my mother had suffered spells of depression, delusions, and long periods as an invalid both before and after I was born. My father had taken care of her until I was ten or so and seemed old enough to replace him. Then my parents separated, and my mother and I lived on our own. Though my parents always made me know that they loved me, and treated me as well as or better than they treated themselves — all very different from the degree of neglect Marilyn had suffered — they still hadn't been able to be real parents much of the time. Basics like regular school attendance, clean clothes, a bedtime, enough money to pay bills, and, after I was ten, any kind of consistent parenting at all, had gone the way of my father's wandering lifestyle. After their divorce, my mother's frequent depressions and need for a caretaker had reversed our roles. Since I always knew they were doing the best they could, I didn't allow myself to be angry — and thus just buried my feelings about what I had missed.

For the first time, I began to wonder what was behind the wall between me and my childhood, and if it hadn't seeped into the present in spite of all my bricks and mortar.

I remembered longing to escape the littered, depressing, rat-infested house where I lived alone with my mother; yet I had recreated an upscale, less dramatic version of it in my own apartment with cardboard boxes, stacks of papers, and long absences.

I remembered worrying as a child about our lack of money and my father's penchant for borrowing it; yet I had saved nothing of what I earned, couldn't resist giving money away, never planned for the future, and often ended up with a familiar feeling of being neglected, deprived, and insecure.

I remembered feeling sad about navigating life by myself, working after school, worrying about my mother, who was sometimes too removed from reality to know where she was, or who I was, and concealing these shameful family secrets from my friends; yet I had chosen to work by myself as a freelancer, and then to do a parallel kind of caretaking for a magazine and a movement. Now as then, I turned away sympathy with jokes and a survivor's pride. In both cases, I was turning away from a well of neediness that I feared would swallow me up if I admitted it.

The parallels were so obvious that even I began to see that I was repeating the painful, familiar patterns of home. In spite of my insistence that I'd put the past behind me, that free will and the realities in which I found myself were the only shapers of my life, it just wasn't so.

I began to follow clues backward. Why was the sound of a radio so depressing, though television and records were not? *Because the radio had been the only sound in the house where I lived with my mother.* Why couldn't I give myself security and a pleasant place to live? *Because they hadn't been given to me as a child.* Why didn't I ask for help from people who would have freely given it? *Because they hadn't been there in the past.* Why had I lived my life so that I would be ready to leave anyplace at any time, even if I didn't actually do it? *Because that was the way I had protected myself against getting attached to places as a vagabond child.*

It may be obvious that we continue to treat ourselves the way we were treated as children, but I lived a diverse and seemingly aware life for more than forty years without figuring it out. I suspect many other people have, too. Only becoming conscious of old and unchosen patterns allows us to change them, and even so, change, no matter how much for the better, still feels cold and lonely at first — as if we were out there on the edge of the universe with the wind whistling past our ears — because it doesn't feel *like home.* Old patterns, no matter how negative and painful they may be, have an incredible magnetic power — because they *do* feel *like home.*

This repetition begins to diminish the moment we're aware of its source, and the more we heal the past so we can respond to the present. As the twelve-step Alcoholics Anonymous–type programs say, "Dig it out or act it out." Though we may repeat some sequence of events and feelings in different ways before they gradually dissolve, at least now the point of power is no longer in others who made decisions for us, but in ourselves.

I don't know whether Marilyn made connections between past and present or not: between her lost father and the "fathers" she kept marrying; between the invisible child she once was and her imprisonment in a very visible image that Hollywood had concocted. Perhaps the patterns went too deep, or perhaps there was too much reward for *not* changing in a world that paid and praised her for staying helpless and childlike. She died before feminism made clear that women have every human possibility, and even before people like Missildine were beginning to write about the inner child. Whether she could have become strong enough to go back and be a parent to her own sad child of the past, we'll never know. But her life story has helped others, if not herself. Certainly, her often repeated plea to be taken seriously reached out to me, made me want to write about her, and thus gave me the great gift of seeing the echoes of her life in my own.

Each of us has an inner child of the past living within us. Those who needed to build no walls have access to that child's creativity and spontaneity. Those who had to leave this crucial core behind can tear down the walls, see what the child needed but didn't have, and begin to provide it now. The more we do this, the more we know that we are worth it.

And that we always were.

Self-Esteem Is Contagious: The Royal Knights of Spanish Harlem

Within walking distance of my Manhattan apartment but also light-years away, there is a part of New York called Spanish Harlem. In many ways, it is a Third World country: infant and maternal mortality rates are about the same as in, say, Bangladesh, and average male life expectancy is even shorter. These facts it shares with the rest of Harlem, yet here, many people are also separated from the more affluent parts of the city by language. When all this is combined with invisibility in the media, the condescension of many teachers and police who work in this Third World country but wouldn't dream of living there, and textbooks that have little to do with their real lives, the lesson for kids is clear: they are "less than" people who live only a few blocks away.

At a junior high that rises from a barren patch of concrete playgrounds and metal fences on East 101st Street, Bill Hall teaches the usual English courses, plus English as a second language to students who arrive directly from Puerto Rico, Central and South America, even Pakistan and Hong Kong. Those kids are faced with a new culture, strange rules, a tough neighborhood, and parents who may be feeling just as lost as they are. Bill Hall is faced with them.

While looking for an interest to bind one such group together and help them to learn English at the same time, Bill noticed someone in the neighborhood carrying a chessboard. As a chess player himself, he knew this game crossed many cultural boundaries, so he got permission from a very skeptical principal to start a chess club after school.

Few of the girls came. Never having seen women playing chess, they assumed this game wasn't for them, and without even a female teacher as a role model, those few who did come gradually dropped out. Some of the boys stayed away, too — chess wasn't the kind of game that made you popular in this neighborhood — but about a dozen remained to learn the basics. Their friends made fun of them for staying after school, and some parents felt that chess was a waste of time since it wouldn't help get a job, but still, they kept coming. Bill was giving these boys something rare in their lives: the wholehearted attention of someone who believed in them.

Gradually, their skills at both chess and English improved. As they got more expert at the game, Bill took them to chess matches in schools outside Spanish Harlem. Because he paid for their subway fares and pizza dinners, no small thing on his teacher's salary, the boys knew he cared. They began to trust this middle-aged white man a little more.

To help them become more independent, Bill asked each boy to captain one event, and to handle all travel and preparation for it. Gradually, even when Bill wasn't around, the boys began to assume responsibility for each other: to coach those who were lagging behind, to share personal problems, and to explain to each other's parents why chess wasn't such a waste of time after all. Gradually, too, this new sense of competence carried over into their classrooms, and their grades began to improve.

As they became better students and chess players, Bill Hall's dreams for them grew. With a little money supplied by the Manhattan Chess Club, he took them to the State Finals in Syracuse. What had been twelve disparate, isolated, often passive, shut-down kids had now become a team with their own chosen name: The Royal Knights. After finishing third in their own state, they were eligible for the Junior High School Finals in California.

By now, however, even Bill's own colleagues were giving him reasons why he shouldn't be spending so much time and effort. In real life, these ghetto kids would never "get past New Jersey," as one teacher put it. Why raise funds to fly them across the country and make them more dissatisfied with their lives? Nonetheless, Bill raised money for tickets to California. In that national competition, they finished seventeenth out of 109 teams.

By now, chess had become a subject of school interest — if only because it led to trips. On one of their days at a New York chess club, the team members met a young girl from the Soviet Union who was the Women's World Champion. Even Bill was floored by the idea that two of his kids came up with: If this girl could come all the way from Russia, why couldn't The Royal Knights go there? After all, it was the chess capital of the world, and the Scholastic Chess Friendship Games were coming up.

Though no U.S. players their age had ever entered these games, officials in Bill's school district rallied round the idea. So did a couple of the corporations he approached for travel money. Of course, no one thought his team could win, but that wasn't the goal. The trip itself would widen the boys' horizons, Bill argued. When Pepsi-Cola came up with a $20,000 check, Bill began to realize that this crazy dream was going to come true.

They boarded the plane for the first leg of their trip to Russia as official representatives of the country from which they had felt so estranged only a few months before. But as veterans of Spanish Harlem, they also made very clear that they were representing their own neighborhood. On the back of their satin athletic jackets was emblazoned not "U.S.A.," but "The Royal Knights."

Once they were in Moscow, however, their confidence began to falter badly. The experience and deliberate style of their Soviet opponents were something they had never previously encountered. Finally, one of the Knights broke the spell by playing a Soviet Grandmaster in his thirties to a draw in a simulation match. The Russians weren't invincible after all; just people like them. After that, the Knights won about half their matches, and even discovered a homegrown advantage in the special event of speed chess. Unlike the Soviet players, who had been taught that slowness and deliberation were virtues, the Knights had a streetsmart style that made them both fast and accurate.

By the time Bill and his team got to Leningrad to take on the toughest part of their competition, the boys were feeling good again. Though they had been selected at random for their need to learn English, not for any talent at chess, and though they had been playing for only a few months, they won one match and achieved a draw in another.

When the Knights got back to New York, they were convinced they could do anything.

It was a conviction they would need. A few months later when I went to their junior high school clubroom, Bill Hall, a big, gentle man who rarely gets angry, was furious about a recent confrontation between one of the Puerto Rican team members and a white teacher. As Bill urged the boy to explain to me, he had done so well on a test that the teacher, thinking he had cheated, made him take it over. When the boy did well a second time, the teacher seemed less pleased than annoyed to have been proven wrong. "If this had been a school in a different neighborhood," said Bill, "none of this would have happened."

It was the kind of classroom bias that these boys had been internalizing — but now had the self-esteem to resist. "Maybe the teacher was just jealous," the boy said cheerfully. "I mean, we put this school on the map."

And so they had. Their dingy junior high auditorium had just been chosen by a Soviet dance troupe as the site of a New York performance. Every principal in the school district was asking for a chess program, and local television and newspapers had interviewed The Royal Knights. Now that their junior high graduation was just weeks away, bids from various high schools with programs for "gifted" kids were flooding in, even one from a high school in California. Though all the boys were worried about their upcoming separation, it was the other team members who had persuaded the boy who got that invitation to accept it.

"We told him to go for it," as one said. "We promised to write him every week," said another. "Actually," said a third, "we all plan to stay in touch for life."

With career plans that included law, accounting, teaching, computer sciences — futures they wouldn't have thought possible before — there was no telling what continuing surprises they might share at reunions of this team that had become its own support group and family.

What were they doing, I asked, *before* Bill Hall and chess-playing came into their lives? There was a very long silence.

"Hanging out in the street and feeling like shit," said one boy, who now wants to become a lawyer.

"Taking lunch money from younger kids, and a few drugs now and then," admitted another.

"Just lying on my bed, reading comics, and getting yelled at by my father for being lazy," said a third.

Was there anything in their schoolbooks that made the difference?

"Not until Mr. Hall thought we were smart," explained one, to the nods of the others, "and then we were."

At first glance, this parable seems to be a simple example of the words of football coach Vince Lombardi: "Confidence is contagious, so is lack of confidence." But that's only one of its lessons. If we think about our own classroom experiences — whether in schools that were far more privileged than those of Spanish Harlem, or just as bad with not even a Bill Hall — we may also remember that we became more or less smart depending on our teachers' vision of us, that we learned better when teachers invested themselves in their subjects and expected us to do the same, and that we knew very well when our textbooks and teachers were excluding us.

In *Transforming Knowledge,* Elizabeth Minnich describes education as the possession of the few — and therefore a miseducation of everyone — as a problem found not only in ghetto junior high schools, but also in elite universities:

> The *root problem* reappears in all fields and throughout the dominant tradition. It is, simply, that while the majority of humankind was excluded from education and the making of what has been called knowledge, *the dominant few not only defined themselves as the inclusive kind of human but also as the norm and the ideal.* A few privileged men defined themselves as constituting mankind/humankind. . . . Thus, they created root definitions of what it means to be human that, with the concepts and theories that flowed from and reinforced those definitions, made it difficult to think well about, or in the mode of, anyone other than themselves, just as they made it difficult to think honestly about the defining few.

To change education, as she says, the goal is "to think ourselves free, to free our own thinking."[7]

Thinking ourselves free starts with questions: *What happened to those girls who left the chess club? Would they have stayed if there had been a woman teacher? What was going on inside that teacher who wanted to be right more than he wanted his student to do well? What was in the texts those boys were reading — the whole world or only certain parts of it, and certain people? When The Royal Knights come home from high school and college, will they be more or less themselves?*

Most important of all: *What was our own education like?*

Self-Esteem Is Self-Discovery: Gandhi, Marilyn Murphy, and Others

When I was living in India on a fellowship after college, a kind Indian friend took me aside and suggested I might consider saying "South Asia," "Southeast Asia," and the like, instead of the "Near" and "Far East." It was the first time I'd ever realized that "Near" and "Far" assumed Europe as the center of the world.

Ever since then, I've noticed that the process of discovering and esteeming a true self is remarkably similar for a person or a race, a group or a nation. When women began to call themselves "Mary Jones" instead of "Mrs. John Smith," for example, they were doing the same thing as formerly colonized countries that stopped identifying themselves in relation to Europe. When India and England continued their Commonwealth and other relationships after India's independence, one might say that, as George Sand once suggested men and women do, they had broken the marriage bond and re-formed it as an equal partnership. When "Negroes" became "blacks" and then "African Americans" in the United States, it was part of a long journey from the humiliation of slavery to a pride of heritage. When I myself started to say "we" instead of "they" when speaking of women, it was a step toward self-esteem that was at least as important as identifying with one's true ethnic heritage. It was also my Declaration of Interdependence.

No matter who we are, the journey toward recovering the self-esteem that should have been our birthright follows similar steps: a first experience of seeing through our own eyes instead of through the eyes of others (for instance, the moment when an Algerian first looked in defiance at a French soldier, or when a woman stops being defined by the male gaze); telling what seemed to be shameful secrets, and discovering they are neither shameful nor secret (from the woman who has survived childhood sexual abuse to the man whose bottomless need for power hides weakness); giving names to problems that have been treated as normal and thus have no names (think of new terms like *homophobia, battered women,* or *Eurocentrism*); bonding with others who share similar experiences (from groups of variously abled people to conferences of indigenous nations); achieving empowerment and self-government (from the woman who has a room and income of her own to the nation that declares its independence); bonding with others in shared power (think of democratic families, rainbow coalitions, or the principles of the United Nations); and finally, achieving a balance of independence and interdependence, and taking one's place in a circle of true selves.

In this spirit of comparing journeys not usually seen as comparable, I've combined two stories that aren't as different as they seem.

Marilyn Murphy was forty-three years old before she began to see the world in color instead of, as she later wrote, "in gradations of grey." Not that she had known what was missing. Growing up as the first of five sisters in a Catholic Irish/Italian working-class family in New York City, she had assumed that, if she couldn't see color, it wasn't there. She went through all the expected girlish stages, from sneaking on lipstick when the nuns weren't looking to fantasizing about being a nightclub singer in a sequined gown. When an experience did stand out in this grey world, she wasn't sure why. After her union-organizer father had moved the family to Tulsa, Oklahoma, for instance, she saw a sign in a local bus: "Colored — Sit in the Back." It burned into her consciousness, so that forever after, she could remember the sick feeling in the pit of her stomach; yet as a white person, she was not supposed to feel this.

At eighteen, she chose motherhood over convent life, the only two options she remembers being conscious of, and by twenty-five, she was the mother of four children. But she continued to feel a mysterious identity with any group or person having a hard time, and this led to one of her many differences with her husband, who ridiculed her attempts to "do something" by calling her "Crusader Rabbit." So she kept living an expected life, trying to see herself through the eyes of others, even dieting her comfortable body down to the shape society said it was supposed to be, with diet pills prescribed by her obstetrician. Only when she was thirty-three and her three daughters and one son were old enough to be more self-sufficient did she enter a junior college near her new home in California where her husband began taking courses, too. Even then, she worried about his resentment of her new interest, so she studied in the bathroom or at night when he was asleep. When she was elected Student of the Year, he put up a large homemade sign declaring her Wife of the Year. Then he told her that it no longer pleased him for her to go to college, that she could finish out the semester — but no more. But somehow, her first personal success had given her the courage to rebel, and by the time she was thirty-five, she was divorced, living on and off welfare with her children, and trying to finish college part time.

When the women's liberation movement began, she read each book, pamphlet, and essay that came her way. Patriarchy and men in power reminded her of racism and whites in power, which began to explain her feelings. If women's position in the home and the world wasn't natural, she hadn't been so wrong to identify with other groups in trouble after all. When her English professor made clear that only men's conflicts were the proper themes of great literature, she decided she was definitely a feminist. In 1969, when Florence Howe, later to become founder of the Feminist Press, came to speak, she inspired Marilyn's first political action: as part of a group trying to get women writers included in the English department curriculum, Marilyn agitated and organized. At the time, she considered herself a heterosexual feminist, and when she met lesbian feminists, they seemed to her "unstable." Their love relationships were not as long as she was accustomed to thinking partnerships should be.

Since she had challenged society's assumptions about women, she began to challenge her own assumptions, too. Perhaps without economic and social pressure to stay in marriages that weren't mutually rewarding, she thought, many heterosexual women's relationships wouldn't be so "stable" either. For all the suffering of living in a way that society didn't legally bless or even admit, perhaps lesbians were not less stable — just more free.

Curiosity has a way of telling us what we need to know. By 1975, Marilyn had separated from a second husband. She was beginning to understand the soul-killing depth of male dominance and could no longer imagine living with a man. Nonetheless, her conscious mind still assumed she was destined to be, as she put it at the time, "that least happy of women — a heterosexual feminist who wants to be sexual, but can't speak to a man without a growl." Then, to her surprise, she fell irresistibly, head-over-heels in love with another woman.

Suddenly, she began to feel an inexplicable sense of rightness and naturalness, as if she was finally living her own life. The world seemed open and "free-form," unlike her heterosexual past in which everything had "rules, guidelines, customs and traditions," as she put it. Lesbians suffered from living outside society, but that meant they invented their own society as they went along. Like so many people who discover their true self, she had the odd sensation of suddenly seeing the world in color, the reverse of many people who become depressed and feel their surroundings fade to grey. As she later wrote:

> I feel about Lesbianism as if I spent forty-three years being color blind. . . . At first I was intoxicated by the sight of the primary colors. I still am, but now I am able to see an ever-widening spectrum. I run around saying, "Look at all the varying shades of green. How brilliant! How subtle!" Some women, having seen color all their lives, are not impressed. "Big deal," they say. "I've seen some shades of green that were positively disgusting."
>
> In my next life when I am a Lifelong Lesbian, I may be blasé about my good fortune, too, though I do not really think so.

She didn't stay with that first lover, but she did form a loving partnership with another "Lifelong Lesbian," as Marilyn would say. In 1976, they were among the founding mothers of Califia Community, named for the goddess of the once-united land of Mexico and California. For a decade, she helped to organize and run week-long women's retreats on the hard subjects of class, race, homophobia, divisions of age, ethnicity, appearance, and able-bodiedness — all the divisions that keep women from working together. About 4,000 women passed through these Califia sessions over ten years, and they continue to play crucial roles in keeping women's groups around the country together, in spite of all the societal pressures trying to break them apart.

As for Marilyn herself, she now travels around the country, speaking, working as a conference organizer with her longtime lover and colleague, Irene Weiss, creating new feminist projects with their vast network of activists and friends, and also visiting Marilyn's seven grandchildren. Since 1982, she has written warm and wise columns that, in *The Lesbian News* and in book form, have helped many other women find their true selves. It is from these essays — along with our telephone talks from her stops around the country — that her words here are taken.[8] One of her chief hopes is to help establish bodily integrity as a fundamental human right: a legal umbrella that would guarantee women's right to make sexual choices without punishment, the right to reproductive freedom, protection for poor women against being used as surrogate mothers, for poor people against pressure to become sources of transplants and transfusions for the well-to-do — all the ways in which bodies are owned or exploited. It would make clear, once and for all, for both women and men, that the power of the state stops at our skins.

Most recently, she has come to see incest and other childhood sexual abuse as, in her words, "a preverbal sexual terrorism that breaks the female spirit, and makes women continue to believe terrible things will happen to them if they tell men's secrets." Neither the new spirit of freedom in Eastern Europe or the older democracy here will mean anything, she believes, as long as "a three-year-old child can't find protection in our courts of law." It's one of the many sources of anger that make her refuse to become "mellow" and insist on "growing old ungraciously."

Marilyn's spiral of self-esteem began, in the time-honored phrase of the lesbian and gay cultures, with "coming out." Our sexuality is such a deep, spontaneous, and powerful part of our core identity that the conscious or unconscious need to falsify it is a little death. But concealing any part of our true self is a partial death, too. The act of "coming out" has been invested with such honesty and courage by so many millions of women and men that it has become a paradigm for discovering a true self. Whether our inner truth is a false childhood shame or a true talent, a group identity or a unique one, we all need to "come out" as who we really are.

About being called "Mahatma," the Great One, Gandhi wrote in his autobiography, "Often the title has deeply pained me; and there is not a moment I can recall when it may be said to have tickled me." His hope and his heart were with average people and ordinary actions. "I have not a shadow of a doubt that any man or woman can achieve what I have," he insisted. Only if we remember his life before he became the man we know can we learn what he wanted to teach.

Mohandas K. Gandhi was born into a family who were, by caste, grocers, at the peak of the British Empire, in an India that was even then in its second century of domination. As a boy, he memorized such sayings as:

> Behold the mighty Englishman
> He rules the Indian small,
> Because being a meat-eater
> He is five cubits tall.

Later, as a teenager, he himself would secretly eat meat for a year, though this meant lying to his family and violating his own morals, even having nightmares about tortured animals; all because he hoped to become superior like the English. Nonetheless, he remained so unconfident that he went home directly from school every day "lest anyone should poke fun at me."

At thirteen, he married a girl of his own age by their parents' arrangement, as was the custom, and did his best to dominate her as a proper husband should. When she was too spirited to obey, he became both jealous of her sexually and envious of her strength. He himself was still afraid to sleep in the dark. When he once went to a brothel, he was so shy that the prostitute lost patience and asked him to leave. "I felt as though my manhood had been injured," as he wrote later, "and wished to sink into the ground for shame." Even his mediocre accomplishments as a student were ascribed by him to luck. "I had not any high regard for my ability," as he later explained. "The least little blemish drew tears from my eyes. When

I merited, or seemed to the teacher to merit, a rebuke, it was unbearable for me."

After graduating from high school, he went on to college with a vague idea of becoming a doctor, but failed every course. Only the financial help of an older brother, plus his young wife's willingness to sell her jewelry, paid for his decision to go to London, where a barrister's degree was notoriously easy to earn and would allow him to put that magical phrase, "England-returned," on his calling card. But once in that cold and unfamiliar country, he was so ashamed of his ignorance of English manners, his embarrassingly homemade suits, and his inability to recite in class that he sometimes went hungry out of reluctance to ask for vegetarian food. Determined to learn the secrets of English superiority, he moved in with a family, bought Bond Street pinstripes and high collars he could ill afford, and even took lessons in French, the violin, and the fox-trot. As he would later admit, he had "wasted a lot of time and money trying to become an Englishman." Even *The Bhagavad-Gita* — the sacred Hindu text that was to become the "truth-book" he read every morning — was encountered for the first time when two English brothers asked for his help with reading it in the original Sanskrit, though Gandhi himself was more skilled in English. Only his continuing ineptitude made him give up his social lessons, sell his violin, and retreat to cheap rooms where he did his own cooking. Gradually, he began to feel more comfortable, as if his failures had been the signals of a true self. Though he maintained his proper English suits for many years, he also began to call his shyness his "shield," for it kept him away from pursuits that felt false, and also forced him into a simplicity of speech.

Once he was back in India after finishing his studies, however, even his London degree couldn't make him a success at practicing law. Finally, he took an assignment in South Africa, and there, his willingness to learn bookkeeping and his fear of conflict combined to produce his first success: a negotiated settlement in a financial lawsuit. It was his second discovery that what seemed a weakness in one context could also be a strength in another. "My joy was boundless," he wrote. "I had learned to find out the better side of human nature and to enter men's hearts . . . to unite parties riven asunder." Flushed with his first success at twenty-seven, he brought his wife and sons to live with him in a large English-style house with servants, a perquisite he had insisted upon as part of his job, and asked that they adapt to this "civilized" (that is, European) way of eating, sitting in stiff-back chairs, and dealing with servants, even though it made them supremely uncomfortable. But one day on a train, Bond Street cutaway, first-class ticket and all, Gandhi ran afoul of the color bar and was thrown off in the dust. It was a rude awakening. No matter how successfully he assumed a false self, he realized, his skin color would always humiliate him, and make him "a coolie" in the eyes of white South Africans. Once that shock was absorbed, he decided that, if he was going to be dishonored as an Indian, he would live as an Indian. Moreover, he would live simply in order to be truly independent. After a racist barber refused to cut his hair, for instance, he began to cut it himself. In order to be free of the need for servants, he began to wash, starch, and iron his high-collared shirts himself.

But even this rebellion was instructed by Western writers like Ruskin, Thoreau, and Tolstoy. It was as if Gandhi needed their theories to support his own values that had begun with vegetarianism and continued in a nonhierarchical view of all life forms. But unlike many revolutionaries, this support for nonviolence made him realize that adopting violent means would be an imitation of his adversaries. Though he challenged the hierarchy of skin color on behalf of Indians only and not the black majority of South Africans, he did become a leader who was known for his ability to bring people together and negotiate with the powerful. He adopted traditional Indian dress, founded a small experimental community in which no person turned another into an inferior as a servant, and won many dignified and successful battles for Indian rights in South Africa.

After almost twenty years of practicing law and social reform, he returned at forty-five to the disunity that was India in 1915. He was something of a hero, but he also looked at the struggling independence movement with new eyes. It would have to unite Indians across many barriers to be successful. There were fourteen major language areas, with at least as much cultural diversity as in Europe, seven major religions with hundreds of caste and other divisions within them, and an economic ladder that stretched from millions of impoverished villagers to the heads of 562 princely states who lived more opulently than (but at the pleasure of) the British Raj. At the same time, the few Indians who went to a university learned more about England than India, and even the independence leaders were urban and English-educated. Many Indians had come to believe in Indian "disorder" versus European "order," in Indian backwardness versus British excellence, and in their own inability to unify versus the tradition of The Crown. Often, they trusted the British more than they trusted each other. It was a colonized mentality that imprisoned this vast subcontinent more effectively than any army.

Gandhi began to travel in rural India and to call on the urban independence leaders to do the same. He campaigned for the unifying dignity of basics for everyone, whether this meant asking rich Indians to give up jewelry and possessions, or giving poor ones the fundamentals of life for the first time. Everyone was to wear homespun *khadi* in defiance of British laws against weaving, which were a way of creating a market for their own manufactured cloth, and to practice civil disobedience to other unjust laws. All castes were to be respected as one, all religions as one. He literally turned the hierarchy on its head, not by giving orders but by himself making the bottom rung his standard of living. He led by example. Even his surprising choice of the Salt Laws as a subject for civil disobedience was meant to unify. Salt was the one staple used more by the poor, who sweated it away by work in the sweltering heat, than by the middle class and rich; yet all Indians were forced to purchase salt from the British instead of harvesting it free from the ocean.

For the first time, there was a movement that began in the villages, not in a British-educated top layer of leaders. A large and populist women's movement also had been struggling for most of a century against such customs as child marriage and *suttee* (the immolation of widows), and Gandhi learned from it and adopted many of its culturally nonviolent methods. (Indeed, Gandhi included women to an unprecedented degree, yet also submerged many women's issues — for instance, family planning, which he opposed in favor of abstinence — thus leaving much to be done by an independent women's movement in years to come.) Even the harijan, or "untouchable," caste was included, and so were the British themselves. Instead of denying the humanity of the oppressor, Gandhi appealed to that humanity. Though long years of British and also post-Independence Indian religious violence challenged his methods of passive resistance, when the British left peacefully after two hundred years of domination, the world learned a new possibility from this first case of a nation that gained its independence without war. It was an object lesson in ending a cycle of colonial violence, and also in self-esteem. Without self-esteem, the only change is an exchange of masters; with it, there is no need of masters.

As for Gandhi himself, he continued to date his life as "before" and "after" what he called "my experiments with truth"; that is, his efforts to give up a false self and learn to trust a true one. Having experienced the humiliation of hierarchy, he eliminated hierarchy, stopped identifying with the oppressor, and in so doing, discovered an important secret: A leader cannot raise a people's self-esteem by placing himself above them.[9]

Nineteenth-century India or twentieth-century United States, a cultural monolith or a sexual one, freeing a country or freeing female minds and bodies: the lives of Mohandas Gandhi and Marilyn Murphy are very different in detail, yet very similar in shape. Both spent half their lives trying to live as a false self, both found their strength only when they followed an inner voice, both taught by example, and both worked to unite people across boundaries. Sometimes, even their provinces are now seen as parallel. The female half of the world is often described as a Third World country: low on capital, low on technology, and labor-intensive, with female bodies controlled as the means of reproduction. It is a psychic nation unifying for a common dream of independence, just as India became a geographical one.

I think if Marilyn Murphy had met Gandhi, she would have recognized a kindred revolutionary. I hope he would have, too. Perhaps when you and I are feeling discouraged, we can think of a radical lesbian feminist as an obedient housewife or Mahatma Gandhi trying to fox-trot in a Bond Street suit, and know that we can find a true strength, too.

Self-Esteem Is Physical:
The Women of Ahmedabad

In modern India, the women who sell vegetables in the street, roll cigarettes or weave baskets for sale while they nurse their babies, carry construction materials on their heads in human chains at building sites, and perform a thousand other individual, piece-work jobs are called "self-employed women." They are the bottom rung of the labor force, but their work is indispensable. In addition to making and distributing many small products, they also mend and resell cooking pots, collect paper from offices and garbage dumps, and pound used nails straight enough to be used again: a human recycling system in a country where everything is used many times.

Not only are they the poorest of India's workers, they are also subject to the special punishments of living in a female body. Girl children are considered so much less valuable than boys that two thirds of the children who die before age four are girls — the result of infanticide, plus saving scarce food and medical care for boys. Girls are so much less likely to be sent to school that the national female literacy rate is less than half that for males (among these workers, often much less), and their humanity is so minimally acknowledged that killing a wife in order to take another wife — and get another dowry — is one of the major sufferings addressed by the women's movement.

In a world that so devalues them, they have little reason to value themselves — which is why there is so much to learn from their successes.

For years, journalists and government officials in industrial cities like Ahmedabad have been condemning the fact that women do such hard physical labor — but nothing changed. Then in 1971, a young Gandhian labor organizer named Ela Bhatt did something new: she asked the women themselves what they wanted.

As it turned out, they had long been amused and angered by experts with soft hands who said women shouldn't do such work. It helped feed their families and gave them a small measure of independence, and they were not about to give it up. What they wanted were better conditions in which to do it: safe places to leave their children; higher wages for their handmade or recycled products and construction jobs; an end to the bribes they had to pay the police for the privilege of selling their wares in the street; and relief from moneylenders who charged murderous interest rates for the few rupees they borrowed to buy vegetables or raw materials each morning and then paid back at the end of each day. Finally, they wanted a secure place to keep their few rupees from husbands who otherwise considered women's earnings their own.

But even as they wished for these things, they also said nothing could be done. They had no faith in each other, no trust in Ela Bhatt, no reason to believe in change. Who would listen to poor and illiterate women?

By the time I first met Ela and some of these women in Ahmedabad in 1978, their Self-Employed Women's Association, whose acronym SEWA also means "service," was about six years old. They had exposed the corruption of police who demanded bribes, started childcare centers and infant crèches, and even persuaded the Bank of India to let them open a special branch for their small loans and hard-won savings. They themselves pounded the streets for members, put two improvised teller windows in a small room, and literally created a bank. (The problem of illiteracy had been overcome by putting a photograph of each woman on her passbook. "Maybe we can't read," as one of them explained with a smile, "but we can think.") To the surprise even of Ela Bhatt's sponsors, a Gandhian textile workers' union that had considered these women too passive and disparately employed to organize, they were doing better than many more educated workers in traditional unions.

What made the difference? First, an organizer who had lived the problems of being a woman herself, and who listened to each woman as a sister. For the first time, they felt worth listening to. Second, their mutual support and their small but growing list of successes when dealing with corrupt police and dishonest employers. As a lawyer and a skilled organizer, Ela knew the importance of both listening and explaining new alternatives in using demonstrations, the media, and even the courts.

But Ela Bhatt herself thought there had been one crucial turning point.

After the work of forming SEWA, Ela suggested the founding group celebrate by taking a holiday together. The women had never done anything separate from their families and children before, but other workers took holidays. Why shouldn't they?

After a discussion, they decided to visit Hindu holy places that were nearby, but farther from home than most of these women had ever been. After much planning and preparation to free them from family obligations, which was not easy to do even for a few hours, Ela hired a rickety bus and they set off.

Everything was fine until they neared a temple that could be reached only by boat. Menstruating women were not allowed in temples, and inevitably, some of the women had their periods. They were sure that if they crossed the river, the boat would capsize to punish them for defying tradition, and since they couldn't swim, everyone would drown.

By appealing to every emotion from curiosity to defiance, Ela finally convinced them to get in the boat and consign themselves to the wide river and fate.

They crossed — and nothing happened. After placing their offerings of fruit and flowers in the temple, they crossed back again — and still nothing happened. For the first time in their lives, they had defied the rules that denigrated them — and they had won.

Somehow, everything was connected to that first defiance and victory. If women's bodies were not so "unclean" and inferior after all, perhaps their work was not so inferior either.

Now, a dozen years later, SEWA is the most powerful women's trade union in India, and one of the largest in the world, with independent grass-roots organizations in nine other regions. It offers revolving loan funds to help women farm, set up small businesses, and carve out a small security in a system that offers little hope to those at the bottom. As for Ela Bhatt, she is consulted by the World Bank on grass-roots economic development and served for a while in the Indian Parliament. But at heart, she is an organizer and still spends most of her time helping to develop strength and leadership among poor women.

SEWA itself has become a model of self-help and economic empowerment for women throughout the Third World. And even in our own industrialized nation, SEWA is often mentioned as an example to follow wherever poor or otherwise powerless women gather to organize.[10]

But these least valued of women should inspire anyone, any-where, female or male, who is devalued so deeply that inferiority seems to be inherent in the reality of her or his own body — whether for reasons of race or appearance, disability or age, or anything else.

If feelings of unworthiness are rooted in our bodies, self-esteem needs to start there.

Self-Esteem Is Love: The Man Junkie

Tina is a friend and a musician who represents for me a kind of miracle. With almost no outside help or support, she rescued her-self from something most women have experienced enough to be ashamed of, and some have never escaped. I speak of that half-a-person feeling so carefully cultivated in females, the one that makes us think we are nothing without a man.

For years, I listened to Tina as she wrote songs of her own and did creative arrangements for other people's melodies. She loved and was good at her work; yet in the middle of any inspiration or dead-line, she would drop everything if a man, almost *any* man, asked her out.

It wasn't sex itself that hooked her. Going to bed with a man was mostly a means of pleasing him. It wasn't company she longed for. She had a lot of women friends and often didn't much enjoy the men she went out with. It wasn't even the hope of marriage and security. She often chose unmarriageable men and then lavished more time and money on them than they did on her. What she needed was the exhilarating "high" of romance. It was magical thinking: *This* man will be different. *This* man will make everything all right.

She moved away, and I didn't see her for a decade. When she reappeared, she had become the person her friends always knew she could be: talented, strong, independent — and very much at ease with herself. It was hard to imagine this new Tina had ever tolerated humiliation or given herself away. What had happened in that in-tervening time?

After so many years as a man junkie, Tina explained, even she couldn't bear repeating her pattern one more time. Her addiction had taken her away from her work and sometimes put her in physical danger with men she hardly knew. The comparison to drug and other addictions had become so clear that she decided on an addict's most drastic cure: cold turkey, total withdrawal. She would see no man for whom she had any sexual or romantic feeling until she felt whole on her own.

For five years she composed, traveled, lived alone, saw friends, but refused all invitations from eligible men. She fixed up her own house, took vacations to new places, and taught songwriting. She lived a full life — but one that did not include sex or romance.

It was very hard for the first two years, Tina said, and very frightening. Without seeing herself through a man's eyes, she wasn't sure she existed at all. But gradually, she began to take pleasure in waking up alone, talking to her cat, leaving parties when she felt like it. For the first time, she felt her "center" moving away from men and into some new locus within herself. And now that she had no man to ask what he wanted, she learned to ask a new and revolutionary question: "What do *I* want?"

In the fifth year, when she was feeling completely content with her life as it was, she met a man she would never have looked at before — he was too nice, too gentle, too attentive. He actually liked her, which would have been enough to disqualify him when she disliked herself. After many months, the empathy between them spread from their minds to their senses. For Tina, it was the first time that sensuality and sex had grown out of friendship. He appreciated her music, asked her opinion of his work, listened without interrupting, and was otherwise unlike the self-absorbed, supermasculine narcissists she had found so irresistible before.

As Tina began to understand, she had been obsessed with egocentric men because she had too little ego. She had sought out selfish men because she had too little self. She had looked for a strength and identity she felt she lacked in herself. In those exaggerations of certain qualities, she had been looking for something unrelated to those men: the rest of herself.

This was the difference between love and romance, she explained. Now, she appreciated the other person. In romance, she had just coveted what the other person had.

Tina and her new friend lived together and then married. They have made a rich mutual life that adds to the life each leads separately. They have also had one child and adopted a second — so far, without unbalancing their partnership, which may be the greatest testimony to its durability.

Of course, no ending is entirely happy — or even an ending. Tina sometimes misses the "high" of romance and the exhilaration of magical thinking. But she doesn't miss the feelings of despair and nonexistence that rushed in when the adrenaline left. She sometimes feels that her years as a man junkie took irreplaceable time away from her music, and wonders what women could be if, as she puts it, "we stopped taking care of men so they will take care of us — and put the same amount of time into taking care of ourselves." But there is a world of songs waiting to be written about experiences other than romance, and Tina is now beginning to feel them. It's a truism that we can't love others until we love ourselves — but truisms are also true.

Self-Esteem Is Cosmic: The Astronomy of the Self

Tom was the violent brother in the family, the bully among his school friends, the child of a frightened and passive mother. He patterned himself on his wealthy father's model of controlling as much as possible of the world.

At least, that's the way he would later describe himself. As the oldest son, he had borne the brunt of his father's discipline and then passed it down the line to his younger brothers, who still remember Tom's vicious taunts and kicks, his domination of childhood games, and his cruelty to the horses and dogs on their family's country estate near London. Classmates in his public school also remember him as the most ferocious paddler of younger boys in hazing rituals, and a student who would obey no one but the headmaster. Like a crown prince, he recognized only the power of the king. He could be charming, obedient, flattering, and even subservient in the presence of his father or the headmaster, but out of it, he was contentious, condescending, domineering, and often cruel.

By the time he had gone to graduate school for astronomy (a field he chose because it would enable him to outdistance in miles, if not in income, the earthbound profession of geology, which had earned his father a fortune in mining), Tom had become the sort of person whom people fear, flatter, or avoid — but rarely tell the truth.

He had also begun to lose the control that was his purpose. Circumstances — and his own character — were defeating him. In his profession, a reputation for being superior and uncooperative had cost him many jobs. He lost a major chunk of his inheritance because no one had the nerve to tell him how bad a particular investment was. And like many narcissists, he was only attracted to women he couldn't have; courted them like crazy — and then ceased wanting them once they wanted him.

Feeling out of control for the first time in his life, he went into a depression. "Hitting bottom" is a crucial experience for many people, and Tom now had his first taste of this painful but necessary way of learning. Since he couldn't talk honestly to women for one reason and to men for another — and since Tom's father would have ridiculed his asking an outsider for help, so therapy was out of the question — he went off on a solitary trip around the world.

Twice during this long journey, he contemplated suicide. Out of passivity and a dearth of any other ideas about what to do with himself, he went to work on an astronomy project in Australia, where there was a famous and powerful telescope that he could, literally, write home about.

At first, contemplating the heavens only made him feel more lost. When he had peered through telescopes before, it had always been with an assignment, a sense of competition, but none of that seemed to matter anymore. Out of depression, he abandoned his quest for control. After all, who could control — or do anything but observe — the vastness of the universe? At last, he wasn't trying to conceal his weaknesses, dominate, or prove his public strengths. He wasn't even thinking about the career use of this work. Without self-consciousness, he just observed. For weeks. For months. For a whole year.

An older professor noticed Tom's solitude and depression, and gave him a piece of advice that, for all his learning, he had never thought about before: "You won't go wrong if you remember two things," the professor explained to Tom, who would later repeat this to his own students. "First, all the potential of the universe is inside you. Second, it's inside every other human being, too." This was a message he was finally ready to hear. All the months of stargazing had been a kind of preparation for it.

That was almost twenty years ago. Now, Tom has become a professor who is also a quiet pioneer in humanizing science, in trying to study everything as field-dependent and connected. It's an obscure and poorly paid calling that wouldn't have satisfied his former grandiosity, but it makes both Tom and his students feel hopeful about the future.

Though still a bachelor, Tom now understands and can occasionally conquer his self-hating conviction that any woman who wants him must be not worth having. To his father's disgust and his brothers' amazement, he often takes care of his youngest nieces and nephews. As a penance for past cruelties to animals, he gives money to an English group that repatriates zoo animals — first to an estate outside London, and then to their native habitat. In fact, he does his best never to bully another living thing. Each one, he knows, contains the universe.

One day, Tom hopes to be able to tell his father — who has retired, and had a stroke and a few bouts with depression himself — how he suffered from impossible standards of control as a child, and how his father is suffering from them, too. Yet even though Tom no longer kowtows to kings, his father still compels more fear than love, and this conversation remains only a goal.

On the other hand, Tom has forgiven his mother for being too passive to protect him. And he has apologized to his younger brothers for the pain and fear he brought into their childhoods.

I don't know how many people come to esteem all living things, and thus themselves, through esteem for nature and the universe, but Tom certainly is among them.

Alan Watts, who was also a philosopher of science, has helped us to see ourselves and each other in this miraculous way. "How is it possible," he asked, "that a being with such sensitive jewels as the eyes, such enchanted musical instruments as the ears, and such a fabulous arabesque of nerves as the brain can experience itself as anything less than a god?" [11]

Two

It's Never Too Late for a Happy Childhood *

"Freedom is what you do with what's been done to you."

JEAN-PAUL SARTRE

* With thanks to Tom Robbins, who ended his novel *Still Life with Woodpecker:* "It's never too late to have a happy childhood."

I *The Child Within*

"Books . . . rarely if ever talk about what
children can make of themselves, about the
powers that from the day or moment of birth
are present in every child."
JOHN HOLT

"The Nature of This Flower Is to Bloom."
ALICE WALKER

In the dedication to an earlier book, I wrote that my
mother had "performed the miracle of loving others even when she
could not love herself." At the time, I thought this was the biggest
and most mysterious gift she had given my sister and me. But in
recent years of listening to stories of other people's childhoods and
reading books on childrearing, I've realized she did something even
more difficult — and more rare. She managed to break the pattern
of her own upbringing and pass on something quite different to us.

In spite of a childhood marked by more discipline than love —
and in spite of the difficulty she and all parents find in giving their
children something they themselves did not experience — my
mother did her best to make us feel unique and worthwhile. Over
and over again, in every way she knew how, she told us that we
didn't need to earn her love. We were loved and valued (and therefore were lovable and valuable) *exactly as we were.*

What seemed to help her in this heroic effort to break with her
own past was a childrearing theory she had absorbed from theoso-
phy, a school of spiritual thought that blossomed in the early twentieth century and survives to this day in the writings of
Krishnamurti, Annie Besant, Madame Blavatsky, and many others.
"Children don't belong to us," she used to say, paraphrasing what
she had learned from this blend of many world religions, especially
Eastern ones. "They are little strangers who arrive in our lives and
give us the pleasure and duty of caring for them — but we don't
own them. We help them become who they are."

Even in the face of some crisis or misconduct, she always tried to make a distinction between the behavior and the child. We weren't "bad girls" because of this or that act, or "good girls" if we obeyed. "I love you very much," she used to say sadly in moments of discipline that were more effective than any harsh words; "I just don't always love the things you do."

This conviction of being loved and lovable, valued and valuable *as we are,* regardless of what we do, is the beginning of the most fundamental kind of self-esteem: what psychologists call "global" or "characterological" or (the term I find most descriptive because it connotes something that comes first) "core" self-esteem.

As infants and small children, we cannot possibly earn our welcome in the world; yet we sense very soon whether we are in fact welcome. The comfort of having someone respond to our cries and needs, the sensuousness of being cuddled and held, the reassurance of seeing ourselves intensely "mirrored" in the faces of caregivers, the sheer pleasure of hearing sounds and, a little later, words of love and encouragement — all these things confirm (or their absence denies) our welcome. Perhaps that's why the most child-loving cultures,[1] and those childrearing practices that seem to produce the most secure children, share a belief: it is not possible to "spoil" a child before the age of two or three. Total dependence on the world creates a corresponding right to feel that it is totally dependable, and that we are the center of it.

Later in childhood, we begin to develop the second and more externalized kind of self-esteem, which psychologists call "situational" — the sort that comes from knowing we are good "at" something, compare well with others, meet other people's expectations, and can complete ever more challenging and interesting tasks for the sheer joy of it. In this phase comes satisfaction with new abilities, a new sense of interaction and community with others, and increased curiosity about the world, which we satisfy with all five senses.

But families and cultures that do not foster core self-esteem — and then ration out situational approval in return for obeying, fitting in, serving the parents' or group's purpose, and doing tasks that are always assigned instead of chosen — produce kids who feel there must be something "wrong" with their own interests and abilities.

They therefore begin to create what psychologists call a "false self" in order to earn inclusion and approval, to avoid punishment and ridicule. Thus, the small boy who is told to do such impossible things as "take care of your mother" or "be the man of the house" is teased and humiliated for showing his vulnerabilities, or is aggrandized and worshiped for a superiority he knows is unreal, often begins the elaborate construction of an "inflated" self, which results in the mostly male problem known as narcissism.[2] And the little girl who is discouraged from strength and exploring, or is punished for willfulness and praised for assuming a docility and smiling sweetness she doesn't feel, often begins to construct a "deflated" self, which results in the mostly female problem of depression.[3]

These kinds of intimate pressures and expectations are almost impossible to resist, even for children with a sound base of love and esteem. For those who do not have that base, it may not even be possible to "go underground," to continue a sense of a true self *behind* the false creation.

Since no amount of situational approval can completely fill the resulting emptiness inside, the need for approbation and community becomes so strong that it can be exploited to make people of any age work, compete, and serve in ways that clearly go against their true self-interests. Cultures and families for whom the main emphasis is on roles, conformity, obedience, or just "fitting in," and who don't develop and reward each child's full circle of unique talents, are penalizing themselves in the long run. Without that feeling of intrinsic value, it's hard for children to survive the process of failing and trying again that precedes any accomplishment. It's harder still to enjoy successes once we achieve them or to support the successes of others.

Indeed, when core self-esteem remains low even into adulthood, no amount of external task-oriented achievement or approval seems able to compensate. On the contrary, the needy child of the past is a kind of emotional black hole into which external rewards disappear — which is why a lack of core self-esteem can produce totalitarian leaders for whom no amount of power is enough, grandiose money-makers or spenders of inherited money for whom no amount of display is enough, and authoritarian parents for whom no obedience is complete.

With some sense of intrinsic worth, however, children can survive amazing hardships. Certainly, my mother's early miracle of unconditional love helped us through the later neglect and hard times that came with her depressions and withdrawal into a private world.

The need for supporting core self-esteem doesn't end in childhood. Adults still need "unconditional" love from family, friends, life partners, animals, perhaps even an all-forgiving deity. Love that says: "No matter how the world may judge you, I love you for yourself." But if there was an early deficit at the core, needs that are appropriate to childhood will constrict and dominate adult life. In any patriarchy, for instance, absentee, inexpressive, or withholding fathers are so much the result of values and job patterns that keep men from taking equal care of small children that two abnormal results are often assumed to be normal: men who keep seeking approval from paternal authority figures, and women who keep looking to their husbands and male lovers for fathering.

Core self-esteem doesn't remain neatly divided from the situational kind, either. Like two sources that flow into one river, they are separate only at the beginning. But the point is: Self-esteem, like everything else about the growing human organism, is developmental. If the individual self inside each child is ignored or punished at age two, or four, or six, some part of us remains two or four or six — until we return, recognize what happened, and begin to re-parent ourselves. It's a version of what Ernest Hemingway wrote in *A Farewell to Arms:* "The world breaks everyone, and afterward, some are strong at the broken places." Those places don't always get broken as early as childhood, but when they do, they hurt more in the resetting and take longer to knit. Perhaps the compensation is that afterward, they become even stronger, just as we form antibodies to a disease once conquered, or defend with scar tissue skin once wounded.

The problem is that if societies produce obedience by withholding core self-esteem, they are likely to discourage its mending, replenishing, and healing, too. The idea of intrinsic worth is so dangerous to authoritarian systems (or to incomplete democracies in which some groups are more equal than others) that it is condemned as self-indulgent, selfish, egocentric, godless, counterrevolutionary, and any other epithet that puts the individual in the wrong. If people feel they have a value that needn't be earned, the argument goes, how can they be made to work? Why should they continue to strive at all?

To answer this question, we need only remember that it is in infancy and early childhood, the period during which we are most likely to feel unconditionally loved, that we learn and stretch our abilities more than at any other time in our lives. No one had to reward us for learning to roll over and crawl, or penalize us for not standing or walking. We didn't need orders to explore the world around us, or a competition to say our first words. These things were learned for the sheer joy of accomplishment, stretching our own abilities, choosing what we wanted to do and then doing it — the surest path to good work at any age. Then, expanding the limits of our bodies and minds, with no false division between the two and even with great risk and effort, was a reward in itself. It still is.

People who are worried about laziness and the work ethic need only look at examples of chosen work versus compelled work, or work for which we feel personal responsibility and pride versus that done in an anonymous group. The truth is that, like every other part of nature, human beings have an internal imperative to grow. With enough sun and water to put down deep roots of self-esteem, children can withstand terrible storms. Without them, the slightest wind will seem full of danger.

II *Finding the Broken Places*

"Break open your hearts
Turn around and go back
across the wintry land."
SHARON DOUBIAGO

If you are reading this book with the double vision of a parent — thinking of the childhood you are guiding as well as the one you experienced — then it's doubly important to remember both the strength of roots and the inevitability of storms.

So much has been blamed on parents, especially on mothers, that we need more realistic and compassionate ways to think about parenting. In the 1960s, psychoanalyst D. W. Winnicott began to use a helpful phrase that is only now entering the language: the "good enough" mother,[4] a relief from the "good mother" ideal that produced guilt in women who couldn't meet its impossible standard of self-sacrifice, and guilt in the children for whom those mothers sacrificed themselves. (Of course, Winnicott perpetuated a big part of the problem by leaving fathers out of the equation, but at least he recognized the limits of mothering and the durability of children.) When used for both parents, his "good enough" concept helps us to realize that, if we love and respect our children as unique individuals, do not neglect them or use them to satisfy our personal hungers, and treat them at least as well as we treat ourselves (something that children, with their innate sense of fairness, are quick to recognize), then we are probably "good enough" parents. There are still the biases and cruelties of the outside world to deal with, but we have probably helped our children to flourish, as it is within their natures to do, and thus to feel angered by bias instead of defeated, and to fight cruelties instead of looking for approval by becoming cruel, too.

But too few childrearing theories start with the *parents'* childhoods. "Treating our children as well as we treat ourselves" is a reversible syllogism: we have to treat ourselves as well as we want to treat our children. For those with a damaged inner child whose needs are not recognized, however, "as well as" may get disastrously confused with "the same as." Think of these three common errors of childrearing:

Giving our children what we wanted and didn't have. This means children get treated *like the parent* instead of *like themselves.* No matter what their wants and needs may be, they are given what the parent wanted years ago. Furthermore, the still-deprived inner child of the parent may feel jealous of this present child and demand compensation in the form of obedience or gratitude.

Using children to live out our unlived adult lives. The father who raises a son to have the profession he once dreamed of, and the mother who uses her daughter as the adult companion her husband is not; the parents who urge their children into accomplishments as status symbols — all these and many more are ways of subordinating a child's authentic self to a parent's needs.

Justifying and normalizing our own childhoods by doing to our children what was done to us. Without a chance to go back, confront, examine, and heal — and without a consciousness that what was done was wrong, undeserved, or not "for your own good" — as parents we tend to continue some version of abuse we ourselves experienced.

In all the above cases, the needy child of yesterday *inside the parent* is dominating a child of today. In the case of intergenerational abuse especially, we're just beginning to see the dimensions of suffering. In the United States, for instance, about one in three women has been subjected to physical, sexual, or psychological abuse before the age of eighteen, and at least one in seven men. If these cycles are to be stopped, parents or others who contemplate raising a child owe it to themselves *and* those unique, individual children in their care to become aware of past damage. W. D. Wall, an English expert in early childhood education, puts it simply, "Children grow well when their parents are growing well."[5]

In *Strong at the Broken Places,* a helpful book for those who have suffered childhood abuse, especially sexual abuse, Linda Sanford offers a useful corollary to the concept of the "good enough" parent: the "bad enough" childhood. If our upbringing was bad enough to cause us to do things that are unchosen or not dictated by the circumstances of our adulthood, it was probably "bad enough" to be taken seriously and confronted as part of a process of self-healing.

The instances of abuse or neglect don't have to be spectacular. Being a very small person in a very big world, but left unprotected by the grown-ups who are supposed to protect us, is quite enough to make us feel that we are not *worth* protecting. As Sanford explains, "A 'bad enough' parent's love is conditional and his protection is in short supply. The 'bad enough' parent does not always injure the child in dramatic or obvious ways."[6]

Nor should we have to win a competition of suffering in order to take our damage seriously. There can be no "competition of tears," in the phrase of Letty Cottin Pogrebin, an expert in nonsexist education. Tears are tears, suffering is suffering, and our feelings are to be trusted. Neglect and abuse suffered in fine surroundings can be just as painful as those in poor ones, and some studies show there may be more sexual abuse of girls in very well-to-do families than at lower economic levels.[7] Furthermore, the workaholic father who constantly looks at his watch while he is with us, or the romance-aholic mother whose lover competes with us for her attention, can be just as damaging to our sense of being worthwhile as a parent who explicitly punishes us.

The more serious the abuse, however, the more difficult it may be to confront. We think: My mother or father couldn't possibly have done that to me — I must be imagining it. Or perhaps the memory has been pushed out of our consciousness completely. But those images and feelings remain alive in our unconscious — and they can be uncovered. Even abuse so long-term and severe that a child survived only by dissociating from it *while it was happening* still leaves markers above its burial ground. Periods of growing up about which we have little or no memory are among the most common such markers. So is self-injury: having learned a form of self-hypnosis to numb ourselves to physical abuse, and still believing we are "bad people" because we must have deserved the bad things done to us, we can grow up with a compulsion to cut, burn, or otherwise damage ourselves. Other frequent signs are childhood convulsions for which there are no medical reasons, a total inability to express anger, parents whom we remember as both terrifying and perfect, the conviction that one either humiliates other people or is humiliated, a sense of observing oneself without emotion, and flashes of images in which we hurt our children, animals, and others less powerful than we are — as we were once hurt ourselves.

Especially when judging criminals, destructive leaders, or even the parents who made us suffer, I know that tracing these roots to childhood strikes some people as "soft," an evasion of personal responsibility. I'm sure sometimes it has been misused in that way. But if we want to diminish violence, not just punish it, we have to take seriously the overwhelming evidence that those whose minds and actions are controlled and whose bodies are invaded and treated with violence in childhood are the most likely to continue wounding others, themselves, or both. The violence may be extreme and obvious, or it may be much subtler and even implicit in traditional childrearing techniques. In *For Your Own Good,* Alice Miller, a pioneer in tracing the origins of destructiveness to childrearing, writes about what she calls "poisonous pedagogy," the process of breaking a child's spirit so that the adult can have easy control — all done supposedly out of love, to save the child from later sufferings due to lack of discipline, and thus, as parents so often say, "for your own good." She sums up the central tenets of childrearing manuals that were popular in Europe — especially Germany — and much admired in this country as well through the first decades of this century. Some are still alarmingly familiar.

1. Adults are the masters (not the servants!) of the dependent child.
2. They determine in godlike fashion what is right and what is wrong.
3. The child is held responsible for their anger.
4. The parents must always be shielded.
5. The child's life-affirming feelings pose a threat to the autocratic adult.
6. The child's will must be "broken" as soon as possible.
7. All this must happen at a very early age, so the child "won't notice" and will therefore not be able to expose the adults.

She also sums up the beliefs that underlie these practices:

1. A feeling of duty produces love.
2. Hatred can be done away with by forbidding it.
3. Parents deserve respect simply because they are parents.
4. Children are undeserving of respect simply because they are children.
5. Obedience makes a child strong.
6. A high degree of self-esteem is harmful.
7. A low degree of self-esteem makes a person altruistic.
8. Tenderness (doting) is harmful.
9. Responding to a child's needs is wrong.
10. Severity and coldness are a good preparation for life.
11. A pretense of gratitude is better than honest ingratitude.

12. The way you behave is more important than the way you really are.
13. Neither parents nor God would survive being offended.
14. The body is something dirty and disgusting.
15. Strong feelings are harmful.
16. Parents are creatures free of drives and guilt.
17. Parents are always right.[8]

Such beliefs were certainly popular in the past. Thanks to well-meaning German nannies who were in demand among upper-class families in the United States for their ability to produce discipline, they had a special influence on children of the powerful who were likely to become world leaders.* Nor are such theories all in the past. The popularity of Alice Miller's books in sixteen languages testifies to the durability of these techniques of childrearing. But Miller argues that they produce citizens who are likely to obey the "always right" leader, that they produced a critical mass of such willingness in Germany and thus were key to electing Adolf Hitler and his National Socialist agenda. Certainly, the imagery of the Nazis appealed to the need for a traditional family, from restoring the Fatherland to sending women back to *Kinder, Küche, Kirche* ("Children, Kitchen, Church"). Hitler constantly appealed to the myth of a pure and healthy Aryan family, one whose return was threatened only by Jews, socialists, feminists, homosexuals, gypsies, the mentally ill, and other unhealthy outsiders.[9] He himself was to be the supreme father. "In my fortresses of the Teutonic Order," he promised a nation still feeling humiliated by defeat in World War I,

> a young generation will grow up before which the world will tremble. I want the young to be violent, domineering, undismayed, cruel. . . . They must be able to bear pain. There must

* In *Little Gloria . . . Happy at Last,* Barbara Goldsmith's biography of Gloria Vanderbilt, an heiress who also grew up under the control of a German nanny, Goldsmith explains that rich families were trying to imitate the upbringing of European royalty. But she also notes that homegrown experts shared the same philosophy. She quotes Dr. John B. Watson, "the most eminent child psychologist of the thirties, [who] recommended total detachment in child-rearing and warned, 'Never hug and kiss them, never let them sit on your lap. If you must, kiss them once on the forehead when you say goodnight.' " He also advocated toilet training

be nothing weak or gentle about them. The free splendid beast of prey must again flash from their eyes. I want my young people strong and beautiful.[10]

In one controversial chapter in *For Your Own Good,* Alice Miller analyzed Hitler's own childhood as the source of the cruelty he then glorified and imposed on others. In so doing, she took on the many analysts who preferred to think of Hitler as an isolated monster whose background was irrelevant, an accident that is unlikely to happen again, and in any case, one about which we can do little except identify, isolate, and punish. On the contrary, she believes, Hitler was not an inexplicable monster, but a product of an extreme version of "poisonous pedagogy." He had a sadistic father who himself had been regularly beaten with a whip until unconscious by *his* stepfather, and who in turn beat young Adolf so viciously that his sisters later remembered trying to restrain their father by holding on to his coat. A neighbor also remembered this father whistling for Adolf, as if he were a dog. And in *Mein Kampf,* Hitler presented a picture of himself as a six-year-old growing up with his parents and four siblings in two basement rooms, watching his father beat his mother and seeing "things which can fill even an adult with nothing but horror."[11] By eleven, he had been beaten almost to death for trying to run away.[12] Later, the only thing he would remember with pride from that childhood was being able to deaden himself so thoroughly that he could take thirty-two whiplashes from his father without making a sound.[13]

Though Alice Miller made clear that not everyone with a sadistic childhood becomes a monster, and that she was trying not to lessen one man's culpability but simply to see the world through the eyes of one tortured boy in order to keep other mass murderers from happening, she still aroused the ire of those whose argument is simple: If *anyone* has survived a sadistic childhood, then the childhood cannot be at fault.

But recently, another firsthand account of a famous "monster" has come along to support Miller's thesis. After thirty years of silence, Peter Z. Malkin, one of a team of Israeli agents who cap-

by six months — which may be a physical impossibility — and recommended punishing babies who did not comply by forcing them to drink castor oil. (New York: Alfred A. Knopf, 1981, p. xii.)

tured Nazi war criminal Adolf Eichmann, has offered his own evidence of a destroyed person who then destroyed others; a conclusion made all the more powerful by the fact that Malkin's own family members were among the millions murdered at Eichmann's orders.

In 1959, Malkin intercepted on a Buenos Aires street this man who had invented the term "the final solution," commissioned the design of the first gas chambers, and directed the murder of more Jews than any other Nazi officer. As his personal captor for several days in a safe house, Malkin talked with Eichmann, in spite of orders not to. His curiosity about this "monster" was too great. What he found was a man cut off from emotion: a man who talked about his mother's death when he was ten, the murdering of millions of Jews (whom he insisted he had nothing against personally, even rather liked), pleasant memories of having traveled to Jerusalem in order to better understand the Jewish culture he was trying to eradicate, and also of a Jewish boy who had been his best friend growing up — all without any emotion at all. Indeed, Eichmann still seemed to believe he deserved praise for having done his job of extermination so ingeniously and followed orders with such carefulness. In turn, he congratulated Malkin on the professionalism with which the Israeli team had carried out Eichmann's own abduction. The only time he ever seems to have disobeyed an order, as Malkin observed, was later when he refused to swear on the Bible at his trial in Israel; apparently because it was a reminder of his father, a cold, remote, devout figure who had been an accountant and an elder in the Evangelical church. The only clue to a buried self in his conversation was an undercurrent of hostility toward and fear of his father, though Eichmann's words remained as matter-of-fact and impersonal as they had been about everything else.

But Malkin's most chilling remembrances are those of Eichmann as a man who could only give or follow orders, be dominant or subservient — nothing else. Though he had been living a "normal" life for fourteen years, for instance, he reverted to this behavior the moment he reentered a hierarchy as a prisoner, and at first he would not eat, drink, or defecate. It took Malkin several days to realize that Eichmann *was waiting to be ordered,* that he had been suppressing the needs of his own body. Even after Malkin had ordered him to seat himself on the toilet, at a time when his bodily excretions had been stored up for so long that he must have been in agony, Eichmann asked Malkin politely, "May I begin?" Then he apologized abjectly for every noise his body made and finally asked permission to wipe himself. This routine continued daily.

In fact, like Hitler, Eichmann in his life as a successful Nazi official had bragged about his ability to cut off pain and proudly showed scars on his knees and elbows from crawling over barbed wire during training as an SS officer. Once imprisoned by the Israelis, he put himself — or the body in which a self must once have lived — under enemy control, almost as if it were as familiar as home. "I was a good son," was the only thing Eichmann would say about his response to his father. "It was not my place to question him." Asked about Hitler, he instantly replied, "The Führer was infallible."

"Why is it," Malkin wrote, "that one person comes of age profoundly humane while someone else, of the same culture and social background, is seemingly impervious to the needs of others?"

> The conclusion I reached, though hardly original, nonetheless still seems far too little appreciated. It has everything to do with how one is regarded as a child. Those who as children are valued and nurtured, loved without expectation and listened to and heard, are likely to become passionate adults who think for themselves and make moral choices. Those many others around whom regimentation is the norm and unconventionality is taken as aberrant are quickly made to understand — by parents, by teachers, by almost everyone in their universe — that they are of worth only as part of the larger whole. As second nature, they learn passivity and obedience, not conscience.
>
> Such an insight would prove useful in my work, helping me to understand those whose behavior sometimes seemed unfathomable. It would come in even handier later, in my own life, when I became a father.[14]

It may happen only occasionally in history that such leaders are elected, but the destruction brought about by tortured children who grow into torturing adults can be read about in our newspapers every day. We know what miracles of courage millions of such children will have to perform in adulthood if they are to stop this sadism in one generation.

And we must remember: any form of abuse that comes from the very people who are supposed to protect us, to whom we have no choice but to make ourselves vulnerable, is the most destructive of self. Until the last decade or so, sexual abuse especially was compounded by the disbelief and blindness of psychiatrists, teachers, law-enforcement officials, social workers, and other parent surrogates to whom children are supposed to be able to turn when the parents themselves are the problem. Imbued with such well-meaning but still "poisonous pedagogy" as the Freudian doctrine that child victims desired and therefore fantasized having sex with adults — perhaps also with many professionals' own need to keep their childhood pain buried — they refused to believe children, who were developmentally incapable of having imagined such adult acts. This unwillingness to take children's testimony seriously still characterizes a court system where young witnesses are refused the right to testify, broken down by lawyers on the stand, and discredited. In fact, studies show they are more likely to be telling the truth than are adults.[15] Nonetheless, children are even less likely to be believed when their stories involve extremes of sadism, collusion among families and communities (sometimes extending over several generations), and so-called ritual or cult abuse — including the torture and killing of animals to frighten children into silence — that are so terrible that authorities decide these things just *can't* be true. Yet many instances of such "incredible" crimes are documented, sometimes by adults after years of suppressed memory, sometimes by authorities who are now beginning to believe children enough to investigate their stories.

Now that women have begun to speak out about past abuse and to believe each other, we have a better idea of the dimensions of the sexual abuse of girls. But sexual abuse of boys is still shrouded in silence when it involves other boys or men, and misinformation when it involves women. Homophobia makes many boys fear being stigmatized if they reveal their abuse, even years later; yet current statistics indicate that about 90 percent of abusers of children in general are men. At the same time, the relatively few cases of adult women who sexually abuse male children get disproportionate attention — especially in films, novels, and plays that sexualize such abuse and downplay its real damage, just as they sexualize young girls with much older men. The cost of this silence is high for both the individuals who suffer it and society. Since men are more likely to respond to past abuse by abusing others, our prisons are full of those who continued doing to others what was done to them.

With so much disbelief around them from so many adult quarters, it's no wonder that children begin to bury and dissociate their own reality — especially when people on whom they are totally dependent say things like:

"This is what all fathers and daughters do."

"I wouldn't want you to learn about sex from a stranger."

"If you say once more that you're going to tell, I'm sending that cat of yours to the pound for gassing." [16]

"You're a slut, you're no good, you asked for it."

"If you tell, it will kill your mother."

Those are real words of real sexual abusers, all of them fathers who abused their own children. But such obvious invasions of a child's self are not isolated events. They are one end of a continuum. "The most common pathogenic parental attitude in America," reports Dr. Hugh Missildine in *Your Inner Child of the Past,* is "overcoercion," a tendency that is

> typically expressed by the parent who constantly directs, supervises, redirects the child with an endless stream of anxious reminders and directions. Because the child's need to initiate and pursue his [*sic*] own interests as part of his own development is ignored by this coerciveness, the child may learn to rely excessively on outside direction. Often, because he must assert his independence as an individual some way, he reacts to this constant coercion by dawdling, daydreaming, forgetting, procrastination and other forms of resistance. [17]

In everyday life, the overcoercion and consequent weakening and shaming of self may be as mundane as being constantly encouraged or forced to imitate, follow, and obey; to always "color inside the lines." It can be as approved as being made to feel intrinsically sinful by one's upbringing, religious and otherwise. It can be as cruel as hearing from one's parent what a burden one is (as in, "If I hadn't had you, I could have been . . ."). Or as damaging as being a little girl whose family wishes she were a boy. It can be as internalized as the bias that causes some Jewish families to be disappointed when children look "too Jewish," and even to urge them toward cosmetic surgery, or that causes some African-American families to favor the child with lighter skin and "good" hair, consciously or not.

But somewhere within each of us, buried at varying depths depending on the age and degree of neglect or abuse, shame or coercion we endured, there is a resistant, daydreaming, rebellious, creative, unique child — a true self who is waiting.

III   *Parables of Return*

"By the shore of the lake there is a girl
twelve years old, watching the water
fold and disappear. I walk up behind her,
I touch her shoulder, she turns her head —
I see my face. She looks through me
up at the house. This is the one I have
come for. . . . She does not know
any of this will ever stop.
She does not know she is the one
survivor."

SHARON OLDS

Given the pain of so many childhoods, there are three riddles: why many people pass the pain on to their children, why many do not, and what makes the difference. Since illness demands and receives more attention than health, there are more answers to the first riddle of why people *do* pass on their legacy of pain:

Because this kind of childhood patterning runs deep in psyches and wide in cultures.

Because when pain has been intertwined with love and closeness, it's very difficult to believe that love and closeness can be experienced without pain.

Because many adults are proud of surviving, and therefore believe the damage wasn't serious, or even that it toughened and helped them.

And perhaps most of all, because our children are the only people on whom we can safely take revenge for what was done to us.

But there is great hope. Though figures vary widely, an umbrella survey of forty studies concluded that only about a fourth to a third of abused children actually grow up to abuse their own children. Linda Sanford cites these figures in *Strong at the Broken Places* out of justifiable concern that survivors may be stigmatized twice: once by their own suffering, and again by societal assumptions that they will repeat it. (For example, she recounts the case of a mother who was deprived of custody of her children in a divorce case — not because they had been abused, but because *she* had been abused as a child.) What made the difference for those who were able to break the patterns in which they were raised was the support of family and friends and an ability to be open and angry about their own past abuse.[18]

Since females are less likely than males to pass on their own violent abuse to others, socializing boys a lot more like girls would probably help to diminish these cycles. Learning to talk about feelings more openly, to solve conflict in nonviolent ways, to reject dominance as part of gender identity, and to be empathetic with the feelings of others — all these are skills of which boys are often deprived. On the other hand, if girls were raised a little more like boys — if they had more right to say no, to declare boundaries, to develop a strong personal identity, to be angry, to rebel — they would be less likely to be revictimized as adults. Studies of battered women show that many were battered in childhood or saw their mothers battered (though, of course, the sheer number of violent men means that many wives and partners will suffer this fate, regardless of their backgrounds). Many studies of female prostitutes have shown that a disproportionate number were victims of childhood sexual abuse. Many also tried to save themselves by fleeing abusive homes, but the feeling of having only a sexual value was even harder to escape.

What makes self-rescue possible, says Alice Miller, is one condition: *at least one person* in our childhood who affirmed our true feelings, and thus let us know that our true self could be seen by others and did exist.

I've come to believe that this hopeful "one person" theory is true. But something more: that even if there was no such person then, it's possible to *become* that "one person" for ourselves now; to journey back to a lost child, recover and experience what that child experienced, and become our own parent.

The stories that follow are of people who went on this journey at very different stages and places of life, sometimes with a guide, sometimes with others on a similar quest, and sometimes as solo explorers.

Robert's Story

Toward the end of the 1960s I watched a little boy who came each day to a storefront childcare center in a crowded, changing neighborhood of New York's West Side. He was a serious child with big, dark, expressive eyes who always stayed separate from the other noisy kids. Mostly, he just watched from a safe place near the wall. When he did play with toys, he touched them as if they might be more alive than he was. As far as anyone knew, this four-year-old had never said a single word.

Each morning, Dorothy Pitman Hughes, the neighborhood leader who had started this pioneering center, would steal a few minutes from her busy day and take him over to a quiet corner with a full-length mirror. Kneeling beside him so that her eyes were on a level with those of his small reflected self, she would go through a quiet litany: "Look at that face. Isn't it beautiful? Do you know there's no other face in the world like it? . . . Now, hold up that hand. See what an amazing hand it is? Those fingers can tie sneakers and draw pictures and do things no one else in the world can do. . . . And see how strong those legs are? They can run and dance and play for a very special little boy. . . . His family loves him very much, I love him very much — kids here would love to play with him. . . . And look at those eyes. There's a very special person looking out of them. He knows things no one else can know. . . ."

At first, Dorothy's patient routine seemed to have no effect at all. Passive and obedient as always, he held up a hand or an arm when requested, but his eyes just watched as if from very far away. Weeks went by with no change.

Then one afternoon when Dorothy was so busy at the center that a day was coming to an end without their private ritual, the little boy tugged at her skirt and led her over to the mirror. It was his first expression that went beyond hunger or the simplest need.

A few days later, he began to anticipate the steps by holding up a hand — then a foot, then a knee — as if to make sure that each part of him was still okay and included. When he heard once more that it was, he smiled without being asked.

Then one morning in the middle of Dorothy's litany, he pointed to the area of his heart and said, "Me?"

"Me," Dorothy confirmed. She asked him to say his name.

"Me . . . *Robert!*" he said. These were the first sounds anyone there had ever heard him utter.

To each of his classmates, one by one, he repeated his name, as if making sure he existed in their eyes, too. With every response from someone who asked him to play, or just said hi, he seemed to take a little more courage. As he once had gone from quiet watching to a conviction that he didn't exist at all, he now reversed his journey and went from saying his name to expressing more and more thoughts to actually responding to playmates and grown-ups alike. With every new bit of impact on the world, his face lit up with a smile of delight. Little by little, Robert became as active and irrepressible as any child at the center — perhaps more so, as if he were making up for lost time.

Now that this boy is a man in his twenties, I'm told that he is married, living somewhere far from New York, and raising a daughter and son of his own. Because Dorothy understood how to value the mind and heart of a four-year-old, two more children are learning that they are unique and valuable, too.

When I checked my memory of Robert's story with Dorothy, who was then my speaking partner in feminist lecture tours and is still a friend and colleague, she remembered much more. Unlike some of the kids in that makeshift storefront center in a neighborhood of both poverty and gentrification, he hadn't come from a home that was either very uncaring or very poor. Unlike a few from both ends of the economic spectrum, he never arrived in the morning with suspicious bruises or with a parent who seemed to resent the effort of bringing him there. He just happened to be the smallest, newest member in a pressured and busy household that included one older sister, three cousins who had been sent from the South for better schooling in New York, and a hardworking, exhausted mother who was responsible for supporting and taking care of them all.

In fact, she was so pulled in different directions, so pressed for time and attention, that she had come to depend on Robert's quiet preference for playing alone, as had his older sister and cousins who looked after him in the long hours after school. A doctor had told Robert's family that there was no physical problem, and they hoped that words and self-expression would come in time. But they also had grown used to him exactly as he was.

Without Dorothy's help, this little boy's sense of his own unique self might have been cut off at the start. When I asked her how she had known what to do for Robert, she explained that she, too, had felt a little invisible as a child in rural Georgia, where schoolbooks showed no black faces and still leaned toward a Confederate version of the Civil War. Her understanding of what to do had come not from any formal training but from her own unschooled, very young parents, who managed to raise eight children with love and confidence at the same time that they were growing up themselves. It was especially Dorothy's rebellious, musically gifted mother, a cleaning woman for white families, who had helped her children feel cherished. She had explained to Dorothy that a lot of white people and even some black teachers just hadn't been raised to understand that black children were important; that this was no fault of Dorothy's; and that, like each of her sisters and brothers, she was deserving, smart, and beautiful.

Without this early belief in herself, Dorothy's childhood would have been more damaging than Robert's. Her schools had been more segregated, her family's poverty more extreme, and her rural area so racist that Ku Klux Klansmen terrorized her own and other black families by shooting into their windows at night. Yet because she was brought up with love and attention in a strong black community, Dorothy learned she was *worthy* of love and attention. Because people close to her made her feel valuable, she didn't have to seek approval by creating an artificial self.

In retrospect, Robert's problem had been less the *presence* of something (prejudice, violence, anger, humiliation) than the *absence* of something (attention, support, response, assurance that he was important and therefore that he existed), and so he almost did not survive at all.

By guiding him back through his short life to the time in late infancy and early toddlerhood when a sense of separate self develops, Dorothy helped him forge a missing link in a developmental chain. She did this without academic instruction, but with what even therapists and scientists are beginning to recognize as a more important qualification: a radical empathy for one's subject. As maverick geneticist Barbara McClintock put it, "a feeling for the organism." With this kind of help, even children often go back to mend the earliest broken places.

Kate + Kathi + Kit = Katharine

The woman who came up to me after a fund-raiser and introduced herself as Katharine was large and rounded, like the Willendorf Venus, dressed elegantly in a pantsuit, and wearing a plastic identification bracelet like those given to hospital patients. She wanted to talk about my reference to Louisa May Alcott and the neglected influence of *Little Women* on generations of little girls. Where else, I had asked, could we have read about an all-female group who discussed work, art, and all the Great Questions — or found girls who wanted to be women and not vice versa?

As we walked to a coffee shop, Katherine explained that only now in her fifties did she know how much Meg, Jo, Beth, and Amy had meant to her. "Jo was my real favorite," she explained. "I had a secret life of writing poems and reading boys' mysteries, and I thought only Jo would understand. But *everybody* in the March family seemed closer to me than *anybody* in my own. I mean, my mother worked as hard at the gas company as my dad did as a printer — so why was she the one who did everything at home? And my older sister seemed younger and sillier than I was. She would ask me which earrings to wear or if I thought some boy was cute. I vowed never to be like either one of them."

Then one day when she was around twelve, everything changed. "My girlfriends suddenly behaved as if any boy were more important than anything we did together," she said. "I started to feel ashamed of my mother because she wasn't thin — before that, I loved sitting on her lap, she was so comfortable. I stopped loving school, I stopped speaking up in class, and I started to be what *Seventeen* called 'a good listener.' The only thing left of my secret life was rescuing injured birds and stray cats. My sister and a boy I liked — I'd started to get crushes, too — thought it was silly but okay, as long as I dropped the part about becoming a veterinarian. Sometimes, I slipped up and became my old opinionated self again, but whenever I did, I felt *unlovable*. I felt *selfish*. I even burned all my poems so nobody could find out who I really was.

"Instead of being 'Kate,' I suddenly became 'Kathi' with an *i* — like all the girls in school named Sandi or Patti or something. We dotted our *i*'s with little circles and — I don't know how to tell you this — with little hearts."

I remembered writing my name with hearts over the *i*'s, too. We fell into a discussion of the sweetness syndrome, a smiling, always cheerful mask we had begun to adopt as teenagers. No wonder girls started turning anger into depression and eating problems — where else could it go?

"And the girls who get depressed are the sane ones," said Katharine. "At least they're rebelling. I just went along. Ever since I'd torn up my poems, I'd been trying to be a new, socially acceptable girl. Unfortunately, I succeeded. I married a socially acceptable man and had four kids. I tried to live through them, which meant I controlled everything they did. I also spent thirty years on a diet so I wouldn't look like my mother. I became 'Kit' then — as if my name and my body should take up as little space as possible. The more I gave up, the more I thought, At last, I'm really a *good woman*.

"Of course, I started to drive my husband and kids crazy. Who wants to be lived through? But worse, *I* was going crazy. I spent ten years on tranquilizers prescribed by some asshole doctor who said I should be happy because I had 'everything.' After the kids were grown up and my services weren't needed anymore, my family didn't know what to do with me, so they put me in a nice loony bin. I suppose after all those years of my controlling their lives, they decided to control mine."

What eventually helped her had little to do with the hospital. While sitting in the lounge waiting for her nightly dose of drugs, she happened to see *Nobody's Child,* a made-for-TV movie about Marie Balter, a woman who had been put in a mental institution as a teenager, mainly because her family didn't want her. She spent more than twenty years in hopeless dependency before a woman psychiatrist thought she saw "a person behind those eyes." I'd seen this movie, too, with a very realistic Marlo Thomas playing the role, and I once had met the real Marie Balter. She had indeed battled dependency on years of drugs given to her in hospitals, plus extreme agoraphobia — that fear of going into the public world that often afflicts people too long kept out of it. Doctors had predicted that she would never be able to live permanently outside an institution, but through a long process of taking college courses, moving in with a sympathetic family, getting her own apartment, and finally earning the academic qualifications to work with people like herself who needed bridges out of hospitals, she became a national advocate for programs to help people make the transition from institutionalized dependency to lives of their own.

I well remembered the final scene in the movie, in which she returns as a lecturer to the same hospital through whose halls she had shuffled for so many years, numbed by Thorazine and lost to herself. "I know that there were some of you, maybe many of you," she said from the podium, "who were *sure* I'd be back. Well, here I am."

That triumphant moment had made Katharine feel she could recover, too, but what moved her even more was a scene of Marie finally embracing the "ghost" of her inner self, the abandoned and terrified little girl of the past. "Marie puts her arms around her," Katharine explained, "and then the little girl and Marie merge into one. Well, when I saw that, I couldn't stop crying. I suddenly thought: Kate is still inside me. If somebody like Marie Balter can rescue herself, I damn well can do it, too.

"Of course, that was a movie version. It took me weeks of going back in my mind to rooms where Kate had lived before she would let me talk to her. But finally one day, she showed me her poems — the ones I had burned — and suddenly, *I remembered every word.*

"After that, I used to start every day imagining myself sitting next to her, waiting to hear what she would say. First, she told me how lonely she'd been. Then she told me I was too thin, how could she sit on my lap and be comfortable? Then she said she didn't understand why I was in a hospital when I wasn't sick — and shortly after that, I went home.

"Now, I don't need to visit her every day. She's just a part of my life. Thanks to her, I decided two things were going to become the size they were meant to be: my body, and my name. I also try to do things I know she would enjoy — which is why I love my job running an animal shelter. But the last time I went back to talk, she said a funny thing: 'You needn't have worried: Jo was taking care of me.' "

As we got up to leave the coffee shop, my eyes fell again on the hospital bracelet. Now that she was out, Katharine told me, she wore it as a sign of solidarity with the women who were still on the ward, despairing, overmedicated, waiting, as Katharine had once waited. "I lost myself a long time ago," she explained, "and now I feel better than I have since I was reading *Little Women.*"

I thought of Kate — and all the Kates within us — when I read *Making Connections,* a collection of studies by Carol Gilligan and her colleagues at the Harvard Graduate School of Education on girls in the pivotal years just before adolescence. Until this groundbreaking effort, most generalizations about adolescence, like other conclusions in psychology, had been drawn from studies of males, and therefore little attention had been paid to the differences between growing into increased freedom and growing into less. Gilligan writes of evidence "that girls' development in adolescence may hinge on their resisting not the loss of innocence but the loss of knowledge." [19] But, as she concludes, early female strengths don't just disappear, they go underground. She points to the number of women novelists, from Charlotte Brontë in *Jane Eyre* to Toni Morrison in *The Bluest Eye,* who have used a nine- or ten-year-old girl as their narrator, their most clear-sighted witness.

I also thought of Katharine — and all the Katharines we're trying to become — when I read *Writing a Woman's Life*, Carolyn Heilbrun's small, laserlike book that explains why so many women become ourselves after fifty. As Heilbrun writes: "Age portends all the freedoms men have always known and women never — mostly the freedom from fulfilling the needs of others and from being a female impersonator."[20]

Perhaps it's not quite "never." There was a time of freedom — not in comparison to males perhaps, but in comparison to women's later lack of it — for many little girls in the years before the feminine role. It is not surprising to learn that there are two times of crisis in a woman's life: when she enters that social role in adolescence, and when it abandons her at around fifty. Perhaps one day, we will have changed society enough so women are never asked to submerge a true self. Until then, those early years are the best guide to the person we can become in that last third of life.

But even that submerged stage of "Kathi" and "Kit" isn't without subliminal, perhaps subversive knowledge. I was looking at photos of prehistoric archeological finds the other day and realized that the heart once symbolized female power. It was a procreative, genital symbol: the female version of the phallic symbol. Though trivialized into romance and deprived of its power by centuries of patriarchy, the heart still belongs to us. In a way, history has progressed oddly like a woman's life: first a time when we were powerful and ourselves, then a long period of patriarchy and forgetting, and perhaps, with this worldwide wave of feminism, an era of rediscovering our power in a new way.

Perhaps the millions of little girls who incorporated hearts into their signatures, as Katharine and I once did, weren't so silly after all.

Alcoholic Parent, Workaholic Child

Bryan Robinson is one of the millions of people who now call themselves "adult children of alcoholics," a term that entered the culture only about twenty years ago. Indeed, in the rural South of the 1950s where Bryan grew up, even the word *alcoholic* wasn't used in polite society. There were just "hard drinkers" who were normal if they were men, or less normal "tipplers" who were

women. Only the town drunk who fell down in the street was recognized as having a problem. Anything that went on behind closed
doors was no one else's business.

Bryan's father, a machinist and sometime inventor, was far
from being the town drunk. He supported his family and was an
affectionate and generous father — when he was sober. But when
he drank too much, he became a paranoid tyrant. Instead of a sane
and loving father coming home from work, Bryan might see a dictator who felt every smile was ridiculing him. Instead of a calm
house after school, there might be a raging battlefield with yelling
parents and overturned furniture. Instead of being picked up in front
of the theater after a weekly movie, Bryan and his sister might be
left to wait so long into the night that a policeman would finally
take pity on them and drive them home. Like so many children,
Bryan internalized all this. "If my father couldn't remember to pick
me up at the movies," as he remembered later, "I figured I must not
be very important."

He also assumed that drinking and violence was a shame
unique to his family. After his older sister escaped the house by
getting married at seventeen, Bryan took over as a prematurely old,
superresponsible child who pulled the curtains so neighbors couldn't
witness his parents' violent fights and swept up the broken glass
afterward. Sometimes he got caught in the violent crossfire, especially when he tried to mediate, but the emotional crossfire was
worse. "I was embarrassed by the way my father behaved and was
afraid people wouldn't like me because of it," Bryan wrote many
years later. "He seemed to care more for his bottle than he did
for us."

Bryan withdrew into the refuge of his room and his imagination. As soon as he could hold a pencil, he began to write stories
because in them, everyone — unlike his uncontrollable father — did
exactly what Bryan said. He also discovered that in school if he
worked hard, he could win approval and thus have something pre-
dictable in his life. Nonetheless, he was always on guard against
revealing his family shame. When his third-grade teacher asked why
he never smiled, for instance, Bryan remembers believing that "she
had detected my hidden secret. . . . I found myself smiling for no
apparent reason — not because I was happy but because I wanted

to hide the fact that I was sad." With all the force of his intelligence and desperation, he created a false self.

After growing up to earn four degrees including one doctorate, Bryan turned the same energy to his work as a teacher and psychologist. Weekends and holidays gave him a feeling of panic, just as they had at home, so he extended his work hours at the expense of time with his family. "I was hooked," he later wrote.

> I had become hopelessly addicted to work. I worked for the sake of work and the superficial, fleeting feelings of esteem and accomplishment it gave me. . . . In work I had found my salvation, my Nirvana — or so I thought.
>
> My behavior was highly rewarded in my job, and I quickly made it through the professorial ranks. . . . I became obsessed with my career. . . . Like an alcoholic, I felt restless and became irritable when I went more than a few days away from my desk. . . . Hardly a vacation passed that a stuffed briefcase of work didn't accompany me as part of my luggage. While others swam and played in the surf, I toiled over my word processor back in the cottage. My family became concerned, and after many stormy protests, work was no longer allowed on vacations. My response was what any normal work addict would do: sneak it into my suitcase. I hid my work as my father had hidden his bottle.

Gradually, his addiction had reached such a level, and such a clear parallel with his father's life, that Bryan himself began to realize he was out of control. Though his father had died a lingering and painful death five years before, he was continuing to dominate his son's life. Moreover, Bryan's drug of choice was all the more seductive for being the only one an addict is paid and praised for taking.

But the pattern of addiction is the same whether it attaches to alcohol or cocaine, food or work — a growing realization that has caused self-help programs like Alcoholics Anonymous to diversify into everything from Overeaters Anonymous and Workaholics Anonymous to groups for those whose lives are affected by the addictions of people close to them. Such programs enable people who've experienced these problems to help each other identify unchosen patterns of behavior, dispel feelings of shame and isolation, and begin to change, "one day at a time." When he began going to these groups regularly, Bryan made discoveries:

- that he felt panic without work because his childhood days away from school had been filled with terror of his unpredictable father;
- that he had imagined everyone else must have a perfect family in which no one disagreed, but that the freedom to express feelings, even to disagree, was a valuable part of a healthy family life;
- that his childhood had given him strengths as well as problems; for instance, an ability to understand the similar experiences of other people that was more powerful than his academic training.

The interesting thing is that after the shame goes, the strengths remain. Dr. Bryan Robinson now considers all that he is and does "a culmination of having lived in an alcoholic family and having worked for twenty years in the helping professions as a teacher, counselor, family researcher, therapist, and professor of child and family development."

To bring his personal and professional life together, he wrote a small book about work addiction, with an intimate first chapter from which I have been quoting here. Though not something professionals have traditionally adopted, the use of the personal is what gives his work its power.[21]

Perhaps you know, are living with, or are yourself someone for whom this parable has echoes. I know I feel them. I remember so well the dread of not knowing who I would find when I came home: a mother whose speech was slurred by tranquilizers, a woman wandering in the neighborhood not sure of where she was, or a loving and sane woman who asked me about my school day. I, too, created a cheerful front and took refuge in constant reading and after-school jobs — anything to divert myself (and others) from the realities of my life. Years later when I became a writer, I mined my life for amusing anecdotes. Only in my forties did I begin to leave that false self behind by using some of the grimmer experiences in my writing.

In the early days of that change, I remember comparing child-hoods with Julie Andrews, not yet a movie star, but already a stage success in *My Fair Lady* and *Camelot*. I was amazed to discover that inside this calm, talented, beautiful woman there was still a very unpretty, isolated, prematurely old twelve-year-old whose hard work and freakily adult soprano voice had supported her own un-inhibited mother, her alcoholic stepfather, and two young half brothers. Like Bryan Robinson, she had concealed this totally out-of-control life by writing in-control stories; in her case, an almost entirely false diary in which she made up a "vibrant and jolly" fam-ily life, hour by hour, day by day.

I never forgot this contrast between a small, sad grown-up with very real duties and the carefree child she had created. While she changed the "nappies" of her two half brothers, toured as a per-former to pay the family bills, and was unable even to attend school with her contemporaries, Julie was also creating a cheerful and elab-orate fiction because, "If someone found the diary, this is the life we were supposed to have."

When I asked her if I could include this story, she said yes, that psychoanalysis had finally given her a way to look on both her child-hood and her parents with compassion. "I only began to feel grown-up — truly in charge, as if I had grown into my own skin and bones — about ten years ago," she explained. In retrospect, she felt that two things had given her "something to hang on to in all the chaos": the accident of a singing talent that was part of the reason for her plight, but also gave her an identity; and the faith of her father, a schoolteacher who told her when she was fearful about the future, "Darling, your own good brain will tell you what to do when the time comes."

Even now, when she explains why she hasn't yet written about all this — unlike her friend Carol Burnett, for instance, who was also a superresponsible child in an alcoholic family and wrote a very moving book about it[22] — one can still hear the uncertain little girl: "My biggest cross is a lack of education." But there is also a resolve: "I'd like to write again — truthfully this time."

In the United States, one in eight adults is the child of an al-coholic household.[23] Combined with drug addiction, illness, vio-lence, sexual abuse, and all the other reasons why children create false selves to survive, this sensation of hiding behind a "normal" facade may be the majority experience. Though these sad statistics are often greeted with a nostalgia for simpler times, there is no reason to believe that children were treated with more respect in the past. What seems to be an increase in sexual abuse, for instance, may actually be an increase in reporting it, or even remembering it. Certainly, in my own unscientific sample of interviewing women of seventy or eighty, the numbers are about the same. And in *The Secret Trauma,* Diana Russell reported a rise in statistics since the early 1900s, perhaps due to such factors as an increasing number of stepfathers, but also pointed out that the only *de*creases had taken place when millions of men were gone during two world wars. Perhaps a major part of the increased suffering of children is that the nuclear family, a new construct of the last century or so, has increased their vulnerability by making them exclusively dependent for the first time on only one or two adults.[24] The rescuing grandfather, the loving aunt, the mother down the road who takes in a neighbor's child as her own — that one person who, Alice Miller tells us, is crucial if only as a witness — is an increasingly rare phenomenon.

There may be an even greater need now to let the child within us know: You're not alone anymore.

Leaders as Guides of Return

Bell, a town in a rough and rural part of eastern Oklahoma with about 300 mostly Cherokee families, had no school that went above the eighth grade, little indoor plumbing, a lot of conflict, and widespread hopelessness. Because residents were dependent on government handouts and treated as invisible to the outside world, they had come to feel powerless over their fates; adults with all the vulnerabilities of childhood and none of the rewards. The few who managed to escape were often ashamed to admit they had ever lived in Bell.

When Wilma Mankiller, a Cherokee community renewal leader, said she wanted to start a project there, she received two warnings from people who knew Bell: first, "these people" would never work, much less volunteer, to help themselves; and second, she shouldn't stay in town after nightfall.

Nonetheless, she posted notices in Cherokee and English asking people to come to a town meeting to discuss "what you would like Bell to look like in ten years." No one came. She called another meeting. A handful of residents came, but only to complain. She called a third, and convinced now that she really wanted to listen, about a dozen people showed up.

"I've always trusted disenfranchised people to come up with their own ideas," Wilma said later. Therefore, she didn't dictate or even suggest. She just asked a question: "What single thing would change this community the most?"

The answer was not a project for school dropouts or any other program to help young people who still had a hope of escaping Bell, which was what Wilma had expected. Instead, they chose something that was more democratic and crucial to everyone, regardless of age or intention to leave: a water supply that was connected to every house, plus indoor plumbing. This would cut school dropout rates, too, as they explained to Wilma. Their kids had to bathe in polluted streams or in water carried from a single spigot outside the schoolhouse, and when they failed to bathe as often as their less poor classmates in Stillwell, a neighboring town with the nearest high school, they were ridiculed.

Just as Wilma had started this process with a question that gave residents the power of choice, she continued it with a bargain that gave them an equal role in what they had chosen. She would get the supplies, federal support, engineers, and other experts — but only if the residents built the water system themselves and also helped with the fund-raising. After generations of broken promises, they were full of skepticism about outside help, and after generations of passivity, also full of self-doubt. Nonetheless, they named themselves the Bell Water and Housing Project, and began.

Each family was assigned a mile of pipe to lay. Those who knew English also worked on fund-raising plans, and those who spoke Cherokee did everything from marking the path of ditches to carrying sand for backfill, but all knew their jobs were vital to the project. Though the women had been "just part of the woodwork," as Wilma put it — and were also convinced they were too weak to carry pipe or do construction tasks — they soon discovered it wasn't any harder than water carrying and their usual household chores. Wilma knew the group's spirits had begun to rise when families started a relay race to see who could lay pipe the fastest.

Though failure had been the unanimous prediction of Bell's neighbors, people from surrounding communities came to see what was happening. So did several foundation executives who viewed this renewal project as an example of Third World development; certainly few places in the world were poorer than Bell. When a local CBS television crew — attracted by Bell's reliable scenes of poverty — came to film powerlessness, they played an inadvertent role in changing the situation by letting residents see themselves on the evening news and begin to feel less isolated. Soon, even the non-Indian residents of Bell were saying positive things about this water project in the newspapers, and the Indian community began to feel visible for the first time. Most important, they had become visible through something they were doing for themselves.

The next fourteen months encompassed a novel's worth of personal change and problem-solving, but by their end, the water system was complete. The CBS crew returned to document success, and the seven-minute story that resulted appeared on "CBS Sunday Morning" with Charles Kuralt. Now known as "the town film," it is often replayed with pride.

Having grown from the dozen residents who attended the first meeting to a group that included most families, the Bell group now decided to start its next project: housing. Again, Wilma got federal funds — but no federal contractors. The residents were to do the work themselves. "Even if families didn't like each other," as Wilma explained, "they were learning to work together. They were beginning to bond as a community." Because federal funds had been earmarked for Indians only, the five or six *non*-Indian families in Bell weren't eligible for housing funds. After careful discussion, the Cherokee community decided to hold fund-raisers so those families could benefit, too, even though some had behaved badly toward them in the past. As always, self-esteem had created an ability to be generous: in this case, it began to restore the Indian principle of reciprocity, wrongly characterized as "Indian giving" by whites but really a balance of giving and receiving.

At that first meeting in 1979, the most often heard sentiment had been: "It's always been like this; nothing will change." Now, it was: "Look what we've done; what else could we take on?" Since renovating Bell's housing, members of the steering committee have overseen a senior citizen education project, an annual "fund-raising powwow," a speakers' bureau that carries Bell's lessons to other rural communities, and a bilingual education program to help preserve the Cherokee language and culture. The school dropout rate has fallen, and other nearby communities like Burnt Cabin and Cherry Tree have begun water and housing projects, too. Those who were once ashamed of living in Bell have become proud.

But for Wilma, watching individual people flower was the greatest reward. Sue and Thomas Muscrat, a Head Start worker and farmhand respectively, had been too unconfident and skeptical to speak up at all in the early meetings. They became members of the school board and the speakers' bureau. With beadwork, drawings, and elkhorn carvings they had always made but realized had value only after outsiders commented on their beauty, they opened a craft store. Because their one son had grown up before this change in their lives, they decided to share their good fortune by adopting a child, an abused, part-Cherokee little boy from Dallas.

As for Wilma Mankiller herself, you may have heard of her. In 1987, the Cherokee Nation — which includes many residents of Oklahoma and five more states — elected her Principal Chief, the first woman to hold this office that carries more responsibility than those of state governor and U.S. senator combined. One of the eleven children of a Cherokee farmer turned longshoreman and an Irish-Dutch mother from Stillwell who had defied her family to cast her lot with the Cherokees, Wilma is a political activist as well as a gifted organizer, mother, administrator, and creative leader.

Still, she was criticized by some in her nation who said a woman shouldn't be chief. Though in the old days a council of grandmothers had chosen the tribal leaders, even decided if wars should be fought, many Cherokees have absorbed the values of the male-dominant society around them in the centuries since then. When she ran again in 1991, Wilma was opposed as Principal Chief by two male candidates, but most Cherokee people knew she was giving them back the most precious possession: their self-esteem. She won reelection by an unprecedented 83 percent of the vote. The projects she has helped to start during her reign as chief range from adult literacy programs to a communally owned manufacturing plant, and she oversees a total annual budget of $54 million, more than half of which is now self-generated by the Cherokee Nation. Before community renewal programs began, 80 percent of all funds came from the federal government.

Wilma Mankiller became the best kind of leader: one who creates independence, not dependence; who helps people go back to a collective broken place and begin to heal themselves. Though there is a long way to go before the Cherokee Nation restores in a new form the dignity and self-sufficiency it knew 500 years ago, before the terrible centuries of genocide and the banning of even the Cherokee language and religion, now there is a way of making progress that is their own.[25]

Teaching What We Need to Learn

No one has written more revealingly about hidden or blatant cruelty in childrearing than Alice Miller. As a psychoanalyst for more than twenty years and author of a half-dozen books, she has had an enormous impact on both professionals and ordinary readers looking for help. It's not an exaggeration to say that her work has saved lives.

One of her most common experiences over the years has been the reader who says: "You described my childhood exactly — how could you know?" Until recently, she had no answer. She just had a ready empathy with children who had undergone those too-common methods of teaching and parenting that assume children must be tamed, or that they are blank slates on which adults can write anything. She knew how to help others, but this did not prevent her from clinging to the belief that her parents had provided her with loving care and had made every effort to give her everything she needed as a child. This remained true through all her academic training, years of clinical work, successful books, and two full analyses. "Even in my second analysis," she revealed, my mother appeared only as a somewhat oversolicitous woman with good intentions who had tried to do her best. It didn't fit in with the training or ethical attitudes of either of my therapists for them to acknowledge that her pedagogic efforts had served *her* interests and the conventional ideas of her day while ruthlessly violating her child, whom she considered her property. . . . I still took pains to try to be understanding of my mother, to forgive her for her subtle psychological cruelty, which kept appearing in my dreams.[26]

Though she had no memory of the first five years of life and memories of later childhood were sparse, and though she knew as a professional that this was a sign of strong repression ("something that never," as she had warned others, "occurs without good reason"), she remained the dutiful daughter who forgot her own feelings and remembered only her mother's version of the past.

But in the early 1970s, she embarked on a personal avocation that was quite separate from her professional life. She began to paint. Without training or any need to be realistic, she produced small paintings that were both abstract and personal: brilliant blotches of color faded into darkness, and dark, snakelike forms ran throughout the colors. Gradually, she realized that she was painting the hidden emotions of her childhood.

"Now it was up to me," as she knew, "to take the first step myself — to listen to the child in me — and this meant exposing myself to all the pain once inflicted on her, which she had had to bear all alone, without witnesses, without words, without hope of ever being understood."[27]

This spontaneous painting continued off and on for thirteen years as she became more conscious of the reason for the emotions she was reaching. But in the meantime, the painting process was freeing her unconscious enough to help her make an empathetic connection with other abused children and to inspire her to pursue it with all the force of her considerable intellect.

Gradually, it also helped her to recover shreds of memories. Though her mother had once confided with pride that she had toilet trained her daughter by the age of five months — an act that is almost unimaginable — even the professional part of the daughter's mind hadn't been ready to admit what kind of minute control and discipline that required. As she grew up under her mother's roof and thumb, no part of her life had been her own. Everything she did was to be a proof of her mother's prowess, especially her youthful intellectual accomplishments. Only because her painting had never been possessed by her mother could it become a path to her emotions of the past.

"Was this an unusual situation?" Alice Miller asked years later.

> By no means. Of course, not every mother channels all her ambition exclusively into bringing up her children — thank goodness; and sometimes there are fathers or older siblings who come to the child's rescue. But it was not at all unusual for a daughter who had no rights and was under the thumb of her parents and brothers — the way my mother had been as a child — to seize the sole means of gaining power that society traditionally offered women as a "reward" for all the humiliation that had been heaped upon them. In the form of absolute control over the body and soul of her child an immense kingdom was granted her.[28]

It was this setting free of past emotions and events by her painting that gave her the courage to try the new therapy of J. Konrad Stettbacher, a Swiss psychotherapist, who has evolved a process for recovering memories in a safe environment, so that the adult can become an advocate for an inner child of the past. In her most recent book, *Breaking Down the Wall of Silence*, she has finally uncovered *all* the terrors. Her mother not only controlled her every thought and action, but sometimes refused to speak to, or even look at, her daughter for days on end. And when the little girl tried desperately to know what she had done wrong, how she should change, her mother only insisted that it was her further fault for not knowing and for thus being without conscience. It was a punishment Miller compares to Kafka's *Penal Colony*, in which a prisoner learns his lesson only from having it etched over and over again in the skin of his back. Yet as she points out, "I couldn't say: 'I'll find another mother, someone who talks to me and respects me, a woman who doesn't treat me like so much air but lets me know what she is going

through — a woman who knows because she is living consciously.'
As a child I had no choice but to suffer my mother's vindictive silence, and, because I was blind to her dishonesty and thirst for
power, to blame myself."[29]

Now, Miller is passionately devoted to the cause of helping to
eliminate such horrors from the lives of future children, a goal she
believes can only be achieved when each adult stops denying, forgetting, or justifying his or her childhood, and thus stops repeating
it out of revenge or unconscious patterning. Believing that the intellectual process of psychoanalysis is not only unhelpful but damaging, she has stopped using that professional identification and
resigned from its associations. Instead, she explains the healing process of remembering (and has written the accompanying text for
Making Sense of Suffering, a book in which Stettbacher outlines a
process for remembering that can be done on one's own if a group
or therapist is not available[30]), and campaigns to change childrearing practices that she believes create leaders whose inner rage en-
dangers us all.

> Today I know that it was not the books I read, it was not my
> teachers or my study of philosophy, nor was it my training to
> become a psychoanalyst that provided me with this knowledge.
> On the contrary, all these together, with their mystifying con-
> ceptualization and their rejection of reality, prevented me from
> recognizing the truth for years. Surprisingly, it was the child in
> me, condemned to silence long ago — abused, exploited, and
> turned to stone — who finally found her feelings and along
> with them her speech, and then told me, in pain, her story.[31]

Though the pain of her childhood had been without witnesses,
she had trusted her own interests and impulses — first intellectually
through her work, then emotionally through her painting, and later
with the force of a true self made whole by memory — until she
became that witness herself.

IV *Reparenting Ourselves*

"There is a secret person undamaged in every individual."
PAUL SHEPARD

The unconscious is timeless. A taste or smell or sound that accompanied strong emotions of the past can renew those forgotten feelings — just as the sound of a radio in an empty room once did for me. So can an innocent event that triggers some past anger, embarrassment, or pleasure. The holograms of all past experiences that were important to us are stored in our brain cells, just waiting to be reentered. When we find the path into them — whether we stumble on one accidentally or consciously search for it — past time is suddenly the present.

There is no single way of reentering the past. Often, a teacher, therapist, or trusted friend becomes a surrogate parent who makes us feel safe enough to begin the journey. For some, hypnosis is a time-honored bridge. For many others, meditation, a gentle form of self-hypnosis, allows us to turn inward. (You will find a sample induction at the back of this book.) Often, the company of others with similar experiences helps to build a bridge over the shame or fear that has been blocking the path. Sometimes, a whole group begins to change, and because we share that group identity, paths for our own change are opened up, too. These and other ways of journeying backward in time are discussed in chapter 4.

If the broken places are so deep and painful that the conscious mind resists in order to keep functioning — just as the child also covered them up in order to function and survive — their existence may be more difficult to explore and may need a safer environment and more consistent process, as Alice Miller's personal example shows us. In general, the deeper the wound, the more an empathetic guide or at least a personal commitment to a trusted process is necessary before the unconscious that has protected us all these years will make the journey home.

But the point of the journey is not just healing. It's also recovering the truest, most spontaneous, joyful, and creative core of ourselves.

If any of the stories you have just read strikes an emotional chord, that's a possible signal from your inner self. If anything in the present brings you unreasonable pleasure or sadness, that's a clue, too. The important thing is to make the connections between past and present. And, of course, not everything is in our power to know. We need faith in a future that will redeem the past.

When I think of my mother, for instance, who was my parent but could not be her own, I find comfort in these lines from Cherokee poet Marilou Awiakta:

> MOTHEROOT
> Creation often
> needs two hearts
> one to root
> and one to flower
> One to sustain
> in time of drouth
> and hold fast
> against winds of pain
> the fragile bloom
> that in the glory
> of its hour
> affirms a heart
> unsung, unseen

If all of this talk of reparenting oneself still seems mysterious or unlikely, just start with one exercise: Write down on this page, in whatever order or way they come to you, the things you wish you had received in your childhood — and did not:

You have just written what you should do for yourself.

Three

The Importance of Un-learning

"We are governed not by armies and police but by ideas."

MONA CAIRD, 1892

"For seasons and seasons and seasons all our movement has been going against our self, a journey into our killer's desire."

AYI KWEI ARMAH

I *Parables of Town and Gown*

> "I have been a member of the Columbia University community for thirty-five years, and I can only consider myself to be speaking as what Lionel Trilling called an opposing self, opposed to culture, in this case, the culture of the university."
> CAROLYN HEILBRUN

> "To finally recognize our own invisibility is to finally be on the path toward visibility."
> MITSUYE YAMADA

> "I was a modest, good-humored boy; it is Oxford that has made me insufferable."
> MAX BEERBOHM

Once we are old enough to have had an education, the first step toward self-esteem for most of us is not to learn but to *un*learn. We need to demystify the forces that have told us what we *should be* before we can value what we *are*.

That's difficult enough when we have been misvalued by an upbringing or social bias that is clearly wrong. But what happens when this wrongness is taught as objective truth? When the most respected sources of information make some groups invisible and others invincible? When we are encouraged to choose between "bettering" ourselves and becoming ourselves?

I never asked any of these questions during my various years of schooling. To get an education was an end in itself; its content was beyond questioning. Not until decades after I had left all formal education behind did its impact on me — and its purpose in general — seem open to challenge. Perhaps "real wisdom," as author Joan Erikson said, only comes from "life experience, well-digested."[1] I know that my own questioning was fueled by two chance experiences that occurred within weeks of each other several years ago.

First, I went back to Toledo, where my mother and I had lived when I was in junior high and high school. The occasion for this trip was a women's conference at the university on the "good" side of town, but I couldn't resist wandering around the streets of East Toledo and our old neighborhood the night before. There were the same small houses, the same bars and churches in equal numbers, the same Polish and Hungarian social clubs. A few more black families had moved in, and Puerto Rican workers were bringing a new layer of ethnicity, but what looked like the same tricycles were rusting in the front yards, the same wash was flapping on the lines, and the same big TV antenna dwarfed each roof, as though life here could only be bearable if lived elsewhere in the imagination.

Certainly, my teenage self had been totally consumed with escaping. If I had written any book then, it would have been titled *Getting Out* — and most of my friends felt the same. Our dreams of escape from the neighborhood kept us from focusing on our probable fates as lifetime factory workers who rebelled only on weekends, or homemakers who played pinochle, went bowling, and sometimes got a beating on Saturday nights. Our imaginations rarely went beyond the two escape routes we knew: sports (if we were boys) and show business (if we were girls). In fact, we could point to two local celebrities to show that we also had a chance: a guy who had gone to a university for a year or two on a football scholarship before coming back to the neighborhood as a factory foreman, and singer Teresa Brewer, who had won the Ted Mack Amateur Hour while still in high school and never come back. Mostly, though, we were responding to the media. Sports and show business were the only places we saw people like us who seemed to be enjoying life and not worrying about next week's paycheck.

I always felt both odd and lucky because I had the possibility of an additional way out: getting a college education. It was a path first to an interesting job and ultimately to a better class of husband (or if the husband should lose his job or die, it was "something to fall back on," as my mother always said) — and that was enough. Getting out of our drab, hardworking neighborhood and into the beautiful, carefree suburbs that we saw on television was all we had in mind.

I had this encouragement because my mother was the only parent in our group who had graduated from college. She had even spent a little time in graduate school. Of course, she ended up much poorer than the factory workers in this neighborhood where she grew up, and living in her family house, which was by then a ramshackle structure teetering over a major highway; a place so depressing that it was hard to rent out the first floor so the two of us could survive on the second. Yet this daily reality never changed my dream of how "college people" lived, and it certainly never interfered with my mother's faith in the redemptive powers of an education. Just as her own mother had instilled this faith in her, she handed it down to me. When our house was condemned and the land beneath it sold to the church next door, my mother used this windfall to pay my tuition at a "good" college, and I left what I thought were my less fortunate friends behind.

The day after this visit to my old neighborhood, however, I saw some of my East Toledo contemporaries at the women's conference where I was speaking. A few faces I remembered, but as we talked, we realized many of us had lived the same lives and gone to the same schools, whether or not we knew each other then. But they entered adulthood early by marrying right after graduation, or before if they "had to" (our neighborhood counted the months from wedding to birth), raising their families, and perhaps helping to support them with a part-time "pink-collar" job for the phone or gas company. But by the feminist 1970s, when new opportunities for women were being publicized on TV talk shows, their children were self-sufficient, and they were ready to seize on these new possibilities with their whole hearts.

At a time when the housewives of the "feminine mystique" were still getting out of the suburbs and into the labor force — and when I and other white-collar women workers were still trying to "deserve" the unequally paid professional jobs we thought we were so lucky to get — these women had begun to demand equal treatment with men, and by the time I encountered them again, they were getting some of those opportunities. The few women who had been able to get comparatively well paid jobs in local factories could see that the guys standing next to them on the assembly line were doing exactly the same tasks for fatter pay envelopes, so they had brought one of the earliest sex-discrimination suits. By organizing with more traditional family-planning groups, some of the others had just won a citywide referendum against an anti-abortion measure disguised as a "maternal health ordinance," and defeated it two-to-one in their mostly Catholic, blue-collar precincts. Still others were starting their own small businesses, planning the campaign of a woman mayor (who was to win and become a first in Toledo history), and organizing battered-women's programs instead of assuming that Saturday night beatings were inevitable. A few were running for the school board and other local political offices, and almost all had gone back to school for a degree or professional training as what the University of Toledo referred to as "nontraditional students," and what the women themselves called "retreads."

But what most separated all these women from the girls I remembered and their own younger selves was their spirit. They were full of rebellion, humor, energy, and a certain earthy wisdom that seemed to say, "I'm myself now — take it or leave it." One of them summed up her reasons for going back to school after forty by posting this motto on her refrigerator door: "Free your mind — so your ass can follow."

Of course, there were also many casualties. They told me about one of my best friends in high school whose children had been born so close together that her small body had run out of calcium. She lost her teeth and her hopes, and settled into the life of an old woman. Another classmate had been so shamed by her family for being "an old maid" at twenty-five that she married a man who was younger, concealed his violence toward her out of gratitude that he had married her at all, and finally became so depressed that she was institutionalized. Yet another had spent so much of her life inside one of the tiny row houses in our neighborhood that she became terrified to leave it. A doctor prescribed tranquilizers, not freedom.

But by the time we finished the conference and went to a local television station to do an interview about it, I was feeling great pride in the women who had stayed in this neighborhood that I once lived, dreamed, and breathed of escaping. They were self-confident, productive, bawdy, and very much themselves. When an angry male viewer phoned after the show to denounce the conference as "anti-family," and me in particular as "a slut from East Toledo," I suddenly remembered how devastating those words would have been to my teenage self. But all these years later, they caused less pain than laughter: he didn't have the power to define me or any of us anymore. We were defining ourselves.

As we toasted each other as "the sluts from East Toledo" with coffee and beer after the interview, I thought: Not a bad thing to be. Maybe I'll put it on my tombstone.

But the full meaning of what my classmates had achieved wasn't clear until I saw the difference between them and the college graduates I had been so eager to join. Because my twenty-fifth college reunion came only a few weeks later, the contrast was inescapable.

On the New England campus of Smith College, I realized again the great distance between this idyllic scene and my old neighborhood. Green lawns, landmark buildings, new graduates carrying long-stemmed roses, and smiling alumnae in summer dresses — all seemed evidence of assurance and good fortune. But underneath, there were doubts and tensions. And underneath was where we had been trained to keep them.

For instance: A classmate who had tried unsuccessfully to create panel discussions on aging, violence against women, equal rights legislation, and the like concluded that topics were chosen for safety and obscurity. (My personal favorite was "Tropism or Refraction?") As she said, "What do you expect? We were taught to revere Aristotle, who said females were mutilated men and could tarnish a mirror."

For instance: At our class dinner, the first woman president of Smith College addressed the problems of women combining career and family — yet never suggested that men might play an equal part at home. Indeed, she implied that she had been able to have a successful career because she *didn't* have children.

For instance: Of those who responded to our class reunion questionnaire, 98 percent had supported legal abortion. Having grown up in the era of *illegal* abortion, many of us had experienced this danger firsthand. Nonetheless, when a group of us showed up for the Alumnae Day Parade with pro-choice signs, we were told we couldn't march with our class. Why? Because there might be *even one person* who disagreed. Instead, our class carried committee-approved signs that made jokes about our age, eyesight, and waistlines, as if self-denigration and silliness were things with which no one could disagree.

For instance: Even among the new graduates, the most rebellious were still debating whether to display a banner protesting U.S. policy in Central America, with the same ladylike worry that a few people might disagree. The idea that it was okay to disagree, that people would carry whatever signs they wanted to, hadn't been part of the either/or discussion. Moreover, issues of special importance to women were clearly less serious, even to the rebellious, than foreign policy issues seen as important to men.

I'd forgotten the seductive power of niceness and unanimity. Our courses had not been dedicated to "freeing our asses." As a result, we had a hard time assuming our own centrality. Would graduates of a black college forbid civil rights signs at a reunion because *one person* might disagree? Would Jewish graduates take foreign policy toward Latin America more seriously than policy toward Jews?

It seemed that for women of all races and classes, education had separated *what we studied* from *how we lived.* It had broken the link between mind and emotion, between what we learned intellectually and what we experienced as women.

Of course, there were Smith women who were spirited, self-confident, and active in everything from politics and business to education and the arts. Individually, many were doing brave and remarkable things. But as a group, they seemed less strong, funny, joyful, and free than their East Toledo sisters; more apologetic and self-blaming; more distant from themselves. If divorced, they were more likely to have lost their identity along with their husbands. If married, they seemed more identified by their husbands' careers. The difference was not only in what they said, but in how they said it. "I want . . . I know . . . I hope . . ." was how East Toledo women started their sentences. "They say . . . It may be true that . . . It's probably only me, but . . ." was how Smith women were more likely to preface their thoughts.

When I mentioned this contrast in writing about the reunion at the time,[2] I assumed the difference was economics. Since more East Toledo women had to work to help support their families, they also were forced to discover their strength and independence. Since Smith women were more likely to have husbands who could afford a dependent wife, on the other hand, many had been deprived of the self-confidence that comes from knowing you can support yourself. And, of course, neither group had been encouraged to value and give an economic worth to their work of maintaining a home and socializing the next generation. That was a patriarchal rule that crossed class boundaries.

Now, I still believe class often works in reverse for women. There's a bigger power difference between a tycoon and his wife (or wives) than between an average husband and wife, and even a male professional is likely to have a job that's the main chance, unlike a blue-collar man, and thus to have a wife whose work is secondary (a "jobette," as one of them described it ironically). But economics doesn't explain the whole difference between my two very different groups of contemporaries. After all, some of those Smith women had come from poor and working-class backgrounds, others were single and supporting themselves, and a few had high-powered careers. By that twenty-fifth reunion, about 40 percent of respondents to the questionnaire were doing paid, full-time work.

No, I think the deeper explanation lies in the kind of education we college women had absorbed. Its content — and our lack of the reality checks those East Toledo women had by virtue of taking courses later in life for pragmatic reasons — had made us more vulnerable to lethal underminings like these:

- Being taught to revere "the classics" of Western civilization, most of which patronize, distort, denigrate, or express hatred for the female half of the human race.
- Learning systems of philosophy that depend on gender dualisms at best and female inferiority at worst; surveying a tradition of art in which women are rarely artists and often objects; studying biology that focuses more on human differences than on human possibilities; absorbing ethical standards that assume masculine values; and learning theologies that assume all-male deities.
- Reading history books in which almost all power and

agency is assigned to men and being graded for memorizing male accomplishments — with the deep message that we can learn what others do, but never do it ourselves.

- Seeing fewer and fewer females in authority as we climb the educational ladder: fewer as faculty, fewer still as deans and presidents, and fewest of all in the fields of science, engineering, politics, business, foreign policy, or other specialties valued by the world at large. And if we are of the "wrong" race or class or sexuality, perhaps seeing no one we identify with at all.
- Being told we are "subjective" if we cite our own experience; that the "objective" truth always lies within the group — and the group is never us.
- Finally, being isolated from other women — perhaps resented by them — because we are educated like men.

Of course, men are also separated from their less well educated brothers by elitist educations — which is part of the same problem — but men are not an insurgent group. For women, the tragedy is closer to that of Latin, African-American, or just plain poor students who get separated from their communities and families. Women go to college and learn about economics in which the work that our mothers do at home (which is worth about 25 percent of the U.S. gross national product) isn't counted at all, and human rights that include protections against group hatred based on everything except sex. The fact that we may love college and feel grateful for being there — as I certainly did — only means we internalize these messages more eagerly.

Fortunately, all of us can unlearn. Thanks to the good luck of living in an era when women are questioning lifetimes and even millennia of lessons, I have faith in that possibility. I've also noticed that self-taught people who didn't learn the system in the first place are often our best teachers. Without time-consuming detours through this or that theory, terms-of-art that only the initiated can understand, and intellectual jousting with the ghosts of ancient authorities, they go to the heart of what they need to know.

In the 1970s, for instance, at the first feminist conference ever held by, for, and about women in Appalachia, I met women from

West Virginia, Kentucky, and Tennessee who came out of the hills and hollows in buses and pickup trucks, in shared cars or on foot, to gather on the campus of Marshall University. In the course of discussions, a craft fair, and workshops, I noticed that many of these women had a head start on things that it had taken me years to figure out:

- Never having been taught to separate "art" (what mostly men do) from "crafts" (what mostly women and natives do), they just assumed that their quilts and wood carvings were art. Which they were.
- Never having learned from Marx and other economists that women were the same class as their husbands, they assumed that women shared a culture and situations that were a little different from those of their respective men. And we did.
- Never having defined civilization as man's conquering of nature — and living close to nature themselves — they opposed the rape of the land and were ecologists. From experience.
- Not being Freudian, they envied not men's anatomies, but their male-only earning power in the coal mines. They set out to integrate those mining jobs. And a few years later, they did.
- Never having heard of a "feminist issue," they chose their own: contraception and drivers' licenses — control of their bodies and the family pickup truck. Both meant freedom.
- Not being prosperous enough to have churches and ministers to intervene between them and the Bible, they read the verses that supported them and ignored the rest.
- Never having learned to separate mind and body, thought and emotion, or intellect from the senses, they trusted their own experience.

Perhaps it's an exaggeration, but in retrospect, I felt I had learned more that was *of use* in that one long weekend than in a year of college. More about nature, art, justice, power, and fairness. Certainly more about my own strength.

II   *A Lot of Learning Is a Dangerous Thing*

"Of all the injuries inflicted by racism on people
of color, the most corrosive is the wound
within, the *internalized* racism that leads some
victims, at unspeakable cost to their own sense
of self, to embrace the values of their
oppressors."

H. JACK GEIGER, CIVIL RIGHTS WORKER

"The study of women's intelligence and
personality has had broadly the same history as
the one we record for Negroes. . . . In drawing
a parallel between the position of, and feeling
toward, women and Negroes, we are uncovering
a fundamental basis of our culture."

GUNNAR MYRDAL

If anyone had told my generation of college women that
sex paralleled race, we might have listened politely (we listened politely to almost everything in those days) and gone straight back to
our preoccupation with finding some nice, upwardly mobile young
man to give us a life. It takes more than a fact or two to break
through the lessons of culture.

But the educational shame was this: no one *did* tell us. Gunnar
Myrdal's *An American Dilemma* had long been accepted as a defin-
itive work on race in America, but the parallel it drew between race
and sex was ignored. Also absent from my textbooks were the nineteenth-century works of white and black feminists, from Elizabeth
Cady Stanton to Frederick Douglass, who had explained this race-
sex parallel at learned and courageous length in the suffragist and
abolitionist movements. I was told only that women were "given"
the vote, a one-sentence distortion of a century of struggle that did
nothing to shake my assumption that power was located somewhere
other than within myself. With the exception of a martyr here or a

revolutionary there, white women weren't serious, and women of color were supposed to honor the suffering of men of color more than their own. Since the consciousness of injustice is a step toward justice *and* self-esteem, our educations had reduced our potential for both.

I think there were two other factors that kept us from knowing how much trouble we were in at the time, and that continue to lull women into a false feeling that all is well. The first is that we get good grades, often better than those of our counterpart males. Since grades are the measure of academic life, they obscure the larger question of what is being learned; that a female student may be getting an A-plus in self-denigration. Second, many of the personality traits holding us back are seen as inherent in females. If self-sacrifice, a lack of personal will, living through others, fear of confrontation, and a need for approval are considered part of women's "natural" self, there isn't much reason to search for other causes.

Fortunately, feminist scholars and a shrinking world have produced evidence of confidence and power among females in our own history and in other cultures. The gradual introduction of some courses in Women's Studies, African-American Studies, Asian-American Studies, and even occasional acknowledgment that many of our heroes of the past were gay or lesbian and that gay culture is a frontier of influence in history — in other words, all the courses that might better be called Remedial Studies — have begun to diversify the narrow academic canon. Though such courses are still poorly financed and rarely part of the core curriculum, they hint at the dimensions of what we've *all* been missing. European Americans can now wonder why our textbooks didn't explain the ways in which Europe underdeveloped Africa (for instance, Tanzanians of 2,000 years ago were making carbon steel with a method not matched in Europe until the midnineteenth century), and men can ask why they were more likely to learn about Socrates than Aspasia, the great woman scholar, who even in a very unequal ancient Greece he called "my teacher" — and countless more such educational deprivations.*

There are also now a few researchers beginning to plumb the reason why, to differing degrees, females of all races and groups

---

* For remedial reading, see Appendix II, *History As If Everybody Mattered.*

seem likely to experience the anomaly of high academic achievement and low self-esteem. Though the problem gets worse as the education level gets higher, most research is still directed at elementary students. For instance: One study of books from fourteen U.S. publishers found that, in the process of learning to read, a little girl is exposed to more boy-centered stories than girl-centered stories by a ratio of five to two, to folk and fantasy tales with four times more male characters, and to biographies that are six times more likely to profile males than females. Even animal stories are twice as likely to feature male animals.[3] In the classrooms of the United States and Britain, a cross-cultural study found that boys are twice as likely to be seen as model students and praised by teachers, five times more likely to receive a teacher's attention, and eight to twelve times more likely to speak up in class.[4]

Even when educators survey grade school texts and create new bibliographies to help teachers include Asians, Eskimos, and other Americans, females in and out of those groups may be downplayed or forgotten. When education researchers Myra and David Sadker surveyed nine reading and language arts texts, for instance, they found that four of them ignored girls' unequal presence in the curriculum, four devoted less than two paragraphs to it, and one actually furthered it by noting that "it has been found that boys will not read 'girls books' . . . therefore the ratio of 'boy books' should be about two to one within classroom library collection."[5]

Then there is the crucial question of speaking up in the classroom. We know that boys are called on more often and talk more in their average response, yet when the Sadkers showed teachers films of classroom discussions in which boys outtalked girls by a ratio of three to one, the teachers — including feminists — still perceived the girls as talking more.[6] We are so culturally trained to think that females talk too much, that we should be "good listeners," that we seem to measure ourselves against those expectations, not reality.

There is also the problem of instruction through "positive reinforcement," as psychologists say. Boys tend to be praised for achievement, while girls are praised for interacting well with others. And there are distinctions among girls, too. In one study of kindergarten through the third grade, teachers tended to praise European-American girls for helping others with academic problems, and African-American girls for helping others with personal or emotional problems.[7]

Thus, even though girls get good grades, learn how to read sooner, and have an edge over boys in verbal skills, the question we really need to ask is: *What are these girls learning?*

According to a study commissioned by the American Association of University Women and released in 1991, a large part of the lesson is to undervalue oneself. As nine-year-olds, for instance, 67 percent of girls and 60 percent of boys said they were "happy with the way I am." By the time students were in high school, however, only 46 percent of boys said they felt that way — also a tragedy that needs every attention — and the girls had plummeted to 29 percent. Though African-American and Hispanic girls retained somewhat higher levels of self-esteem than European-American girls did, it was at the expense of distancing themselves from the educational system: both groups reported more feelings of alienation from schools and teachers than their white counterparts did.[8] As Herbert Kohl explained in *I Won't Learn from You!*, there is such a thing as willful "not-learning" that is different from failure and may even "clarify one's definition of self" — which is perhaps what these students of color were choosing when faced with an educational system that denigrated them — but it is still a choice between bettering oneself and being oneself that no one should have to make.[9]

Thus, in high school, where the gender gap in math and science begins to open up or widen, the problem may be more girls' view of themselves than the subjects. As Carol Gilligan has pointed out in her study of girls' loss of confidence as they approach adolescence, the same students who have been quite outspoken and sure of themselves up to then suddenly begin to say "I don't know."[10] Janet Golden, a science teacher in Georgia, has found that "when students struggle in science, the boys blame the materials, the girls blame themselves."[11] Perhaps the simplest statement of the price of girls' low self-esteem comes from two studies that experimented with removing the "I don't know" option from multiple-choice tests. Since girls choose this option more than boys do, especially when the question is couched in sports or other terms that make them feel it doesn't "belong" to them, researchers wanted to see what would happen if girls were forced to make an informed guess, to trust their knowledge and instinct. In science, a study of thirteen-to-seventeen-year-old girls found that the gender gap disappeared when the "I don't know" option was taken away.[12] When that option was removed from math tests, seventh-to-tenth-grade girls were found to do *better* than boys.[13] In a world heavily dependent on tests, this self-esteem gap continues to obscure what females really know.*

These problems aside, however, grade schools — and even high schools — are usually places where male and female students study the same academic subjects. Even shop and home economics are now often combined into one life-skills course, thanks to women's movement efforts toward nonsexist education. They also see many women in authority (as teachers if not principals), and tend to feel a fairly equal ownership of learning. When some of those female students go to college, however, much of this will be reversed. They will see fewer female role models in classrooms, read histories and other college texts that include even fewer active females than their early readers did, and be introduced to specialties in which women have little or no visible power.

At the same time, these women are no more likely to get class-room attention than they ever were — and maybe less. Bernice Sandler, longtime director of the Project on the Status and Education of Women for the Association of American Colleges in Washington, D.C., reports studies showing that women are called on less in class, get fewer direct responses, and are interrupted more often, while "men receive more eye contact from their professors than women, are called on more often and receive informal coaching from their instructors."[14] Since college faculty are heavily male (and in the U.S.,

* In the all-important Scholastic Aptitude Test (SAT) for college entrance, a monitor reads instructions like the following from the 1988–89 *Supervisor's Manual:* "Scores on these tests are based on the number of questions answered correctly minus a fraction (¼ point per question) of the number of questions answered incorrectly. Therefore, random or haphazard guessing is unlikely to change your scores." Because girls are more likely to follow instructions — and more hesitant to guess when they're not *positive* of the answer — they often penalize themselves by failing to follow a hunch as much as boys do on the SATs. As Carol Gilligan put it, "This test is a moral issue for girls; they think it is an indication of their intelligence, so they must not cheat. Boys play it like a pinball game." Phyllis Rosser, *The SAT Gender Gap: Identifying the Causes,* Washington, D.C.: Center for Women Policy Studies, April 1989, p. 64.

90 percent white), the comfort level of interacting with the familiar seems to penalize all women and men of color. Because the accomplishments of former students is one measure of professorial success — and because males are seen as more likely to "do something" with their educations — faculty of both genders often consider males a better investment of time and attention.

Many studies indicate that going to a women's college can make a big difference. More than their sisters in coeducational institutions, students there feel positive about their classroom experience, speak up in class, excel in science and other nontraditional subjects, become leaders (both on campus and in later life), complete their degrees, and go on to graduate schools. They are also more likely to maintain or increase their intellectual self-esteem, and to report satisfaction with their college experience.[15]

Some of these differences may be socioeconomic or a function of the kinds of students now choosing the few women's colleges that are left: with feminism came new motives. "Parents who once sent their daughters to be protected," as one education writer put it, "are now sending them for leadership experiences they're unlikely to get anywhere else."[16] Yet even at colleges like Smith that now have more consciousness about educating women, higher education has a long way to go. A longitudinal study of 200,000 students at 300 institutions in all undergraduate categories showed that women across the board reported a major increase in "self-criticism" between entering and leaving college, a trend that may be mitigated by women's colleges but can't be eliminated without major changes in what is being studied. For male students, on the other hand, intellectual and interpersonal self-esteem is maintained or strengthened — *even when their grades are lower than women's.*

When an increased belief in personal autonomy and women's equality did result from these four years, among men or women, Alexander Astin, the author of this massive study, found that the first was "almost totally attributable to societal changes" and the second was "a mixture of societal and college influences." Astin concluded: "Even though men and women are presumably exposed to common liberal arts curriculum and other educational programs during the undergraduate years, it would seem that these programs serve more to preserve, rather than to reduce, stereotypic differences between men and women in behavior, personality, aspirations, and achievement."[17] Clearly, that "common" curriculum belongs more to one group than the other.

For the last ten years, researchers Terry Denny and Karen Arnold from the University of Illinois have been measuring just how bad it really is. In 1981, they began to follow eighty high school valedictorians: thirty-four men and forty-six women; white, African-American, Hispanic, and Chinese-American; from a wide variety of economic backgrounds. All graduated at the top of their class and went on to fulfill their promise at a wide variety of colleges, universities, institutes, and later, in many cases, at graduate and professional schools. In fact, the women valedictorians, greater in number from the start, also had college grade averages slightly higher than those of the men.

After two years of college, however, intellectual self-esteem among the women had plummeted. Though 23 percent of the males and 21 percent of the females had described themselves as "far above average" in intellect when surveyed after high school, by sophomore year in college, that proportion had remained at 22 percent among the men — but dropped to 4 percent among the women.

By the time these students graduated, 25 percent of the men had an estimate of themselves as "far above average" — but *none* of the women did.[18]

"The dramatic difference between men and women who were high school valedictorians," Arnold concludes, "is not what they achieve in college. They both continue to get good grades, to earn conspicuous honors, and to receive scholarships based on outstanding academic performance. Women choose the difficult curricula and the prestigeful careers as often as do their male counterparts."*[19]

The difference seemed to be that, with each additional year of higher education, the women saw less of themselves, and less chance

---

* Other interesting findings: women's career plans became more limited than they had been at college entry; and "religiosity is negatively correlated with women's presence in nontraditional majors . . ." (p. 17). The Astin study showed that women in coeducational schools also became *less* politically liberal than they had been, while men became *more* liberal. At single-sex colleges, women complained *less* about the absence of men than men did about the absence of women.

of being themselves. In the academic canon and in the classroom, their half of the human race was underrepresented in authority, often invisible, sometimes treated with contempt, perhaps treated as if success were "unfeminine," and denied even the dignity of a well-recognized suffering. And since the great majority were in coeducational schools — and studies report that male classrooms are more "competitive" while female classrooms are more "cooperative" [20] — women of all races were having to function in an alien and often hostile culture.

It makes sense, then, that more education and even good grades could add up to lower self-esteem: the lesson these students were so conscientiously learning was their "place."

"We have long known that rape has been a way of terrorizing us and keeping us in subjection," writes the distinguished historian Gerda Lerner. "Now we also know that we have participated, although unwittingly, in the rape of our minds." [21]

While the problem for women has been largely invisible, the impact of education on racial and ethnic self-esteem has been more readily acknowledged — though little more has been done about it. From the days when teaching a slave to read was illegal, to the Black Studies scholars, bilingual Hispanic educators, and Native-American students, who have only recently been able to learn about their own culture in some tribal schools, there has been a clear understanding that the content of education is just as crucial to these discriminated-against groups as access to it.

In 1931, for instance, a black leader named Dr. Carter G. Woodson grew so alarmed at the European-centered, self-hating attitudes being imparted to his people in schools and colleges that he wrote a book called *Miseducation of the Negro*. The majority of educated Negroes, Woodson wrote, were "all but worthless in the development of their people." He urged that progress be measured by what was being read, not just by how many people were able to read it. "When you control a man's thinking," Woodson explained, "you do not have to worry about his actions. You do not have to tell him not to stand here or go yonder. He will find his 'proper place' and will stay in it. You do not need to send him to the back door. . . . In fact, if there is no back door, he will cut one for his special benefit. His education makes it necessary."[22]

In *Black Bourgeoisie,* an intellectual broadside that shocked and sobered reform-minded readers when it was published in 1957, sociologist E. Franklin Frazier blamed the content of education — as well as all the more obvious forms of discrimination — for creating a group that was often divided within itself along color lines, did not return often enough to help less fortunate blacks up the ladder, and was sometimes addicted to conspicuous consumption. "The black bourgeoisie," wrote Frazier, "the element which has striven more than any other element among Negroes to make itself over in the image of the white man — exhibits most strikingly the inferiority complex of those who would escape their racial identification."[23]

Though it's been almost thirty years since Frazier's death put a premature end to his leadership of the sociology department at Howard University — and though his argument was mitigated by black college students who became activists in the civil rights movement — his book can still arouse anger among those who fear he gave ammunition to racists. But in fact, his observations are just as true of any group whose core self-esteem is low and who therefore crave situational esteem and approval from those "above" them. If *female* is substituted for *black,* for instance, the subject might become "Queen Bees" of every race: educated and successful women who feel they must separate themselves from other women and get status from being one of the few women among men. The marks of self-hatred are the same: acceptance of an internal ranking system based on approval from the powerful, refusal to help or identify with one's own group, and an obsession with fashion, appearance, and other forms of conspicuous consumption. Though Frazier himself drew comparisons only with other racial groups, his painful description could be used for almost any discriminated-against group that — through education and other means — internalizes society's low estimate of itself and therefore identifies "up," whether it is a lack of woman-pride, a feeling that being bilingual is insufficiently "American," or an ominous silence about being gay, lesbian, or bisexual.

But when one member of a group changes, the balance shifts for everyone, and when one group changes, it shifts the balance of society — just as a few molecules shift the whole. New pride among African Americans inspired a contagion of changed consciousness in the national family. It helped women of all races to see the parallels of racial and sexual discrimination and also led to an atmosphere in which many ethnic groups found more pride, from Jews who reconsidered changing their names in spite of continuing anti-Semitism to Italians who protested stereotyped associations with organized crime. One group's efforts often directly benefited the next: for instance, Native Americans, whose history and languages were forbidden in schools well into the 1970s, were aided by bilingual education laws that Hispanic Americans initiated.

The amazing thing is the difference that even a small amount of new information can make. I remember listening to a white college football player talk about James Agee's *Let Us Now Praise Famous Men.* Before reading that ode to ordinary men, he said, he had felt "you weren't really a man unless you made a lot of money." After reading it, he began to see that, "it is what we do, not what we have," that matters. In the early seventies, when Women's History courses were rare, Gerda Lerner held ad hoc ones in New York for anyone who wanted to come. "Even short-term exposure to the past experience of women, such as in two-week institutes and seminars," she reported, "has the most profound psychological effect on women participants. . . . Women's History changes their lives."[24]

The buried history of each group can have a similarly powerful effect. Judy Grahn, the poet and writer, described what it meant to her ten years ago to learn about the traditional and honorable roles reserved for lesbians and gay men in the ancient cultures of more than eighty of North America's Indian nations:

A huge burden, the burden of isolation and of being defined only by one's enemies, left me on that enlightening day. I understood then that being Gay is a universal quality, like cooking, like decorating the body, like singing, like predicting the weather. Moreover, after learning about the social positions and special offices fulfilled by Indians whose tribes once picked them for the tasks of naming, healing, prediction, leadership, and teaching precisely because they displayed characteristics we call gay, I knew that Gayness goes far beyond simple sexual/ emotional activity. What Americans call Gayness not only has distinct cultural characteristics, its participants have long held positions of social power in history and ritual among people all over the globe."

This distant fact was so affirming that, as she confessed, "I put my face into my hands and sobbed with relief." * As late as the 1960s, she had gone to the Library of Congress to ask for books about homosexuals and lesbians and had been told that they were locked away and available only to psychiatrists, lawyers, and other experts.

Yet in the suffragist wave and in this feminist one, activist women especially have often been more likely to demand equal access to existing education than fundamental changes in what is being taught. Even an intellectual pioneer like Simone de Beauvoir talked about women's rebellion as if it were present and future, and raised no demand to restore evidence of rebellions in the historic past. Elizabeth Cady Stanton, who had the temerity to rewrite the Bible *as if women mattered,* was criticized by other suffragists. Perhaps it's significant that Stanton had little formal education, and de Beauvoir was very highly educated indeed. Stanton just assumed that women must have played a part in history but de Beauvoir had been taught otherwise.

Now, mainstream education is still somewhere between cautious experimenting and hostile resistance to what should be called remedial studies — those efforts to help students to see all of the past and present world instead of just those parts of it that are in keeping with current power structures. As I write this, there are mainstream educators trying to discredit efforts to diversify the academic canon by giving them the dreaded label "politically cor-

* After this realization, she blended personal history and historical research to write *Another Mother Tongue: Gay Words, Gay Worlds* (Boston: Beacon Press, 1984, from which the above quote was taken, p. 105), a book that gives readers a glimpse of the importance of gay culture.

rect" — now known familiarly on campus as "P.C." (which, as Robin Morgan has pointed out, might well stand for "Plain Courtesy") — as if centuries of exclusion had not been the height (or depth) of politics. *Excellence* has also become a code word for exclusion, as if the more important question were not "Excellent at *what?*" Perhaps these protests are a reaction to a new understanding that change means more than just integrating females and people of color into the curriculum, or into any existing structure, whether it is the work force or a view of history. It means learning to see with new eyes — to question the very idea of "norms" against which all other experience is judged. If race is only discussed in relation to African Americans and other people of color — though it's equally or more important as a factor in the world view of European Americans — then the discussion only serves to reinforce racism. If an analysis of sexism takes place only in relation to women, it adds to women's feeling of burden and fails to alert men to the ways in which they are being limited, too. And where is the routine study of social forms other than hierarchy, patriarchy, and competition — or even an understanding that they exist? Where are the campuses as pioneers of the powers of self-esteem and human possibilities?

A first step is acknowledging the ways in which our current education is suppressing self-esteem by treating students as if they were empty vessels, without a great deal of wisdom that's already there. That itself would relieve many people who are feeling alone, at fault, a little crazy.

For instance: One recent University of Chicago survey looked at 70,000 schools in an effort to identify the major factors affecting students' success in the classroom. The high dropout rate among black students (nearing 50 percent, according to the U.S. Department of Labor) and their poor reading skills (more than 40 percent of black seventeen-year-olds are unable to read beyond a sixth-grade level) had made this study of particular importance to the black community. Many observers expected it simply to point to the same culprits blamed by other experts: the high proportion of impoverished female-headed households and too little money spent in disproportionately black school districts.

In fact, however, single-parent families, no matter what their socioeconomic status, turned out to be a very distant third on the list of problems, and the per-pupil amount of education spending was only a poor second. The single most important factor in student accomplishment was an intangible: teachers and parents who had high expectations of the student.[25]

In a way, the rush to blame poor and female-headed households, so much more likely to be African-American families, is just racism — and sexism — in a more liberal guise. For one thing, many high achievers have come out of female-headed households and beaten the societal odds. For another, well-to-do suburban kids from "intact" European-American families have drug problems, eating disorders, dangerous behavior patterns, and a sad proof of low self-esteem, high suicide rates — indeed, far higher than among the very poor. Those facts should tell us that we're not asking the right questions: What hopes does a single mother have for herself and her child? Do the suburban kids *or* the poor ones have someone who listens? Who tells them they're special? Do kids in elementary schools see nurturing women *and* men as role models? Are their teachers excited by their students — and vice versa? Is at least some learning fueled by the students' own interests? Whatever the problems, do kids see them as challenges or personal faults? Do they have teachers who treat them as unique unfolding mysteries — or as people who must constantly "measure up"?

Here is one study's sad answer: When leaving their homes and starting the first grade, 80 percent of children in a diverse sample were found to have high self-esteem. By the fifth grade, that proportion was down to 20 percent. After finishing high school, only 5 percent still possessed it.[26]

Though this and other studies disclose different percentages, depending on how questions are asked and many other variables, there is an unusual amount of agreement on their conclusion: schools cause self-esteem to plunge for almost everyone.

We need to unlearn some of our respect for education, since it has undermined our respect for ourselves. It's worth taking a little time to demystify it.

III   *The Seduction of Science*

"It is the theory which decides what can be observed."
ALBERT EINSTEIN

About twenty years ago, I picked up a book called *Apes and Angels* published by the Smithsonian Institution in Washington. It is a modern compendium of the scholarly, scientific, and popular evidence — ranging from comparative measurements of skull sizes and arm lengths to anthropological surveys and popular caricatures — that had been originated by nineteenth-century scientists and popularized by journalists to "prove" a respectable and popular thesis: the Irish had descended from apes only a few generations before, while the English were descendants of man created in God's image and thus "angels." [27]

In addition to impressive forensic evidence, scientists of the day could point to the proof around them. Most of the Irish were poor — and therefore overrepresented in prison populations — at a time when being poor or criminal was itself thought to be genetic. In England, Irish workers were often illiterate and at the bottom of the social hierarchy, but in Ireland, English families were powerful and prosperous. Even in the United States, many Irish immigrants were laborers or indentured servants, and in cities like Boston, they competed for jobs with free blacks.

What is most interesting about this biology-based argument is its academic and social respectability at the time. That's what makes its parallels with other biology-is-destiny theories about sex and race so striking. Freud, for instance, was actually very clear about his adversarial stance to women's equality. "We must not allow ourselves to be deflected . . . by . . . the feminists," he wrote to his colleagues, "who are anxious to force us to regard the two sexes as completely equal in position and worth." [28] Yet his theories have been cited for most of the last century as objective. Thanks to that retrospective look at apes and angels, I began to realize that even the most objective areas of education need always to be questioned; the more they present themselves as value-free, the more the need for questions.

Think about science. It has become the most powerful influence on the ways our minds and capabilities are valued and the ways we ourselves value them. But the scientific methods on which we now rely to verify and explain our personal experience are not so time-honored as we like to think: only about three or four hundred years old, they are newcomers in human history. Moreover, during most of that time, science was conducted within centers of learning run by religions that often discouraged or punished secular challenges to religious beliefs about human origins and relative worth. (We have only to look at fundamentalist Christians still teaching creationism in schools, or at other contemporary fundamentalists interpreting Islam, Judaism, Shintoism, and other religious doctrines, to understand the resistance to any view of human beings as part of a continuum of nature.) Even among scientists who pursued secular inquiry, often at great personal risk, a total rejection of cultural assumptions was impossible. If all women and various races of men were said by religion to have no souls, for instance, you could be pretty sure that science would soon discover they were "less evolved" as well. The theory came first, and evidence in its support was mustered afterward — not necessarily in a dishonest way, but as a result of selective vision.

As nineteenth-century materialism and travel to other cultures weakened the church as a practical authority, however, scientists began to achieve more independence from it — but also to inherit some of its seductive power. Now, *they* were expected to become society's explainers, justifiers, and providers of rules. If converting the heathen to Christianity was no longer a sufficient rationale for the colonialism that had become the pillar of European prosperity, for instance, then science was expected to supply equally compelling reasons why such a system was positive, progressive, and "for their own good."

This interest in ranking by race and ethnicity gave birth to craniology, the father of many prestigious and influential specialties devoted to documenting and measuring human differences. By elaborate measurements of cranial capacity, this new branch of science set out to assess brain size, relative development of different areas of the brain, and thus (it was assumed) intelligence itself.

In context, craniology must have seemed humane after many seventeenth- and eighteenth-century beliefs: for instance, that intelligent women were the work of the devil (a belief that had helped to justify killing nine million women healers and other pagan or nonconforming women as witches during the centuries of change over to Christianity),[29] or that an individual's physical and mental problems came from an imbalance of the four cardinal "humours" of blood, phlegm, choler, and bile (the reasoning behind the standard medical practice of "bleeding" patients to restore the balance). Instead, craniology offered the reward of simple, clear, replicable proofs of human hierarchy and its mental manifestations.

From the beginning, it was clear that men as a group had more "cranial capacity" than women as a group — a fact that was both origin and verification of craniology's basic premise that greater skull size meant greater intelligence. After many wide-ranging studies that compared multiple measurements-per-skull by race and ethnicity as well as by sex, craniologists were also able to report that the average cranial capacity of the white race was larger than that of Africans, Asians, and even Southern Europeans.

These discoveries squared with other mainstream scholarly conclusions of the day. From anthropology to neurology, science had demonstrated that the female Victorian virtues of passivity, domesticity, and greater morality (by which was meant less sexual activity) were rooted in female biology. Similarly, the passive, dependent, and childlike qualities of the "darker races" (then still called the "white man's burden") were part of their biological destiny. Evolutionists also chimed in with a reason for all this: men who were not Caucasians and women of all races were lower on the evolutionary scale. In the case of race, this was due to simple evolutionary time, since it was then believed that European civilizations were the oldest. In the case of Caucasian women — who obviously had been evolving as long as their male counterparts — there was another rationale. The less complex nervous systems and lower intelligences of females were evolutionary adaptations to the pain of childbirth, repetitive domestic work, and other physical, nonintellectual tasks. Naturally, females of "lower" races were also assumed to be inferior to their male counterparts.

Then as now, the biologically based myths that resulted from these theories of sex and race were parallel. Men of color, and all women, Caucasian and otherwise, were said to be childlike, governed by their emotions, closer to nature, limited in intellect, in need of simple rules to follow, suitable for physical tasks, and so on. These myths diverged only slightly to justify different functions and economic uses — greater physical strength for men of color, greater strength to bear pain and childbirth for all women — and together, they worked efficiently and well to legitimize white male supremacy.

Elizabeth Fee, a scholar of nineteenth-century craniology, has gathered representative quotes like these:

- In 1863, James Hunt, President of the London Anthropological Society, proved definitively that sex-plus-race made women of color doubly inferior: "There is no doubt that the Negro's brain bears a great resemblance to a European female or child's brain and thus approaches the ape far more than the European, while the Negress approaches the ape still nearer."[30]
- In 1866, F. Pruner, a French craniologist, wrote about the social results of this sex/race parallel: "The Negro resembles the female in his love for children, his family, and his cabin." And: "The black man is to the white man what woman is to man."[31]
- By 1879, G. Le Bon, another French craniologist, had no doubt: "In the most intelligent races, as among the Parisians, there are a large number of women whose brains are closer in size to those of gorillas than to the most developed male brains. This inferiority is so obvious that no one can contest it for a moment; only its degree is worth discussion."[32]

As a new and increasingly popular branch of science, craniology added impressive human data to older plant- and animal-based arguments for breeding only with "one's own kind." This proof of the influence of both racial purity and superiority had special importance in the United States, where a Civil War against slavery, a domestic movement against women's status as the legal chattel of fathers and husbands, and the joint fight of these movements for universal adult suffrage were threatening to undermine the entire sexual and racial caste system. Craniology reinforced the need to restrict the freedom of white women — the means of reproduction for the white race — and to outlaw "miscegenation," "race mixing," or "race mongrelization." Though such antimiscegenation laws were not used against white men who fathered children with women of color, even by force, they did prevent legitimizing any such union, thereby perpetuating a racially "pure" system of inheritance.* And they were used with full effect against any bonding between white women and men of color.

Craniology was flexible enough to survive many internal disputes — and some external ones. In the second half of the nineteenth century, for instance, neuroanatomists believed that higher mental activities were located in the frontal lobes of the brain. Not surprisingly, craniologists confirmed that those areas were larger in male skulls than in female ones, and that the less important, parietal regions at the top and sides of the skull were smaller than in females. Toward the turn of the century, however, neuroanatomists revised their opinion: higher intellectual abilities were located in the parietal regions after all. Soon, craniologists had discovered that their earlier measurements had been inaccurate: males actually had *larger*

---

* Until the civil rights movement of the 1960s changed the racial atmosphere and the laws, "miscegenation" was one of the most inflexibly punished crimes, without even the extenuating circumstances allowed for murder. Black men accused of it could be lynched, with or without trial. During slavery, if white women entered an interracial relationship willingly, they could be imprisoned or sold off as indentured servants and their mixed-race children sold as slaves. Post-slavery, such women became social outcasts unless they testified that they had been taken by force. (See *In the Matter of Color: Race and the American Legal Process* by A. Leon Higginbotham, Jr., New York: Oxford University Press, 1978.)

Among the many victims of such antimiscegenation laws were Asian men brought to this country by the thousands in the nineteenth and first half of the twentieth century as workers — forbidden to bring wives from their own countries, and also forbidden to marry non-Asians here — some of whom are still living.

parietal lobes than females, and the newly unimportant frontal regions were *smaller*.

Eventually, craniologists had to modify their focus on sheer brain volume as the primary indicator of intelligence. Otherwise, whales, elephants, and other possessors of much-larger-than-human brains would have had to be counted as potentially more intelligent than Homo sapiens. The obvious answer was to take body size into account, but there was an internal split on how to do it. Should scientists use the ratio of brain weight to body weight (which would have made women as a group *more* intelligent than men as a group)? Or should they use the ratio of brain surface to body surface (which proved women's intellectual inferiority but also made white males inferior to men of some other races)?

Alas for craniology, there was no one answer that met the demands of both logic and politics. In addition, there were scandals: some scientists had just been *assuming* that the skulls and brains they used in laboratory experiments were from male or female cadavers, based on their own tautological criteria, and others were comparing the wrong numbers within the up-to-5,000 measurements of one skull. In a back-to-basics effort to save their profession, some craniologists returned to a simple hierarchy of skull and brain size. After all, that was easily understood and met the commonsense criterion of explaining male superiority.

Soon, however, new data on mental patients disclosed the alarming fact that many of these "inferior" people had large skulls. Since women who didn't conform to their gender roles were (as we now know) more likely to be judged insane, there were a disproportionate number of females among the mental patients in general, including the large-skulled ones.

Ingenious explanations were devised. Some scientists argued that a large skull indicated both a greater mental capacity *and* an increased danger of madness. Because males had stronger characters, they were better able to develop the former and resist the latter. Females, well known to be weak and subject to hysteria because of their female organs, were incapable of using the intellectual potential and likely to fall victim to the instability. Among the proofs presented was the case of an exceptionally large-brained female graduate student who had committed suicide after failing her exams.

With one expedient theory of the differential impact of large skulls on males and females, craniologists had managed to explain away three facts: why mental patients were disproportionately female, why all geniuses were male, and why females were more likely than males to attempt suicide.

But even such ingenuity couldn't save craniology from the weight of its own contradictions. By the early twentieth century, scientists were in disarray from the cumulative impact of in-fighting and public problems with their criteria.* One of its death blows had been dealt in 1901 by Alice Lee, a London mathematician who did a study comparing the skull sizes of female medical students (presumably sane, since they had been accepted into such august company) with those of respected male faculty members. Since some of the female students had larger skulls than some of the male authorities, the distinguished men had to choose between their own intelligence and accepted craniological theory. (As Lee pointed out, the theory couldn't be true of an entire sex unless it was also true of individuals.) As a student rigorously trained by Karl Pearson, a respected male biometrician, Lee also noted that most skull differences fell within the 3-percent margin allowed for error. Her paper was so criticized by craniologists that, like many women academics today, her work had little impact until a respected male academic defended her; in this case, a spirited defense by Pearson himself, a supporter of female emancipation.[33]

In later years, larger and more random samples were to confirm what we now know: there are no racially consistent differences in average brain size; and neither male nor female skull or brain size, as long as it is within a normal range, has any relationship to intelligence. Craniologists had defeated themselves from the start by working backward from the false hypotheses of male and Caucasian

---

* Another ill-fated craniological effort tried to relate facial planes and intelligence. The forehead slant and protruding nose of white males — compared to the smaller nose of females or flatter nose of African and Asian males — was thought to signify mental power. This theory foundered on the fact that animals also had protruding nasal structures; for instance, anteaters.

One argument that was never resolved: Were female skulls inferior to those of white males because they were more round (like children's) or more elongated (like Negroes')?

superiority.* But all the respectable biases leading up to the flowering and acceptance of these theories, as well as their long century in the sun, produced too many casualties to number.

John Hope Franklin, a modern African-American historian at Duke University, gives such beliefs as much credit for keeping African Americans in slavery and out of the U.S. Constitution as the economic motives more often cited. "We don't really know, we only think we know," he points out, that the Constitution could not have been ratified if it outlawed slavery. He blames "the notion that Africans were inherently inferior and, consequently, slavery was a satisfactory, even desirable status for them."[34]

Even after such biological arguments had been discredited at a scientific level, they continued to enjoy an afterlife in political and social agendas — in Nazi Germany, for instance. And only in 1991, thanks to a new spirit of openness and *glasnost,* did citizens of the Soviet Union discover that a Brain Institute had been working away in Moscow for sixty-seven years, trying to prove Stalin's thesis that "the New Soviet Man" could be bred by developing brain weight as a measure of intelligence (and where Stalin's own brain, as well as those of Lenin and even of dissident Andrei Sakharov, had been faithfully weighed and preserved).[35] In this country, such beliefs no longer have much open support, but they still crop up in the cruel jokes and cartoons that sometimes depict African Americans as monkeylike; and the beliefs that still confront women with arguments that "femininity" and intelligence are somehow contradictory, and that women's biology restricts rational thought. An updated version of this bias is the notion that women's advances are damaging our health. Though longevity and mental health of women of all races have actually increased in the twenty years of the latest wave of feminism — and though poor black women, not white male

---

* Other assumptions were errors, too. Later clinical tests showed females in general to be *more* sensitive to pain, and to sound and touch, than males in general; a difference that itself turned out to be environmental, not innate. Parents tend to "toughen" male babies by ignoring their cries and by holding and cuddling them less than females. The evolutionist assumption that Northern European cultures were the oldest and most evolved has been overturned by such discoveries as the oldest known human skeleton, a woman named "Lucy" by paleoanthropologists, who lived on the African continent some three million years ago.

executives, have always had the greatest incidence of tension-related diseases in any case — there is a premise that doing "men's jobs" will give women "men's diseases"; a not-so-subtle threat that "success will make you sick."

In general, however, craniology and other nineteenth-century theories of group differences seem ridiculous now. That's why it's so important to understand that they were once respectable, and to look with healthy skepticism on currently accepted theories that may turn out to be just as seductive, dangerous to self-esteem, and wrong.

In 1981, anthropologist Stephen Jay Gould set out to mend some of the damage done by his profession. In *The Mismeasure of Man* (a title that, ironically, once again omits women), he retraced early craniological studies to show the careless, biased, even fraudulent methods with which their massive samplings had been gathered. Nonetheless, Gould found that, for the most part, this was not done with any malice or even consciousness; an important testimony to the culture-bound assumptions on which science may rest. Theories are most successful, Gould concluded, when they enable millions of people to believe "that their social prejudices are scientific facts after all."[36]

IV *Modern Measuring*

"As long as there are entrenched social and political distinctions between sexes, races or classes, there will be forms of science whose main function is to rationalize and legitimize these distinctions."

ELIZABETH FEE

The diminished credibility of craniology did not in any way spell an end to the attempts to "scientifically" rank human beings by group of birth. From Charles Darwin to Havelock Ellis, the theory that male animals manifested more extremes of behavior and development than did female animals was used to explain the supposed ordinariness of females versus the extraordinary range, from defectiveness to genius, of males. Other scientists hypothesized that every cell in the male and female body and brain must reflect the difference between ova (limited in number and passive) and sperm (plentiful and active). Still others measured the knowledge with which children entered school and concluded that, in the words of G. Stanley Hall, the father of modern developmental psychology, "the easy and widely diffused concepts are commonest among girls, the harder and more special or exceptional ones are commonest among boys."[37]

But none of this was helpful in predicting individual variations within the sexes. In the United States, the post-slavery debate on whether education was "appropriate" for Negroes, the successes of the suffragist movement in achieving citizenship for women of all races, the constant pressure of new waves of immigrants, and most of all, the promise of meritocracy, were combining to make unprecedented demands on the educational system. Some way of making undemocratic decisions that was *not* based on group of birth was urgently needed.

An answer was inadvertently created in France at the turn of the century when Alfred Binet devised simple aptitude tests to identify learning disabilities in very young children, with the sole purpose of giving them remedial help. His method of testing general knowledge plus reasoning skills offered a welcome relief after the tortuous and mostly discredited path of extrapolating mental ability from physical characteristics.

By 1916, when the first Stanford-Binet Intelligence Quotient (IQ) test was published in the United States, however, Binet's original purpose of remedial help had been left behind. The test was greeted with enthusiasm as a mass-producible yet individualized way of predicting and, contrary to Binet's purpose, providing a rationale for excluding. Moreover, if the results didn't turn out "right" from a group point of view, the content of the test could always be adjusted. After the first version of the Stanford-Binet IQ scale produced a small but stable margin of female superiority, for instance, the test was modified in 1937 by adding more items favoring males — mostly about sports.[38]

From the start, there were also race-based cultural biases in the definition of what "general knowledge" was, as well as in the interpretation of test scores. After the first mass experiment with IQ testing of army recruits in World War I, for example, results were said to demonstrate that Alpine and Mediterranean races were intellectually inferior to Nordic races, and that blacks were inferior to whites. Later, this turned out to be a bias in interpretation: regional, economic, and educational differences actually had a greater impact than race. "Nordic" soldiers from the South made the lowest scores of any white soldiers in America, and black soldiers from the North scored higher than whites from the South.[39]

Nonetheless, these scientifically designed, easily graded, mass-produced tests caught on like wildfire. By the end of World War I, hundreds of psychologists and educators had become skilled in administering them to soldiers, as well as to four million schoolchildren. In the 1920s, eugenicists successfully used the demonstrably false army tests to set immigration quotas that lasted through two decades, and that kept Southern and Eastern Europeans out of the U.S., most crucially when they were trying to leave in anticipation of the Holocaust. Even while Northern European quotas went unfilled before World War II, quotas based on those meaningless tests kept out as many as six million refugees. As Stephen Jay Gould comments, "The paths to destruction are indirect, but ideas can be agents as sure as guns and bombs."[40]

By the 1950s, with pressure on schools increased by postwar prosperity and returning veterans, various scholastic aptitude, achievement, and intelligence tests had been integrated into every level of education.* For parents, students, and educators alike, the idea that each person had an "IQ," an intelligence quotient that dictated her or his destiny and value, had entered the popular culture.

This system of assigning each person a number based on blind

---

*Because the G.I. Bill of Rights provided encouragement and subsidy, veterans were often admitted regardless of test scores. In the eyes of some educators, that group's record of later accomplishments proved that motivation is a better predictor of performance than aptitude and IQ tests. Of course, severe limits on women's participation in the military had kept them out of this postwar flood of free education, too, just as "veterans' preference" for jobs advanced men in the workplace.

testing seemed more democratic than past biology-based categories, and indeed, it was not as airtight as they had been. *Some* females might do as well as *most* males, for instance, or *some* members of racial minorities might be found to have IQs higher than *some* whites (though as we now know, cultural bias in the test content made this difficult). It's probably a backhanded compliment that test results no longer sufficed, and outright bans or quotas became necessary to keep Jews, blacks, women, and other "out" groups from taking places in colleges, universities, and professional schools that were assumed to be better used by white Christian males.

But there were many resemblances between these paper tests and their craniological predecessors. Both took measurements that had nothing to do with the subject's performance in a practical situation. Both were dedicated to quantifying presumed differences, not to demonstrating that those differences were relevant, or even that they existed outside the realm of the tests themselves. Both were often formulated and interpreted in biased ways. And both generated data used to make group judgments, even when the results did not warrant them. One has only to think of the late sixties when Arthur Jensen and others were still linking IQ and scholastic-achievement scores to race to understand the level of the damage done. Though later and considerably less well publicized studies found that the education level and even religion of the mother were greater determinants of IQ than race, the purpose of supporting an existing social order had been served.

More than twenty years of criticism of such tests as biased, inaccurate, self-fulfilling in their predictions about groups as a whole yet simultaneously useless in predicting the long-term success of individuals, have begun to have some effect. In 1989, a Federal District Court ruled that the exclusive use of SAT scores to award merit scholarships (as much as $8 million annually in New York State alone) had discriminated against women.[41] As a result of so much effort on the part of research and social-justice groups, reliance on test scores for college admission has diminished. Other criteria have become important parts of the mix, ranging from previous academic records, personal interviews, and autobiographical essays to the well-roundedness of the individual and the diversity of experience she or he might bring to other students at the school. In answer to the inevitable question of replacements for these inaccurate tests, there are many solutions: for instance, the so-called "portfolio method" in which students are judged on a variety of work on a particular subject over a period of time, including their own notes on why they chose a method, or what they learned from an essay or experiment.[42] Nonetheless, paper tests remain the single most important element in college-admission decisions, especially for the top fifty schools, and the notion that each of us is measurable by a numerical IQ is still a part of the culture.

As for the tests' content, some cultural biases have been corrected — but others have not. In the Scholastic Aptitude Test, for instance, a majority of reading-comprehension passages use descriptions of accomplishments in science, politics, sports, and the like, thus becoming more "user-friendly" to many white, male, and middle-class test-takers than to others. Even the math and reasoning problems are often expressed in impersonal, distant-from-life examples that are more part of male than female socialization. Phyllis Rosser, an expert on the gender bias of SATs, has documented the negative impact of these masculine contexts on female test-takers.[43]

David White, a Harvard Law School graduate in California who coaches candidates in the fine art of surviving the LSATs for entry into law school, says that efforts to make the questions more hospitable to women and people of color sometimes reflect limited thinking in themselves. Having noticed that the word *feminism* only appeared in wrong answers, for instance, he offered a dollar to any student who found it in a right one — and he didn't have to pay off until 1989. White also points out LSAT questions like the one asking for logical arguments *against* slavery, but in the context of statements from slaves who support it; or in which the test thesis is women's damage to the country and to children when they are in the paid labor force.[44]

An African-American critic named Robert Williams introduced some humor into the testing debate by inventing the Black Intelligence Test Counterbalanced for Honkies: BITCH. "Is it more indicative of intelligence to know Malcolm X's last name," he asked,

or the author of Hamlet? I ask you now when is Washington's birthday? Perhaps 99 percent of you thought February 22. The

answer presupposes a white form. I actually meant Booker T.
Washington's. . . . What is the color of bananas? Many of
you would say yellow. By the time the banana has made it to
my community, to the ghetto, it is brown with yellow spots.
What is the correct thing to do if another child hits you . . . ?
. . . For survival purposes, children in Black communities are
taught to hit back; however that response receives zero credit
on current intelligence tests such as the Stanford-Binet.

But his point and conclusion are serious. "The Black child does
quite well in coping with his home and neighborhood environment,
but does poorly in the school system. He clearly shows every indication of brightness at home. It is incumbent upon educators to develop appropriate learning experiences . . . and not the other way
around."[45]

The defense of testing is often as tautological as craniology's
assumption that smaller skulls must have been female because female skulls are smaller: If female, nonwhite, and lower-class test-
takers don't do well with material dictated *by* the mainstream, say
the tests' defenders, then they won't do well *in* the mainstream. The
undiscussed question here is who and what defines *mainstream*. Females of all races, men of color, plus men of a different class or
sexuality make up the huge majority of the country; yet they are
supposed to let a small (white, male, middle-class, heterosexual) minority decide what is important to know, think, and value.

In other words, to do well on such tests, many of us are creating
a false self for test-taking and educational purposes, and submerging
a true one.

All criticism and legal challenges notwithstanding, paper tests are
still the single most powerful, socially approved tool of human dif-
ferentiation. And even when tests are downplayed as part of affir-
mative-action programs, there is often some stigma of lowered
standards *even though they have little relationship to academic performance and none to accomplishment after graduation.*

But perhaps more tragic than their external use is the influence
these scores have on students' self-estimates. "All the things an ad-

olescent can be," mourned Thomas Anthony, dean of admissions at Colgate University, "are reduced to a three-digit number."

Testing has lost some of its ability to justify hierarchies, however, and so yet another branch of science has been born. In 1975, "sociobiology" was officially named and defined as "the study of biological bases of human social behavior." Though this new specialty bows to social change by regretting rather than celebrating birth-determined hierarchies, it still devotes itself to proving their inevitability. Here are some quotations from the latest scientists of human difference: [46]

- Richard Dawkins: "The female sex is exploited, and the fundamental evolutionary basis for the exploitation is the fact that eggs are larger than sperms."
- Edward O. Wilson: "It pays males to be aggressive, hasty, fickle, and undiscriminating. In theory it is more profitable for females to be coy, to hold back until they can identify males with the best genes. . . . Human beings obey this biological principle faithfully."
- W. D. Hamilton: "I hope to produce evidence that some things which are often treated as purely cultural in man [*sic*] — say racial discrimination — have deep roots in our animal past and thus are quite likely to rest on genetic foundations."
- Lionel Tiger and Robin Fox: "Nothing worth noting has happened in our evolutionary history since we left off hunting and took to the fields and the towns. . . . We are still man the hunter, incarcerated, domesticated, polluted, crowded and bemused."

It isn't difficult to counter arguments like those. For instance: Eggs are actually hardier and longer-lived than sperm. If a female is interested in searching out a male with the best genes, she is being active rather than passive and "coy." If racial discrimination were genetic, why would so many barriers against intermarriage have been necessary? If biology rules, where does the will *not* to have children come from? Or the determination to regulate fertility? And finally, men were never *all* hunters in every culture, humans were never all men, and the question of what is "worth noting" depends on who's doing the noting.

But why should we *have* to counter these arguments? The very purpose of sociobiology is one that we should question. Its raison d'être in the world at large is to explain and support group differences; that is, to prove that the existing social order, unjust or not, is pretty much inevitable. But since the differences between and among individuals *within* any group are greater than the differences *between* groups, why focus on birth-determined categories at all? Fortunately, challenges have been mounted, and thanks to a new confidence brought by social-justice movements, often with humor. When the "math gene" argument for male high achievers surfaced again in the media in the late 1980s, for instance, Jane Pauley, then the cohost of *Today* on NBC-TV, discomfited her two biodeterminist guests by asking if this meant males who were bad at math were not "real men."

The hormone-influenced, "right-brain" (masculine) "left-brain" (feminine) theory that is the most popular concept of modern biodeterminism is also under attack. By using biofeedback, women and men have been able to shift the balance of electrically measured brain activity back and forth between hemispheres at will. Moreover, the left hemisphere is specialized to analytical and logical tasks that are "masculine" as well as verbal skills that are "feminine," while the right hemisphere governs spatial and visual tasks that are math-related and "masculine," but also intuitive or associative thinking of a kind supposed to be "feminine." Thus, in cultural terms, each hemisphere is androgynous.

But there is a predisposition toward theories that justify a current power structure — the familiar problem of "If you're so smart why aren't you rich?" Even when the scientist in question tries to make clear that a physical, brain-centered finding may be the result of either nurture or nature, behavior or birth, there is a tendency to distort the meaning. For example, when Dr. Simon Le Vay of the Salk Institute of California, himself a homosexual, announced in the fall of 1991 that a salt-grain-sized part of the hypothalamus was found to be slightly smaller in gay men than in heterosexual men (on the basis of autopsies performed on nineteen gay and sixteen heterosexual men who had died of AIDS), much of the media misinterpreted these findings to mean that gay men were "born that way" (though Le Vay himself made clear that he did not know whether this difference was present at birth), and also that these results included lesbians — who were not part of the study at all. Even worse than this distortion, however, were the uses to which it was put. As Frances Kunreuther of the Hetrick-Martin Institute in New York, a social-service agency for gay and lesbian young people, pointed out in the midst of this media controversy: "The issue is not what causes sexual orientation, but the reaction to it. And that reaction leads to suicides. It causes gay people to be beaten up, to be thrown out of their homes, to be in incredible isolation."[47]

Rita Arditti, a biologist who is innovating forms of instruction that are experiential, not just intellectual, looks forward to a new kind of education that frees us to trust our instincts, expand our capabilities, and study human possibilities instead of limitations. "Today in science," she points out, "we know 'more and more' about 'less and less.' . . . The emphasis on the analytical method as the only way of knowing has led to a mechanistic view of Nature and human beings." As she and many other new scientists believe, the point is linking, not ranking, a dissolving of boundaries and categories, not an argument over where individuals or kinds of knowledge fit. In her words: "The task that seems of primary importance — for women and men — is to convert science from what it is today, a social institution with a conservative function and a defensive stand, into a liberating and healthy activity. Science needs a soul which would show respect and love for its subjects of study and would stress harmony and communication with the rest of the universe."[48]

Until education is reformed along the lines suggested by Rita Arditti, being alert to its problems is a first step. Neither people it falsely aggrandizes nor those it falsely deflates are being allowed an authentic self and individual response. I was reminded of this when I met a young, highly educated, well-to-do young man who told me that he was spending one entire year without reading books, reviews, or anything else of an interpretive nature. He wanted to discover his own responses and to experience life unmediated.

But for those who are diminished or excluded, this awareness is especially important. Those least likely to be included in the current curriculum are also most likely to need degrees to move upward. I remember feeling that need strongly when I was in college and heard about a New York law school that had an experimental program: students could enter as juniors and turn their last undergraduate year into their first year of law school. Surely, a law degree would be the ultimate protection against ending up back in Toledo or in a life anything like my mother's, I thought, but when I talked to my college vocational adviser, she explained that women lawyers usually did research or wills and estates. ("No client or a dead client," as I later heard this rule explained.) Thus, I could end up doing research in the back room of some big law firm, or, as she pointed out cheerfully, I could graduate from Smith and do research right away. Suddenly, a law degree didn't seem so attractive after all.

But now, for those who are forewarned and trust their own responses, education can be a very different experience. I heard that kind of story from an elegant black woman in her late thirties while I was visiting Detroit. This woman explained that she had first seen *Ms.* magazine in a Michigan prison when she was serving time for prostitution. After reading an issue or two, she had begun to wonder: "Why am I in prison, but my customer and my pimp are not? If prostitution is a crime, why is the seller arrested — but not the buyer?"

Remembering a movie about a prisoner who had read law books and become his own advocate, she went to the prison library. In her state, she was told, only men's prisons had law books. Made more rebellious by this news, she organized a few other women prisoners to protest. When the state's criminal-code books finally arrived, she began reading, and soon she was answering questions for other prisoners about their problems of regaining custody of children put in foster homes, or getting children job training to support themselves. Once out of prison, she went to a local women's law firm for a clerical job. Knowing motivation when they saw it, they hired her.

To make an extraordinary story short, she passed a high school equivalency exam, entered college at night, and gradually moved from filing, to secretarial, and then to paralegal work. Some years later, she finished law school itself.

"So now I'm a lawyer," she explained with a smile. "I thought you just might like to know."

That story made me think about the contrast between my own easy "giving up" and this woman's tenacity. Because she was motivated by the human impact of her learning, she had inspiration and purpose. Because she hadn't been educated in why the system was right, she could more easily see where it was wrong. Because she had little outside authority to unlearn, she could trust authority within herself.

But whoever we are, we can go beyond learning with no will of our own — and beyond what Herbert Kohl called willful "not-learning" — to following our interests and passions. We, too, can decide how to value our educations — instead of letting them value us.

Four

Re-learning

"A man who had studied at many metaphysical schools came to Nasrudin. . . . 'I hope that you will accept me, or at least tell me your ideas,' he said, 'because I have spent so much of my time in studying at these schools.'

"'Alas!' said Nasrudin, '*you* have studied the teachers and the teachings. What should have happened is that the teachers and their teachings should have studied *you*.'"

SUFI WISDOM
from *The Pleasantries of the Incredible Mulla Nasrudin*

THIS chapter describes a variety of paths that people have followed on the way to relearning their true selves. Perhaps one of these paths will attract you, or two or three can be combined into a journey of your own devising — or you may reject all of them, yet find they serve as catalysts to the imagining of still others that work for you.

Whatever your response: trust it. Each of us has an inner compass that helps us know where to go and what to do. Its signals are interest, excitement, the joy of understanding for its own sake, and the sort of fear that is a sign of being in new territory — and therefore of growth. ("Feel the fear," as psychologist Susan Jeffers says, "and do it anyway.") Honoring and following these internal signals is itself the beginning of the journey.

By definition, there is no one way, or even one exactly replicable way, of relearning who we are. There is something more important: your way. I hope this chapter will start you on it.

I   *Believing in the True Self*

"If you bring forth what is within you, what
you bring forth will save you. If you do not
bring forth what is within you, what you do not
bring forth will destroy you."
JESUS
*The Gnostic Gospels**

Why does one baby reach for certain toys, while another doesn't? Why does one respond more to touch and another to sound? Or one thrive on company and another on calm? No one

---

* The Gnostic Gospels — written about two centuries after the death of Jesus, rediscovered only in 1945, and not fully translated until the 1970s — are the record of a Jesus who presented himself as a teacher, not the son of God, and taught that God is within each of us. For background and major quotations, see Elaine Pagels, *The Gnostic Gospels*, New York: Random House, 1979; Vintage, 1981. For a

knows — but we do know that frequent frustration of these preferences will make an infant irritable and angry, then uncertain, passive, and finally unlikely to initiate anything at all.

Why does one child choose to color with paints while another builds with blocks? Why does one create adventures in the imagination while another seeks them in the outside world? No one knows — but we do know that children who are encouraged to follow their own interests actually learn more, internalize and retain that learning better, become more creative, and have healthier and more durable self-esteem than those who are motivated by reward, punishment, or competition with other children.[1]

Why do some adults absorb information better by hearing it than seeing it? Why does one sibling remember stories and ideas while another remembers names and numbers? Why are some people gifted at languages, and still others drawn to anything mechanical? Why do some have perfect pitch and others have "green thumbs"? Why are some of us alert in the morning and others hopeless until noon; some gregarious and others shy; some sexually attracted to the same gender, some to the opposite gender, and some to the individual regardless of gender? No one knows. But we do know that, like children, adults whose innermost feelings and preferences are ignored, ridiculed, punished, or repressed come to believe that there is something profoundly, innately "wrong" with them. And conversely, those who are able to honor these inner promptings know what it is to feel at home with themselves.

Several millennia worth of observers have believed that a unique and true self resides in each one of us. It may be suppressed or nurtured, thwarted or developed — but it is there. Anthropologists, philosophers, and other close observers of humankind have tended to agree with Plato: "The soul knows who we are from the beginning."

Science and scientists, however, being new to human history, have tended to dismiss the time-honored testimony of the unique self and in-tuition; literally, self-teaching. It is not replicable in laboratory conditions, defies analysis, and is actively hostile to the tam-

---

complete text, see James M. Robinson, editor, *The Nag Hammadi Library*, New York: Harper & Row; Toronto: Fitzhenry and Whiteside, 1977.

ing, shaping, quantifying, and categorizing that are the foundation of science. But even some of the most skeptical scientists are now being jolted out of their hierarchical and group-based assumptions by recent revelations that the universe itself is a nonlinear, chaotic balancing of overlapping energies in which, as Marilyn French puts it in her summation of the new physics, "Nothing rules, yet there is peace, as each segment follows its own course and exists in coop-erative relation with everything else."[2]

Since each individual is a literal microcosm of all the forces in the universe, it is not a long stretch to a view of human beings in all their infinite and irreducible variety as being part of and con-stantly influencing as well as responding to the larger universe. Our newfound ability to map the living brain confirms this new view by showing how context-sensitive are its workings and neural path-ways, how profoundly it adapts to and is organically changed by different environments, and how inexhaustible are the possible gene combinations that produced each unique brain in the first place. So scientists, too, are beginning to acknowledge the existence of a unique, genetically encoded mystery within each of us, and to un-derstand the value of those methods of education and childrearing that honor the essence at the core of each human being. In so doing, they are likely to produce more quantum leaps of scientific under-standing; for those have tended to come from a radical empathy with the subject plus intuition, whether it was Darwin's vision of a human tree that led to his theory of evolution, or Einstein as a six-teen-year-old envisioning himself riding a beam of light into the uni-verse and thus achieving the core idea that led to his great paper on relativity ten years later. As René Dubos, the discoverer of the first antibiotic, pointed out in *The Dreams of Reason,* it's these "inspired guesses" that generally lead to a breakthrough in theory: "The mod-ern scientific techniques have served merely to verify the theory and to elaborate its details."[3]

"Educating through individual interest" is the heart of these self-valuing methods, but I had never seen it in practice until I visited an elementary school founded by parents of children who had grad-uated from Dorothy Pitman Hughes's childcare center described in chapter 2. Because their kids had emerged from that center with spirits unbroken and therefore no patience for the conformity demanded by conventional schools, a group of families had started the Children's Community Workshop School, an alternative school for grades one through six, in an old neighborhood brownstone.

On the day I visited, two children were explaining their special projects. An eight-year-old boy who loved trains was plotting out a coast-to-coast trip. By reading maps and calculating the engine's need for fuel, he had already learned geography and math far beyond his grade level — and he'd only gotten as far as Chicago. But intellectual learning was not all this experience had given him. He looked forward to coming to school; he had come to respect his teachers for the knowledge they shared with him when he needed it; he now knew how to use a library card and find information on his own; and most important, he had a growing confidence in himself.

The second child was a nine-year-old girl who had fallen in love with Greek myths. To make them more relevant to her own life and those of her friends, she had adapted and rewritten her favorites. Vocabulary, spelling, grammar, and clear handwriting had become welcome tools because they helped her to express herself. By turning the story of Aphrodite into a delightful musical play she called "Afro-dite," she was adding her own vision while introducing the whole school to the universality of myths.

Watching these children, I finally understood how pleasurable and self-enhancing an education could be. It was the very opposite of conventional methods so well described by Emma Goldman: "Since every effort in our educational life seems to be directed toward making of the child a being foreign to itself, it must of necessity produce individuals foreign to one another, and in everlasting antagonism with each other." [4]

With instruction from sources as diverse as Plato, the Jesus of the Gnostic Gospels, Emma Goldman, and the Community Workshop School, we could make this vision a reality:

- Religions could stop telling us we are innately sinful, and encourage the godlikeness and self-authority in each of us instead.
- Business could depend less on titles and taking orders, and

more on the satisfaction of work that is self-governed, rewarded, and well done.

- The military could ask us to live for a cause, not die for it,
  and save their promotions for those who solve conflicts
  without violence.
- Prisons could provide positive ways of showing individual
  worth instead of stripping inmates of all identity, without
  even the group pride that soldiers are offered in return.
- Most of all, children could feel loved and valued *from the
  beginning.*

I know these goals seem unrealistic, especially for those of us
who have grown up believing that religion is about obedience, business about status, the military about conquering, prisons about punishment, and parenthood about owning. But those elaborate,
oppressive systems are just as difficult to create as their supposedly
unrealistic alternatives — perhaps more so, since no uniform system,
no matter how repressive, has ever completely succeeded in producing uniform people.

One thing is clear: The human mind can imagine both how to
break self-esteem and how to nurture it — and imagining anything
is the first step toward creating it. Believing in a true self is what
allows a true self to be born.

II *Voyaging to Time Past*

"I believe that this neglected, wounded inner
child of the past is the major source of human
misery."
JOHN BRADSHAW

Feeling half ridiculous and half scared, I am sitting in the
office of psychotherapist Nancy J. Napier, an experienced travel
guide for journeys into the unconscious — that timeless part of our

minds where events and emotions of our personal past are stored along with the wisdom of our species.

My surface thought is: This inner-self stuff will never work for me; I'm just here to research it for other people. My underlying fear is: What if I remember the painful past — and can't get out of it?

Nancy tells me that we are about to embark on what is called an induction: a series of simple, clear, positive instructions that help to relax the body, focus the mind, and enter a state variously known as meditation, trance, or self-hypnosis.

These words sound exotic, but, as she explains, there's nothing unusual about the state they describe. Each of us has entered a version of it many times: when reading, only to find ourselves in the middle of a paragraph and realize our mind has turned inward and missed its meaning; while concentrating on a task with such intensity that we fail to hear someone speaking to us; or when arriving at a familiar destination with no conscious memory of how we got there — all because we've been in a daydream but functioning on "automatic pilot." It is this capacity for deep focus that allows athletes to "become one with the ball," writers to experience characters "coming alive" in their heads, and musicians to "enter the music." In fact, anytime that our attention is turned inward with enough intensity to outweigh the sensory input of the outside world, we are in some degree of trance.

This internalized state should not be frightening, for the slightest hint of need or danger will cause our conscious self to resume control — just as the smell of smoke, the presence of someone threatening in the room, or the cry of a baby with whom we are bonded can wake us from the deepest sleep. And the ability to tap the unconscious can be a great gift, for it gives us access to powers of the mind that are constant as well as timeless. Many people have had the experience of going to bed with a problem and waking up with the solution, for example, because the deeper part of the mind kept working while the surface slept.

The purpose of an induction is to help us evoke the trance state consciously, without having to wait for the accident of its occurrence. With the help of an exercise called a guided meditation, the unconscious can then be focused on anything we choose. I have come to Nancy for help in retrieving a past and forgotten self — the self of my childhood.

My induction begins with Nancy's calm voice giving a series of simple, positive instructions: "Breathe deeply, relax into the support of the chair, slowly raise your eyes to the ceiling, and slowly close them. . . ." I feel my body and mind beginning to calm, or "settle," as Nancy calls it — and I become more aware of her words. She tells me to "imagine a safe place that is beautiful and private"; then she spends some time directing me to imagine its details.

After there has been time to focus inward and conjure up a setting, she suggests I let an impression of myself as a child rise up to the surface of my mind, like an image that will gradually appear on photographic paper. Don't force it, she tells me, just accept whatever comes. What gradually surfaces is both familiar and strange: the image of a child as she appeared in an actual photograph, a little girl I remember but feel distant from. Nancy asks me to describe the child — where she is, what she is wearing, if she looks happy or sad — and this makes me draw closer to her. Though I never lose awareness of the room in which I sit with closed eyes — not feeling "hypnotized" at all — my perspective changes. I am still my present self sitting with Nancy, but I can also look around the yard where the photo was taken. I feel the puppy the child is holding in her arms and sense my father standing on the balcony above me with his camera. I both observe the little girl and see through her eyes.

Nancy suggests that I visit this little girl where she lives. This seems hopeless at first. Nothing comes. Then I am in a small room with white walls dappled in summer sunlight. It is hot. There is a little girl of five or six, wearing a worn-out red bathing suit, lying on the cool sheets of a bed where she feels relaxed and poured out like molasses. I know she's been outside all day catching turtles that she keeps in a tub in the backyard, then lets go again at summer's end. Her hair is a mass of snarls and tangles that haven't been combed in weeks; I remember the tears I cried when my sister, with great patience, made the effort. The sight of that bed also brings back the sensations of nights too hot to sleep and the cooling drift of talcum powder on my skin. It also brings an image of being awakened by my father for a midnight swim, then tiptoeing downstairs, feeling grown-up because things look strange in the moonlight and my father wants my company.

Mostly as this little girl, I feel filled with the pleasure of a good tiredness, going barefoot; feeling unself-conscious and being at home in my body. The words *Wild Child* come into my mind — and make me smile.

At Nancy's suggestion, I sit down next to this little girl and wait for her to talk to me — but it's too soon. She doesn't trust this older person who has left her alone for so long. For now, I'm filled with the reality of a part of my past that I had completely forgotten. I tell her I'll come back again — and I know I will. I would like this Wild Child to be part of my life.

Brought back to the present by the simple means of Nancy's instruction to slowly open my eyes, I feel alert and interested, as if I've just had an absorbing conversation. I'm sure that I was in no trance at all, yet I've experienced a long-ago scene as if it were the present.

It was odd to discover this untamed and spontaneous child: someone who existed *before* the terrifying years of living alone with my mother, and who was shut out when I built a wall to protect me from remembering what happened a few years later. She is so much more physical, confident, and true to herself than I am. It's hard to imagine *her* being discouraged from law school, intimidated in a hotel lobby, or transformed into a female impersonator. How could I have lost the freedom and willfulness this little girl had?

Before the session with Nancy, I had talked with many people who said their "inner child" was the source of their most spontaneous, creative, daredevil self, that reclaiming this inner reality had been their reward for confronting the past — but it all sounded mysterious and simple-minded to me. Now I was beginning to understand what they meant. My ability to shut out feelings and survive hard times — once a great gift and a necessity — had closed the door on a part of myself. It would take not just time but work to change this strong habit of my conscious mind, but the difference was that now I could sense the rewards.

As I return home after this hour of inward voyaging, I feel a greater clarity and awareness while doing the simplest things: walking, running an errand, looking at people in the street.

Despite my conscious self, which remains skeptical, I think: There must be something to this timeless-unconscious stuff after all.

I've continued this time travel. It's like diving for pearls in an ocean of the unconscious: Sometimes you come up with a gem, sometimes you don't, but either way, you emerge renewed.

If you're interested in such explorations, you'll find a sample induction and guided "inner child" meditation in Appendix I, as well as a list of helpful books, including Nancy Napier's own *Re-creating Your Self*, and others that offer help in using this trance state for purposes ranging from lowering blood pressure and strengthening the immune system to retrieving and healing past traumas. In many of the world's major cities, there are also free or inexpensive public courses on various meditation and self-hypnosis techniques. Ancient yogic practices, modern therapists trained in hypnosis, high-tech methods using biofeedback, self-hypnosis taught one-on-one, or instruction from the many Transcendental Meditation centers — all are paths to the inner self.

But no path is right for everyone or immune to adaptation. Allow your feelings to guide you, learn to experiment, combine, change, and come up with inductions and guided meditations of your own. Some people silently repeat a mantra (one or two meaningless syllables whose sound resonates within the body) to calm and relax the conscious mind so the unconscious can surface. Others do "affirmations," the repetition of a phrase with positive personal meaning (for instance, "I am valuable," "I am well," or just "I am"). Some imagine that each breath is taking in peace and expelling confusion, or inhaling confidence and expelling fear. Many visualize a flower or bright light that emanates from a center just above the eyes — the so-called third eye that is said to activate the midbrain — which has been described historically as a doorway to the unconscious or the soul. Still others visualize a color that fills their bodies, is exhaled with each deep breath, and surrounds them in a cloud that creates a private world.

The key is regularity and a routine that acts as a signal to the unconscious. Just as nightly rituals let your body know it is time to sleep, a meditation routine can signal your conscious mind that it is safe to relax and let a deeper self emerge. Practiced for twenty minutes at the beginning and end of each day, which seems to be the optimum for real change (though even once a week is helpful), meditation is a healthful and well-marked path to the recovery of the inner self.

If you're skeptical about the existence of such a trance or meditative state, consider the physical evidence. Almost any level of this focused attention — even when bodily tensions or other distractions prevent it from going very deep — produces measurably slower respiration, lower blood pressure, and longer brain waves than do many sleep states. In deep trances, these differences can be very pronounced. Studies show that the regular practice of meditation can lower cholesterol levels, regulate blood pressure, diminish the need for many medications, increase creativity and efficiency, sharpen memory, and heighten perception. In fact, the evidence has been so widely proven that it now takes an entire book, *The Physical and Physiological Effects of Meditation*, to survey and sum up the results of 1,200 such studies conducted over the last sixty years.[5]

And if you're *still* skeptical, just proceed *as if* you believed it. Your unconscious may surprise you.

In addition to all its other benefits, access to your unconscious can retrieve repressed trauma — a process that is vital to freeing yourself from old patterns but also means experiencing repressed pain. If you fear that buried beneath the surface there are episodes too painful to deal with on your own, honor these feelings and find trustworthy help before embarking on your journey. As mentioned in chapter 2, there are telltale signs of such buried trauma: an easily tapped rage that is always just beneath the surface or a fear of expressing anger at all; substantial childhood periods of which you have no memory of emotions or events, or ongoing severe memory lapses with or without drugs or alcohol; episodes of incapacitating depression; flashbacks of being confined, beaten, abandoned, tortured, or humiliated sexually; a feeling that responses received from other people are inexplicable, as if they were being directed toward a different person; severe eating disorders; easy "startle," that is, reacting to any small physical surprise with automatic defensiveness; episodes or fantasies of injuring oneself, animals, or other people; or perhaps a flat, too-perfect-to-be-true version of childhood about which you feel little emotion.

Trust these clues — there is statistical as well as personal evidence that the conditions they point to are widespread. Perhaps a third of the children in the United States (and many other countries as well) have been subjected to sexual and other kinds of severe abuse or neglect, and there are many other causes of what is now called posttraumatic stress disorder: serious accidents, domestic violence, political torture, war experiences, rape, and prison abuse — to name a few. Frequently, such memories are so painful that they don't surface fully until years after the events occurred. The more extreme and erratic these events, the younger we were when we experienced them, and the more dependent we were on the people who inflicted them, the more repressed they are likely to be.

The good news is that there are now many more therapists who are experienced and empathetic in recognizing the causes and helping with the results of such trauma. And there is a much greater likelihood, thanks especially to international movements of and for women, children, and crime and torture victims, that people who have experienced these things will be believed.

To find a personal guide to recovering the past, interview therapists until you find someone you trust and feel safe with. Don't be hesitant to ask friends with similar experiences for their recommendations, and to ask questions of therapists themselves. Look for signs of compassion: If a therapist reacts with sadness when you tell him or her a story that makes *you* sad, it's as important a proof of empathy as it would be with a friend. Look for signs of personal security: If she or he encourages your questions and challenges, it's a good indication that your independence is the therapeutic goal, not your dependence on the therapist. And remember that credentials may have meaning, but none can substitute for what you feel. If a therapist puts you at ease, gives you the freedom to express yourself and the confidence that you are understood and *believed,* and also challenges you and cares, she or he is the right therapist for you.

If you can't find a guide or group you trust, *Making Sense of Suffering,* a book by J. Konrad Stettbacher, the Swiss therapist whose thoughtful process for recovering and healing past pain was so helpful to Alice Miller, is also listed in Appendix I. From preparing for this process with rest and sleep to making floor plans of the rooms in which you lived as a child, he offers a practical and sensitive succession of steps to follow.

I've saved until last the most amazing property of the unconscious: its timelessness. It is this property that allows us not only to retrieve the past, but to *reshape* it: to go back to a place of pain or deprivation and alter the way it affects us, a method psychologists call "corrective regression." Precisely because past emotions and events are stored timelessly, we can enter that realm of the unconscious and reprocess them.

Nancy Napier writes about the case of a pregnant woman who was severely neglected as a child and feared that she would not know how to be a good parent. She wanted to give her child what she hadn't received, yet she had no model, no emotional memories of what this intimacy might feel like, stored in her brain cells.

During a long series of trances, psychologist Milton Erickson, a pioneer of corrective regression, guided her return to various stages of her growing up. As she reexperienced an early birthday, Erickson joined her as an imaginary friend of her father's: someone who cared about her very much, who encouraged her to express herself, and who praised her interests — in other words, a nurturing parent. Because her unconscious responded to this experience as if it were "real" (just as we respond physically to strongly imagined danger or food or sexual fantasies as if they were real), he was able to help her reprocess old memories and actually create new ones.

This "February Man" (as she called her nurturing friend in honor of the month of her birthday) visited her often and lovingly in different places and times of her childhood. At a conscious level, she knew this parental figure didn't exist. But at an unconscious one, she experienced the reality of his love and caring. When her own child was born, she was able to pass on the nurturing that she had experienced. As Napier reports: "She had learned from her interactions with her father's 'friend' how it felt to be cared about, what it was like when her experiences and thoughts were regarded as important."[6]

Many people have been able to reparent their inner child on their own. Having recognized and emotionally felt what their child of the past needed but did not receive, as adults they were able to reenter childhood scenes in their unconscious and become their own rescuer and loving parent. Most seem to find that this process takes a long series of regular meditations, but some are helped by just developing "affirmations" to comfort their wounded child when a present event triggers an unresolved fear; for instance, "It's okay to be scared," "You didn't cause your father's anger, and you aren't causing this person's anger now," or just, "I'm here to take care of you now, and I'll never leave you."

The years of your childhood you need to recall may be very clear to you consciously, or perhaps your unconscious is letting you know by producing feelings of great tenderness when you see a child of that age. If there are no such signals, you might read compassionate books on child development (see Bibliotherapy in Appendix II), then figure out consciously the stage in which your present problems are rooted, and call up scenes from that time in guided meditation. More and more, popular books and even therapy series on television are interweaving child development and adult self-healing techniques into a process of self-parenting.[7]

Odd though it may sound to those who haven't tried it, this idea is not new. Many writers and artists have left records of their child-adult dialogues, and some have needed to face early fears to be able to perform at all. Enrico Caruso, one of the greatest operatic tenors, was paralyzed with stage fright that recreated a childhood experience of choking. His shouted exchanges with his child self, in full hearing of stage hands, were legendary — and for him, they worked. At the opposite extreme is Virginia Woolf, whose childhood sexual abuse by her two older half-brothers began at age six and remained the undercurrent in her life and work until she committed suicide by drowning at fifty-nine; yet it is only now being understood and written about.[8] With more ability to disclose, return, and heal, we might have had this great writer with us longer.

If we ever have a second chance at the past, it is the unconscious that gives it to us. We *can* go home again — because a part of us never left.

In whatever form you make this journey, consider keeping a journal of your most subjective, uncensored, free-form thoughts. These are the gifts your unconscious brings you. Just by setting aside time for such explorations, you are saying: My inner life is real; I am real; it is worth my time and attention. You are affirming the importance and uniqueness of your authentic self.

As a reward, you may not only heal wounds, but find treasures. Indeed, the most creative people seem to be those with the easiest access to their unconscious. Einstein was so sensitive to its gifts that he had to be careful while shaving. Otherwise, new ideas surfaced with such speed that he cut himself in surprise.

Paradoxically, only journeying backward in time and reentering the home we once knew allows us to go forward to the home we've always wanted — as the people I describe below have begun to do in many different ways.

III   *The Writing/Painting/ Laughing/Singing Cures*

"The act of writing is the act of discovering
what you believe."
DAVID HARE

A woman thrust an envelope in my hand after a recent lecture, and when I opened it on the plane, I discovered an essay called "Finally First at Forty-One" by Christine Bergman.

"One day," she wrote, "a small voice inside just said no more . . . The End, Finale, Terminus, Kaput, FINIS!" To the amazement of her colleagues, and with only a part-time designing job as an excuse, Christine quit her very responsible position as a unit secretary at a major hospital. She didn't know what she wanted to do, only what she *didn't* want to do: go on meeting other people's expectations as a "Scullery Maid (Cinderella) to Doctors, Nurses, Patients, Visitors . . . helping them all get ready for the Ball."

"After much writing, exploring, researching and reading (and napping with the cat when I could think no more)," she wrote, her "true voice" began to come clear on paper.

She wrote first about the beliefs she had absorbed in school:

"That everyone was expected to be alike, follow the rules, that there would be no allowances or nurturing for the creative nature. . . ." Then she wrote about the beliefs that had been fostered in her family. As the daughter of an alcoholic father, she had been made into the "black sheep" for attempting to "turn on the lights in a family of denial." As a result, her mother took her to a child psychiatrist who was very judgmental, and Christine learned "just how important it was to look good, and fit in, especially when you are the small one. Otherwise, you might end up in a really crazy place."

Once she had understood this creation of a false self, fairy tale–like myths began to rise from the back of her mind. They revealed a child within who felt "seven again. Very small and fragile, and afraid"; an inner critic who called her "stupid" and said she couldn't learn anything; and the woman she had become, who knew the only escape from this negativism was to "let the truth out and shatter my silence" — but who was also afraid. The more she wrote, the more she understood her bond with a philosophically inclined father, who, like her, had loved words, but who anesthetized his fear of failure with alcohol. Seeing the world from "similar places of woundedness" had been their connection, but her father had never been able to face and thereby heal his past — which she was doing by writing.

Gradually, her fairy tales began to collect themselves into a kind of mythological autobiography. "I come upon a symbol or word in my outer world which connects directly with an inner issue," she explained, "and in a daze I sit in front of the typewriter and the story types me."

At the end of the essay she had given me, she described the days of writing she supports with a variety of jobs as a writer, storyteller, and leader of writing workshops:

> Now, I'm a woman who gets up every morning, usually pretty early, and walks myself to the kitchen, where I go to work at my desk. There I meet with my self, as the authority, to sniff out the day. I whirl through my projects, each flowing one to the next, with a sense of spirit, of adventure, of sleuthing. . . . From the inner world of richness and vast treasures come these ancient and sacred fairy tale–like truths.

"What I write," she concluded, "is exactly that which I need to know."

Experiences like Christine's are not uncommon. Writers from Thomas Mann to Virginia Woolf, Joyce Cary to Maxine Hong Kingston, have described being "visited" by their characters, and "making up" things that turn out to be true. Ancient and modern mystics have often described "automatic writing": words that come from a place so deep that they feel another person is writing "through" them. Many psychologists have recognized the "writing cure" as well as the "talking cure," and many professional writers would agree with Tennessee Williams that they write to stay sane. "We do not write in order to be understood," as C. Day Lewis put it; "we write in order to understand."

Though we know about the few who publish their results, we rarely hear about the many who do not — and they may be even more likely to be writing from the soul without censoring themselves. Forgetting about shortcomings of skill or grammar and writing entirely for oneself can transform the often difficult task of putting words together into a way of tapping the unconscious. Many methods have been devised to trick a critical mind into relaxing enough to let this inner voice emerge:

- Using a bedside notebook to scribble down whatever fragments of dreams you recall at the moment of waking, even if only the emotions the dream left behind.
- Using the same bedside book to record whatever feelings, images, and thoughts float up at the moment of waking, before a conscious self has been called into action by the day.
- Writing with the "wrong" hand, thus occupying the conscious mind with a physical effort (and often invoking the child self who first learned to write) while the unconscious operates unimpeded. (If you or important people in your household spoke a different language, return to that language you first heard.)
- Carrying a notebook with you wherever you go and jotting down key words or images that come to you in various sit-

uations or with different people — then reading it over at
the end of each week to see what patterns emerge.
• Writing so quickly and in such quantity — as much as is
physically possible for a set period of time — that censoring
by a critical self becomes simply impossible.

Each of these methods provides a unique kind of access. Writing with the nondominant hand so often invokes the inner child that some people refer to it as the "honest" hand. For instance: Try using your nondominant hand when answering the question about your childhood at the end of chapter 2. Or conduct an internal child/adult dialogue by writing a question with one hand, its answer with the other — and then reversing the procedure. Jotting down thoughts on first awakening can capture the webs of consciousness through which you have just risen. Battered women, prisoners, and other people deprived of self-expression — often for so long that they believe there is no self *worthy* of expressing — have found that keeping any journal, perhaps sharing it with others in a similar situation, is the first step to believing their own voices. Writing in great quantity is a technique recommended by many teachers of creative writing. Maxine Hong Kingston, author of *The Woman Warrior* and *China Men,* tells her students that this quantity-writing reveals a voice both unique to each person and expressive of one of the universal biological rhythms that are, Kingston believes, the source of classic literary forms. Each sonnet is a writer's unique message, but its rhythmic structure, Kingston says, is the pulsating of the human heart.

Perhaps the oldest of these methods of tapping the unconscious is dream recollection. Australian aborigines use "dreaming" (*tjukurpa*) to refer to the wisdom of the timeless past, including still-followed migratory paths once made by totemic beings — events thought to be alive and still affecting the present. ("Those who lose dreaming," says an Aboriginal proverb, "are lost.") On this continent, many Native American cultures make "dream-catchers," small circles of twigs or metal with cobweblike strands of leather stretched across them, and place them at bedside as a reminder. Modern therapists suggest a dream journal as a way of capturing important images and emotions. From Rabindranath Tagore in India to Truman Capote in the United States, writers have learned that taking notes on their dreams keeps them in touch with their creative core and exercises their powers of description at the same time.

Whatever the purpose or tradition, there is one thing diverse cultures agree upon: the more you cultivate the habit of dream-memory, the stronger it becomes — and the greater your access to the true self. When we write down our dreams or any unconscious wisdom, perhaps we literally write our souls out — putting them down on paper where our minds can see them.

Painting

"We talk too much; we should talk less
and draw more."
GOETHE

About a decade ago, Judy Collins told me she had taken watercolors with her on vacation. I accepted this as news from a different species. In addition to singing, playing the piano and guitar, composing many of her own songs and lyrics, and touring the world as a modern troubadour, she had now become An Artist. No matter how she tried to explain that this was simply a way of expressing herself — that she couldn't draw, that she just spread big sheets of paper on the floor and filled them with whatever shapes and colors she felt attracted to — I assumed that this occupation took her beyond me.

It was only years later while reading Alice Miller's description of painting as the path to reexperiencing and healing her own over-controlled, spirit-breaking childhood (see chapter 2) that I began to understand what Judy had been trying to tell me. After all, Miller was not An Artist, but she had used the process of creating visual images to make a breakthrough that had evaded every intellectual attempt at retrieval. It was only the free, tactile act of painting that finally broke through a protective shield of denial.

When I talked to Judy about my belated understanding of the universal need to create images, she said that she, too, had waited a long time before trying it. Not only did she have a mystique about painting, but her own talented and self-sufficient father had been blind — and so making visual imagery had seemed a betrayal of him. It was no accident that her first attempt to make anything but music had been the tactile art of pottery. Only years after she had become a successful musician and composer — and had written poetry, kept a dream notebook, and tried other paths to the self — did she take up watercolors.

"I finally realized that it isn't just dilettantism," she explained. "Visual images are part of our genetic heritage. In other cultures, we would have been decorating our houses and our bodies, making pots because we needed them, singing songs to pass the time, weaving fabric for our clothes; everything. We have five senses because we're supposed to use them. I think we each come out of the womb with some unique way of looking at the world — and if we don't express it, we lose faith in ourselves."[9]

Since that conversation, I've noticed that most art in the world does not have a capital "A," but is a way of turning everyday objects into personal expressions. With no thought of critics or museums, it is perhaps the truest art: Bedouin weavings and American quilts are abstract paintings, simple Amish furniture and native American pottery are beautiful sculptures, Hopi sand paintings and Palestinian embroidery often invoke healing, the painted symbolism of Mithila women in India and bushpeople in Africa speak for the same collective unconscious, and abstract paintings redone casually and routinely by West African women on their mud-walled houses after each monsoon could put many of the canvases in modern museums to shame.[10]

Art can be such a vital part of daily life that the !Kung bushmen of Africa carry their painting tools in their belts, to have them always at the ready, and young women of Turkey and Afghanistan weave their hopes into the traditional *kilims* that will hang in their doors and cover their floors after they are married. Even in the United States, artists from frontier and Native American cultures, the ethnic traditions of Mexico and South Asia, Africa and the Middle East, are beginning to take art out of museums and into personal and community life. As Lucy Lippard explains and illustrates in *Mixed Blessings: New Art in Multicultural America,* this is an art about naming experience, representing the self, storytelling, and dreams.[11] It is about art that has burst out of museums and entered real life.

As it turned out, Judy's experience was personal — but it was also universal. Once I stopped thinking of image-making as a rare-fied pursuit, I began to notice it everywhere. Within a few months, these examples had crossed my path:

• A Chicana teenager in East Los Angeles whose self-esteem was so low that she rarely made any definite statement — until a *barrio* program encouraged her to "paint what you see when you close your eyes." She produced paintings of such sliding, eliding, colorful beauty that even she began to believe there was a worth-while world within herself.

• A young friend in New York, an anorexic former dancer who gained weight and health during six months of flinging paint on big canvases, then troweling it into the shapes of larger-than-life wom-en's bodies. Having created females who had breasts and hips and were still strong, beautiful, and safe, she stopped starving herself out of being a woman.

• An Iowa farmer who painted huge, colorful, imaginary birds on the side of his barn. He told me that this "crazy period" had been brought on by his wife's rebellion and departure over his dis-tance and coldness; a crisis that made him realize he had become like his own cold and distant father (who had forced him, among other cruelties, to kill his pet birds). His wife never came back, but this man became closer to his own sons; now, they paint the barn with new bird-spirits every spring.

• An account of Winston Churchill's long years of disgrace and exile from political power, a period in which he wrote memoirs and did paintings of the English countryside. He emerged from this in-ward journeying with a new strength and maturity that helped to sustain England when he became its leader in wartime.

• A book published by psychotherapist Peg Elliott Mayo after the suicides of her husband and son. In it, she used her own expe-rience of grief to create rituals and images that others could use to unearth their feelings about death.[12]

• A teenage boy I met in a folk art gallery in St. Paul, Minne-sota, who had been thrown out of his farming family's house be-cause he had been honest about his gayness. After months of living in the street, he had begun to draw with colored chalk on sidewalks to the delight of passersby, and only then did he stop his plans for suicide.

• Art historian Robert Farris Thompson's remarkable book, *Flash of the Spirit,* in which he connects African and Afro-American art, philosophy, and music. It is, as one reviewer said, "art history to dance by." [13]

If everybody from Winston Churchill to an Iowa farmer has discovered the importance of image-making, why do I and so many others grow up believing that painting is a never-never land from which non-Artists are forever barred? Perhaps it has come with the long separation of art from daily life, and the denigration of useful art as "crafts," or perhaps it's the encouragement to desire the mass-produced. For whatever reasons, using paint, crayons, and clay has become something many of us do *before* we're old enough to read and write — and then abandon. Only indigenous cultures, futurists, and a few pioneer educators seem convinced that we need to use *all* of our senses if we are to value *all* of ourselves.

So give yourself an opportunity to discover your own imagery. Walk through an art store and see what attracts you: using a sketch-book and soft pencils, getting your hands in wet clay, smelling oil paints on real canvas, sloshing brushes over watercolors, feeling finger paints, or scrawling with big crayons. The images you create can bypass the intellect and go straight to emotion, and so can the tactile feel of the medium you make them in.

Whatever you end up creating will be as universal as a human hand and as unique as your fingerprint. The more regularly you create, the more you will notice an image often repeated in varying ways. That is your true self made visible.

Laughing

"When we see how funny we are, we see
how dear we are."
ANNE WILSON SCHAEF

Think of the feeling of laughter — helpless laughter. It starts in the mind, spreads irresistibly to the body, and involves the whole self. It drives out other thoughts as surely as an orgasm, more surely than sleep — and can be as restorative as either.

Laughter has many poor relations: smiles that ingratiate or deceive; giggling at our own embarrassment or at someone else's expense; grinning with victory or defiance; chuckling with appreciation; smirking with prurience; simpering with need for approval — and many more. But only laughter is something you "burst into" with complete spontaneity. Sleep can be induced, even an orgasm can be faked — but not a good laugh. False laughter just isn't convincing. It can't be planned or even predicted, coerced or compelled. It just *is:* a flash of recognition; a moment of perfect balance between inner and outer worlds; a fast dip into the unconscious that the whole self revels in. In many cultures, laughter means health, balance, self-acceptance, even a flash of cosmic joy.

Often, the absence of laughter and humor is a sign of mental and emotional illness. Those who are stuck in the inner world may become severely depressed and a danger to themselves, while those who live only in the outer world may be psychopaths and a danger to others, but neither can let inner and outer worlds meet and produce the contradictions that create laughter.

Students of physical illness have learned that laughter can be literally health-giving. Even limited experiments in which one group of patients watched a laughter-inspiring film and another group did not have shown that the immune systems of the first group became measurably stronger for a period of hours afterward. Laughing also calls up endorphins, the body's natural shields against pain, with none of the side effects that artificial painkillers bring with them (for instance, suppression of protective cells that impede the growth of tumors). Norman Cousins, who was a modern-day prophet of laughter, discovered its beneficial effects during a long and life-threatening illness. A few minutes of laughter gave him a few hours of pain-free sleep without medications and strengthened his body's ability to fight beyond medical predictions. He lived fifteen years after that illness: more than long enough to write about his experience, persuade many hospitals to include humor, films, and literal "living rooms" in their medical programs, and to see his controversial theories confirmed. In 1989, the staid *Journal of the American Medical Association* published this conclusion from a Swedish study: "A humor therapy program can improve the quality of life for patients. . . . Laughter has an immediate symptom-relieving effect."[14]

Like any expression of the true self, laughter is radical and revolutionary, and it upsets conformity. As Robin Morgan explained
in *The Demon Lover:*

> When you try to stifle laughter, it just gets worse. It gurgles and
> bubbles and rises until you're ready to explode with it — like
> in church or in a judge's chambers or in a business meeting.
> . . . You can gulp back tears if necessary. You can certainly
> swallow words you know will get you into trouble if you speak
> them. You can grind your teeth and not cry out in pain. But
> there's no way to swallow laughter, real laughter.

I say all this to convince you that there is such a thing as a path
of laughter. As far as we know, it is unique to human beings — a
flash of consciousness, a clue to who we are.

Singing

> "I celebrate myself, and sing myself."
> WALT WHITMAN

Each of us with hearing and vocal cords can sing, yet
many of us have been embarrassed out of this primordial pleasure
by self-consciousness and shame at the sounds we make. Our critical, conscious self literally stifles our voice. And, as with any other
human capacity, the less we use it, the less we believe it to be worth
using.

An inability to sing *even for oneself* has become so common
that there are now classes, camps, and retreats to help people make,
hear, and appreciate the sounds of their own voices. Paul Winter, a
gifted musician and composer, often holds summer singing camps
for adults. Though he travels and performs internationally to bring
musical traditions of different cultures together, and has pioneered
the use of natural sounds in his compositions, he finds that getting
the silent to sing is as gratifying as anything else in music. With the
simple act of doing this intimate thing they were convinced they
could not do, people's lives change.[15]

Perhaps this need to use *all* our senses explains why a decrease
in such school "extras" as music, art, dance, and gym often seems
to parallel the loss of student self-esteem described in chapter 3.

And as adults, we tend to narrow our forms of self-expression even more.

Any one of our human capacities, if unused out of fear or shame, leaves a small hole in the fabric of our self-esteem. Think of the times you have said: "I can't write," "I can't paint," "I can't run," "I can't shout," "I can't dance," "I can't sing." Since this was not literally true, you were really saying: "I can't meet some outside standard. I'm not acceptable *as I am*."

IV   *Creating Psychic Families*

"Only connect."
E. M. FORSTER

Five years ago, I received this letter from Victoria Hawks in Douglas County, Oregon:

> My daughter, age 20, high school dropout, single parent of an 18-month-old, [was] dealing with a dead-end relationship with her child's father; a low self-image; and an inability to see a positive future for herself and her child; . . . she came from a "broken home"; had none of the material advantages of many of her peers; early on a stepfather who both physically and mentally hurt her mother, her brother, and herself; then she saw another divorce; got into drug, alcohol, and sexual abuse of herself; and beginning at age 15, left home many times (finally and forever at 17).
>
> All the strikes were against her, it seemed, save one: I love her and wanted her life to be better than mine had been.
>
> [Now she is] a very different person. She smiles more; she speaks up and lets people know she has valid opinions; she has specific plans for future education and career ideas; and she is more self-assured and positive than I ever imagined she could become. As a side effect, she has decided to take on the re-education of her 23-year-old brother, who is a very negative

thinker (obviously obtained through the same life experiences and dilemmas). Although he is a junior at the University of Oregon, he too is unable to project a positive self with a bright future. . . . She may have a setback day now and then, but assuredly most of her days are forward. Her whole family, including a new stepfather who cares deeply for her as well, is pleased that she will never again be the self-sorry, self-deprecating, lost soul she once was. . . . My Laura with the beautiful face, who felt cast-off and left out of the greater world, [now has] the tools to become a shining star for all to see, but more importantly, to finally see for herself.

What made the difference for Laura? Three months of going to something called the Confidence Clinic, a group of single mothers and other women who were divorced, widowed, deserted, and often on welfare. They understood her feelings and gave her a trustworthy place where she could share them in a group that was committed to mutual help. She found what I call a psychic family.

When I first heard about the Confidence Clinic, a successful program in a rural and isolated part of southwestern Oregon, it had already closed for lack of money. Ironically, the features that made it successful were the same ones that made getting public funds difficult: it was staffed by women who had conquered similar problems (and therefore were not seen as properly professional), its headquarters were noninstitutional and homelike, and it respected the privacy of the women it served, even when public agencies requested information. That's why the clinic was applying for a grant from the Ms. Foundation for Women, a national multi-issue women's foundation, and one that focuses on grass-roots self-help projects. As its staff had explained when they asked for help in reopening, the "heart" of their program was a series of support groups of a dozen to twenty-five women who met regularly for at least three months. Its "legs" were twelve-week, five-day-a-week courses in job skills, legal rights, survival as a single parent, assertiveness training, money management, and preparation for the outside world that included a clothes bank so women could dress suitably for job interviews.

The clinic's record spoke for itself. Of those many women who arrived without a high school diploma, 98 percent had earned one in twelve short weeks. Within a year after leaving, most clinic graduates were employed, in training for a specific job, or in college — a stunning leap for women who had been isolated, despairing, and dependent, and certainly a *much* better success rate than for conventional programs aimed at getting women and their children out of poverty.

Clearly, the Confidence Clinic deserved — and got — a Ms. grant, but before it had reopened, its past work was identified by the American Institute for Research as one of a hundred successful programs in the United States. Finally local government, United Way, and small foundations began to support its work. Since 1971, when a handful of women first decided that what they most lacked was confidence — and so opened a Confidence Clinic — more than 1,500 women have passed through its support groups, the "heart" that makes this program unique and now it has become a model for other programs.[16] Like a real family, women stay in touch with other members of their small groups or drop in to the homelike atmosphere of the clinic to share the news of their lives. Now, the clinic is struggling to find money to help women *before* they're on public assistance; women who "fall through the cracks" by being ineligible for government-funded programs.

Five years is a long time in the life of a young single mother with many miles to travel, but when I called to see how Laura was doing, I discovered that she was a junior at the University of Oregon — a feat accomplished with scholarships and welfare money — and that her own little girl was in the first grade. Her goal is to help women like herself who end up on drugs or in prison because that's all they think they deserve.

"She told me yesterday," said her mother, "that *I* should go to the Confidence Clinic. I told her it's too late for me."

Having rescued herself, Laura is now the rescuer.

Psychic families exist for almost every situation and experience, from small groups of women who make a space for themselves outside patriarchy to men and women who support each other's abstinence from alcohol or drugs; from people trying to maintain their self-respect while homeless or living on welfare to those working to conquer agoraphobia, fear of flying, or eating disorders. We may describe these groups in New Age–style terminology — self-help, support, consciousness-raising, twelve-step, networks, and so on — but comparable affinity groups existed in the past in the form of quilting bees, book clubs, immigrant and other ethnic associations, underground cells, settlement houses, or just the guys at the barbershop or women like those celebrated in *Steel Magnolias*. They are built into older cultures, whether among Pakistani village women whose communal clothes-washing becomes a support group (which have been known to collectively thrash a man who has been abusing his wife), or among adolescent boys in many African tribes who gather in special houses during their passage into adult responsibility. New or old, these affinity groups are a recognition that the biological family isn't the only important unit in society; that we have needs and longings that our families cannot meet. Indeed, in some cultures, the community is more important than the family.[17]

In general, the effectiveness of a psychic family depends on four principles: that someone who has experienced something is more expert in it than the experts; that shared experience and desire for change can bind us to each other; that mutual confidentiality and commitment are to be honored; that everyone participates but no one dominates. Size has a lot to do with how feasible it is to put these principles into practice: the healers and wise women of pagan times knew what they were doing when they made covens of thirteen witches — small enough so everyone could talk, large enough for diversity, and an uneven number so decisions were not deadlocked.

There is also a potential for exploitation in these groups, just as in real families. In Alcoholics Anonymous–type groups that are mostly male, "thirteen-stepping" became a shorthand way of saying that women members were being pressured sexually. On the other hand, many such groups, especially for eating disorders, now have so many women members that they have rewritten the twelve steps — originally designed to break down the ego so the addict can admit addiction — to better suit the needs of women with too little ego. Again, trust your feelings.*

---

* For a discussion of addiction adapted to women, see *Women, Sex, and Addiction: A Search for Love and Power* by Charlotte Kasl, New York: Ticknor & Fields, 1989.

Like the Confidence Clinic, some groups combine internal support with external action, but it's the inner half that is the key for self-esteem: a group that is entirely activist and externally directed may be very productive, but it doesn't offer the bonding and growth that is possible in a psychic family. Since growth depends on growing pains, however, there shouldn't be too much comfort. As Bernice Johnson Reagon of the singing group Sweet Honey in the Rock says: "If you're in a coalition and you're comfortable, you know it's not a broad enough coalition."

When evaluating your existing group or one you're thinking of joining, you might ask:

- Can each person speak and really be listened to often enough to feel a sense of ownership of the group?
- Does having this group in your life make you feel more empowered and challenged than you otherwise would?
- Do you look forward to meetings as something *for you,* not just one more obligation?
- Can you be honest inside it? For instance: Can you be angry? be vulnerable? trust the responses you get?
- Does being part of this group lead you to positive and independent action *outside* it?
- Does the group honor the departure of old members and welcome new ones?
- Does it give you pride in your own identity — without putting others down for theirs?
- Do you feel accepted *as you are?*
- Does it make you stretch and become better than you thought you could be?
- Is there a balance over time between what you're receiving and what you're giving to others?

If you can't answer yes to most of these most of the time, you may need to find — or create — a different psychic family. Here are a few more descriptions to give you faith that there is or could be a group that speaks directly to you:

- When executives retire, it's easy for them to lose self-esteem along with the community leadership positions, speaking invitations, charity drives, private cars and planes, or other privileges that may disappear when the position does. Some corporations are beginning to encourage the forming of executive support groups *before* retirement, including as mentors those who already have made this not-so-easy transition.

• Parents of gay men and lesbians face homophobia in society, perhaps even in themselves; yet they probably have fewer opportunities for support and learning what gayness really means than do their daughters and sons. In addition, they may have special problems: the mother who believes a son or daughter's sexuality must be her "fault," or the father whose own sense of "masculinity" is threatened by having a gay son. In most major cities in the U.S. and many other countries, there are now networks, special groups within religious and ethnic organizations, even branches of national or international gay organizations, that bring parents together so shared support and wisdom can replace isolation, bias, and guilt, and so parents are better able to connect with their children — and vice versa.

• People who love to dance don't always have partners or friends who feel the same, and dancing has been a way of lifting the human spirit since the beginning of time. Swing dance societies, tango clubs, waltz groups, lunchtime discos, square dances, Latin nights, ethnic dance groups — all are places to find kindred spirits who come together for no purpose other than the sense of well-being they find in moving to their own kind of music.

• One in three people in the United States will have cancer at some time in their lives. Nonetheless, each person who hears this medical verdict hears it alone. Survivor and "wellness" groups break this isolation, share treatment knowledge, support each other through changes in appearance and identity, challenge poor medical practice, explore causes of incidence and recurrence, and share feelings that one who hasn't absorbed the word *cancer* into his or her life might not understand. Since research shows that the state of our minds and emotions affects the immune system's ability to battle this or any other disease, these groups may be literally life-giving.

• Daughters born into families of inherited wealth and power — families that often have a stronger bias in favor of sons, or even sons-in-law, than families with less power at stake — are seeking each other's help in breaking trusts, taking a rightful place on family boards, learning to run family businesses, dealing with lawyers and advisers, and generally trying to control their own lives. In this rarefied world, isolation can be great, and understanding from people who haven't experienced powerful patriarchies at an intimate level can be scarce or turn to resentment. Small confidential support groups of women trying to control their own financial resources — and to use them to help other women in the process — now exist in several major U.S. cities and are often findable through local women's foundations.

• When researchers in California set out to find the reason for Asian-American students' disproportionately high achievement in math and science, they discovered only one likely answer: study groups. Unlike their peers who studied on their own, the Asian-American students shared their strengths by studying together, so that the strength of each was taught to all. Like similar groups in law schools, there is a commitment to each member's success.

Given the diversity of groups already in existence, one that's right for you is likely to be among them. And if not, you'll be helping your psychic siblings if you bring them together. From the consciousness-raising groups that became the cell of the feminist revolution to sexual abuse survivors who learn they are not alone, there is no greater magic than shared experience.

V *The Uses of Parallels*

"I am myself plus my circumstance, and if I do
not save it, I cannot save myself."
JOSÉ ORTEGA Y GASSET

The unconscious and the conscious are not separate compartments but ends of a continuum in which influence flows both ways. Methods that begin with the unconscious mind are the first to reach barriers to self-esteem formed in our earliest and most intimate lives. Methods like those that psychologists call "cognitive" — which enter at the intellectual or conscious end of the continuum — are the first to reach barriers that have been erected by culture and society.

Suppose, for instance, we are members of a group treated as unequal or invisible by some or all of the society around us. Whether we come from the "wrong" race, sex, caste, class, ethnicity, or sexuality — whether our inner or outer selves just aren't the "norm," or our circumstances have changed in a way that temporarily shakes our self-esteem — we probably have internalized some of this low opinion. In addition, we may feel "crazy" when we try to express our true selves, because the dominant system treats our point of view and experiences as invisible or unimportant. Two kinds of parallel therapy can help break through this visibility barrier.

First, we can explore the parallels between our own experiences and those of another discriminated-against or undervalued person or group whose sufferings society takes more seriously. Letty Cottin Pogrebin used this kind of parallel therapy when she wrote about the similarities between anti-Semitism and woman-hatred. Starting with the often-quoted statement that "women are the Jews of the world" (and vice versa), she listed parallels:

> Just as woman comes in two opposing archetypes, Madonna and whore, so is the Jew split in two: victim (Anne Frank) and victimizer (Shylock).
>
> The myth of "female power" (in terms of sexual or maternal omnipotence) re-casts the male in the vulnerable role and thus justifies discrimination against women; the myth of "Jewish power" re-casts the Christian majority as pawns, and helps justify repression of the Jews.
>
> "Jews really control the press," "White women really control the wealth," and "Black matriarchs really control black men" are three equally inaccurate clichés invented to mask the overwhelming concentration of power and money in the hands of *white Christian men*.
>
> The existence of some leisured women and some affluent Jews is claimed as proof that *all* members of both groups are privileged.

. . . The mystique of the *intrinsic* sexual-psychic evil of both women and Jews makes plausible periodic purges of Jews and bizarre accusations against women.

"Women are too powerful" was the underlying impetus for the slaughter of 9 million "witches" and the advancement of a repressive patriarchal religious establishment. "Jews are too powerful" was the argument Hitler used to promote himself as champion of the working class against rich "Jewish bankers."

Every so often, when times are especially hard, Jews get identified as "the problem" . . . so do women. Times are harder now — and both anti-Semitism and antifeminism are on the rise.[18]

This exercise was written to help women understand anti-Semitism within the women's movement, but it also helped women, Jewish and otherwise, to see their situation from the outside, cognitively, and thus to take antifemale discrimination and stereotyping as seriously as they would take the same treatment of Jews.

There are hundreds of other pairings that can be used to illuminate the shared experiences of apparently disparate groups. In authoritarian societies that try to channel all sexuality toward childbearing, for instance, independent women and homosexual men both stand for subverting the "natural" purpose of sex (that is, the production of children within patriarchal marriage), and both undermine the basis of the sexual caste system by putting men in a nondominant role. Even now, fundamentalist religions condemn feminism and homosexuality in the same breath, but the parallels between them were even more painfully clear in the past. In medieval Europe when the Inquisition conducted centuries of witch-burnings in order to wipe out those women leaders and healers of the preexisting pagan faith, for instance, homosexual men were often burned at the stake first to make the fires "hot enough" to burn a witch — hence the derogatory term *faggots*.

For challenging the kind of socially sanctioned invisibilities, denigrations, and divisions described in chapter 3 — and thus relearning our own worth and the worth of other devalued groups — this first form of parallel therapy can work wonders. Empathy is the most revolutionary emotion, and parallel therapy can help to create it.

The second kind of parallel thinking is more ambitious. Instead of making a comparison between two discriminated-against groups, try putting the powerful in the place of the powerless. It's a great reality check.

Take language, for instance. Many women feel invisible or aberrant when they are subsumed under a masculine term that is supposed to be universal; yet they are often made to feel trivial and nit-picking if they object. But look at it this way: Would a man feel included in "womankind"? Would he refer to himself as "chair-woman," "Congresswoman," or "Mr. Mary Smith"? If a male student earned a "Spinster of Arts" degree, a "Mistress of Science," or had to apply for a "Sistership," would he feel equal in academia? If men had grown up seeing God portrayed only as Mother and She, would they feel an equal godliness within themselves?

The same linguistic concerns hold true for race and religion. If titles like "novelist" and "engineer" were perceived as black unless otherwise stated — if "white novelist" or "white engineer" were necessary qualifiers — would whites feel equal ownership of those professions? If political issues put forward by white male citizens were called "special interest" and those of women and people of color who are the majority were the mainstream, who would feel themselves marginalized? If white people were defined in the negative as "non-black," or Christians were defined as "non-Jews," who would see themselves as the norm of society?

Or take homemakers, a group generally described as "women who don't work." In fact, homemakers work longer hours than any other class of worker. So do the women in agricultural countries who work in the fields and grow the family food — but they're not counted as workers, either. Suppose we started counting all this work at its salaried replacement value? Women who work outside the home would benefit from this altered perception, since they're usually working *two* jobs, one that is salaried and visible and one that is neither. If, on the other hand, men were valued according to female definitions of work, think what would happen. Most men would be described (and paid) as "part-time workers" — they are productive outside the home, but not in it.[19] As a bonus, the Gross National Product of the U.S. would go up at least 25 percent — and certainly the gross national self-esteem of homemakers would increase, too.

If parallel therapy seems too abstract, try using it in everyday life. When reporters focused on what I wore or why I wasn't married instead of what I said, for instance, I used to think that it was either my fault or just somehow in the nature of things. Then I began to make a mental parallel with a man who was exactly my age and also unmarried: consumer advocate Ralph Nader. In each instance, I asked myself: Would these reporters ask Ralph Nader why he wasn't married? Would they preface what he had to say with remarks about the cut of his hair and the color of his suit? The answer was usually no. I began to feel less at fault, and more able to explain the imbalance — and to give reporters a logical argument for changing it.

The ultimate in parallel thinking is the Golden Rule — providing it is read *both* ways. The traditional sequence assumes a healthy self-esteem and asks for empathy: "Do unto others as you would have others do unto you." But for many people whose self-esteem has been suppressed, the revolution lies in reversing it: *Do unto yourself as you would do unto others.*

VI   *The Great Paradigm Shift*

"That's what learning is. You suddenly
understand something you've understood all
your life, but in a new way."
DORIS LESSING

"You can't beat something with nothing." That street wisdom also applies to habits of the mind. You can't lose old and negative ways of thinking until new and positive ones replace them.

The biggest and most far-reaching kind of cognitive therapy is a paradigm shift: a change in the organizing principle that underlies the way we think about ourselves and the world. It is a pattern so ingrained that we may consider it "natural" and be unaware of its existence.

In societies shaped by patriarchy and racial divisions, the prevailing paradigm comes in three parts.

The first is the either/or way of thinking that divides almost everything in two. "Masculine" and "feminine," subject and object, light skin and dark skin, dominant and passive, intellect and emotion, mind and body, winner and loser, good and evil, the idea that there are "two sides to every question" — all these are the living results of bipartite thinking. In older and more subtle cultures, each half was equally necessary to the other (as in the yin and yang of Eastern thought), but even that division had its origins in the division of human qualities into "masculine" and "feminine." The more unequal this genderized dyad became, the more it turned into the next part of the paradigm: linear thinking. Rating and grading people, the notion that all accomplishment lies in defeating others, even a linear view of abstractions like time and history — all these things were organized by the same paradigm. Since a straight line was too simplistic to be practical for most human interactions, however, it split into the third and last part of the paradigm: hierarchy. The pyramid or the classic organizational chart became the grid through which many cultures were to see the world for centuries: from a "male-headed" household to corporate structures in which all authority flows from the top; from hierarchical classrooms to religions in which God's will is interpreted by a pope or ayatollah.

It isn't that a binary, linear, and then hierarchical paradigm is always wrong. Some things really have two parts, competition can be used to press individual boundaries, and a hierarchy is well-suited to firefighting, surgery, or anything else that requires quick action.

But as a universal pattern with almost no alternatives, this paradigm limits us at best and destroys us at worst. It turns most human interactions into a contest that only one or a few at the top can win, and it teaches us that there is a limited amount of self-esteem to go around; that some of us can only have it if others do not.

Fortunately, this is just a cognitive construct. There is nothing biological or immutable about it, and therefore it can be changed.

In other times and cultures, there have been cyclical and regenerative paradigms, unitary paradigms, and pantheistic ones in which each living thing had a spirit of its own — to name just a few. Especially for those of us who have been looking at everything through a linear and hierarchical grid — perhaps no more aware of alternatives than a fish is aware of alternatives to water — it's important to let other possibilities into our minds. Since we are living in a time when the foundations of the old paradigm are cracking anyway, there are motives for changing it and glimpses through the cracks of what the future could be. Perhaps the most obvious motive for change is the ecological crisis. Disasters like pollution, a new species extinction every few hours, biospheric degradation, and the threat of nuclear annihilation are all powerful reasons to overturn the centuries of the either/or, Man-against-Nature paradigm that got us here. To think about taking our place in nature instead of conquering it is a deep change in the way we see ourselves and the world. It means changing from binary and linear thinking to a cyclical paradigm that is a new declaration of interdependence.

Another motive is the movement against internal colonialisms of sex and race. Superior/inferior, light skin/dark skin, masculine/feminine divisions are being replaced with the idea that each person has a full circle of human qualities in unique combination. Instead of defining power as domination, it is being redefined as self-determination. Instead of outstripping others, the goal is completing oneself. Since the sexual caste system is the most ancient form of oppression and the one on which all others are based, changing it is like pulling the rug from under the whole hierarchy. As physicist Fritjof Capra writes in *The Turning Point,* feminism "will have a profound effect on further evolution" because patriarchy "is the one system . . . whose doctrines were so universally accepted that they seemed to be the laws of nature."

The communications revolution has eroded hierarchy by giving the bottom as much information as the top — and also by letting all parts of the hierarchy *see* each other (which is why computers and photocopiers are outlawed in totalitarian regimes, and access even to phone lines extremely restricted). Long-term hierarchies have produced a few people at the top who use power poorly, a lot of people in the middle who wait for orders and approval, and many more at the bottom who feel powerless and resentful. But from Eastern Europe to South Africa, democratic uprisings are softening and humanizing hierarchies into more circularity. Smaller, more lateral and cooperative units are emerging for diverse purposes, from Japanese corporate management to Gandhian village economies.

Even the sacred cow of competitiveness is getting to be less sacred. In *No Contest,* psychologist Alfie Kohn poses the question: *"Do we perform better when we are trying to beat others than when we are working with them or alone?"* After looking at many studies, he concludes: "The evidence is so overwhelmingly clear and consistent that the answer to this question already can be reported: *almost never.* Superior performance not only does not *require* competition; it usually seems to require its absence." In fact, a competitive system perpetuates itself by keeping self-esteem low and making even the winners constantly needy of more success. As Kohn writes, *"We compete to overcome fundamental doubts about our capabilities and, finally, to compensate for low self-esteem."*[20]

Rather than finding a source in competition, self-esteem and excellence both come from the excitement of learning and pressing individual boundaries; a satisfaction in the task itself; pleasure in cooperating with, appreciating, and being appreciated by others — and as much joy in the process as in the result.

As each person completes herself or himself and contributes what is authentic, a new paradigm emerges: circularity. At rest, it is a circle, and in motion, a spiral. When we look more closely at each part, it is a microcosm of the whole. If we consciously take this as our organizing principle, we come up with very nonbinary, unlinear, nonhierarchical results. For instance:

If we think of ourselves as circles, our goal is completion — not defeating others. Progress lies in the direction we haven't been.

If we think of families and nurturing groups as circles, the sum means maximizing each part — not restricting others or keeping secrets. Progress is appreciation.

If we think of work structures as circles, excellence and cooperation are the goal — not competition. Progress becomes mutual support and connectedness.

If we think of nature as a circle, then we are part of its reciprocity. Progress means interdependence.

If we respect nature and each living thing as a microcosm of nature — then we respect the unique miracle of ourselves.

And so we have come full circle. Self-esteem is not a zero-sum game: by definition, there is exactly enough to go around. By making the circle the organizing image in our minds, a prison of lines and limits will gradually disappear.

 Your Future Self

All fuses now, falls into place
From wish to action, word to silence,
My work, my love, my time, my face
Gathered into one intense
Gesture of growing like a plant.
MAY SARTON

In that first session with Nancy Napier, I had bypassed the hardest years and found a Wild Child from an earlier, happier time. It was as if my subconscious had given me an immediate reward as a way of encouraging me to continue returning. But meditating by myself, I still found that my mind glanced off the years that came later, when my mother and I were living on our own, as if they were behind an invisible shield. I feared that, if I allowed myself to feel the emotions this little girl had worked so hard to suppress — the heart-piercing sadness of watching my mother as she tried so desperately each day, like a bird with a broken wing, and the panic of trying to be her caretaker when I was too young to care for myself — I would fall into an old and familiar well of invisibility and aloneness.

For the first time, I would have to admit just how much I had missed having a mother.

It was a fear I first had noticed in my relationship with an older woman whom I trusted, loved, and depended upon in a way unique for me, and for that very reason I couldn't hug her in the easy way I could hug my other women friends. She played a "mother" role toward me, and I wanted that so much I feared I would dissolve. This fear was, I realized, why I had chosen to play a sister role with all the women in my life. I didn't know how to be a daughter and accept help and nurturance — though I wanted them desperately. And to become a mother would have meant getting lost in caretaking again, and perhaps becoming as broken-spirited as *my* mother.

When I explained this to Nancy, she suggested that I introduce a new image into meditation. After the usual induction, she asked that I see myself walking on a path through a natural scene that I found beautiful and safe: a forest or meadow, the seashore or the mountains — anything that rose up from the back of my mind. She encouraged me to make this scene real by asking questions: What were its sounds and fragrances? Was there sunlight or shade? How did the path feel beneath my feet? I realized she was calling up all five senses in order to find the strongest bridges to the unconscious, but even this outside observation didn't keep her questions from working.

I began to see a forest of pine trees with a path that seemed to parallel an ocean, yet also drew closer so that, in the distance through the trees, the ocean itself was visible. As usual, my visual sense was strongest, but I had intimations of the crunch of pine needles beneath my feet, the tang of salt and pine in the air, and the feel of dappled sunlight under trees. Those faint perceptions added to a sense of being *present* in the scene.

This path was a part of my life's journey, Nancy explained. My conscious self was an observer, a passenger, and my deeper self was the voyager. Ahead of me on the path was someone walking where I had yet to travel. It was my future self, the person I wanted to become, an optimal self who was leading me. She suggested that I look more closely at this distant woman: What did I notice about this future self? How was she different from my present-day self? When I looked at her, how did I feel?

Though all I could see was a shadowy figure, I was surprised to feel a kind of strength and clarity emanating from it. As Nancy's questions progressed, I could see that this future self was wearing some sort of long, dark cape that flowed down from hair pulled back in a bun or braid. Looking at her made me feel inspired, yet uncomfortable, as if she were desirable but cool and unfamiliar at the same time, but there was also an implicit inner yes, as if I had accidentally stumbled on the right answer. Only one detail was clear and it made me smile: She didn't have on shoes like those I was then wearing, with low heels but heels nonetheless. Her feet were planted firmly and *felt* the ground.

As if reading my mind, Nancy asked me to imagine myself *inside* this future self and to note the differences between her body-feelings and mine. I felt the sure-footedness again, and also a spareness and simplicity, as if this future self had been reduced to essentials by the elements. In her body, I seemed to be standing straighter, to be both myself and androgynous in a way that made gender seem irrelevant. "Your body," Nancy explained, "is learning something important about how to recreate this future self in your daily life. It will remember." Again, I recognized this as a posthypnotic suggestion; yet I could feel my body remembering.

Then she focused my attention on other questions: If you were able to look through the eyes of your future self, how would the world look different from the one you experience now? . . . Look back at your present self — what do you see? . . . Inside this wiser and more mature part of you, what emotions do you feel toward your present-day self? . . .

Though I hadn't been able to imagine the face of my future self, I could look though her eyes — and suddenly the trees looked more sharp and green, and I could glimpse the brightness of the ocean in the distance. When I looked back at my present-day self, she seemed lost in the shade of confusion and encumbered with unimportant things. I felt a heart-turning-over compassion for that figure behind me, much more than I thought I could feel for myself.

From now on, Nancy explained, I would be able to call on this future and optimal self in daily life. If I called her up through my body's memory of how her body felt, she would be there to lead me. With that inner "click" of something fitting into place, I knew this was true. She was a real and unreal image at the same time; a magnet that seemed to collect inner and unknown strengths around it; a far-off view that gave perspective to the present.

One more thing, Nancy explained: "If your present self is too afraid to go back and comfort your inner child, send this stronger, wiser self back to the child. She will go where you cannot."

I sensed that this was right: until those childhood emotions had been lived through, my future, stronger self *could* go where I was still afraid to travel. She was ahead of me on the path.

As I left Nancy's office this time, I thought: Perhaps that little girl has found a mother after all — the only mother who knows her.

Since that day, I've revisited my inner child — though still as my future self. Occasionally, I've painted or drawn what I saw; for instance, the basement room where a scared eleven-year-old lies on the top of a bunk bed while her mother sleeps beneath. Though stick figures are all I can manage, I find it's the colors that count. *Gray* is for the ceiling that the little girl stares at to pretend nothing else exists, *dark brown* is for the horizontal figures of her and her mother lying on their narrow beds — and *purple* is for the healing witness of my future self who is entering the doorway.

I've also tried to use those future and different body-feelings in times of crisis or confusion. It doesn't always work, of course, but I find that imagining a greater groundedness beneath my feet, a body that feels more spare and erect, does call up some deeper well of strength and focus — a sense of knowing what is important and what is not.

And sometimes when I feel a current blow hitting a childhood bruise, I do send that future self backward in time as a grown-up witness who knows what happened, but who is less afraid that it will happen all over again.

Since these voyages began, I've also talked to diverse people who use this "future self" in their daily lives. One young woman imagined her future self meeting the man she was about to marry — and realized he could not know or love the woman she wanted to become. It helped her understand that she had been pretending to be the person he wanted, not who she really was.

I know an older woman who placed photos of herself at each of several difficult stages of her life on the bedside table. By looking at them every morning with the more compassionate eyes of her future self, she dissolved her guilt at having "deserved" such hard times, and also retrieved strengths she had forgotten.

A middle-aged man with a badly damaged little boy inside himself — and a young son he was damaging in turn — imagined in meditation a laserlike beam of light emanating from the heart of his future self, passing through his present self, and illuminating the little boy on the path behind him. He realized that by focusing all his childrearing efforts on undoing the damage his father had done to him, he had been trying to father *himself*.

Because this process goes deeper than intellect, it often brings surprises. Some years ago while using this imagery, Nancy Napier had seen her future self in city clothes, lecturing in a conference room. Since public speaking terrified her at the time and she was working at an experimental psychology center in rural New England, this seemed unlikely; yet what she experienced when she *envisioned* that future self was an inner power and ease she hadn't known existed. "I spent the next months imagining 'her' every morning," she wrote in *Recreating Your Self*, "either visualizing the image or experiencing the feeling of *being* her." After the center closed, she moved to New York and began consulting. One morning as she was standing in a conference room, talking to a large group of executives, and "doing it *comfortably*," Nancy realized that she had indeed become her future self.

I've heard many other such stories:

• The mechanic and carpenter in Northern California who was an unhappy, paper-pushing Los Angeles executive until he realized that his future self had dirt under his nails, tools in his hands, and a smile on his face. In real life, this transformation took seven years, but it brought the satisfaction of working for himself. It also brought new self-esteem to his blue-collar father who had thought his son disdained working with his hands.

• The teacher in Montreal who consciously set out to approach his future and most authentic self by reentering his own childhood — at each developmental stage. With the knowledge he had gained from his years of teaching children, he supported that inner infant, toddler, child, and adolescent, until he had succeeded in literally reparenting himself. It also made him a better teacher, he said, one who could better empathize with his students.

• The teenager from Boston whose present self could not confront her sexually abusing father, even though she knew that her younger sister was being abused, too. Only after her future self had taken her terrified child-of-the-past to a safe place, where the father

could never hurt her again, could she start the present-day proce-
dures that saved her sister — and started her own healing.

• The documentary filmmaker in Rome who invoked a future
self, and then made in her mind her own autobiographical film, thus
viewing her life with form and perspective.

• The homemaker in Tokyo who saw a future self leading other
women — and who began a newsletter for other homemakers struggling to educate their children in a competitive system and to break
time-consuming traditions of homemaking at the same time.

• The union organizer from Detroit who kept seeing a future
self surrounded by kids — even though his own grown-up children
had been estranged from him for years — and so became a foster
parent of five "hard to place" kids. The last time I saw him, his own
children still had not forgiven him for giving strangers a father they
had missed, but he felt happier than he'd ever been.

Not everyone used meditation to reach a future self. For some
it made a spontaneous, one-time, life-changing appearance. For others, it had always been an organic part of daily life, something they
never had to be taught. But given the external focus of modern life,
most of us probably have to make a conscious effort to search for
it, allotting a set period of time each day for writing, dream-captur-
ing, meditation, or whatever else works. Many therapists, shamans,
and other wise women and men recommend checking in with that
future self often, perhaps each morning as part of a daily meditation.
Nancy suggests adding the inner child to that routine, so there is
contact with both the creativity that our child-self represents and the
strength and wisdom of our future self.

Integrating a future self into the present is very different from
the time-wasting, life-wasting habit of thinking about the future instead of the present; of indulging in magical thinking about what
could happen; of living a deferred life. By definition, one can only
live in the present — and time is all there is.

But each of us is a hologram. That means we can only perceive,
understand, and value ourselves by looking from all sides; from a
continuum of past, present, and future. They are all within us right
now.

Five

Bodies of Knowledge

"The unified field . . . vibrating at a high frequency, creates mind, resonating at a lower frequency, precipitates into matter."

DEEPAK CHOPRA, M.D.

I   *Starting with the Body*

"Great ideas originate in the muscles."
THOMAS EDISON

During lectures, I sometimes ask people in the audience to stand up for a moment — without explaining why. (If you want to try this experiment, stand up now, too.) Then I ask them to look at how their bodies are placed in space.

Many people, especially women, discover that they are standing with feet together, head inclined slightly forward, arms folded across chest or hands clasped in front of them so their bodies are covered and they take up as little space as possible. Others, especially men, are standing with feet apart, head up and back, with arms at their sides or perhaps with one hand braced against their body so an elbow juts out, taking up the maximum amount of space.

Then I ask these groups to exchange styles and see how it feels. When people in the small-space group expand their stance, they often say they feel odd or exposed at first, then stronger and more confident. When those in the big-space group contract their bodies, they often report feeling childlike at first, and then less powerful, even less visible.

This experiment began as a way of demonstrating how quickly "feminine" and "masculine" stances can influence state of mind. Women in particular need to understand how something so simple as physical posture can undermine, or enhance, self-confidence. In the unified body-mind field of the self, the movement of any molecule shifts the others. But I soon understood that women — and probably many men, too — weren't comfortable taking up too much space; certainly, that wasn't the goal. Since we had done *thesis* and *antithesis* but no *synthesis,* I added a third stage of asking people to close their eyes and let their bodies gravitate into the most comfortable way of standing, with no effort to please, displease, or displace others. Within a moment or two, both groups were reporting a greater sense of ease and well-being, as if their bodies had a wisdom

199

of their own when habits of mind stopped intervening. The point is: How we stand says something not just *about* us, but *to* us.

As someone who has always tended to live in my head, I didn't realize how powerfully our sense of ourselves resides in our body until I was on a trip to Japan. While walking through the crowded streets of Tokyo, I suddenly realized I was feeling safe and comfortable in a way that was quite remarkable in a country so different from my own, and I couldn't account for it. Then I realized the source: for the first time in my life, I was taller than most of the men in the street. My mind had been reluctant to register how much this difference mattered, for that would mean confronting how on guard I felt in the streets of my own country, how endangered I and many other women sometimes feel in "public" spaces.

The idea that muscles and sinews instruct our minds is often assumed to be anti-intellectual or childlike. Because Western dualism values *mind* over *body*, *thinking* over *feeling*, most of us end up ignorant or skeptical of the idea of *soma* and *psyche* as a unified energy field. Even when we do acknowledge the existence of body-mind links, the ones that get the attention are usually those in which the mind speaks to the body: for instance, stress-reduction techniques such as meditation and visualization to help reverse the effects of heart disease;[1] or the amazing "placebo effect," in which a harmless sugar pill has the same effect as the medication both patient and doctor believe it to be.[2]

What gets downplayed or ignored, however, is all those phenomena that suggest body-mind communication is a two-way street; that mind-change can *begin* with body-change. Here are some examples ranging from the simple to the complex, the transitory to the long-lasting.

BREATH   *The way we breathe can influence our state of mind.* Though in many cultures, the very word for breath implies this knowledge — *chi* in Chinese, or *prana* as in *pranayama* (breathing practices) in Hindi — in our modern Western culture, we rarely go further than acknowledging the importance of breathing in sports (where the E-E rule tells us to exhale on exertion) and in childbirth (where special techniques ease the pangs of labor); as if the physical act of breathing could only aid a physical process. In fact, it is the single function that most influences all others — including mental and emotional ones — and because it is the one autonomic process that can easily be regulated, it can and should be a bridge to exploring many of our untapped powers. For instance: *exhaling* more slowly than we inhale calms the mind; *inhaling* more slowly than we exhale energizes it; and *balancing* the two breaths also balances the right and left brain. Simple deep breathing — and focusing on those breaths — is a bridge to the meditative states that are described in the preceding chapter. The ancient yoga practice of alternate-nostril breathing will "center" both mind and body: just press one nostril closed while inhaling deeply through the other for one count, press both nostrils closed while holding that breath for four counts, and then press the other nostril closed while exhaling for two counts — or any timing in a 1-4-2 ratio. Repeat at least a dozen times until the rhythm feels natural, and then be conscious of those moments of total stillness in midcycle. Yoga tells us this time of being full of breath, full of spirit, is a moment of feeling the true self; the soul.

TOUCH   *Being touched and held is our earliest source of self-discovery — and a continuing need.* We know that infants deprived of daily touching fail to thrive, even when their nutritional and other basic needs are met. Without frequent and direct contact with other living beings, nerve endings communicate fewer signals to the brain, and development is slowed — even stopped. This has been proven over and over again in foundling homes where infants were clean and well fed but rarely held, as well as in the efficiently run *Lebensborn,* the Aryan "baby farms" of Hitler's Germany, where the rates of stunted growth, retardation, and even death were very high. These real-life evidences of the importance of touching counter Freud and other theorists who believed that feeding was the infant's most crucial need and primary source of bonding. In the 1950s, however, animal-learning theorist Harry Harlow set out to prove the importance of touch all over again with animals. In a famous and cruel experiment still taught in many Introductory Psychology courses, he took rhesus monkeys away from their mothers a few hours after birth, then gave the newborns a choice between one artificial "mother" made of baling wire and another made of terry-cloth. So great was the infants' need for warmth and comfort that, *even when the wire figure contained the only feeding nipple,* they preferred the one made of cloth: its softness offered at least a hint of the touch and cuddling they craved (though not enough to make them useful as breeders, as Harlow had hoped they would be).

Only recently has science begun to prove the importance of touch with experiments in enrichment instead of deprivation. When Tiffany Field, a psychologist at the University of Miami Medical School, changed the usual "minimal touch" rule for premature infants in incubators and massaged them gently three times a day, they gained weight faster and were released earlier, thus aiding the infants and reducing hospital costs. When normal babies were allowed more skin-to-skin contact in the first six months, they developed better mentally.* And when some rabbits were fed a damaging high-cholesterol diet but developed 60 percent fewer symptoms than other rabbits from the same litters, experimenters were mystified until they discovered the answer: the healthy rabbits were the ones in the lower cages, thus the only ones reachable by the lab technician, who had been petting and cuddling them each night. Later, controlled experiments produced the same results.[3]

New techniques for tracking the development of the living brain suggest that touch is the primary source of neurochemical changes in infancy. We also know from anecdotal evidence that massage is effective against depression and hypertension, and that cuddling and sleeping skin-to-skin can do everything from lowering blood pressure and lengthening brain waves to strengthening the immune system.

SEXUALITY   *Orgasm and other forms of sexual expression are such a source of self-affirmation that two thirds of psychiatrists believe people "nearly always or often" lose self-esteem when deprived of a "regular outlet for sexual gratification."*[4] In fact, it is so central to our being that, as countless studies have shown, masturbation is instinctive from a very early age. In later life, sexuality and sensuality are also ways we express ourselves and "talk" to each other: unlike other animals, for whom sex seems to be focused in times of "heat"

---

* "In most parts of the world, people massage babies," as Field observed. "The Western countries are about the only place this is not routine. . . . We touch each other too little." (Daniel Goleman, "The Experience of Touch: Research Points to a Critical Role," *New York Times,* February 2, 1988.)

or estrus when conception is most likely, human sexual pleasure exists independent of conception, and so is a way we communicate as well as procreate. Given gender politics, however, men may be so genitally focused that they miss whole-body sensuousness, while women may focus so much on sensuous cuddling that the sense of inner power that orgasm brings is underplayed.* Once again, progress lies in completing the circle, exploring in the direction we have not been.

The point is that sexual and sensual pleasure is often a spontaneous signal sent out by the deepest self. Women with low self-esteem may miss it by "listening" more to their partner's body than to their own. Men with low self-esteem may "listen" to external standards of sexual performance at the expense of their partner's pleasure, and often their own. In fact, like love and laughter, real pleasure is an emotion that can't be compelled — and thus is an expression of the authentic self. If we trust it, follow it, listen to it, our body will take us places the conscious mind could not have imagined. "When I speak of the erotic," as poet Audre Lorde explained, "I speak of it as an assertion of the life force of women; of that creative energy empowered, the knowledge and use of which we are now reclaiming in our language, our history, our dancing, our loving, our work, our lives." And as novelist Christopher Isherwood wrote, "Sensuality is . . . like a mine. You go deeper and deeper. There are passages, caves, whole strata. You discover entire geological eras."

PHYSICAL IMAGERY   *The body seems to have its own antennae that can sense the degree of esteem — or contempt — in which similar bodies are held.* Regardless of how distorted and self-hating our body image may have become, our real bodies seem sensitive to the fate of others like them. Think of the impact of "Black Is Beautiful" or any comparable message on a group whose physical appearance — whether because of sex, race, ethnicity, age, or ablebodiedness — has been key to its devaluing. Stand outside the rare movie with a strong and daring female protagonist, and watch

---

* "The elimination of clitoral sexuality," as Freud wrote in *Sexuality and the Psychology of Love*, "is a necessary precondition for the development of femininity." As in so many areas, women were asked to choose between "femininity" and self-esteem.

women emerging with higher heads, stronger walks, and greater confidence. Consider the importance of a sports champion who comes from a group that has been made to feel it can't win, a popular movie in which American Indians are finally the "good guys," a violinist whose music soars while he sits onstage in leg braces, a deaf actress who introduces millions of moviegoers to the expressiveness of sign language, and even one woman who remains joyous, free, sexual, and good at her work after sixty or seventy. The images of power, grace, and competence that these people convey have a life-giving impact — just as trivialized, stereotyped, degrading, subservient, and pornographic images of bodies that look like ours do the opposite, as though we absorb that denigration or respect through our nerve endings.[5] Wherever negative physical imagery has been part of low self-esteem, a counterpoint of positive imagery can be part of raising it.

MOVING IN SPACE   *Freedom to explore our environment and develop our bodily abilities is a link to intellectual development.* We now know that physical freedom in the earliest years develops spatial-visual skills that are important in math, in many kinds of problem-solving, and in what psychologists call "field independence" (the ability to think for oneself). Such skills are equal in boys and girls until about the age of eight, which is when girls typically begin to come under more physical restrictions. After that, their skills diverge slightly, the gap between them becoming especially pronounced at adolescence, when the restrictions on girls' freedom to explore and master environments also become more pronounced. That this relates to socialization, not inherent ability, seems clear from the fact that boys who have been allowed less mastery of space will tend, like girls, to show signs of less developed spatial-visual abilities and field independence. For example, one study that compared kibbutz-raised boys and girls in Israel with their counterparts in Western and other Middle Eastern countries showed that the kibbutz children had the edge, presumably because they enjoyed more physical freedom. In another study of children's visual-spatial abilities, Eskimo boys and girls — whose culture allows children of both sexes a high degree of autonomy, including going on long hunting trips — showed no sex difference in intellectual skills. On the other hand, a study of the Temne culture in Africa where females *are* more restricted showed a familiar male intellectual edge. Cultures as otherwise disparate as a town in New England and a Bantu-speaking society in Kenya, when they shared this gender-bound difference in freedom to master space, also shared gender difference in intellectual skills. Though there is certainly more than one cause for such intellectual differences, Susan Saegert and Roger Hart, the two scholars who collected and evaluated these studies, concluded that "the very different opportunities given to girls versus boys to freely manipulate the environment must surely affect their cognitive representations."[6]

Since in all these cultures fear of molestation and other safety concerns were high on the list of reasons for restricting the freedom of girls, the frequent experience of feeling endangered in a female body — a feeling I realized only when it lessened in the streets of Tokyo — turns out to have penalties that stretch far beyond the immediate. As Alison Stallibrass points out in *The Self-Respecting Child,* a compassionate classic based on her years of experience with play groups, both boys and girls who are discouraged from developing their physical confidence tend to compensate by overvaluing words, by booing or bullying others, or by preferring the company of adults to that of children. Though adults may reward the verbal child, as she points out, "a child whose mental activity is predominantly verbal is living at secondhand."[7]

The good news is that remedial programs in physical skills seem to benefit less active children very quickly, as if their potential were stored up and waiting. When adults have a safe place to make themselves vulnerable, they also can return to this developmental "broken place" and restore a neglected physical skill. More good news is that the redundant backup systems of body and brain tend to compensate if any faculty is lost. Thus, children who move through space on crutches or in a wheelchair also develop the spatial intellectual skills that another child does while running and climbing. And it has recently been discovered that deaf babies of deaf parents begin to babble with their hands — to make gestures that are clearly more organized and repetitive than the random gestures of hearing babies — at about ten months, the same age at which hearing babies begin to speak in syllables in imitation of *their* parents.[8] The point is to develop and value our bodily abilities, whatever they are.

But we have no idea what might happen if both girls and boys were allowed to be adventurous and exploring in safe and enriched environments; or if adults whose childhood freedoms were restricted were encouraged to "go back" and give themselves another chance to throw a baseball, hike in the wilderness, perfect a swan dive, dance the soft-shoe, run a marathon, take up archery, ski cross-country, learn to skateboard, climb a rock face, study t'ai chi, or do whatever else it is they felt attracted to but couldn't try.

If we had a culture that nurtured the intelligence implicit in blood and bone from infancy on, we wouldn't need remedial efforts, and there's no telling how far we might advance. Nonetheless, many people have made big changes in later life by learning how to honor the wisdom of their bodies, like those in the three parables that follow. In the fourth, there is a glimpse of what can happen when one's life from the very beginning includes that body-wisdom.

• All children are born with a unique self, but some have families that require conformity. For Patti Davis, this was the constant tension of her childhood: feeling different in a setting where "difference" was wrong. In a family that occupied posh California houses and eventually the governor's mansion, she felt more at home in her friends' warmer, messier, less affluent homes. In a meat-eating household that took pride in serving game raised on the family ranch, she remembered the animals' names, and became a vegetarian. With parents too secretive to tell her that she had a half sister, her father's daughter by his first wife, she was the child who was always curious.

These and other differences brought punishment from Patti's mother, perhaps herself living out the legacy of a cool and often absent mother. When Patti began to develop breasts early, her mother seemed to become even angrier and dressed her in clothes that disguised her body. Patti retreated into a world of her own, often pretending she was an Indian running through the forest, sometimes fantasizing "real" parents who would rescue her.

But though her imagination found refuge, her body still betrayed its desire for acceptance. "We wear our attitudes in our bodies," as Patti explained to me recently, "and I grew up looking like a question mark: Am I okay? Do you approve?"

At nineteen, she moved away from home. Her father — himself the child of an alcoholic father and trained in denial — insisted that everything was just fine, but Patti's mother eventually disinherited her. Meanwhile, Patti made a living as a waitress, changed her name to avoid people who wanted to use her either for or against her powerful father, and created a family of friends. Eventually, she married and began to find her voice as a writer of novels, but she still feared public places, disapproval, and even success, since that went against her mother's predictions for her and thus didn't feel "like home."

One day, her husband invited her to go with him to a gym, since at thirty-two, she still was reluctant to venture into new places alone. She began to learn the weight-training techniques of body-building, including ways to direct one's mind "into" a specific muscle, so that blood and energy were directed there, too. Though she had been warned that this process could release old toxins stored in the muscles, she had such strong responses of nausea and light-headedness that she wondered if all her childhood pain might be stored there. Nonetheless, she persisted, and by focusing in this way, she gradually began to feel as if she were *inside* her body instead of fantasizing her way *out*. Unlike dressing up and other kinds of body care that reminded her of her mother — indeed, that made her fear becoming her mother — this one had no sad echoes of the past. Unlike the symbolic running she had done as a little girl pretending to be an Indian, this new strength made her feel she could stand her ground.

But even before Patti noticed differences in her body's strength, her husband noticed changes in her behavior. She was willing to go to the gym on her own, sometimes even to more public places, and she began to speak in a more definite way. "I suddenly realized," she says now, "that all my life, I'd been the Queen of Apology." She felt proud of new muscle in a body that had been round-shouldered and fragile. As this transformation continued from the inside out, she began to feel more at ease on her own, less fearful and cowering, more able to say what she was feeling.

After seven years of exercising every day and weight-training several times a week, Patti's body is no longer a question mark. "I realize that even my first novel, which I wrote before I started body-building, was apologetic," she says now. "There was a big difference in my second one, which took on violence in Nicaragua and so forced me to look at conflict." In her third novel, *House of Secrets,* she was able to deal with conflict in a family setting, though still in fiction. Now, she is at work on an autobiography that will examine the effects of her family's habit of denial on her own life and, since her father, Ronald Reagan, was President of the United States, the effects of his need to insist "everything is fine" on the nation's political and economic life, too.

Sitting across from Patti at a restaurant where we've just been talking, it's hard to imagine this tall, strong, beautiful woman as the round-shouldered and fearful little girl she once was. In the few years I've known her, she has always looked like an artist's rendering of a woman *after* the revolution: arms strong, hair flowing, striding in comfortable boots through her city or mine. Only when she talks about the fragile, cowering little girl does she begin unconsciously to hunch her shoulders and shrink slightly in her chair, as if her body were also remembering. For women to enjoy physical strength is a collective revolution. For Patti, overcoming the feelings of weakness and body-fear that had put her at such a disadvantage as a little girl with a punishing mother and a distant father was the beginning of inner strength, too.

• As a smart and sensitive child, John understood what was expected of him by the time he was four. The son of parents who always said, "He's no trouble at all," John played by himself under the racks of clothes in his family's dry-cleaning store. He learned all the don'ts: "Don't make noise . . . Don't bother the customers . . . Don't be conspicuous . . ." He also absorbed his parents' mix of shame and rage for having been imprisoned in California's internment camps for Japanese Americans during World War II. It seemed to be the source of his mother's fearful injunctions to keep his opinions to himself, to be, in her words, "like a ghost."

But as John later remembered, this message wasn't unusual in his neighborhood of immigrants. His best friend's family was Polish, and they also told their kids: "Don't ask questions . . . Don't think you're like other kids . . . Don't trust outsiders . . ." When that friend disobeyed and got beaten, John admired the defiance with which he insisted, "I didn't feel a thing." At twelve, John began to break from his parents by joining the underground of the boys in his neighborhood. Together, they joked and bragged about sex, masturbated in the darkness of a neighborhood movie, and at fourteen, went to local prostitutes together. Though John still disliked his body for being shorter and having less body hair than his non-Japanese friends, he began to think of sex and manhood as his escape; the only part of himself that was strong enough to rebel against his family's sadness and rescue him from difficult feelings.

When he joined the army reserves to get an education, John at first felt uncomfortable when drill sergeants made them chant: "This is your cock, this is your gun, one is to kill, one is for fun." Soon, however, he began to feel like one of the guys — the first member of his family to become a real American. Still, he couldn't quite imagine that a non-Japanese girl would want to go out with him. He eventually fell in love with and proposed to a young woman from a respected and well-to-do Japanese-American family in San Francisco. It was as far as he could get from his family's shadowed immigrant past.

Within a year after their marriage, however, he was feeling mystified by this bride. She wanted him to take Japanese-style communal baths, to massage his feet and forehead and then have him do the same to her, and to "cuddle." He tried to comply, but it made him feel like a child again. After all, the only difference between closeness to his mother and to another woman was sexual: he was always impatient for the powerful orgasm that got him out of those unmanly danger zones of childhood vulnerability. When his wife finally got up the courage to complain that their lovemaking was just "mutual masturbation," he felt hurt and puzzled: What else should it be?

When their son was born, John's self-doubts surfaced again. He loved this baby so much that he felt as if their bodies melted into each other when he held him. John's own father had paid little attention to him until he was old enough to help out in the store, and so John assumed this was how fathers and sons were supposed to be. He began to stay later at work to avoid the unsettling emotions he felt when with either his son or his wife. In this way, they fell into a routine of almost entirely separate worlds that continued for a dozen years.

But when John was in his thirties, he began to notice a pins-and-needles tingling in his arms and legs, and then a numbness. Tests revealed very high blood pressure, poor circulation, and other precursors of serious problems. When his doctor included daily whirlpool baths and massages as part of his treatment, John was scared enough to comply.

One day while sitting in a therapy tub, he remembered that his parents had gone to traditional Japanese baths. As he lay on a massage table, he also remembered the old woman masseuse who had "walked" on his parents' backs, Japanese style, and who always hugged him and gave him sweets. The odd thing was that with each new feeling in his body, there came a new memory of something from childhood. By blotting out the painful events, he had also forgotten that his parents had given him pleasure.

John began to ask his wife for massages — for purely medical reasons, of course. He installed a wooden, Japanese-style hot tub at home and asked her to join him in it after work. While the water swirled around them, they talked about nonroutine things for the first time since their courtship. Gradually, he found himself looking forward to this sensuous end of the day. After their bath, they began a gentle, languorous kind of lovemaking that he hadn't experienced before; certainly not with the prostitutes he had been visiting ever since his son was born. Sometimes, they just lay on the bed and took a nap curled up against each other like spoons.

One day, John brought his wife a quote from a magazine: *The fundamental error is believing that touch is a means to an end. It is not. Touch is an end in itself.* Understanding that this was a tacit apology, she gave him a subtle present in return by reading aloud to him in Japanese from an ancient guide to sexual pleasure. It said exactly the same thing as that Masters and Johnson quote, but in a much more poetic way. John found himself wondering: Who is this fascinating stranger I've been living with all these years?

Because he had missed the childhood of his son, who was now a teenager with a life of his own, John found himself watching babies in the park who reminded him of that frightening, magnetic, body-melting emotion. Would another baby give him a second chance — just as his own body seemed to have given him one? He asked his wife if she would consider giving birth again, but said he understood if she wouldn't. He thought: If she trusts me enough to do this, I'll be the father I couldn't be until now — and wished my father had been.

A few weeks later when he and his wife were making love in their new, unhurried, sensuous way, John realized that he, too, could have multiple orgasms if he just surrendered his whole body to her touch, and that not every orgasm had to be preceded by an erection. His wife said her erotic readings had led to this discovery. John said it had nothing to do with sex but more with the tears he had finally been able to shed for his parents and for his own numbed years of living "like a ghost."

But whatever the reason, it didn't matter. As his wife said as she told me this story — for it was she who had been telling me why she had decided to have a second child — they agreed on a Japanese proverb: "A circle needs no beginning."

• Like many women whose beauty makes others assume they need no help, Phyllis Rosser got more envy than understanding. We were friends in college, and I admired Phyllis's sensible attitude toward food, her translucent skin, and her ability to get her papers done on time. Indeed, she generously helped the rest of us who put off everything until the last minute, and was the sort of person her classmates trusted, even when we didn't trust each other.

After graduation, Phyllis married and moved to a New Jersey suburb. When we did meet at reunions, she seemed to be the same serene, quiet, beautiful woman she had always been. Once I glimpsed her in an airport with her husband, the two of them walking to a gate with their arms around each other's waist, and I thought: What a good marriage. What a nice man.

But inside Phyllis, something very different was going on. "I felt trapped in a life I had never planned," she told me recently. "I had no clear idea what I wanted, just something beyond the narrow life I was living. After college, I took acting lessons — but I ended up in a suburban backwater with nothing of my own anyway. I loved my husband and kids, so I blamed myself — I thought I just lacked the courage to break out into the wider world. By the time I had my daughter, our third and last child, I was really depressed. Once, Bill told me he was afraid he'd come home and find me and the baby dead on the floor — that's how bad it was."

To her sympathetic husband, this must have seemed doubly mysterious because, from his point of view, their life was going just fine. She remembers his telling her: "Your problem is that you should like yourself better." Of course, he was right — but how could she like herself when she felt she had no self?

It was a measure of her desperation that her calm broke, and she had an impulse to do an impractical and possibly dangerous thing: learn how to fly. Even in retrospect, she's not sure why. Perhaps it was her recurring nightmare of running on a beach while being chased by an airplane from which her parents were trying to shoot her, or perhaps it was the sheer outrageousness of the idea. Or perhaps it was as simple as her one conscious thought at the time: If I have the courage to fly, I can do anything.

She took lessons, and fell in love with the language and symbolism of flying. "There's something you learn to do in the air called 'breaking out of a pattern,' " she explained, "and that's exactly what I wanted to do. Given where I was, it was also important that I keep 'taking off.' And finally, there was 'soloing.' What could be more symbolic than that?"

Months later, when she had trusted her body's competence and learned to fly, she found that her mind began to take off, too. She had been coming in from the suburbs to volunteer in the chaotic offices of *Ms.* magazine — which was how we had made contact again — and I noticed her increased interest and energy but didn't understand its source. It was then the early 1980s, and she suggested covering an upcoming conference on Scholastic Aptitude Tests, those sacred measures of academic accomplishment that were already under challenge for race and class bias. Instinctively, Phyllis felt they had a gender bias, too. She herself had done well on them, but they reminded her of the aptitude tests she had taken in college that had been administered with great authority but had done nothing to help her find her talents.

After that conference, Phyllis began to do soloing of an intellectual kind. She put in several years becoming a self-taught expert in the rarefied field of standardized testing, "even though," as she explained, "I was an art major with no training in psychometrics." Her subsequent reporting in *Ms.* helped bring the gender bias in the SATs to public attention, and she was commissioned by the National

Center for Fair and Open Testing to study the impact of test biases on women's educational opportunities. Two years later, in 1987, she published her report *Sex Bias in College Admissions Tests: Why Women Lose Out* and was asked to testify before the House Judicial Subcommittee on Civil and Constitutional Rights. That was followed by a grant from the Department of Education's Women's Educational Equity Act Program to study exactly how sex bias is embedded in the questions of standardized testing. In 1989, her report *The SAT Gender Gap: Identifying the Causes* was published by the Center for Women Policy Studies.

Partly as a result of her work, many schools began deemphasizing such tests, and some states, either voluntarily or under court order, stopped using them as a basis for distributing public scholarship funds. But to help the majority of students who still have to take the tests, and whose futures are held hostage by their scores, Phyllis contributed an introduction to the 1990 book *The Young Women's Guide to Better SAT Scores: Fighting the Gender Gap.*

In the same years she'd been doing this important intellectual work, Phyllis had been exploring emotionally, too, by experimenting with meditation and other self-therapy techniques for depression, "methods that seemed very 'far out' and 'New Age' at the time," she remembers. That self-inquiry helped her identify a deep yearning that vocational tests had missed. "I realized," she said, "that a part of me was in mourning for the artist I had never become." She began to take sculpture classes at the New York Feminist Art Institute and to work in a studio she set up at home. As I write this, her years of study and solitary work are bearing fruit. She has had a one-woman show and is looking forward to a future of this work that wholly involves both her body and her mind.

In retrospect, her husband, Bill, says that he, too, was afraid in those dark early years: afraid that if Phyllis found a life of her own, she would "just leave me sooner," as he put it, or that she would find someone else. But, of course, the opposite happened: because they allowed each other to become more themselves, they are still together.

Like so many women, Phyllis is becoming herself after fifty.[9] And as for many, the process began with physical risk-taking, perhaps the body's way of breaking out of the calm and ladylike restrictions she had faced from girlhood on. What's amazing is how often bodies choose the perfect symbolic act, the one that speaks most particularly to an inner need. Phyllis's choice of flying gave her the overview of life she had feared belonged only to her parents, and an artist's ability to make shapes out of endless detail; to see the forest *and* the trees. Like a sculptor stepping back from a work in progress, she had begun to see the shape of her life.

• What could we become if we had a whole-body, all-five-senses upbringing? Only children of the future may know, but for now, we have an inspiring clue in the life of anthropologist Margaret Mead.

From infancy, she was encouraged — by her mother, a sociologist, and especially by her paternal grandmother, an innovative schoolteacher and free-thinker — to explore the world around her in every way she or they could imagine. Diverse toys and physical challenges, colors and textures, music, art, and perhaps most important, permission to get dirty and make a mess — all these were part of Margaret's preschool life. Each night her grandmother talked to her about the day's events while she brushed the little girl's hair, giving her the experience of being treated as an equal that is a shared theme in the childhoods of many "gifted" children.[10] By four, as Margaret later wrote, "I was treated as a full person, whose opinions were solicited and treated seriously."[11]

She also memorized poems and maxims by "seeing" their images, thus acquiring a prodigious memory — and, as she would later realize, integrating both sides of her brain. Because of these skills, she never forgot any of the apparently nonsense verse that her grandmother taught her. At four, she could recite:

> I'm sitting alone by the fire
> Dressed just as I came from the dance,
> In a gown, Frog, even you would admire —
> It cost a cool thousand in France.
> I'm bediamonded out of all reason,
> My hair is done up in a queue,
> In short, sir, the belle of the season
> Is wasting an hour on you.[12]

And for the rest of her life, she was able to convince both men and women that she herself was "the belle of the season."

Because Margaret's grandmother believed in learning every aspect of a process, from beginning to end, at eight Margaret built a loom on which she wove textiles of her own design. Knowing how self-alienating school could be, her mother and grandmother often kept her at home to learn carpentry, wood carving, basketry, dancing, and many sports. She also learned spelling and arithmetic by setting them to rhythmic patterns; another whole-body, whole-brain technique. She could imagine the aroma of a color and describe the taste of a room, a gift for synesthesia, or cross-sensing, that persisted for the rest of her life. She could, for instance, smell fear and anger (an acrid odor), remember on her skin the touch of a friend's hand for hours afterward, and sense whether someone she knew had been in a room.

With such body-mind unity, she also moved in and out of her unconscious with ease. She might decide what to dream about and then do so, often solving problems in this way. Or she might examine her dreams to see what treasures her creative unconscious had come up with on its own. When planning a speech, she first saw images; and when asked to describe people or a culture, she focused on precisely how they did their work, built their fishing boats, or raised their children — a love of the particular and ordinary that helped make her a brilliant anthropologist.

As her friend and student, futurist Jean Houston, characterized Margaret's education: "Dualisms were discouraged; she was trained to accept the unity of mind and body, thinking and feeling." [13]

As one result, when Mead's abilities were measured at Jean Houston's Foundation for Mind Research, her fine eye-to-muscle coordination surpassed that of almost anyone else ever tested. As another result, Houston wrote: "A neurologist who examined Margaret for a head injury reported that according to his instruments she had the least empty mind he had ever encountered." [14]

Margaret Mead became a force in her profession while still in her twenties and built an empathetic bridge to other cultures that endures to this day. She was able to absorb complex realities so speedily that some anthropologists doubted her studies were all her own. As her coworker and former husband, Gregory Bateson, explained to her when she was hurt by such doubts, "The reason people don't believe you is that they don't know how fast you work." And, as he testified, you had to see it to believe it.[15] She also lived a full life as a lover, wife, and mother, without being submerged by any of those roles, at a time when this was even more difficult than it is now. Yet given her childhood, perhaps it's not surprising that her sense of herself was so unified and strong; that she was a pioneer in recognizing the relationship between culture and personality; or that she overturned conventional hierarchies and maintained a passionate curiosity about ordinary people and daily life. Certainly, she understood that childrearing was a subject more worthy of study than any other.

"If you ask Western people where 'I' exists, many point to their foreheads," Houston wrote, but "if you asked Margaret Mead that question, she responded matter-of-factly, 'Why, all over me, of course.' "[16]

Perhaps Margaret Mead wasn't so extraordinary after all. Just an ordinary woman with chances we all should have.

II   *Judging the Beauty Judges*

"Just one. I wish I'd been prettier."
ELEANOR ROOSEVELT (WHEN ASKED IF SHE
HAD ANY REGRETS ABOUT HER LIFE)

"Any man with $42 million looks exactly like
Clark Gable."
DON KING (WHEN ASKED ABOUT MIKE TYSON)

Society's standards of physical perfection seem immutable and "right." Our bodies seem variable and "wrong." But once we see the machinery behind the facade of perfection, society turns out to be, like the Wizard of Oz, a frightened little man behind a curtain. We can change him. Indeed, we *are* him. Consider these examples:

• In poor and agricultural countries, plumpness is so much a part of the "feminine" ideal that thin women are often seen as un-sensual or poor childbearing risks, and young girls may be prepared for courtship by an especially rich diet. Similarly, a wife's girth is considered such a tribute to her husband's wealth that rich men have been known to force-feed their wives in order to possess proper sta-tus symbols. In rich and industrialized countries, the ideal "femi-nine" body is so thin that on any given day, most women are dieting, just ending a diet, or on the verge of starting one.

• Thin was not always desirable in this country. When North America was poorer and the goal was to populate the frontier, large families were the ideal, and so were large, voluptuous breasts and hips. After the frontier closed and manufacturing became the main source of wealth, the national preference for buxom women like Lillian ("Diamond Lil") Russell changed, too. The ideal breast and hip size diminished during the suffragist movement and World War I, stayed small during the 1920s craze for the flat-chested flapper, increased again when the bosomy look made a modified comeback in escapist Hollywood movies during the Depression, shrank again in the 1940s when women went to work in defense plants, and re-turned complete with waist cinchers and padded bras after World War II, when women were supposed to replenish the population. Once that need had been met, however, the Marilyn Monroe curves of the 1950s gave way to the Jackie Kennedy look of the 1960s, and its apotheosis, the androgynous Twiggy.

• There is one "feminine" trait shared by all of the styles pre-ferred in all of the above-mentioned eras, whether in Europe, North America, or the Third World: weakness. Rich cultures may prefer thin women and poor cultures may prefer fat ones — because as far as possessions go (and women *are* still possessions) whatever is rarest confers the most status — but all patriarchal cultures ideal-ize, sexualize, and generally prefer weak women. Even women la-borers who must be strong are often made to envy and imitate the fragile, delicate appearance of women of the upper classes. Only rebellions that come from women ourselves seem to mitigate this idealization of weakness. Nineteenth-century feminists protested the wasp-waisted look that forced women into corsets, fainting spells, and pulmonary problems, and put women on bicycles and the tennis court instead. Modern feminists protest the you-can't-be-too-thin cult, encourage sports and muscle-building, and stress access to non-traditional jobs, even combat. But strength is not part of any "femininity" that male-supremacist systems encourage.

• Since men's bodies are valued more as instruments of power than of attraction, men are much less likely to be judged by their appearance. If a man wins at money-making, sports, war, and so on, that's what counts. Nonetheless, ideals of "masculine" appearance do change with caste, class, and the kind of behavior society wants. For instance, the high heels and powdered wigs of French courtiers, the long nails of Chinese mandarins, the foppish fashions that came and went in the upper classes of this country, all proudly announced a distance from physical labor. In an age when most work is done at desks, however, male muscles have become a luxury that announces leisure, discipline, sexuality, and fitness. Some young men have begun to experiment with steroids, and older ones with muscle implants.

• Hierarchies of skin color and racial features are sad testimonies to racism's power to undermine self-esteem, and thus to maintain a racial status quo. Not only are women of color subject to white ideals of beauty — from Caucasian models in Japanese fashion magazines to the blond ideal in the mostly nonblond United States — but within the African-American community here, inside India, Brazil, and anywhere else that racial oppression and colonialism have run deep, the ruling class's valuation of appearance is internalized to the extent that it is often hard to reject, even when the reasons for it are clear. Only increased power on the part of the "wrong" color group can change these externally imposed ideals. African-American novelist Ralph Ellison was one of the first to comment on the relationship between power and appearance when he suggested in the early 1960s that white kids would eventually imitate black appearance. At the time he was laughed at, but that's exactly what happened with Afro hairstyles, dress, dance, music, rap, and other parts of black culture — a clear departure from the days of slavery when straight hair and white skin were worshiped. Globally, movements for independence and racial pride are making more and more people see black (as well as brown, red, and yellow) as beautiful.

• Clothes and body ornamentation follow the same political rules as male strength and female weakness. Female versions restrict the body, and male versions allow freedom of movement. Thus, in Ethiopia or other areas of Africa, and some parts of Asia, women are adorned with neck rings and heavy soldered-on metal anklets that inhibit movement, and the gap-toothed look considered beautiful is achieved by extracting a few crucial teeth — not incidentally those necessary to chew meat, thus leaving the limited protein supply for the men. Male decoration is usually confined to body painting, ornamental scarring, or clay that shapes the hair; nothing that restricts nutrition or mobility. In Moslem areas of the world, women are often required to wear a *chador,* a full-body veil first seen on the wives of upper-class men, and then on poorer women to whom it was presented as a symbol of protection, status, and, more recently, nationalism. Like versions of the painfully bound "lotus feet" of upper-class Chinese women — a lifelong torture that was eroticized as beautiful and made a precondition of marriage — women's marks of beauty involve restrictions of freedom, and often pain and health deprivation as well. In the West, the difference is one of degree, not kind: little girls learn passivity from having to stay neat and clean, and helplessness from dresses that button in the back, while grown-up women limp along on spike heels and are hobbled by tight skirts. By contrast, even the most vain of "masculine" fashions allows freedom and comfort of movement. As Phil Donahue puts it: "Men may do some silly things, but you won't catch them walking in a snowstorm with a cute little hole at the end of their shoe."

• Perhaps the most universal of gender-related beauty standards has to do with age. Obviously, youth in women is considered more beautiful wherever their primary importance is as sex objects and childbearers — which means everywhere except in those cultures where age is venerated so much that even women benefit. But even in such youth-worshiping lands as this one, some women have begun to carve out their own power, with the result that we now see two things happening. The age limit of beauty is moving up (think of Cher, Goldie Hawn, and many others over forty, or Sophia Loren, Tina Turner, Jane Fonda, Cicely Tyson, and others over fifty, in a film industry that once discarded stars at thirty); but meanwhile, some men are resorting in a kind of backlash to child-women (think of teenage models and actresses, "kiddie porn," and twelve-year-old prostitutes).

Sex isn't the only reason for valuing youth in women. With age comes authority, and beauty standards are often a way of getting rid of women just as they are attaining real power. Thus, while more women have become visible as television newscasters, they are also much younger than their male counterparts and subject to much stricter appearance requirements. Men on television remain acceptable about twenty years longer. When men *are* held to youthful physical standards, however, these standards serve the same function as they do with women — they enable well-paid, more experienced workers to be replaced by lower-salaried, less experienced ones. But the double standard is still obvious: women age, but men mature.

Those examples are just the tip of an iceberg that spreads out wide and deep beneath the surface of our culture. We need to take the politics of beauty seriously because it affects every part of our lives, from our vision of who can be powerful to the comfort of our feet and the freedom of our hair. As Alice Walker has written, "Oppressed Hair Puts a Ceiling on the Brain."

Once we look behind the curtain and see that the Wizard of Oz is just a scared society — that beauty standards change with what society wants or fears — we see that beauty is less about looks than about behavior. For women, the behavior is more sexual and reproductive, and for men, it's more economic and productive. Though we are supposed to think that standards of beauty conform to an objective aesthetic handed down from history or the heavens — which is how society shirks the blame for creating them and makes us feel intrinsically wrong for not conforming to them — they are capricious, perishable standards that people made and people can unmake.

With this concept in mind, we can thread our way through confusing imperatives and cultural differences. Once we get a grip on an understanding that, for males or females, *standards of beauty are really about what society wants us to do or not to do*, then we can affect them by taking power into our own hands and altering the way we behave. Indeed, ideas of beauty are regularly turned upside down from one culture to the next, from one era to the next: behind the *form* of what is considered beautiful, there is always the *function* of what is considered acceptable to do. Thus, before we accept a standard of beauty for ourselves, we can ask, "Do I really like the behavior it symbolizes?"

If we could be taught in school about the politicization of beauty, it would help to create a healthier diversity in the United States, where a majority of black children still choose white dolls (sometimes even saying that black dolls are "dirty")[17] and seven-year-old little girls of normal weight think they are "too fat."[18] There has been some change. The ever-popular Barbie doll now comes in different skin colors and with an optional astronaut suit, but she still has the equivalent of a thirty-six-inch bust and an eighteen-inch waist, legs so long they are deformed, and itty-bitty feet that are impossible to stand on.[19]* The ultimate purpose is to help each child know that he or she is beautiful in a unique way, and that means placing the power to decide what is beautiful *within ourselves*, not in some all-powerful "they" out there. It means deciding what behavior is healthy and what bodily expression is appropriate, comfortable, celebratory, or joyous, *for us*. What's at stake is no less than the ability to see the beauty of our authentic selves.

Our health may be at stake, too. In *The Beauty Myth*, a smart and angry exposé of the ways in which beauty standards coerce women into changing themselves to fit the world, instead of vice versa, Naomi Wolf likens this pressure to conform to the medieval instrument of torture known as the Iron Maiden: a body-shaped casket that slowly starved or quickly impaled the unlucky prisoner locked within. On its cover was painted the face and body of a beautiful young woman.[20]

Consider the disease of anorexia, in which people — over 90 percent of them young females — starve themselves into thinness and may literally die for an ideal of perfection. "Anorexia nervosa"

*The late Jack Ryan, designer of the Barbie doll and Chatty Cathy for Mattel, Inc., also helped to design the Sparrow and Hawk missiles for Raytheon, a major military manufacturer. He was once married to Zsa Zsa Gabor. (Obituary, *New York Times*, August 21, 1991.)

was named and identified as a disease by Western physicians in the 1870s;[21] and both Eastern and Western history are full of accounts, even personal diaries, of teenage girls who starved themselves in the name of a god or devotion to a saint, thus rebelling against arranged marriages and other forms of female bondage with the only thing within their power: their own bodies. This obsession with starving themselves into a perfect, permanently adolescent body had the same sorts of goals then as it does now: controlling and putting off their destiny as females.

In this country alone, according to the American Anorexia and Bulimia Association, about 150,000 females die of anorexia each year — and they're often the female version of "the best and the brightest": intelligent and sensitive young women who want to use their talents, yet are still in an economic class and culture that pressure women to be decorative and "perfect." As Naomi Wolf asks on behalf of her contemporaries, "How would America react to the mass self-immolation by hunger of its favorite sons?"[22]

Because the average weight of teenagers is going down, thus leaving less margin for safety, the lethal potential of anorexia and other starving diseases is increasing. In other rich, industrialized bastions of the thinness cult, the Iron Maiden's victims are increasing, too. In England, Japan, and many areas of Western Europe, eating disorders are about as prevalent as they were in this country ten years ago — and catching up fast.

Plastic surgery for questionable or obviously unhealthy reasons is becoming an epidemic, and the average age of patients is getting ever younger. In the U.S., 87 percent of all those who have undergone plastic surgery are females. Though some of this disproportion is attributable to the childhood sexual abuse that causes more women than men to "blame" their bodies and try to change them,[23] much of it comes straight from the double standard of beauty. (And, of course, the sexualization of very young women by the beauty myth connects those two causes.) A few of these cosmetic assaults have been reduced by feminist-inspired changes in the idea of what a female body should look like — for instance, some young girls thought to be "too tall" were once subjected to the surgical removal of leg-bone sections or to growth-arresting estrogen treatments —

but many more are on the increase, from breast implants to jaw wirings for the purpose of ensuring weight loss.

Some of the Iron Maiden's most lethal punishments are alternatives to eating, especially smoking, which is perceived (and marketed) as an aid to being thin. Young women are the only group in the United States among whom smoking is actually on the increase, and the reason most often given is a desire to lose weight or a fear of gaining weight if they quit — motives that cigarette ads exploit by depicting slender and beautiful women, and by using words like *slim* and *thin* in their brand names. Since it would be difficult not to be aware of the danger of smoking, many women are valuing thinness over life itself.

Of course, the Iron Maiden was an equal-opportunity torture device, and many men are also trapped by its rigid standards of appearance — though not to the extent women are. The equivalent for men is the Iron Man, powerful, strong, and handsome: a symbol designed to keep almost all men trying vainly to measure up. In the United States, for instance, the average male height is five nine, yet the ideal goes right on being six feet and over. To take the average of many studies, 70 to 90 percent of all males would like to change something about their appearance, a third would consider cosmetic surgery, and more than half don't like how they look naked — perhaps a result of the cruel emphasis on penis size. Since men's bodies are more instruments of power than ornaments, their behavior and expressions are more the focus of control than their appearance. Of the four intonation levels of voice commonly used in daily speech, for instance, both men and women are capable of speaking in them all; yet men almost never use the highest one, thus limiting their own expressiveness in order to avoid sounding in the least "feminine."[24] Men are discouraged not only from crying, but even from smiling too much. In the military, sports, and other areas of "masculine" power, smiling may be seen as a sign of ingratiation and weakness.

Conversely, women, as well as male members of discriminated-against races, often have to adopt pasted-on smiles, lest they be seen as not sufficiently eager to please, or even threatening. It's a phenomenon that spreads from slavery and class subservience to the

female variety of "smiling" jobs in which body control is a requirement, or to the man in the street who feels the right to demand,
"Why-aren't-you-smiling-honey?"

*If even our bodies — their health, their freedom, their adorn-
ment, their uses — are not our own, what is?*

It's a question that men of color have asked in many anti-
colonial movements, from Gandhi in British India to Steve Biko,
who founded the Black Consciousness Movement in South Africa —
a message of autonomy and self-respect for which, even in 1977, he
was imprisoned and beaten to death. Blacks with the self-esteem to
look to themselves for a sense of what was beautiful and proud were
too threatening to the white minority regime.[25]

It's a question that women in every country are asking as they
defy customs and laws that control female bodies for sex and reproduction; a control sometimes instituted by men of a different race
to limit reproduction, and sometimes by men of their own race to
force reproduction. Whether an older woman is going under the
knife for cosmetic surgery because she fears losing her husband, or
a younger one is forced to undergo a clitoridectomy because she is
not marriageable without it (in many parts of the world, cutting out
the clitoris is done at about eight, usually brutally and without anesthetic, as a traumatic lesson in social ownership and the excision
of sexual will), females rarely own their own bodies.[26] In the United
States, too, a woman may be told she is too fat for a job, be kicked
off the airwaves for being too old, be reduced by economic need to
selling her body for sex or surrogate motherhood, be forced to seek
approval from the state for an abortion because she is too young,
suffer the common body invasion of rape and be blamed for inviting
the crime by the very fact of having a female body, and be con-
strained in a thousand other ways. The basic message is the same:
A woman's power is not supposed to extend as far as her own skin.
Which is why, as Adrienne Rich wrote at the end of *Of Woman
Born,* "The repossession by women of our bodies will bring far more
essential change to human society than the seizing of the means of
production by workers."

It's a question that women who love women and men who love
men are also asking when they overturn homophobic, pronatalist
punishments that subject the most private uses of our bodies to the

most public laws, or when they agitate for the right to be affectionate with each other at high school proms and anywhere else that
heterosexual couples are. They are struggling against a bias so extreme that in the United States almost half of gays have experienced
violent attacks from strangers, peers, or their own families — and
are six times more likely to attempt suicide than their heterosexual
counterparts — even while they are still adolescents.[27] Now in the
era of AIDS, the unfair stigma of "carrying" a disease is a danger
both to self and to self-esteem.

It's a question that many men of supposedly powerful groups
are asking, too, when they challenge everything from laws on the
length of their hair to the largely unnecessary rite of circumcision;[28]
from standards of height to hierarchies based on muscles, prowess
at sports, and ability to fight each other; from an assumption that
they must be willing to die for state-approved purposes to one that
they will kill for them.

The answer to the question of who owns our bodies lies in
establishing the legal, moral, and social principle of bodily integrity,
so that each person controls the universe within our skins. It lies in
getting rid of both the Iron Maiden and the Iron Man so we can
have choice, not compulsion; more beauty in our lives, not less;
pleasure, not constraint. In Naomi Wolf's imagery, we are changing the self-consciousness of a spotlight *on* the body for the self-
confidence of a light radiating *from* the body.

That's the shift of paradigm here: Instead of a light that is directed at us by others, a light that shines from within.

To embody this contrast in a more familiar way, I often think of
Margaret Mead and Eleanor Roosevelt. Both were brilliant and beloved, both had a lasting impact on their times, and neither was
beautiful by conventional standards. In fact, both were often ridiculed for the way they looked. Yet Margaret grew up confidently
and as far removed from the Iron Maiden's influence as any young
girl could, while Eleanor was made to feel she should fit its con-
straints. A mother who was a great beauty herself, a debutante upbringing, and a socially correct, flesh-denying grandmother had seen
to that. From earliest childhood, Margaret simply convinced people
she was beautiful by being so magnetic, sensual, and entirely herself

that even men who most disdained "a lady intellectual" fell under her spell. She lived an adventurous and satisfying life with three husbands and many lovers, both women and men, and succeeded in her work partly because she was secure enough to empathize with the sexualities of different cultures. Margaret Mead simply refused to let the Iron Maiden rule, and was gloriously herself. I used to see her in my New York neighborhood, stalking along with her big, forked walking stick, coming to a beauty parlor on my corner to have her hair done each week; as unself-conscious about this female ritual as about her country walking stick in the city.

Eleanor grew up feeling shy and gawky, too tall and out of place, simultaneously disdaining her mother as superficial and reproaching herself for not measuring up to her great beauty. ("My mother," Blanche Wiesen Cook quotes Eleanor as saying at the beginning of her long-awaited biography, "was the most beautiful woman I ever saw." [29]) After the early deaths of her mother and her adored, handsome, womanizing father, Eleanor tried vainly to fit her tall and angular body into the ladylike image her grandmother taught, and even forced her voice to a higher register, thus giving it the odd crackling sound that was to be so ridiculed by her critics. After she had married her charming and politically ambitious cousin Franklin, she struggled with both her own shyness and her overbearing mother-in-law. Later, when Eleanor discovered Franklin's long-term affair with a "prettier" woman (who would not be the last), she was humiliated, undone, as if she had been betrayed by both her husband and her father at the same time, for they were in that way so much alike. From photographs taken during this period, Blanche Cook theorizes that Eleanor may have become anorexic; certainly, her frequent inability to keep food down in times of emotional conflict is well documented in her letters.

Though she rose above these betrayals, her restricted upbringing, and her own shyness to become one of the most compassionate and humane leaders of her time — and though one hopes for her sake that she did have the affairs with a man and perhaps a woman friend or two that her letters and photographs hint at — Eleanor Roosevelt's triumphant and world-respected later years were still haunted by an uncertain, unpretty girl of the past.

It would have been unworthy of Margaret Mead's life if she

had ended it with the regret for not being "prettier." It was unworthy of Eleanor's life, too.

It would also be unworthy of yours or mine.

 III *The Body in Our Minds*

"It seems that whatever goes into my mouth
makes me fat, just as whatever comes out of it
embarrasses me."
GABRIEL GARCIA MARQUEZ

"She had on a red bikini bottom, I remember,
and no top, and she stood off to one side,
watching us. She had these deep lines under her
eyes, not ugly I thought, but striking and sad.
She refused to speak to anyone all day."
A FRIEND DESCRIBING THE LATE CHRISTINA
ONASSIS AT NINE

I never questioned the wrongness of my body image until
I was in my thirties and saw myself on television. There was this
thin, pretty, blondish woman of medium height who spoke in a boring monotone and, through lack of animation, seemed calm, even
blasé in a New York way. This was a shock. What I felt like *inside*
was a plump brunette from Toledo, too tall and much too pudding-faced, with looks that might be pretty-on-a-good-day but were
mostly very ordinary, and a voice that felt constantly on the verge
of revealing some unacceptable emotion. I was amazed: Where had
this woman on television come from? She was so different from the
way I felt that I almost resented her — though she did give me some
valuable insights into what other people were responding to.

It's taken me the last twenty years to realize that I might better
have asked: Where did that woman in my mind come from? For
each of us, the answer to that question is different, but it's astonishing how universal the experience of such distortions is — and how

hard it is to bring image and reality closer together, especially for women. The first step is to realize that our body image *isn't* reality — in fact, that it often departs from anything that might be considered objective reality.

When fifty women staff members at a London hospital were asked to estimate the width of a box by duplicating it on a bar with movable margins, for instance, they were right on target. But when they were asked to estimate the width of their own bodies at bust, waist, and hip level, they *over*estimated by about 25 percent. Even those who were at their ideal weight or under by medical standards felt they needed to lose. When these results were compared with a parallel study of women who were bulimics — who binge on food and then purge by vomiting — the "abnormal" women were no more likely to overestimate their body size than were the "normal" ones.[30] In this and many ways, women with body-image or eating disorders are not a special category, just more extreme in their response to a culture that emphasizes thinness and impossible standards of appearance for women instead of individuality and health.*

In *Bodylove,* a book whose title reflects the goal of its author, Rita Freedman, a professor of psychology and women's studies, there is a roundup of studies that show just how negative — and remote from reality — females' body images often are. For instance: a majority of ten-year-olds rated themselves as the single *least* attractive girl in their school class; half of a group of teenage girls said they frequently felt ugly; fewer than half of college-age women felt good about their appearance; a majority of adult women considered themselves heavier than they really were, as well as heavier than the ideal they thought men preferred; and women considered "pretty"

---

* A factor not included in this experiment was bulimia as an index of suspicion in sexual abuse. Because the vaginal and anal openings of infants and small children are too small for an adult penis, mouths are often the focus of sexual abuse. As Dr. Jean Goodwin, a professor of psychiatry at the Medical College of Wisconsin in Milwaukee, reports, "Victims with bulimia may experience eating and regurgitation as a repetition of the sensations they underwent while performing fellatio." (Jean Goodwin and Reina Attiasr, "Eating Disorders in Victims of Multimodal Childhood Abuse," *Festschrift for Cornelia Wilbur,* Richard Kluft, editor, to be published.) In many eating-disorder programs, half of all participants are sexual-abuse survivors — compared with about a third in the general population — and a disproportionate number have been abused orally.

by others were just as likely to be dissatisfied with their looks as were women considered "plain." As Dr. Freedman summarized, "There's hardly any connection between a woman's actual physical attractiveness (as rated by others) and her satisfaction with body image . . . and feelings of self-worth. . . . There *is* a strong relationship, however, between body image and self-esteem."[31]

Men also tend to have an inaccurate body image — but in the opposite direction. Every study I found showed that males in general are more satisfied with their overall looks than women are with theirs (for instance, 75 percent of the men in the college study cited above expressed such satisfaction, versus only 45 percent of the women), and that they consider themselves closer to the ideal than their vital statistics reflect. Men also feel they weigh less or are closer to normal than they actually are, and they generally rate themselves as being at least as attractive as others, male and female, rate them. In *The Beauty Myth,* for instance, Naomi Wolf reports that only one man in ten is "strongly dissatisfied" with his body as compared to one in three women; and also that about a third of men are overweight by medical standards, yet 95 percent of people enrolled in weight-loss programs are women. As Wolf summarizes: "Studies show that while women unrealistically distort their bodies negatively, men distort theirs positively."[32] It's also a fact that punishes men, too, by perpetuating overweight and contributing to men's lower life expectancy.

Gender differences in this respect are so pronounced, Wolf concludes by comparing studies, that many able-bodied women have a more negative body image (and thus lower self-esteem) than do many disabled people — the results would have been more striking if able-bodied women were compared only to disabled men. In a male-superior culture, it seems that men are almost always okay no matter how they look, while women are rarely okay no matter how they look, and thus feel constantly in need of "fixing." This sense that women's bodies are less valuable is reinforced by everything from getting paid lower wages than men (and realizing that our work raising families is unpaid and invisible) to, as Wolf writes, a "Western legacy of religion based on men resembling God" and women having sinful or unclean bodies.[33]

As Linda Sanford and Mary Ellen Donovan conclude in

Women and Self-Esteem, a practical and helpful book that resulted from their years spent leading self-esteem-enhancement seminars: "It is difficult to dislike your body or a specific part of your body and still like yourself."[34] Conversely, if you do like yourself, you are likely to feel good about your physical appearance, and often to cause others to do so as well. The French have a term for this phenomenon: *jolie-laide,* beautiful-ugly, as in a woman who is not conventionally beautiful but who *becomes* beautiful by the way she presents herself.

Aging only adds more proof that the body in our minds is often quite different from the one we're walking around in. For both men and women, body image remains fairly constant, in spite of the drastic changes that occur as we grow older,[35] just as so-called core or global self-esteem tends to remain constant. Studies show that age plays little role in whether or not women report satisfaction with their bodies. For example, women under twenty-four are *more* likely to want to change parts of their bodies than older women are.[36] As *The Lancet,* a British medical journal, reported: "We may indeed have opinions of our capacity at cricket, and at maths, and at doing the cha-cha, but we also have a global opinion of our general worth."[37] And it's this global or core opinion that correlates with body image.

Perhaps most surprising, this positive image can persist in spite of many external biases that favor those judged to be more attractive. One's body image can be positive enough, and rooted deeply enough in childhood, to remain positive even in the face of society's quite different evaluation. For instance, physically appealing children tend to be given more attention by teachers, nice-looking people are often perceived as intrinsically "good," fat people are stereotyped as lazy, inefficient, or self-indulgent,[38] and dark skin or kinky hair may be so looked down upon in a racist culture that those words become epithets. Nonetheless, even a recent issue of *Vogue* reported: "When researchers surveyed several hundred women of all ages, they found no connection between fatness, thinness, and psychological well-being, even in overweight young women whom we might expect to be the most vulnerable."[39]

This is not to say that either our body image or our core sense of self-worth to which it is linked remains rocklike and constant.

Our physical self is a living part of each of us. Illness, aging, injury, or anything that shakes some pillar of our identity can unsettle it for a time. Even such subtle things as someone telling us we "look rested" or "look tired" can shift our body image for that moment. But the big difference is that, if we have a basically positive feeling about our bodies and ourselves, we don't "catastrophize"; that is, we don't extrapolate from a negative event or comment, from the effects of illness or aging, to a devastating feeling of despair about the whole self. With a basically poor image, on the other hand, each blow becomes proof that our bodies (hence ourselves) are defective or worthless, each compliment is interpreted as a friend's kindness or insincerity, and each day becomes a challenge to conceal our real selves (that is, what we think we look like) behind a facade. If they saw us as we "really" are, we believe, others would reject us.

So if we didn't internalize a positive body image in childhood, how can we begin to acquire it now? To start with the "don'ts" first: dieting and cosmetic surgery don't seem to work very well, at least not without serious inner work at the same time. It isn't that there is anything intrinsically wrong with them — each may be dangerous or helpful, depending on its content and our motive — but ultimately, they don't reach the image in our mind's eye. At best, they become to body image what money and possessions are to self-esteem: they may help us gain approval from others, but they rarely contribute to a feeling of being valuable *as we are*. At worst, they become addictive in the same way that money and possessions can be addictive when combined with low self-esteem. There seems to be a Law of Intentionality: changes undertaken to please others do that but no more; changes undertaken to please ourselves do that and no less.

If this sounds too contrary to the popular wisdom about the self-image improvements that come with diets and cosmetic surgery, consider that, if dieting could slenderize the image of the body that lives in the mind, 95 percent of adult women wouldn't be overestimating their body size, and 45 percent of *under*weight women wouldn't consider themselves *over*weight.[40] And if cosmetic surgeons could operate on self-esteem, it wouldn't happen so often that the result of such surgery doesn't even confer enough confidence to allow people to tell the truth about having had it. In fact, many people have done such drastic things as dieting away fifty pounds, surgically altering a racial characteristic, acquiring silicone breasts or transplanted hair, and still found themselves with exactly the same self-esteem problem. On the other hand, others have done such seemingly minor things as talking to people who share the same life experiences, exercising every morning, joining a big-and-beautiful group for large-size women, or honoring their own racial and ethnic heritage with people who share it — and learned to feel much more positive about themselves, inside and out.

The only practical, permanent solution to poor body image seems to be turning inward to ask: *Where did it come from?* What subtle or blatant events gave birth to it? What peer pressure nurtured it? What popular images make our real selves seem different or wrong?

It was only when I looked for the *why* of that big, plump, vulnerable girl in my own head — who had made me do everything from becoming stoop-shouldered in an effort to be shorter to hiding behind any available screen of hair and huge glasses — that she began to change at all, and she's not completely there yet. I had left her for too many years sealed up and alone, a chubby girl growing up in an isolated family whose food addictions and body image she absorbed.

I think of my father, who weighed over 300 pounds most of his life, got in the car even to mail a letter, and organized his days around food. He knew every restaurant with an unlimited buffet on his peripatetic sales route from the Midwest to the West Coast, and when we saw each other, our emotional connections always took place over double-thick malteds or apple pie à la mode. I loved him for his sense of adventure, for looking after me when I was very little and my mother could not, and for so much more; yet I was often ashamed of his huge size, his inability to fit into movie seats, his suits and shirts that often bore clear traces of the last meal, and his habit of falling asleep in any company after the soporific of food. At the time and for years after his death, I thought I was separate from him — but of course, I was not. I am his daughter. Like a recovering alcoholic, I'm a foodaholic who can't keep food in the house. I'm still trying to stay healthy, one day at a time. As Gabriel

García Márquez says through one of his characters in *Love in the Time of Cholera:* "I am not rich. I am a poor man with money, which is not the same thing." Well, I am not a thin woman, I'm a fat woman who's not fat at the moment.[41]

I also think of my mother, whose problem was her sad heart and undervalued head, not the rest of her body, yet her soft maternal hips and breasts seemed connected in my child's mind to her fate of sadness. I realize that I've continued to worry about and feel protective of women who are big-breasted and vulnerable, at the same time that I've longed for a more slender, boyish body to distance me from my mother's fate. But when I did begin to lose some plumpness after childhood, it was because I shot up to my full height of five feet seven by the time I was ten or eleven, which made me tower over my girlfriends and internalize a sense of being huge and galumphing. Still, this new height did reward me by enabling me to look older, and thus make money dancing at local clubs, a small-time version of the show-business career that seemed the only way out of our neighborhood. In retrospect, however, this was also a case of growing up too soon that probably added to my feelings of loss as my mother's caretaker. By fifteen, I was pretending to be eighteen in order to enter a local talent/beauty contest and feeling inordinately depressed when I failed to win a chance to compete in Florida for a title I recall as "Miss Capehart TV." When I belatedly began ballet lessons to add to the tap dancing I'd been learning, my ballet teacher also dimmed my dreams of dancing my way out of Toledo by saying I was too tall *en pointe* for most male partners. Since I never questioned the need to be shorter than dates and an eventual husband, a lifetime of creative slumping stretched before me.

Later, when college had got me out of Toledo, I gave up dancing — my only exercise. All other forms seemed beyond me. I thought tennis was for rich kids, field hockey was for prep-school girls, and besides, I'd never learned a sport. In high school, the only desirable sport for girls was being a drum majorette or cheerleader, both of which I envied but didn't attempt. Each time I tried one in college, the instructors — perhaps unaccustomed to having to start from scratch — suggested I try something else. Furthermore, I was downright shocked the first time I heard someone say "I'm going for a walk" when she didn't have to. In my neighborhood in those prefitness times, having a car signaled prosperity and walking meant poverty. College only confirmed my habit of living in my head: I just studied, ate, and gained my part of what was known as "the freshman ton." If there had been a sport called sitting-and-reading, I would have been an all-time champion.

By the time I was out of college, back from a two-year fellowship in India, and trying to make a living as a freelance writer in New York, there were media images that gave me other ways to distance myself from my background and my family. I remember crying over Audrey Hepburn in *Breakfast at Tiffany's* because I identified with the poor and prematurely responsible childhood she had escaped by walking down a dirt road a little farther every day — until finally, she just kept going. I laced my dark hair with obvious blond streaks, just as she had done. The kerchiefs she wore turned out to be perfect for hiding my fat cheeks. I also copied her huge sunglasses in order to hide the fleshiness left over from a chubby childhood that overhung my eyelids and displaced my contact lenses so often that I gave up wearing them. Short skirts like hers were also satisfyingly unladylike and showed the one part of me still fit from dancing: legs. I realized that, if I patched myself together with just the right combination of flaunting and hiding, I could be counted as pretty, even though I was far from that in my mind. A friend from that era described me as a mousy girl with harlequin glasses and a ponytail who had turned herself into a mysterious Holly Golightly overnight.

Thus, I inched along that narrow you-can't-win continuum of female images, escaping from 1950s "collegiate" into 1960s "rebellious" without once thinking who *I* was.

Fortunately, feminist ideas began to explode at the end of the 1960s and helped us all to realize that we shared an overarching problem: being judged on how we looked instead of what was in our heads and hearts. Thanks to this unifying and liberating revelation, we began to rebel against the more obvious forms of imprisonment, like feeling we couldn't go to the grocery without lipstick, or giving more thought to what we wore than what we read. I abandoned clothes anxiety with relief and evolved a simple, comfortable, jeans-sweater-and-boots uniform that I wore for one entire decade. Somehow, it took me that long to burn the cheap dressing-up of

Toledo plus the expensive dressing-down of the Ivy League out of my brain.

Only in the last decade have I been able to achieve what I really enjoy; what Marge Piercy described so well in her futurist novel, *Woman on the Edge of Time:* soft, comfortable, semiandrogynous clothes for everyday, and a pool of fanciful clothes shared with friends so we can all decorate ourselves for an occasional party or dancing at night. Perhaps the one attitude that has persisted from Toledo days is my fear of looking ladylike: then, because the wives of the factory owners looked that way (and unfortunately, I thought of them as the enemy); now, because those fussy clothes seem like a prison. I noticed several studies remarking on the frequency with which women's dreams involve feeling imprisoned by their clothes — and I believe it. I'd like to print cards for little girls in button-in-the-back frilly dresses (as well as for their grown-up sisters suffering in their own versions of those dresses): *Help! I am a prisoner in my clothes.*

But though I was rescued by feminism, it had one result for which I was ill prepared: finding myself referred to as "the pretty one" — jeans and all. Rationally, I knew it was a response of surprise, based on what the media thought feminists looked like (if a woman could get a man, why would she need equal pay?), and this was especially clear to me because I was judged much prettier *after* I was identified as a feminist than I ever had been *before.* Identifying women by appearance again, flattering some and insulting others, was a way of reducing feminism to form without content — and dividing us. Since I didn't feel prettier (or even pretty), I didn't trust the press's image of me, and I just kept hiding out in my uniform of jeans, hair, and sunglasses, hoping that other women wouldn't be alienated by what the media said.

Because the internal image was so much realer than reality, it never occurred to me to question the childhood roots of that self-image — to ask myself why I hid my face, stood round-shouldered, always felt enormous, and when someone complimented me, gave them reasons why they were wrong — instead of just saying thank you.

It was in that stage that I saw my real physical self on television. (This is a self-revelation now available to anyone with a video camera, and one that I highly recommend; somehow, it's much more powerful than looking in a mirror, perhaps because our media craziness makes us think what we see on a screen is almost more real than reality.) Once I got past the shock of wondering who that was, I had to admit there was something called body image. Seeing myself looking so calm on the screen, and knowing that I had been petrified inside — paradoxically, it takes a little confidence to reveal one's *lack* of confidence — also gave me more sympathy for other people. I began to do less envying, judging, or worrying about women based on their appearance, since it now dawned on me that one can never know how others see themselves.

But once I realized that image was different from reality, I also began to wonder how my own mother had seen herself. One of my earliest memories was of brushing her hair or dabbing powder on her pale cheeks while she sat docile as a child, depending on me to "fix her up" for a rare outing. By the time I knew her, she was a woman who paid almost no attention to her physical self. Before those long years of depression, how had she seen herself when she was a young girl?

As we sat in her basement apartment in my sister's house — for my mother still could not live alone — she described how rawboned and gawky she'd felt next to her littler, rounder, "prettier" sister, and how angry she had been at her mother for giving them both a message that women's bodies were shameful. She had eloped with my father because he made her laugh, but also because she was grateful to be chosen. It was the first time in our lives we'd ever talked about anything as basic as our feelings about our bodies, and my mother, then in her seventies, surprised me by saying she wanted to do something about what she called "my dewlaps," loose facial skin that was the result of a hard life that included several years in mental hospitals, and little self-care. For years, I'd noticed that she told new acquaintances she was much older than she really was, and I suddenly understood why: she'd been trying to match inner and outer reality. Now, there was a spark of hope that made her want to *be* that inner person. In spite of my skepticism (then a bias) about plastic surgery, I encouraged her and set about making the necessary arrangements; it was so clearly a sign of hope that she wanted it. But when we talked again, all her old anxieties and depression had returned. Nothing I said could convince her that her body was worth any attention at all. Our talk had come too late.

I look at the photograph she gave me that day, and when I see the tall, spare, "gawky" young woman that my mother was in her early twenties, I realize with irony that she was exactly the free, androgynous image I would later try to become. When I was in my mother's body, had I absorbed this authentic self emanating from her bones? Are there generations of daughters, each one rebelling against the false image forced on the generation before, never knowing that we would have loved and admired our mothers all the more if they had been able to blossom as their true selves?

Over the years since my mother's death, I've been trying to enjoy and appreciate my own authentic body, and to learn what it has to teach. "The body never forgets" is the motto of therapists who help people use somatic memories as bridges to the past, and I've come to believe that the body image never forgets either. I know a woman who saw herself with such shameful and distorted breasts that she wanted to have breast surgery. She remembered only a week before her scheduled operation that her grandmother had made her wear painful bindings as a developing girl, and that she had assumed this was necessary to keep her safe from boys at school. Suddenly, she saw that surgery was not the healing she needed. But I wonder: How many people try to change the part of the body that is only trying to help them remember?

As for myself, I'm still learning. I only recently understood, for instance, why nausea has always felt like the end of the world to me; so much so that I once endangered my health by resisting the need to throw up with food poisoning. By focusing on one current feeling of nausea, I rediscovered the day that I realized I was solely responsible for my mother. My father, long separated from her, had driven me home from Girl Scout camp, and after he had dropped me off, I was alone with my very depressed mother. As I felt the fear of understanding there was no one to turn to, I also felt in my stomach the malted and hamburger my father had bought me. They seemed to remain in the pit of my stomach for days.

But once I had followed this thread to the past, its fearfulness began to dim. The amazing thing is this: The moment we find the true reason for some feeling that has an irrationally powerful hold over us, whether it has to do with body image or anything else, the spell is broken. It may take a long time, but the negative grooves it has left in our minds can be filled in with conscious and positive affirmations. With our ideas about our bodies, as with all things human, saying yes works better than saying no. So I've been trying to recall positive parts of my family legacy and then expand on them.

While working on this book, for instance, I've been thinking how grateful I am to my parents for respecting my body as a child and never making me think it deserved spanking, hitting, or abuse of any kind. This has helped me not only to be rebellious on my own behalf, but to believe in and to fight against abuse experienced by others — for I have no personal stake in denying its reality. I've also tried to focus on parts of my body that I like, and to imagine expanding that empowering feeling to the rest of me. I recently realized that the one part of my body of which I am unequivocally proud is the hands I inherited from my father. They are long, tapering, graceful hands, something about him of which I was never ashamed. Just imagining how this self-esteem might feel if expanded to my whole body gives me a glimpse of how energizing true body-pride could be. I think of all the women I know who take pleasure in their bodies but are made to feel guilty about it, as if they were giving in to a culture that has used women's bodies for fetishes and consumerism. I think of other women who give up body-pride and even jeopardize their health by ignoring their physical selves, retreating into their minds, and trying to defeat the culture by treating flesh and skin as unfortunate necessity. What wonders have they and all of us been missing? What might we become if we were body-proud from the beginning?

The whole answer remains for future generations to discover, but I've found my own small beginning. Sometimes when my hand rests on a surface, I see the middle finger tap involuntarily, exactly as my father's used to do. For that one second, I feel his visceral presence. I hope he knows that I'm no longer ashamed — of either of us.

I don't mean to suggest that changing our bodies can never make us feel better about ourselves; only that, to make sure it will, we do need to know our own motivation. Do we want to make the change out of feelings of hope or fear? a longing for self-expression or a need for other people's approval? pleasure or pressure? Keeping these fundamental questions in mind can help us thread our way through the morass of media images and body-changing techniques to find only what is healthy and empowering — and reject the rest. Plastic surgeon Thomas Rees, a pioneer in the field of what is known as aesthetic surgery, is one of the few who seem to use such questions as criteria in selecting patients for whom the surgery will be helpful. In an article addressed to his colleagues, he warns against the teenager whose nose is being changed to suit the wishes of his or her parents; the woman who seeks breast enlargement because her husband wants other men to envy him when they're sitting around the swimming pool; the perfectionist who can never be pleased; the patient who has just gone through the death of a loved one, a job loss, a divorce or other major transition, and so may be looking to surgery for an unrealistic rescue; and even the patient who betrays a self-esteem problem by being over-flattering to the surgeon but rude to the receptionist.

"Despite all that has been published about self-image," he warns, "our knowledge of it is exceedingly superficial. It is often astonishing to the young surgeon to find out just how people visualize themselves, and how far removed this self-visualization can be from the interviewer's or surgeon's evaluation."[42]

It's a sign that self-image is negative and self-esteem is low when cosmetic surgery becomes just one more occasion for shame and thus for lying. I think of socialite Sunny von Bülow, who had a face-lift, apparently because her husband was having affairs with younger women. She swore her personal maid to secrecy with such desperate vehemence that even after she lay in a permanent coma and her husband was on trial for attempting to murder her, the faithful maid went on trying to conceal "my lady's" face-lift. Conversely, the very act of openly seeking such surgery can be a sign of self-esteem. I think of the teenage boy I read about whose face was ravaged by smallpox and acne, and whose fundamentalist Christian parents would not let him erase this evidence of "God's punishment." He held himself blameless enough to seek permission for surgery from a judge, but he was denied; yet for him cosmetic surgery could have been a great blessing.

I think, too, about the contrast among three women I know, two of whom had breast-reduction operations in their twenties to change the physical discomfort of backaches and street harassment and to feel more of the comfort and freedom they believed they deserved. The third had breast implants in her fifties, still trying to make up for being a flat-chested adolescent whose father teased her by calling her "my son," while marrying a succession of ever-younger and more bosomy wives. For all three, the results of the surgery were implicit in the motive: the first two started out feeling positively about themselves and became more so; the third started out negative and felt even worse afterward. When last seen, she was worried about whether her lover "knew."

Real-life examples like these — not unrealistic, intellectual positions that are totally *against* or totally *for* cosmetic surgery or other body changes — can lead us to the right questions. For the answer, we can turn inward and listen to an always honest inner voice.

1. Will we be uncomfortable discussing this change with people whose opinion we respect? (If we find ourselves not only denying it, but reproaching others who have done the same thing, we know we are dealing with self-hatred, and need to look for its cause within ourselves.)

2. Do we understand that we are equally valuable *with or without it?* (If the answer is no, then the external change won't work; at least, not unless an internal one precedes and accompanies it.)

3. Will this change make us more or less able to change society's standards for us and others like us — whether the standard has to do with age, ethnic appearance, or anything else? It's true there are real biases out there, and we may have to contend with them in the job market, but surgery is very intimate and permanent. If we're just capitulating by saying, "If the shoe doesn't fit, I'll change the foot," we should reconsider.

Among women, especially on the culturally loaded subject of our bodies, there is always a danger of diminishing each other's self-authority. Therefore, the point is not to give each other answers, but to share questions and experiences. So let me be clear: I'm still trying to thread a path between outside images and inner self, and this is just a progress report. For instance: I'm still suspicious of the degree to which I make choices that society rewards. (When I lived for two years in India, I loved wearing saris and kohl on my eyes; I know that, wherever I am, I absorb the going aesthetic.) I'm still angry when people ask me accusingly: Why are you thin? Would they ask a recovering alcoholic why she isn't drinking? Nonetheless, I answer because I know this is a serious question for women: I'm thin mostly because of my family history, but also because I listened to my body and discovered the weight at which I feel best (which, interestingly, turned out to be the same weight prescribed by a medical fat-to-muscle test), and more and more, because I'm enjoying the feeling of being thin-and-strong as opposed to being only thin — a benefit of my belated discovery of exercise and weight-training. I'm still getting over my bias against any body change that isn't "necessary," however, and it took me twenty years to walk two blocks for a simple office procedure to remove some of the fat over my eyes so that now I can wear sleep-in contact lenses. Seeing the ceiling when I look up at it from my bed in the morning and my feet when I look down in the shower — not to mention having peripheral vision, when you've worn glasses since the sixth grade — is a big treat. It's also meant that I could get rid of those big glasses I'd been hiding behind for so long. Of course, now I get letters asking: Whatever happened to your big glasses?

Finally, I'm still uncomfortable talking about all this stuff and look forward to the day when the bodies of women in public life (and private life) are no more subject to scrutiny than men's are. I got two calls in one day, one asking if I was pregnant (the press has a fragile grip on age and biology), and the other asking if I'd had a face-lift. So for the record: No, I'm not pregnant or likely to be, unless there's another star in the East, and no, I haven't had a face-lift — I'm just now getting used to the face I have and don't plan on changing it. I'd like to help push the age barrier. This year, however, my favorite press question was: Why do you part your hair in the middle? Now, *that's* a secret I'm keeping to myself.

But this is self-description, not prescription. As Naomi Wolf says: "A woman wins by giving herself and other women permission: to eat, to be sexual, to age, to wear a boiler suit or a paste tiara or a Balenciaga gown or a secondhand opera cloak or combat boots, to cover up or go practically naked; to do whatever she chooses in following — or ignoring — her own aesthetic. A woman wins when she feels that what each woman does with her own body is her own business."[43]

I'm still not quite the winner that I want all women to be, but it's amazing how much the body is willing to respond to healthy motives at any age. Recently, a woman I didn't know came over to compliment me on my muscle definition, the result of my recent conversion to both yoga and weight-training. *Muscle definition!* It was a compliment that made me more body-proud than all media references to "the pretty one" combined.

IV *Age — and a Blessing*

"We grow neither better nor worse as we get old, but more like ourselves."
MARY LAMBERTON BECKER

Dorothy Dinnerstein, the sociologist and author of *The Mermaid and the Minotaur*, once said that growing up in a family teaches us two crucial things: how to get along with and love people who don't share our interests, and what to expect from the various stages of life.

I was struck by the wisdom of the first part of her remark and bored by the second. Didn't everyone know about "the stages of life"?

Well, everything sounds trite before we're ready for it. Almost two decades later, I realized I didn't understand the process of aging at all. Thanks to my very small family, the patterns of my parents' lives, and the fact that I've worked mostly in movements where age differences melt in a furnace of shared interests, I had never thought about or lived with the surprising, upsetting, implacable, and irrevocable mystery of aging. Instead, I had been behaving as if the long plateau of an activist middle of life went on forever.

Though my circumstances set me apart from many of my friends — for instance, I hadn't chosen to have children and so didn't have their growth as a measure of time — I discovered that few people I knew had a vision of anything but a cliff at the end of this plateau. The rarity of extended families, the lack of multigenerational communities, and too few media images that extend beyond forty or fifty — all these things had stopped our imaginations. Meanwhile, my apparent belief that I was immortal, with all the time in the world, was causing me to plan poorly — to put it mildly.

Fortunately, our bodies are great teachers: even their smallest intimations of mortality are shocks we never forget. I remember having my hair washed at a shop in another city, apologizing as usual for having long hair that is time-consuming to dry, and being told cheerfully, "That's okay — it's rather thin." Then there was the moment when I realized I could only count on going sleepless for one night — not two — when I needed to meet a deadline. And my always nearsighted eyes began to get farsighted at the same time. "I always thought my patients were exaggerating," the optician said when I asked him if I was going blind or just aging, "until I passed forty — now I know exactly what you mean."

These bodily signals sent me into the first stage of dealing with aging: denial. I was going to continue living *exactly as I always had* — and make a virtue of it. If age were ever to interrupt sexual life, for instance, I would just continue it in a different way. After all, the world could use a pioneer dirty old lady. Dorothy Pitman Hughes and I began fantasizing a future as bawdy old women sitting on bar stools in skirts that were too tight, sending out for an occasional young sailor. (Of course, neither one of us drank, or felt attracted to members of the opposite sex who hadn't lived through at least some of the same history — but the fact that dirty old men were almost our only role models was a measure of how finite we felt our options to be.) If I ever grew too infirm to work and my delusions of perpetual youth had still prevented me from saving any money, then I would just become a bag lady. It was a life like any other, and I could always help organize the other bag ladies.

Gradually, this first stage of denial blended into a second, more energized one: defiance. Two of my role models for this future were George Burns, who had just signed a contract to play the Palladium in London on his hundredth birthday (he was well into his eighties at the time, a bravado which made me overlook his not-so-great sex jokes about young women), and Ruth Gordon, who wore miniskirts in her eighties, had a younger husband (playwright Garson Kanin), and acted up a storm in movies (remember *Harold and Maude?*). She also said satisfying things like "I think there is one smashing rule: Never face the facts."

In this spirit, I celebrated my fiftieth birthday in a very public way by turning it into a feminist benefit (which I hope my funeral will also be), and tried to offer some encouragement to other women facing the double standard of aging by getting as far out of the age closet as possible. Of course, I continued to hear "fifty" as old when applied to other people and had consciously and constantly to revise my own assumptions. Though I began making an effort to use time better and to understand that my life wasn't going to go on for-ever — that is, to use turning fifty to good purposes — my heart wasn't in it. In fact, I didn't revise one single thing about my living habits: no exercise except running through airports; no change in my sugar-addicted eating habits; no admission that this long plateau in the middle of my life might be leading into new terrain. In a way, I felt I *couldn't* acknowledge limitations or any of the weaknesses to which the flesh is heir; the everyday emergencies of a magazine and a movement were all-consuming, and I didn't think I could stop swimming in midstream. But to a larger degree, I just didn't know how. I didn't have a model of how to get from here to there; from where I was to seventy, eighty, and hopefully beyond. I needed a model not of *being old,* but of *aging.*

Thanks to good genes, I got away with all this defiance for quite a while — which may be exactly why I needed the word *cancer* to come into my life. Nothing less than such a bodily warning would have made me think about the way I was living. Sleeplessness and endless stress, a quart of ice cream at a time, and my lifetime rule of no exercise: I was so unaccustomed to listening to any kind of messages from within that I'd ceased to be able to hear even a whis-per from that internal voice that must ultimately be our guide. In fact, I had no patience at all with anyone who suggested it was there to be listened to.

Cancer changed that. It gave me a much-needed warning, and it taught me something else: it was not death I had been defying. On the contrary, when I got this totally unexpected diagnosis, my first thought was a bemused, "So this is how it's all going to end." My second was, "I've had a wonderful life." Such acceptance may sound odd, but I felt those words in every last cell of my being. It was a moment I won't forget.

Eventually, that diagnosis and my reaction to it made me realize that I'd been worrying about aging; that my denial and defiance were related to giving up a way of being, not ceasing to be. Though I would have decried all the actresses, athletes, and other worshipers of youth who were unable to imagine a changed future — a few of whom have even chosen death *over* aging — I had been falling into the same trap.

For this health warning — plus the dawning of an understanding that to fear aging is really to fear a new stage of life — I was fortunate to pay only a small price. Thanks to the impact of the women's health movement on at least some of the health-care system, my treatment consisted of a Novocain shot and a biopsy at a women's clinic, while I watched an infinitesimal lump being removed in what turned out to be its entirety — rather like taking out an oddly placed splinter. Since the mammogram had shown nothing — 15 percent show false negatives, which is another reason for self-examination — the diagnosis of malignancy was a shock. But what came after was not nearly as difficult as what many women have faced. First, there was a lymph-node sampling that did require going into a hospital, but didn't interfere with going dancing the evening I got out. Since the sampling was negative, the rest of the treatment consisted of six weeks of lying like the Bride of Frankenstein on a metal slab each morning while I got radiation treatments. My self-treatment was much more drastic: doing away with all animal fat in my diet, and getting less stress and more sleep. All this has helped me remain cancer-free for the last five years.

Nonetheless, I was frightened enough by this timely warning to start doing what I needed to do, indeed what I should have been doing all along: listening to what my physical self had to say. Perhaps one of the rewards of aging is a less forgiving body that transmits its warnings faster — not as betrayal, but as wisdom. Cancer makes one listen more carefully, too. I began to seek out a healthier routine, a little introspection, and the time to do my own writing, all of which are reflected in these pages.

Now, I've come to believe that bodies know whether their times of transition are leading to something positive or negative. If I tell you that menopause turned out to be mainly the loss of a familiar marker of time, plus the discomfort of a few flushes and flashes — and that to me, the ease of this transition seems related to the much-longed-for era of relative peace and self-expression it ushered in — you may think I've gone off my rocker. But consider the results of a 150-nation menopause study: negative symptoms *increased* when women went from more to less social mobility and power, but *decreased* when women's power and freedom grew. In the United States, where women are valued for youthfulness, for instance, there were many negative menopausal symptoms, but in countries like Pakistan, where women are restricted during childbearing years but allowed more authority and social mobility after menopause, women had very few. Within this country, African-American women reported the fewest negative symptoms and Jewish women reported the most; arguably because of the relative importance of the role that older women play in those communities.[44]

In fact, when a medical anthropologist named Yewoubdar Beyenne came here from Ethiopia, she was so surprised by all the negative attributes of menopause that she did a study of its impact in a wide variety of countries and concluded that it is a "biocultural phenomenon." As she put it, "Coming from a non-Western background, I was not aware that menopause causes depression or any other emotional or physical illness. I only knew that menopause was a time when women in my culture felt free from menstrual taboos." From Mayan women in Mexico to blue-collar and professional women in Britain and Hawaii — all of whom had lives to look forward to that were active and free compared with their own premenopausal pasts — the crucial question was: What kind of era is menopause ringing in?[45]

I'm fortunate to have a future of active work I love and look forward to, but the most crucial element in all these studies seems to be an increase in self-expression and freedom, whether it's part of our work or not. Once again, it's the importance of moving closer to the true self, regardless of our age. When male and female college students were asked to write for just twenty minutes a day, for each of four days, about a traumatic personal experience, for instance, the result was everything from a better emotional state to a strengthened immune system. When the same test was repeated with instructions to write only about trivial events, there was no change in mood or immune response at all.[46] The result is not so different from the Pakistani women in that 150-nation menopause study who could finally get out of isolation and into conversation in the marketplace.

For me thus far, the only disappointment with this new country called aging is that it hasn't liberated me from that epithet of "the pretty one" — though in the past, I sometimes pleasurably fantasized about getting old to get rid of it. If that sounds odd, think about working as hard as you can, and then discovering that whatever you accomplish is attributed to your looks. The up-side has been a better understanding of women who really are great beauties — not just feminists who don't fit a media stereotype — and who are treated without reference to their inner reality, as well as denied sympathy. Perhaps a more personal up-side is seeing age as freedom.

In my current stage of aging and listening, I've learned the importance of starting with the body and all its senses. Which is why I go to my body to ask what this new country of aging will be like.

I look at my hands of which I am so proud, for instance, and seeing their backs sprinkled with small brown age spots is shocking at first. So I ask them what they have to say for themselves. "A banner held in liver-spotted hands," they reply. I get a title for a future article, plus my first inkling that liver spots have a sense of humor.

I notice that the hormonal changes of menopause seem to have freed a part of my brain once preoccupied with sex — thus bringing a more relaxed, I-enjoy-it-when-it-happens-but-don't-obsess-about-it attitude — so I ask these brain cells what they're planning to do with the extra time. "Celebrate not being stuck with bars and sailors," they say. Suddenly, I feel liberated.

I wonder if I should let the bleached streaks in my hair grow out after all these years. I don't want to put "a ceiling on my brain," as Alice Walker would say. Then the phrase "punk-rock purple" comes out of nowhere. Maybe even aging hair doesn't have to be serious.

Looking in the mirror, I see the lines between nose and mouth that now remain, even without a smile, and I am reminded of a chipmunk storing nuts for the winter. This is the updated version of my plump-faced child. When I ask what they have to say for themselves, nothing comes back. They know I don't like them, so until I stop with the chipmunk imagery and learn to value them as the result of many smiles, they're not communicating. I'll have to work on this — and many other adjustments of aging still to come.

But I have a new role model for this adventurous new country I'm now entering. She is a very old, smiling, wrinkled, rosy, beautiful woman, standing in the morning light of a park in Beijing. Her snow-white hair is just visible under a jaunty lavender babushka. Jan Phillips, who took her photograph, says she was belting out a Chinese opera to the sky, stopped for a moment to smile at the camera, and then went on singing. Now, she smiles at me every morning from my mantel.

I love this woman. I like to think that, walking on the path ahead of me, she looks a lot like my future self.

This is the wisdom: If we bless our bodies, they will bless us. In Robin Morgan's poem, "Network of the Imaginary Mother," there is her own version of a pagan prayer:

> Blessed be my brain
> that I may conceive of my own power.
> Blessed be my breast
> that I may give sustenance to those I love.
> Blessed be my womb
> that I may create what I choose to create.
> Blessed be my knees
> that I may bend so as not to break.
> Blessed be my feet
> that I may walk in the path of my highest will.[47]

Six

Romance versus Love

Romance. *A tale in verse, embodying the adventures of some hero of chivalry. . . . A fictitious narrative in prose of which the scene and incidents are very remote from those of ordinary life.*

Love. *That disposition or state of feeling with regard to a person which . . . manifests itself in solicitude for the welfare of the object, and . . . delight in his* [sic] *presence.*

THE OXFORD ENGLISH DICTIONARY

I Unlearning Romance

"I *cannot* live without my life! I *cannot* live
without my soul!"
HEATHCLIFF

"Nelly, I *am* Heathcliff!"
CATHERINE

What do you remember about the story of *Wuthering
Heights*, whether from the novel, the classic movie, or the myth that
has become a part of our culture?

I remember the yearning of two people to be together — and
the intensity, the merging, the loss of boundaries when they were.
There was an obsessiveness and a sense of fate about these two lifelong lovers that made even the romantic yearnings of Romeo and
Juliet seem pale.

In Emily Brontë's novel, their romance begins when they are
children. From the moment Heathcliff, a dark-skinned urchin found
wandering the streets of Liverpool, is rescued and brought home as
an adopted servant by little Catherine's father, they are soul mates.
But divided as they grow up by chasms of class and race, their union
as adults seems so impossible that Catherine agrees to marry a kind
and wealthy neighbor. Humiliated by her idea that marriage to him
would "degrade" her, Heathcliff runs away to sea, and Catherine
nearly dies from a fever that is an almost literal lovesickness. By the
time a newly prosperous Heathcliff returns three years later, it is too
late: Catherine has married Edgar Linton. Heathcliff rages, swears
vengeance, and marries Linton's sister to get control of her property
and to spite the family — but Catherine knows she is the cause of
all this suffering. Torn between her alter ego and her kind husband,
and also pregnant, she falls ill but lives long enough to give birth to
a daughter.

It's one of the departures of this novel that its heroine dies
halfway through it. We then see almost twenty years of Heathcliff
raging, mourning, and trying to control everything Catherine ever

touched. When he finally succeeds, he seems to will himself to die, as if this obsession had been the only thing keeping him alive. At his request, he is buried next to "my Cathy" at the edge of the moors where they once roamed happily as children, with the facing sides of their coffins cut away so nothing will separate them for eternity.

When this magical novel was first published under the pen name of Ellis Bell in 1847, English critics were shocked by its intimate, romantic focus; a departure from the big canvas, many characters, and broad issues that characterized the Victorian novel. When the author was revealed to be the reclusive daughter of a country clergyman, a woman who had died at thirty from consumption and what we would now call anorexia, and who had little experience of life apart from what she had gleaned from voluminous reading, there began generations of scholarly efforts to understand how such a woman could have produced this masterful novel — the first in English, one critic was to say a century later, "which invites the same kind of attention that we give to *Macbeth*."[1] The most fervent part of the search was for the man who was the model for the passionate, brooding, and very "masculine" Heathcliff.

Some literary investigators theorized that Emily Brontë must have carried on an affair with one of her father's curates, almost the only unrelated men around, though there was no evidence for it. Others thought that, like her contemporary Charles Dickens, she had observed a variety of lives around her, copied down character names from gravestones, and stitched together a novelistic quilt from scraps of reality. Still others assumed that Heathcliff's excesses had been copied from Emily's tormented brother, Branwell, who died young from an excess of gin and opium. Whatever his source in reality, many called her an immoral woman for including such a character as Heathcliff in her novel at all. As one scholarly introduction to *Wuthering Heights* admitted: "Those critics who feel compelled to 'explain' a work of art by tracing it to its origins and who assume that the imagination simply adds up experiences in the external world are ill at ease with this novel."[2]

Only when the most recent wave of feminism brought a less traditional view of women's inner lives into the mainstream of criticism did there begin to be a body of scholars who believed *Wuthering Heights* could have come from one isolated woman's imagination. Long ago, she had given us a major clue when she said, in the guise of Catherine, "I *am* Heathcliff." Emily Brontë was *both* the capricious, suffering girl who could not escape the restrictions of a female life, and the dark, adventurous, rebellious outsider. Like each of our true selves, her nature was *both* "masculine" and "feminine," but unlike most of us, she lived in such isolation that, far from being handicapped, she seems to have preserved more of that wholeness. Growing up outside schools and conventional society, choosing to be reclusive even by the standards of her own isolated family, she was free to commune with nature on the moors, to turn inward, to learn from an inner universe. Though she read a great deal — novels, poetry, and the many political journals her father brought into the house — she missed the social training that convinces women we must not identify with men — and vice versa.

As her older and more gregarious sister, Charlotte Brontë, explained about both Emily and their younger sister, Anne, who also died young: "Neither Emily nor Anne was learned; they had no thought of filling their pitchers at the wellspring of other minds; they always wrote from the impulse of nature, the dictates of intuition." [3]

But it was in Emily that "masculine" and "feminine" seemed most perfectly blended; Emily who was the most creative of a gifted family; and Emily in whom Charlotte, herself to become the author of *Jane Eyre* and other classic novels, found endless fascination. "In Emily's nature," Charlotte wrote, "the extremes of vigour and simplicity seemed to meet. Under an . . . unpretending outside, lay a secret power and fire that might have informed the brain and kindled the veins of a hero." This fascination began the moment Charlotte found Emily's secret stash of poems and persuaded her retiring sister to let them be published under a pseudonym. As Charlotte later explained, "Something more than surprise seized me, — a deep conviction that these were not common effusions, or at all like the poetry women generally write. I thought them condensed and terse, vigorous and genuine. To my ear, they had also had a peculiar music — wild, melancholy, and elevating." Her obsession with Emily's enigmatic strength and independent spirit continued long past her sister's death from consumption. After watching Emily hasten her demise by refusing to eat, a means she had often used to gain control over her otherwise dependent life, Charlotte wrote: "Never in all her life had she lingered over any task that lay before her. . . . She made haste to leave us. Yet, while physically she perished, mentally she grew stronger. . . . I have seen nothing like it; but indeed, I have never seen her parallel in anything. Stronger than a man, simpler than a child, her nature stood alone."[4]

A few years later, when *Wuthering Heights* became popular enough to be reissued in a new edition, Charlotte wrote a preface in which she tried to disarm its critics by first joining their disapproval of its tortured hero ("Whether it is right or advisable to create beings like Heathcliff, I do not know: I scarcely think it is"), then defending her sister by explaining, "The writer who possesses the creative gift owns something of which he is not always master — something that, at times, strangely wills and works for itself." Heathcliff, she makes clear, is "a man's shape animated by demon life." That demon lived within her quiet sister, who "rarely crossed the threshold of home."

Charlotte also defended Emily for endowing Catherine's husband with such "feminine" traits as "constancy and tenderness."

> Some people will think these qualities do not shine so well incarnate in a man as they would do in a woman, but Ellis Bell [Emily's pseudonym] could never be brought to comprehend this notion: nothing moved her more than any insinuation that the faithfulness and clemency, the long-suffering and lovingkindness which are esteemed virtues in the daughters of Eve, become foibles in the sons of Adam.

Clearly, Emily believed in the presence of *all* human qualities in both men and women. At the very end of the novel, when Catherine's daughter marries a cousin raised by Heathcliff, thus uniting the two families he had sought to divide and destroy, the union seems to symbolize Emily's hope for future wholeness in both women and men. The romance between Catherine and Heathcliff had been the result of an inner void within each of them, and the story tells of their impossible effort to fill it with the body and soul of the other. Indeed, in Heathcliff, Emily created the perfect vision of a self in which the "masculine" is totally bereft of the "feminine": energetic, focused, strong-willed, controlling, even violent, unable to empathize beyond his own boundaries or to love without possessing. Catherine embodied the fate of the "feminine" without the "masculine": vulnerable, diffused, too connected, more aware of the needs around her than of her own.

In Emily herself, of course, there were both; yet this unity was forbidden. The bond between the lovers who were born of her imagination, as poet and theorist Adrienne Rich has written, "is the archetypal bond between the split fragments of the psyche, the masculine and feminine elements ripped apart and longing for reunion."[5]

No wonder the romance of *Wuthering Heights* endures — as do romantic myths in almost every culture. Indeed, the more patriarchal and gender-polarized a culture is, the more addicted to romance. These myths embody our yearning to be whole.

No wonder romance so often begins at a physical distance or across a psychic chasm of class and race,* and thrives on death and separation. Projecting our lost qualities onto someone else can be done more easily from a distance.

No wonder romance grows weaker with closeness, dailiness, and familiarity. *No one can be or give to us the rest of our unique self.*

No wonder many women need romance more than men do. Since most human qualities are labeled "masculine," and only a few

---

* Emily Brontë may have had in mind a racial distance greater than that between the gently bred Catherine and a "dark-skinned gypsy," as Heathcliff was described. Jamaican-American writer Michelle Cliff points out in her unpublished essay, "Caliban's Daughter," that Liverpool was a center of the slave trade, where discarded Africans, perhaps also children fathered by slave traders, lived in the streets. Catherine's father brought home this boy who was "dark as if it came from the devil" and speaking "some gibberish that nobody could understand" only after he had unsuccessfully "enquired for its owner." Later, when Heathcliff runs away to become rich enough to marry Catherine, what trade other than slave ships could have earned him such a fortune in three years? And if that self-betrayal was the source of his wealth, no wonder he was in such pain when he returned to find that even this blood money couldn't give him Catherine. Perhaps Emily Brontë, wandering over moors she must have known were part of a slave trader's estate, was drawing parallels between a Heathcliff who could be bought (and forced to sell others) and a Catherine who could be sold in marriage. Or perhaps as an outsider by sex who had written imaginary stories about Africa as a child, she was simply finding within herself the emotions of an outsider by race — just as Aphra Behn, the first professional woman writer in England, had done almost two hundred years earlier.

are "feminine" — and even those are marginalized — *women have an even greater need to project life-giving parts of themselves onto another human being.*

No wonder that, while it lasts, romance brings such an explosive feeling of melting, merging, and losing boundaries. *We are making love to the rest of ourselves.*

Do you fall in love when you're feeling vulnerable or not so good about yourself? When you fall *out* of love, do you "crash," as if you had been on a drug? Have you noticed that friendship, shared values, working together, almost *anything* is more likely to lead to a lasting love than the usual romance — yet you still find yourself thinking *this* romance will be different? Are you waiting to make basic decisions in your life because those should be determined by a future partner? If you already have a partner, do you spend more time thinking about pleasing and/or improving him or her than pleasing and/or improving yourself? When you're not in a romance, are you prone to too much eating or drinking or other addictions? If the person you are in love with would only change or solve his or her problems, do you feel your problems would be solved, too? Do you feel a "rush" of adrenaline and power when a coveted person agrees to go to bed with you (more usual for men) or professes love for you (more usual for women)? In general, is your sense of well-being determined more by the state of your love life than by your own life?

If you can answer yes to any of those questions — as so many of us can — then you are still playing a role in some version of the classic script in which romance blooms at a distance, bursts into obsession, and then diminishes into ordinariness — or perhaps unrequited pain. In the true sense of the word's root, *addicere*, "to give oneself up" or "to devote or surrender oneself to something habitually or obsessively," romance can become an addiction, and this cycle can repeat itself again and again. That twelve-step program originated by and for alcoholics, and then expanded to include many other addictions, has now been adapted by those addicted to sex and romance.

But like other addicts, many of us are still in denial: we still believe we can find the rest of ourselves in a foreign substance; that is, in the body and mind of another person. But we didn't invent this dilemma.

Think about it: On the one hand, each of us is born with a full circle of human qualities, and also with a unique version of them. On the other hand, societies ask us to play totalitarian gender roles that divide labor, assign behavior, provide the paradigm for race and class, and are so accepted that they may be seen as part of nature. Societies have been so intent on creating an elaborate difference where none exists that in many languages, even inanimate objects are genderized; thus, one kind of pen may be "feminine" (*la plume*) and another "masculine" (*le stylo*). Yet despite all of these pervasive efforts to categorize and limit everyone and everything, the little boy who is ridiculed for crying "like a girl" doesn't stop feeling sad, he just buries that emotion; and the little girl who is punished for willfulness as a "tomboy" just takes that spirit underground. Later, since both have been told that some parts of themselves are appropriate only to the "opposite sex," they will look for them in other people. In search of inner wholeness, they will try to absorb and possess someone else as Catherine and Heathcliff did — and as you and I probably have done, too.

This polarization of "feminine" and "masculine," this internal mutilation of our whole selves, would be cruel enough if its effects went no further, but the two halves aren't really "halves" at all. Male dominance means that admired qualities are called "masculine" and are more plentiful, while "feminine" ones are not only fewer but also less valued. Thus, boys as a group have higher self-esteem because they are literally allowed more of a self *and* because the qualities they must suppress are less desirable, while girls as a group have lower self-esteem because they are expected to suppress more of themselves *and* because society denigrates what is left. Once adolescence and hormones hit, this lack of a true self in both sexes, this feeling of being incomplete and perhaps also ashamed of parts of oneself that "belong" to the opposite sex, combines with society's intensified gender expectations to make many of us construct a false social persona — in a big way. The boy who has been allowed to retain more than the usual amount of self-esteem by his upbringing may resist this tendency, or only pretend to conform; especially if he has an adult model to follow, support for some "unmasculine" talent, or perhaps a racial, sexual, or other status that strengthens an "outsider" identity. The girl with exceptional self-esteem may get away with such "masculine" qualities as assertiveness and tomboyish behavior — after all, imitation is the sincerest form of flattery, so it's more okay for girls to imitate boys than vice versa — as long as she compensates by becoming a female impersonator in romantic and other social areas. But with low self-esteem, both males and females are likely to seek refuge and approval in exaggerated versions of their gender roles, and thus to become even less complete as they grow up. Inflexibility, dogmatism, competitiveness, aggression, distance from any female quality or person, homophobia, even cruelty and violence, become the classic gender masks of low self-esteem in men. Submissiveness, dependency, need for male approval, fear of conflict, self-blame, and inability to express anger are classic gender masks of low self-esteem in women.

This means that, with low self-esteem, men and women grow more polarized and have more suppressed parts of themselves to project onto others. They then become the objects of an affair, romance, "falling" in love — all the words we instinctively use to describe the addictive "rush" and withdrawal of adrenaline that is so different from the steady well-being of love. In a survey of 400 U.S. psychiatrists by *Medical Aspects of Human Sexuality,* for instance, the majority reported that both women and men with low self-esteem were more likely to be promiscuous, to have difficulty finding fulfillment in sexual relationships, and to be *less* likely to fall *deeply* in love.[6] Even among women and men with healthy self-esteem, a temporary setback or insecurity can increase the appeal of romance, whether it's the scared young man going off to war who falls in love with someone he's only known a few days, or the scared pregnant woman who falls in love with her obstetrician. Indeed, any strong gender trigger may create a romantic chimera for a while, from the woman who gets a crush on a man because he leads masterfully on the dance floor, to the man who falls in love with a secretary who is being paid to support him.

In her novel *The Company She Keeps,* Mary McCarthy described this phenomenon in her heroine: "Now for the first time she saw her own extremity, saw that it was some failure in self-love that obliged her to snatch blindly at the love of others, hoping to love herself through them, borrowing their feelings, as the moon borrowed light. She herself was a dead planet."

Playwright Sherwood Anderson confessed the same thing from a man's point of view: "I've never been able to work without a woman to love. Perhaps I'm cruel . . . I'm like an Irish peasant taking potatoes out of the ground . . . I take from her. I know damned well I don't give enough."[7]

But if romance has its source in an incompleteness of self, it's unlikely to turn into love: the neediness and low self-esteem of the lovers is the worst adversary of anything deeper and more lasting. As Linda Sanford and Mary Ellen Donovan report in *Women and Self-Esteem,* low self-esteem is perhaps the single greatest barrier to intimacy. It makes a woman "terrified of letting someone get too close lest they discover the real her and reject her."[8] And, of course, men experience the same terror, and often an added fear that dependence on a woman or the discovery of "feminine" feelings within themselves will undermine their carefully constructed facade of manliness.

Obviously, jealousy also springs from these feelings of inadequacy and incompleteness. It increases as self-esteem diminishes. The more incomplete we feel, the more obsessed we become with owning someone on whom we've projected all our missing qualities, hence the more jealous we become. Yet gender masks of low self-esteem also make us feel more interchangeable with any other woman or man.

This cycle of gender roles, low self-esteem, romance, jealousy, lack of love and intimacy, even lower self-esteem, *more* exaggerated gender roles, and so on, can be dangerous in every way. As four family therapists found in a study of abusive relationships, it is precisely when men and women conform to traditional roles most rigidly that abuse is most likely to occur. In their words: *"Abusive relationships exemplify, in extremis, the stereotypical gender arrangements that structure intimacy between men and women generally."*[9] And, of course, this violence also has the larger political purpose of turning half the population into a support system for the other half. It polices and perpetuates gender politics by keeping the female half fearful of the moods and approval of the male half. In fact, patriarchy *requires* violence or the subliminal threat of violence in order to maintain itself. Furthermore, the seeming naturalness of gender roles makes male/female violence seem excusable, even inevitable. As G. H. Hatherill, Police Commander of London, put it: "There are only about twenty murders a year in London and not all are serious — some are just husbands killing their wives."[10]

Romance itself serves a larger political purpose by offering at least a temporary reward for gender roles and threatening rebels with loneliness and rejection. It also minimizes the very antipatriarchal and revolutionary possibility that women and men will realize each other's shared humanity when we are together physically for the sexual and procreative purposes society needs. Finally, it privatizes our hopes and distracts us from making societal changes. The Roman "bread and circuses" way of keeping the masses happy — and the French saying that "marriage is the only adventure open to the middle class" — might now be updated. The circus of romance distracts us with what is, from society's point of view, a safe adventure. When it fails, we blame only ourselves.

Perhaps the greatest testimony to the power of this "feminine/masculine" romantic paradigm is that even same-sex couples are not immune to it. Though lesbians and gay men often create more equal partnerships that opposite-sex couples would do well to learn from — especially now that both feminism and the gay movement have challenged old gender roles — we are all living in the same culture, and most of us were born into families where this pattern was assumed to be the only one. Sometimes, gender roles produce an exaggerated version known as doubling, in which two men together may become twice as aggressive, unempathetic, unavailable for intimacy but promiscuous about sex; or two women together may become twice as passive, dependent on one another, and focused on intimacy, with or without sex. For all the internal and external sufferings of same-gender couples in a biased culture, however, at least society doesn't polarize the partners when they leave home every day, and that in itself allows more freedom to explore new forms of balance.

In short, the internal wholeness that allows one to love both one's self and another, freely and joyously, is hard to find anywhere. On the other hand, the personal wreckage caused by romantic obsession is a feature of our everyday landscape. We have only to open a newspaper in any country of the world to read about someone who has been murdered, beaten, or imprisoned in what is known as a "crime of passion." In more than twenty years of speaking on campuses here and in other countries, for instance, I've yet to find one where, within the memory of current students, there wasn't at least one young woman murdered by a jealous lover. Statistically, the man most likely to physically attack or even murder a woman is not a stranger, but someone to whom she is romantically attached. The most dangerous situation for a woman is not an unknown man in the street, or even the enemy in wartime, but a husband or lover in the isolation of their own home. Though women mainly become violent in self-defense or in defense of their children, the power of romantic obsession is so great — and women are so much more subject to it — that even "feminine" nonviolent conditioning can be overcome. When women *do* commit violent crimes, they are even more likely than a man's to be attributable to romance rather than to economics, whether that means the rare crime in which a woman kills out of jealousy or the more frequent one in which a woman is an accessory to a crime initiated by her husband or lover.

What's wrong with romance is neatly summed up by the Valentine's Day 1991 statistics given to me by a judge in Tennessee. In his county courthouse that services Knoxville and environs, there were on that one day: 30 applications for marriage licenses, 60 applications for divorce, and 90 applications for orders of protection against violent spouses.

Will self-esteem cause the withering away of romance? Yes — but only in its current form. After all, romance is one additional very important thing: the most intense form of curiosity. If we weren't so needy, so full of illusions about a magic rescue, so hooked on trying to *own* someone — in other words, if the conscious goal of romance were stretching our understanding of ourselves and others, and not, as it was for Catherine and Heathcliff, looking for the completion of our souls — romance could be a deep, intimate, sensual, empathetic way of learning: of seeing through someone else's eyes, feeling with their nerve endings, absorbing another culture or way of life from the inside, stretching our boundaries, and bringing into ourselves a wider view of the world. If there were equality of power and high self-esteem among women and men, or between two lovers of the same gender, both could have the pleasure of learning and of teaching in this all-five-senses way — without feeling incomplete, angry, or abandoned when romance has run its course.

In the meantime, romance remains among the experiences most written about but least understood. But it's beginning to be demythologized and taken more seriously. Psychologist Charlotte Davis Kasl compares its symptoms ("mood swings . . . distortions of reality") to those of manic-depressive disorders.[11] In many cultures it is "a sacred form of insanity, as sacred as cows are in India," as family therapist Frank Pittman has written.[12] Like every other kind of illness, romance tells us a lot about what is lacking in us — and what to do about it. If, for example, we think about episodes from our own personal romantic histories, we can learn what we're missing, and then consider what we need to do to grow and change. I've contributed a memory of mine in the hope that it will lead you to meditate on one of your own.

Like Heathcliff as a lost child and Catherine as a six-year-old, or like Dante who fell in love with the real Beatrice when both were only eight, children, too, are vulnerable to romance. They're too young for sex and hormones to have much to do with it, but not too young to be restricted by gender and so begin to yearn for wholeness. I remember spending second-grade recesses watching a kind, quiet, dark-haired boy as he ran in the cold with no mittens and a hand-me-down coat. It's the first time I remember feeling "in love," and we exchanged serious valentines. Only now do I understand that I was watching a part of myself race across that playground reserved for boys while girls played quietly by a wall, or that his poverty made him an outsider, and therefore someone I could identify with. Only now do I notice that this first romance came just after a teacher had insisted I could not possibly have written my Thanksgiving poem because its refrain (something like *Not only for the dead but for the living*) was too "adult."

I realize that I kept on falling in love with men who were outsiders, particularly those doing work I longed for myself but assumed I could only do by helping them. I also fell in love with their families, since I was longing for parents, too. Fortunately, I chose kind men with good hearts who loved me back — whether due to good luck or the self-respect my mother had tried to instill in me — and so we remained friends even after the intensity of romance was gone. In this way, I proceeded through college and beyond, trying on the name and life of each man I thought I might marry — thought I would *have* to marry eventually if I was to be a whole person — and acquired one of women's survival skills: getting men to fall in love with us, a form of self-protection that is also a female version of men's sexual conquering. (I'm sure that, as long as shopping and romance are two of women's few paths to a sense of power and well-being in this culture, both will continue to be addictive — and for the same reason.) But since we really believed then that a husband would decide the rest of our lives, marriage became a decision almost impossible to make. If it closed off all other decisions, then it was like a little death. *I'll definitely get married,* I kept thinking, *but not right now. There's this one thing I want to do first . . .* Fortunately, feminism came along to help me and millions of others try to become ourselves, with or without marriage; to understand, in the brilliant phrase of some anonymous feminist, that we could "become the men we wanted to marry." I realized that everyone didn't *have* to live the same way, and this led to a more personal discovery: *I was happy.* If life is what happens while we are making other plans, I had found work I loved and a chosen family of friends while I was waiting for a mythical future.

But sometimes in the middle of life, as Dante said, we come upon "a shadowed forest . . . dense and difficult." That's where I found myself at the end of my forties. Having chosen a particularly insecure, stretched-thin kind of life in a movement trying to change the oldest power difference, but with relatively little power to do it, I had spent most of two decades getting on a treadmill of traveling, organizing, fund-raising, lobbying, working on *Ms.* magazine, and generally doing a triage of emergencies every morning — then falling off the treadmill into bed every night only to get back on it the next day. Though I was privileged to be working in this movement that had given me life and friends I loved, I had less and less time to replenish lost energy — or even to pick up my dry cleaning. Pressure is cumulative. In retrospect, I was redoing the grisly experiment in which a frog, dropped in hot water, jumps out and saves itself; but a frog put in water that is heated *very gradually* stays there and boils to death. After many years in varying kinds of hot water, I was well on my way to becoming the second frog.

Into this time of exhaustion came a man different from others I had known. Instead of working in fields where progress was measured by change in people, he lived in a world where progress was measured in numbers and things. Contrary to my habit of keeping former lovers as chosen family, which seemed odd to many people, his alienation from women who had been his important romances seemed odd to me. Unlike other men in my life, who were as interested in my work as I was in theirs, and who took as much pleasure in finding books, articles, or movies that I might like as I did in doing the same for them, this man answered questions about his own life and childhood, but didn't know how to ask them of someone else.

On the other hand, he had traits I found magnetic. For one thing, he had enormous energy and a kind of Little-Engine-That-Could attitude toward his work that I found very moving. Being work obsessed, too, he didn't mind all my traveling and crazy schedules. For another, he made every social decision (via his staff), so all I had to do was show up, look appropriate, listen, relax at dinners, dance, laugh at his wonderfully told jokes — whatever was on his agenda. I found this very restful. Since I had been helplessly re-creating my caretaking pattern left over from childhood, he seemed the perfect answer: someone I *couldn't* take care of. For a third, he was miserable and said he wanted to change his life, to use his considerable power in new and creative ways. Since I was hooked on helping people change as a way of proving that *I* was alive and valuable, a man who said he was miserable was irresistible. Finally, I was just so . . . *tired.* When I arrived at the airport late one night to find that he had sent a car, its sheltering presence loomed out of all proportion. Remember the scene in *Bus Stop* when Marilyn Monroe, a desperate singer in a poor café, wraps herself in the warm, rescuing sheepskin jacket of her cowboy lover? Well, that was the way I felt sinking into that car.

So I reverted to a primordial skill that I hadn't used since feminism had helped me to make my own life: getting a man to fall in love with me. As many women can testify, this is alarmingly easy, providing you're willing to play down who you are and play up who he wants you to be. In this case, I was aided by my travel and his work and social schedule, which left us with little time to find out how very different we were. And also by something I didn't want to admit: a burnout and an erosion of self so deep that outcroppings of a scared sixteen-year-old had begun to show through. Like a friend who lost weight and, with the burning away of her body fat, reexperienced an anesthetic that had been stored in it from an operation years before, I had lost so much energy and hope that I was reexperiencing romantic rescue fantasies that had been forgotten long ago.

The only problem was that, having got this man to fall in love with an inauthentic me, I had to *keep on* not being myself. Thus, I had to ignore the fact that the cost of a casually purchased painting on his wall was equal to what I had come up with for movement groups in years of desperate fund-raising — and was by a famously misogynist artist at that. I had to suppress the thought that his weekend house cost more than several years' worth of funds for the entire women's movement in this country — and maybe a couple of other countries besides. If I was to be his companion, I had to ignore how obliterated most of my chosen family felt in the company and conversation he enjoyed; indeed, how marginalized they made me feel, too. If I was to be properly appreciative for the advice he gave to me and some of the women I worked with — advice I'm sure he thought of as helpful — I had to forget that, like a gourmet recipe for people with no groceries, it had no practical application. Indeed, even the laughter we first so delightfully shared turned out to be generated by very different senses of humor: his centered around jokes he collected in a notebook and recited wonderfully, complete with ethnic accents; mine was improvised and had a you-had-to-be-there perishability.

I'm sure you know what's coming. So did all my friends. But it took me much longer. Having for the first time in my life made a lover out of a man who wasn't a friend first — my mistake, not his, since I was the one being untrue to myself — I had a huge stake in justifying what I had done. When he supported the same policies and hierarchies that I was working to change, I thought: Nobody said we had to have the same views. When I told him about a trip I'd made to raise a few thousand dollars for a battered women's shelter that was about to close down, and he in the next breath celebrated an unexpected six-figure check that, he joked, would buy a good dinner, I said to myself: It's not his fault he can't empathize — and besides, everyone can change. When a small inner voice began to miss the comfort and eroticism that comes with empathy and sensuality, I thought: If I treat him as I want to be treated, this can change, too. In other words, I made all the classic errors of romance, including one I'd never made before: loving someone for what I *needed* instead of for what *he was*. Far from being a light in my Dantesque "shadowed forest," this relationship became a final clue that I was really lost.

I got lonely and depressed — and then more lonely and more depressed. When I finally tried to voice these feelings that I'd been having all along but *not* voicing, he got mystified — and then angry. But there's something to be said for hitting bottom: as with swimming, it may be the only way to propel oneself back up again. To quote Dante, let me "retell the good discovered there."

After two years, when my last bit of energy and faith in my own judgment was fast disappearing, I finally got down past the scared sixteen-year-old, and came to a clear childhood voice that actually said, "Are you going to condemn yourself to this?" It was such a surprise that it made me laugh. Of course, my well-socialized adult self ignored it for quite a while — but it was the beginning.

Slowly, I began to realize there might have been a reason why I was attracted to someone so obviously wrong for me. If I had been drawn to a man totally focused on his own agenda, *maybe I needed to have an agenda of my own*. Finally, I began to make time to write. If I had felt comforted by the elaborate organization of his life, *maybe I needed some comfort and organization in my own*. Therefore, I enlisted the help of friends to take the stacks of cardboard boxes out of my apartment and started the long process of making it into a pleasant place to live. I even began to save money for the first time in my life. If I had been drawn to simple-minded fun and dancing, *maybe I should get off the treadmill and ask myself the revolutionary question: What do I enjoy?* Finally, I interrupted my triage of emergencies and started taking the initiative to do a few things I loved. If I had glossed over the world's most obvious differences in values (for instance, he advocated trade with a government I got arrested for protesting), *maybe I should have a more realistic idea of what distances I could bridge.* I began to focus my energy on what I might be able to do — and to question why I was so often drawn to attempting what I couldn't. Finally, if I had been interested for the first time in my life in a man who really didn't know what other people were thinking or feeling, *perhaps I had to face the fact that I had the usually "feminine" disease of being empathy sick — of knowing other people's feelings better than my own.* It was a crucial signal that I needed to look inward for solutions instead of outward — a change of which this book is a part.

And perhaps most of all, if I had fallen in love with a powerful man, I had to realize that I was in mourning for the power women need and rarely have, myself included.

I don't mean to make this a neat ending. Romances don't have them. I had deceived him by deceiving myself, and I'm still working on what I learned. But I do know that I chose an opposite as a dramatic example of what I missed in myself. Even allowing for my dissembling, perhaps that's what he was doing, too.

Clearly, romance can arrive with all its obsession whenever we're feeling incomplete, at any age or station of life — and as I can testify, even when we know better. We hurt both ourselves and other people when we become who they want us to be instead of who we really are. Nonetheless, the prospect of getting unhooked from this obsession sometimes creates as much anxiety as giving up *any* addiction: Where will that "rush" of excitement come from? Who will we become?

I think the truth is that finding ourselves brings more excitement and well-being than anything romance has to offer, and somewhere, we know that. Think of the joy of self-discovery: solving a problem, making a bookcase, inventing a dance step, losing oneself in a sport, cooking for friends, writing a poem — all by reaching within for a vision and then making it real. As for who we will be, the answer is: We don't know; we *are* on the edge of history. But we do know that growth comes from saying yes to the unknown.

Donna Jensen, a friend and an expert on how we relate to one another — in couples, families, and organizations — gave me this list of past excesses and the golden mean that is the future:

"Masculine" Extreme	*Wholeness*	*"Feminine" Extreme*
Domineering	Creative	Victimized
Angry	Relaxed	Depressed
Dictates	Invites	Begs or schemes
Knows everything	Curious	Knows nothing
Arrogant	Attentive	Shut down, numb
Out of touch with one's own feelings	Draws self-wisdom from feelings	Overwhelmed by one's own feelings
Unwilling to show weakness	Flexible	Unwilling to show strength
Ignores own mistakes or blames others	Learns from mistakes	Makes excuses or obsesses about mistakes
Feels superior	Feels equal	Feels inferior

When the choice is so clear, who wouldn't say yes to a whole self in the center?

To figure out more personally what you need to do to get there, try this exercise:

Write down — in whatever order or form they come to you — all the things you want in an ideal lover.

You have just described the rest of yourself.

II *Learning Love*

"I have now been married ten years. . . . I am
my husband's life as fully as he is mine. . . . To
talk to each other is but a more animated and
an audible thinking."
JANE EYRE

Charlotte Brontë felt so close to Emily that the tragically
bad notices for *Wuthering Heights* kept her from enjoying the generally good ones for her own first novel, *Jane Eyre,* published only
a few months later. For her part, Emily was such a private person
that she talked almost only with Charlotte. And talk they did. Each
evening after supper while pacing around the parlor table "like rest-
less wild animals," they discussed their own writing projects and
their revolutionary theory of the novel. As poets, they wanted to go
beyond the realistic observation of events that had been the novel's
mainstay thus far ("more real than true," as Charlotte once said of
Jane Austen), and try for poetic power in language and psychological
revelation in narrative. These long nightly talks between two im-
mensely talented sisters still in their twenties, as critic Q. D. Leavis
was to observe more than a hundred years later, "led to the novel's
becoming the major art form of the nineteenth century."[13]
But here the similarity between these two women ended. In
spite of sharing everything from parentage to professional dreams,
and even with the uncommon influence each had upon the other,
these two women had such different inner lives — and from them,
created such different characters and ideas of love and power — that
they are still among the best testimonies to the unique self in each
of us. Unlike Emily's protagonists, Charlotte's never searched for
romantic completion through others; and unlike Emily's only novel,
Charlotte's didn't end with the hint that love was a subject for the
distant future. In *Jane Eyre* as in her other novels, Charlotte made

self-completion the goal, the struggle to preserve an independent spirit the underlying tension, and loving oneself the only path to loving others. "One of the impressive qualities of Charlotte Brontë's heroines, the quality that makes them more valuable to the woman reader than Anna Karenina, Emma Bovary, and Catherine Earnshaw combined," as Adrienne Rich wrote, "is their determined refusal to be romantic."[14]

Of course, this may come as a surprise to many who saw the romance-addicted Hollywood version of *Jane Eyre*. It filtered out all but the novel's central episode — and distorted even that. What's left is the barest plotline of a poor young governess who falls in love with her rich employer, discovers he has concealed a mad first wife in the attic, runs away because there can be no legal marriage, and then returns after the wife has been conveniently killed in a fire that also blinds the man, thus giving the governess a chance to be a selfless caretaker for the rest of her life. But if that were Charlotte Brontë's message, she would have gone down in history as simply another creator of the Gothic novel — that poor-young-woman and rich-older-man standby that depends for its zing on sex plus a woman's inability to get rich on her own. Gothic romances provide for many women readers what sports and war stories do for many men: a fantasy of power.

In the real novel, however, Jane doesn't meet Mr. Rochester until a quarter of the way through the story. By then, the reader is already hooked on seeing the world through the clear eyes of a very well centered heroine. *Jane Eyre* is one of the first female versions of the classic hero's journey from adolescence to maturity — and an amazingly up-to-date one at that. From her first appearance as a ten-year-old orphan thrown on the mercies of a well-to-do aunt and cousins who humiliate her, to her graduation from a charity school where poor young women are turned into governesses for the wealthy, Jane shows herself to be one of those rare young girls who escape the fate society holds in store. Perhaps Jane's status as an orphan saved her by giving her such good reason to harden herself against the expectations of others, or perhaps her harsh circumstances placed her as far outside convention as the Brontës themselves were. In any case, she is rebellious from the beginning.

When Jane arrives at her aunt's house as a lonely little girl, for instance, she is advised to put up with anything and act grateful, but her child's sense of honesty won't let her. When "the young master," her teenage cousin, hurls a book at her head to show that she is a beggar with no right to use the family library, she calls him all kinds of imaginative names. When her aunt locks her up as punishment, she gets sick from the sheer injustice of it. Strengthened and emboldened by the motherly affection of a servant, Jane confronts her cruel aunt-by-marriage with all the weapons in her small arsenal: "I'm glad you are no relation of mine. I will never call you aunt again as long as I live. I will never come to see you when I am grown up; and if anyone asks me how I liked you, and how you treated me, I will say the very thought of you makes me sick, and that you treated me with miserable cruelty."

Not only does she express anger, but she's not guilty about it: "Ere I had finished this reply, my soul began to expand, to exult, with the strangest sense of freedom, of triumph, I ever felt. It seemed as if an invisible bond had burst and that I had struggled out into unhoped-for liberty." It's little wonder that women readers taught to swallow angry words have loved this heroine who doesn't.

Branded a liar and sent to a Spartan school whose headmaster wants "to mortify in these girls the lusts of the flesh," she has the good sense to form alliances with a kind teacher and a classmate who help her to survive — a sort of feminist underground within the school's patriarchy. Yet she knows they are not the ultimate authority either. Though still only ten, she has enough moral compass to disagree with this older classmate on the Christian wisdom of turning the other cheek. "I must resist those who punish me unjustly," she explains. "It is as natural as that I should love those who show me affection, or submit to punishment when I feel it is deserved." Indeed, this gift for seeing herself in perspective allows her to be the "I" of her own story. It's almost impossible to imagine Heathcliff or Catherine as a narrator.

At eighteen, having received an education and survived many hazards, Jane explains: "I desired liberty . . . change, stimulus . . . at least a new servitude!" In this spirit of adventure she places an ad for a position as governess and becomes the teacher of a young French girl who is the ward (and illegitimate daughter) of the infamous Mr. Rochester.

As we all know, she falls in love with him. According to Adrienne Rich: "Jane, young, inexperienced, and hungry for experience, has to confront the central temptation of the female condition — the temptation of romantic love and surrender." [15] But even with all the cards of worldly power stacked against her, Jane doesn't project longed-for qualities of her own onto this man: to a miraculous degree for Victorian England, she has refused to suppress them. Instead, she tries to understand him as an individual through long evenings of conversation in which, as intellectual equals despite their twenty-year age difference, they talk about everything from her paintings of internal landscapes to his affair with the woman who gave birth to her young student. When their first love scene does come about, it is after she saves his life, not vice versa. She wakes him from a smoke-drugged sleep (a fire set, as the reader will soon discover, by his mad first wife during a rare attempt at escape). He then confesses that he had known at first sight that "you would do me good . . . delight . . . my very inmost heart."

But, as we come to understand, this romantic focus on his own needs doesn't bode well. He later tries many deceptions: lying about his interest in another woman to make Jane jealous; trying to redesign her with clothes and jewelry; and finally, tricking her into confessing romantic feelings for him. He does succeed in becoming, as Jane says, "my whole world; and more than the world; almost my hope of heaven," but by that time, both she and the reader have the uneasy sense that this romance is doomed. Though the existence of his first wife is revealed only on their wedding day, it isn't just propriety that makes Jane refuse his entreaties to flee to France and live with him. By the time he finally tells her the truth about this invalid wife kept in the attic — a wealthy West Indian he had married partly from greed and partly from lust* — Jane is clear-sighted enough to understand that this romantic story he relates in a last-ditch bid for her sympathies, a tale of instant attraction and eventual revulsion, reveals a pattern that has doomed other women in his life and will doom her, too.

* For a view of this story as it might have looked through the mad wife's eyes, see the Jean Rhys novel *Wide Sargasso Sea*.

"Hiring a mistress is the next worse thing to buying a slave," Rochester had said in explaining his unhappy years in Europe while legally chained to a mad wife at home; "both are often by nature, and always by position, inferior: and to live familiarly with inferiors is degrading. I now hate the recollection of the time I passed with Celine, Giacinta, and Clara." Jane realizes that "if I were so far to forget myself . . . as . . . to become the successor of these poor girls, he would one day regard me with the same feeling which now in his mind desecrated their memory." Even his illegitimate daughter he refers to as "a dancer's bastard." Surrendering to romance, Jane realizes, might eventually reduce her, too, to a mad woman in the attic.

So, though she suffers enormous pain at leaving him, she flees this powerful, fascinating man with whom she has become so enmeshed — not as a Gothic heroine preserving her honor, but as a real woman saving her true self. With just enough money to take the first coach anywhere, she finds herself in a strange village and becomes ill from wandering in the cold rain. A young clergyman and his sisters rescue her. After she is well again and working as a teacher of farmers' children, she dreams of Rochester sometimes — but has no intention of returning. Better to be "a village schoolmistress, free and honest," she explains, than "fevered with delusive bliss one hour — suffocating with the bitterest tears of remorse and shame the next."

There is one more temptation: the very modern one of giving her life to the cause of a high-minded husband. Asked by the young clergyman to marry him and go to India, she recognizes the coldness and egotism with which he assumes that her life should be secondary to his missionary work. "If I were to marry you," she tells him, "you would kill me. You are killing me now." He is shocked and calls her "unfeminine." Shouldn't a woman sacrifice herself to a husband's good cause? It's one of many questions that love would answer differently than romance.

But Jane shows her gratitude to this clergyman and his two sisters who saved her life. When an uncle dies and leaves her a tidy sum of money, she insists on sharing it equally with them. She also keeps enough money to be independent, and refuses to sacrifice herself to her students. "I want to enjoy my own faculties," she explains, "as well as to cultivate those of other people." Thus, she has work, people she loves, and even — that great rarity for a woman — financial independence, when, in a mystical experience, she hears the sound of Edward Rochester's voice calling her name across the miles. She is now ready to hear it.

With the exception of Mister in *The Color Purple,* perhaps no male character is more changed by events over the course of a novel than the one she now finds. His injury and blindness from a fatal fire set by his wife are the least of it. He has a new acceptance of much that is outside his control. Instead of anger at what has been taken away from him, he appreciates what is left, as if blindness had focused his view inward and allowed him to see himself for the first time. For her part, Jane tells him, "I love you better now, when I can be really useful to you, than I did . . . when you disdained every part but that of the giver and protector."

Their sensuousness and sensitivity together are very moving. Their long talks are as interesting as their earlier ones, but without the intellectual jousting. Their whimsy and tenderness together are a long way from the imbalance of a Gothic novel. Because they are two unique people who *act* loving toward each other, we believe Jane when she says, after one child and a decade of marriage at the end of the novel: "To be together is for us to be at once as free as in solitude, as gay as in company."

It's not easy to generalize about love. Like each person who feels its invisible filaments stretching to another person, it is unique in each instance. Unlike romance, whose plots are uniform enough to be conveyed by shorthand — "if-I-can't-have-you-no-one-will," "transitional affair," "middle-age crazy," "the other woman," "wartime romance," and so on — love has no standard storyline and no agenda except to deepen the joys and cushion the blows of very individual lives. As Robin Morgan sums up in *The Anatomy of Freedom,* "Hate generalizes, love specifies." And romance generalizes, too. When we look for a missing part of ourselves in other people, we blot out their uniqueness. Since most of us have been deprived along gender lines, we generalize about the "opposite sex" (or about any group that becomes "the mysterious other"), thus rendering it a blank screen on which we project our hopes (in romance) or our fears (in hate). No wonder romance turns so easily to hate, and vice versa.

But characteristics of love hold as true for lesbian and gay couples, who may be love's pioneers in our own time, as for Charlotte Brontë's daring nineteenth-century lovers. As described by those who experience them, they are remarkably similar to the marks of high self-esteem:

Each partner feels loved for an authentic self. Jane Eyre had to discover the independent part of herself through adventure, and Rochester found the dependent part of himself through tragedy. Romance, on the other hand, is about possessing and changing, and that's the way people discuss it. The man who falls in love with a strong and independent woman and then tries to tame her, for instance, is not loving but conquering; a common romantic plot ever since *The Taming of the Shrew.* The woman who is obsessed by the question "How can I change him?" is not centered in her own life but trying to control his; a plot that's common when women marry their lives instead of leading them.

Each one knows she or he could get along without the other — but doesn't wish to. Free choice is essential to love. We can't say yes to anyone unless we can also say no. Catherine and Heathcliff could do neither. Jane could stay with Rochester only after she was sure she could survive on her own. To be locked in an intimacy one can't leave, for whatever reason, is to eventually feel resentment: what Camus described as "an autointoxication — the evil secretion, in a sealed vessel, of prolonged impotence." Which is why, as Clare Boothe Luce once explained: "With the equality of the sexes, there will be a lot more love in the world."

There is plenty of room for playfulness, lightness, and humor. When two realities bump up against each other in intimacy, romance views the contradictions with anger or disillusionment, but love acknowledges them with humor. Romance is inflexible because it tries to predict and control, while love is open-handed and can improvise. Perhaps that's why phrases like "I married him because he made me laugh," "We laugh a lot," and "Joking about my day with her always makes it better" are so often heard when people try to describe the otherwise indescribable feeling of love. No wonder *Jane Eyre* has passages that make us smile, but *Wuthering Heights* does not.

Each partner feels empathy for the other. Between the "masculine" extreme of focusing only on oneself (for instance, Heathcliff taking out his need for vengeance by marrying Catherine's sister-in-law) and the "feminine" one of focusing only on other people (for instance, Catherine immobilized between Heathcliff and her husband), there is a midpoint of empathy and balance. Each partner maintains a strong internal "center," yet can also see life through the other's eyes. Charlotte Brontë embodies this image quite literally by having Jane "see" for the blinded Rochester. She takes pleasure in reading to him, describing the countryside, the weather — and he, who had been unable to accept help even from his servants, accepts this service because he feels her pleasure in it. Because we can imagine Rochester feeling the same pleasure in being Jane's "eyes" if their positions were reversed — a big change from all the romances that are far too "gendered" to be reversible — we know Jane isn't just one more woman in a caretaking role. As Simone de Beauvoir wrote, "Genuine love ought to be founded on the mutual recognition of two liberties; the lovers would then experience themselves both as self and the other."

Love is not about power. Romance is a means to the end of self-completion, but love is an end in itself. Or, as Margaret Anderson put it, "In real love, you want the other person's good. In romantic love you want the other person." If we love someone, we want them to continue being the essence of themselves. If so, then we can't own, absorb, or change them. We can only help them to become what they already are. When we argue with someone we love, for instance, it's more about trying to make ourselves understood than trying to win. "Perhaps that's what love is," as essayist and biographer Phyllis Rose said, "the momentary or prolonged refusal to think of another person in terms of power."

Of course, everything is a journey, and nothing is a destination. But it seems to be true that, once we are past the early stages of absorbing parental love, some core of self-esteem is a vital preface to allowing ourselves to feel loved by others.

Take, as lawyers would say, a hypothetical case: Suppose the perfect lover were to suddenly appear. Without a core feeling of self-esteem, this perfection would soon be marred: *What if he or she sees beneath my facade to who I really am?* Jealousy would set in: *Some-*

one *"better" than I am will surely come along.* So would posses-
siveness: *If I lose this person, I will lose the only one who loves
me — since I do not.* With really low self-esteem, we might even
bypass these steps and go straight to devaluing the lover: *If he loves
me, there must be something wrong with him. If she went to bed
with me, she would go to bed with anyone.* In the immortal words
of Groucho Marx, "I wouldn't want to belong to any club that
would accept me as a member."

All this sounds like common sense — but unfortunately, it isn't
common. There are many more people trying to *meet* the right person than to *become* the right person. The genius of *Jane Eyre* was
in showing us that the wrongness or rightness of a lover depends
partly on our readiness to appreciate what is unique and best in him
or her. We may turn a wrong one into a right one — and vice
versa — by how we feel about ourselves. But our world is no more
ready to hear that message than Charlotte Brontë's was.

So here we are, locked in ideas of the romantic rescue, the magical "other." Yet without looking inward, an individual woman may
go on choosing angry men because they express the anger that she
holds in. Or a man may go on marrying women he wouldn't hire
because he can't imagine women as equals (think of the loneliness
expressed by Rochester in his speech about mistresses). But even if
we're lucky enough to have been raised in an exemplary way,
women who express anger often get punished, and so do men who
bond with women. We have to face the fact that striving for a whole
self means going against — and thus helping to change — most of
current culture. But however great the struggle, the rewards are even
greater.

In spite of all our gender-role socialization, for instance, sex-
typing scales show that females who are more "androgynous" —
that is, who incorporate more "masculine" qualities along with their
gender-appropriate ones — have considerably higher self-esteem
than those who rate as exclusively "feminine." Perhaps this isn't a
total surprise, since "masculine" traits (for instance, independence
and autonomy) are more valued in a male-dominant society than
"feminine" ones (for instance, interdependence and connectedness).
But the reverse is also true. Males who incorporate more "feminine"
traits actually have slightly higher self-esteem than do those who rate

as exclusively "masculine." This is true in spite of the fact that society creates more behavioral situations that reward "gender-appropriate" traits, and also imposes more social penalties on men who deviate from gender norms than on women who do the same.[16] Even though imitation is the sincerest form of flattery — and it's far worse for men to become "like women" than vice versa — wholeness still has the edge.

Studies of creativity make the same point: creative people have both higher-than-average self-esteem *and* higher-than-average degrees of androgyny. The ability to impose one's own view of reality, as the artist does, requires a degree of self-confidence. Furthermore, creativity is most likely to come from intrinsic interest, not external reward; from a desire to express the true self.[17] It's not surprising that our cultural images of creativity tend toward the androgynous, from the erotic androgyny of the double-sexed god Eros to the Hindu Kama and other gods of love and creation, from the intellectual androgyny of Virginia Woolf and the Bloomsbury group to priests in skirts giving symbolic birth with baptismal/birth fluid, and long-haired male artists.[18]

But for most men and most women, gender differences are only too distinct, and nowhere are the consequences of their differentness more painfully felt than in relations with each other. While women are encouraged to communicate, nurture, and otherwise develop those qualities that have special importance in maintaining loving relationships, men are rarely allowed to put as much energy into their intimate relationships as into their work, or to develop those "feminine" skills that would make those relationships rewarding. One has only to look in a bookstore to see the consequences. I picked up four current books that profess to be for the sensitive "new man," for instance, but not one listed "love" or "romance" in the index. Though there is a new emphasis on men connecting emotionally with their fathers, there is no parallel emphasis on men connecting intellectually with their mothers. Among the more plentiful books for the "new woman," however, there were a dozen that put "love" or "romance" right up in the title; many on mother-daughter problems; and several with chapters on the importance of the father-daughter connection. *Women Who Love Too Much* and other such books are helpful — but why is there nothing called *Men Who Love Too Little?* Until men are as focused on love, connectedness, and relationship as women are, the problems in those mutual areas can't be solved.

If a long-term solution is in sight, it comes from raising children. Men who raise them *do* change. In one study, single fathers and employed married mothers had almost identical levels of "feminine" traits, in spite of all their preceding years of socialization.[19] Charlotte Brontë's transformed Rochester has been ridiculed by critics as a "woman's man," someone symbolically castrated by blindness who thus becomes more sensitive and connected to others. But perhaps he is a harbinger of a future man who will be made whole not by a tragedy, but by the daily needs and joys of nurturing children. Though Rochester was an idealization in Charlotte Brontë's day, he might turn out to be, to reverse her comment about Jane Austen's novels, "more true than real." After all, patience, flexibility, empathy, interdependence — all these things are present in every male child. They only need to be required and rewarded instead of ignored and punished.

What if men not only raised children but were *raised* to raise children — so that even men who are not fathers, like women who are not mothers, still develop these traits that allow them to better connect to other people? As Dorothy Dinnerstein explains in such historic depth in *The Mermaid and the Minotaur,* the imbalance that so pains both sexes could diminish, and so could violence, both public and private. We might realize, as Rilke wrote in *Letters to a Young Poet,* that "the sexes are more related than we think, and the great renewal of the world will perhaps consist in this, that man and maid, freed from all false feeling and aversion, will seek each other not as opposites, but as brother and sister, as neighbors, and will come together as *human beings.*"

Whatever is best for our collective future, we will only discover it by looking with clear eyes at what made love possible in our individual pasts. Here is a story of mine — in the hope of eliciting yours:

When we first met in the late 1960s, he was a quiet presence in a noisy group arguing about the merits of a political campaign. I remember thinking that he looked like a large friendly tree, inclining slightly toward us as he listened intently, with an occasional response when the wind of our talk rustled in his branches.

Later, as our group of political organizers and reporters toured the Southern inner city where this man had been born and to which he had returned as a doctor, I could feel the suspicion in a storefront clinic: Was I, the only person of the wrong color for this neighborhood, just one more reporter come to record poverty and do nothing and leave? After a while, he said quietly in an apparent non sequitur, "She can't help what color she is, you know." The conversation went right on like water flowing over a rock, but the suspicion dissolved.

As our tired group went to dinner at the end of the day, I noted again that, unique among us, he seemed to feel no need to talk, to entertain, to show off what he knew. Some of the local activists began to relax into reminiscing about the great musicians who had been born in this neighborhood, perhaps eaten at these very tables, and both this man and I began remembering favorite lyrics. I realized that we were moved by the same things — and I could feel him sensing this, too. We continued our group conversation, but now, we were really talking to each other.

For the rest of that summer, he came for weekends to my city, I went to his, or we met in between. We walked the hot streets that everyone else was trying to get out of, went to movies, enjoyed free concerts, and ate every possible kind of ethnic food. It felt as if we had always known each other, yet also as if we were just exploring and exploding into a new part of ourselves. Sometimes, we stayed in all weekend talking, making love, listening to the new music tapes we brought each other, watching old movies, and ordering food so we never had to go out. Sometimes, we explored new places to dance, buy old books, or shop for clothes. Always there were just the two of us. Somehow, we felt complete on our own. Once when an older white man in a movie line struck up a conversation with us, he punched my friend in the stomach and asked about "pro ball" (assuming any tall black man must be an athlete), then made a sexual comment to me (assuming any white woman with a black man must be fair game) Later, we talked and laughed about the linkage between those stereotypes. Being together made it possible to laugh.

In spite of our different lives, we discovered just how much we shared: from mothers who got tears in their eyes when they talked about Roosevelt to feeling like outsiders and optimists at the same time. I could see he hadn't known a woman before who was in movement work, too — his wife had left him for a better prospect when he gave up his prosperous medical practice to set up free clinics — and this made him surprised and appreciative when I could help with speeches or strategizing. For my part, I hadn't known a man before who was so comfortable with what were usually female experiences. I was touched when he heard what I said and its emotional subtext, delighted that he enjoyed shopping for groceries or sprucing up a room, and amazed to discover that he noticed the little peripheral things that many men miss.

After meeting his parents, I could see where these companionable gifts had come from. As the oldest child looking after younger ones, he had learned to iron clothes, braid hair, cook very well, and always temper his strength with gentleness. In his parents, I could see the source of his inner strength. They were two deep-rooted trees, too. They had taught him to feel neither higher nor lower than anyone — but as good as anyone; to feel sorry for those who thought some people were born better or worse than others; and to know that he was worthy of the best. The suit they bought him for his grade-school graduation and could ill afford, for instance, was literally the best in the store. It was an object lesson he never forgot: even if you could afford almost nothing, you still deserved the best.

After he met my mother and understood my childhood, I think he also sensed why I had come to be "the man of the family" very young. Though we just enjoyed each other without examining why at the time, I can see now that I was more of a companion for him because of the "masculine" in me, and he made me feel at ease and understood because of the "feminine" in him.

We went on in this way for several years. Then our friendship went through a gradual process of change. I traveled too much; he had too little respite from his work. He was frighteningly ill for a while, and, as I realized later, taking care of him pressed such a painful and familiar nerve in me after the years of caretaking for my mother that I responded to him in the same way: I was right there and responsible, but turned off emotionally — a familiar form of automatic pilot. And then there was a more lasting phenomenon: we worried about such similar things that we each began to need someone with perspective to get us out of deep grooves in our minds.

After a year or so of painful times of which the above is only a summary, we entered into a new era of being each other's chosen family. We both have other partners, which is a private part of our lives, but on all the other basics, we talk. There are many moves I wouldn't make, from political decisions to major life changes, without his advice — and many that he wouldn't undertake without mine. I realize as I write this that in these last twenty years, there hasn't been a week in which we haven't checked in, asked for an opinion, calmed our mutual paranoia that something has happened to the other, shared a joke, commiserated about some injustice, brought the other a present from some far-off place, celebrated a birthday, recommended a book, helped with a speech or an article, taught each other a new dance step, or shared a cup of tea.

I know he is right there with unconditional love and loyalty — and he knows I am, too. Neither of us can imagine growing old without the other. With health and luck, we'll never have to.

Perhaps what characterizes romance is its separateness from other deep feelings — for a friend or a child, for the ocean or a sheltering tree. What marks love is: It's all the same.

We have far better chances for love than in the Brontës' day — yet our consciousness of them lags far behind.

For instance: We still think of love as "happily ever after." That was a myth even in the nineteenth century, when, as Margaret Mead pointed out, marriage worked better because people only lived to be fifty. (Charlotte Brontë herself died at thirty-nine of toxemia during her first pregnancy.) Though an average life span is now thirty years longer in many countries of the world, we haven't really accepted the idea of loving different people at different times, in different ways. It's possible to raise children with a loved partner and then move amicably on to a new stage of life, to love someone and yet live apart, to forge new relationships at every phase of life, even at the very end — in short, to enjoy many different kinds of love, in a way that doesn't hurt but only enriches.

For instance: Many more women now have the freedom that

comes with self-support, not just a few with the unlikely inheritance of Jane Eyre; yet many still assume a man must be older, taller, earn more, weigh more, be the "right" race, class, and religion, better educated, and so on. In other words, we are still looking for forms of security, strength, and social approval that we no longer need — and thus missing love.

For instance: Many women and men who considered themselves heterosexual have found themselves deeply in love with someone of the same sex, and many who considered themselves exclusively gay or lesbian have discovered the reverse. It seems that sexuality is not a label but a continuum. Even Heathcliff's cry, "I cannot live without my life!" was given new meaning by the late writer and peace activist Barbara Deming, who used it to express her right to live openly as a lesbian. Black women in Boston then used it to protest their lack of safety in the streets. If we follow the feeling of love, for ourselves and others, it leads us to many new meanings.

For instance: We are more free to explore sensuality and sexuality as part of the pleasurable language of love. "Pleasure — which includes erotic joy but is not limited to it," as Marilyn French wrote, "is the opposite of power, because it is the one quality that cannot be coerced." [20] Pleasure is an expression of the true self.

We need nothing less than a remything of love. I think this poem by Alice Walker — my favorite love poem — is a good beginning: [21]

> I have learned not to worry about love;
> but to honor its coming
> with all my heart.
> To examine the dark mysteries
> of the blood
> with headless heed and
> swirl,
> to know the rush of feelings
> swift and flowing
> as water.
> The source appears to be
> some inexhaustible

spring
within our twin and triple
selves;
the new face I turn up
to you
no one else on earth
has ever
seen.

Seven

A Universal "I"

"We do not 'come into' this world; we come *out* of it, as leaves from a tree. As the ocean 'waves,' the universe 'peoples.' Every individual is an expression of the whole realm of nature, a unique action of the total universe."

ALAN WATTS

I *Learning Nature*

"i keep hearing
tree talk
water words
and i keep knowing what they mean."
LUCILLE CLIFTON

Alice Walker, the poet, essayist, and novelist whose writing crosses every boundary — even that between humans and nature — found her only privacy as the youngest child in a big Southern, rural family by leaving a crowded house to walk in the fields or sit under a tree to read her much-loved books and write her first poems. Nature was a refuge from the long hours of cooking and cleaning expected of the only daughter living at home with hardworking parents and older brothers. Though she now lives in San Francisco and loves its ethnic variety, she still retreats to the quiet countryside to write and to restore her energy and peace. As the millions who love her work know, trees, flowers, and animals are often sentient characters within her writing. Indeed, it's partly this empathy with nature and with country people all over the world — people who often share more with their counterparts a million miles away than with their own nation's big cities — that have made *The Color Purple* and other of Alice's works just as popular in Japan or Australia, in Brazil, Africa, or China, as they are here at home.

My own childhood was almost the opposite. Our family was small, and there was nothing if not privacy in our house, for my mother had withdrawn into a world of her own and my father was often on the road. The fields and trees outside our house in southern Michigan seemed to be only a colder, emptier extension of the isolation inside, and I longed to escape into the animated world I knew from the movies that I begged my father to take me to, or the radio serials and novels that were my idea of what "real life" should be like. Even after my parents separated and my mother and I moved to an old house in Toledo — next to a vacant lot where she sometimes tried to grow hollyhocks amid the refuse, because she herself loved gardens — I still associated any expanse of greenery with sadness, emptiness, and defeat. I hoped one day to live in one of the world's great cities — New York or Bombay, Rome or Hong Kong — which to me meant freedom, excitement, and all the promise of adulthood. Even today, I still work best and feel happiest when I'm sitting, as I am now, in a corner of an urban room, safe in the knowledge that all the choices of a great city lie just outside my door.

Alice and I find each other's preferences a little mysterious. One constant of our long friendship is our mutual attempts at conversion — my hoping to persuade Alice to come to New York and enjoy the infinite variety and energy of its streets (which she sometimes does, though she always goes home with relief), and her suggesting that I buy land next to hers in the hills of Northern California (which I also visit and enjoy, though some part of me wants to walk to a corner drugstore). Neither of us ever quite succeeds in converting the other.

I say this because I've noticed that, like Alice and me, most people have some early association that either attracts them or drives them away from nature. When it's negative, we often justify it instead of figuring out where such alienation came from. During all my years of trying to ignore my childhood, for instance, I insisted that I had just chosen a different energy source: urban crowds. Like a great waterfall or a stand of pine trees in the wilderness, I argued, crowds of people were also a natural resource from which we could draw strength. There is some truth in this argument — we *do* get energy from groups of our own species — but I doubt that many of us feel renewed by the dead concrete and steel in which they gather. Even urban planners in love with high-rise cityscapes know that blocks of inanimate buildings must be broken up by an occasional park or tree. Try imagining Manhattan without its 843-acre Central Park, Calcutta without its green Maidan and banyan trees, or Buenos Aires without its tree-lined boulevards exactly like those in Paris.

Once I began to uncover the reasons I had invested landscapes with such loneliness, I also realized that there were some parts of nature that had always given me comfort: tropical beaches, any desert, English gardens, the sight of the ocean; in other words, anything that *wasn't* a reminder of my Midwestern childhood. Even two people as different in our experience as Alice and me were attracted to many of the same elements of nature — especially the ocean. As Herman Melville wrote in *Moby-Dick,* "Take almost any path you please, and ten to one" it will lead to water. "Why did the old Persians hold the sea holy?" he asked. "Why did the Greeks give it a separate deity?" Because: "There is magic in it." Standing at the edge of this mysterious three fourths of the planet from which we all evolved, we feel returned to some authentic, calming, inner core of ourselves, as if the mere sight of it could wash away all artifice and confusion. Given the power of my response to the ocean, I always thought it was strange that I also loved the desert, until poet and novelist Leslie Silko — who grew up hearing stories of the earth's origins from her Laguna Pueblo family — explained it to me one day as we rode ponies near her Arizona home. "Of course you love the desert," she said. "It used to be the ocean's floor."

Following an instinctive pull toward this or that part of nature takes us back to our natural roots, but many of us have been so educated out of those instincts that we think all progress lies in leaving nature behind. We've learned to respond to its power with "feminine" distance and fear, or "masculine" aggression and control. Having been led down this nongarden path of separation from nature by learning, however, we can unlearn our way back just by looking at everyday life.

Consider our bodies. Just as the planet is three-fourths ocean, our bodies are three-fourths water. When we shed tears or drops of perspiration, they are salty, too. Like the tides and all living things, our bodily processes are influenced by the moon's gravitational pull. Indeed, from conception to birth, each human embryo recapitulates all the stages of human evolution, from a few cells floating in amniotic fluid to a mammalian creature emerging on land. These and many other physical parallels can show our minds what we know in our bones: that each of our bodies contains all the processes of nature.

Consider our speech. Centuries of societies and religions have tried to separate us from nature, but they haven't eliminated from our common parlance those phrases that betray its magnetism. Even in modern parlance that is most estranged, there are some expressions — "back to nature," "at one with nature," "communing with nature" — that convey the pleasure of being in touch with all that is deepest and truest in our inmost selves. Nature is not a metaphor for us. It *is* us.

Consider our cultures. If people regard themselves as part of nature — from the preindustrial indigenous cultures that still survive on most continents to postindustrial ecological settlements — they tend toward a communal, circular paradigm that is modeled on the cycles of birth-growth-death-and-rebirth. If they measure progress by their conquering of nature, they create a hierarchical paradigm, with groups considered "closer to nature" on its lower rungs. In other words, even if we as individuals don't value ourselves according to our closeness to or distance from nature, the hierarchical societies we live in will do it for us. As Marilyn French wrote in *Beyond Power,* her historian's diagnosis of patriarchy: "No really profound sense of human equality can ever emerge from a philosophy rooted in a stance of human superiority over nature."[1]

Unlearning this cultural paradigm of "Man" versus "Nature" will take even longer than creating cultures that unify the "masculine" and "feminine" parts of our selves, but cracking our belief in its universality begins its destruction. Just as a blade of grass growing through a crack in concrete will eventually shatter it, the idea of each of us as an integral part of nature begins to take root. The self as a microcosm of nature's power is a more life-affirming kind of imagery than the notion that our progress depends on our ability to stamp out the natural forces within us — which is, of course, impossible.

Because males in industrialized countries have been asked to value themselves according to their distance from nature, for instance, they have tried to ignore their biological cycles; that is, cycles that follow the daily, monthly, and yearly movements of the moon and the sun. Though menstruation makes women's cycles more obvious, men also have cycles that can be determined by dividing the number of days since their birth by twenty-eight. When a railway company in Japan asked its male employees to do this to discover the days on which they were more accident-prone, its accident rate was cut more drastically than it had been by any other measure. If men are supposed to be *less* governed by cycles than they really are, however, women are punished by the idea that we are *more* governed than we really are. Thus, men are found wanting when they don't measure up to a rocklike, John Wayne constancy, and women are seen as flawed because we are thought to be hostages to overwhelming biology. The result is that both sexes are penalized, and neither is encouraged to learn how to use cycles by going *with* their natural energy.*

Our sensitivities to the circadian, twenty-four-hour rhythms of light and dark also give us such common experiences as jet lag. Studies of workers who upset their biological clocks by sleeping by day and working by night — especially those who change shifts frequently — show a higher than average incidence of mood and medical problems and accident. Recently, some people suffering from lack of energy and recurring depression in seasons when daylight hours are shorter have been diagnosed as having "seasonal affective disorder" (SAD), a newly named syndrome affecting people who are especially light-sensitive, whose treatment consists of sitting for a few hours daily in front of a special light box that sheds full-spectrum light.

Not only is each human being a microcosm of nature, but so is each living cell, circadian rhythm and all. Healthy cells have a metabolic high and low point of activity during the course of each day. One of the ways cancer cells betray their perversity is by inverting this daily cycle. Thus, when healthy cells are *least* likely to multiply, cancer cells are *most* likely to multiply; a fact with significance for the timing of radiation, chemotherapy, and other treat-

* Dr. Estelle Ramey, professor of physiology and biophysics at Georgetown University Medical School in Washington, D.C., has analyzed many studies on men's monthly cycles, including the 1969 experiment by the Omni Railway Company in Japan referred to above, in which accidents were cut by a third over two years, even though traffic increased over the same period. A sixteen-year Danish study also proved men's monthly cycles by testing hormone in urine. With women's more obvious cycles, however, the difference has been their interpretation. Prepatriarchal cultures and religions, including some remaining tribal ones, worship women's childbearing ability, consider menstrual blood sacred, and believe that women have special powers of perception at the onset of their cycle; a belief that in itself had nurtured such powers.

ments aimed at inhibiting the growth of the latter without damaging the former. Cyclical rhythms have long been taken into consideration when giving medications for "morning" or "evening." The importance of such timing was proven over again when amphetamines were given to rats at the low point of their daily cycle of hormones and body temperature, and 6 percent of them were killed. When the same dose was given to their siblings, but timed to the high point of their daily cycle, more than 75 percent were killed. During that daily peak, their brains had been producing their own amphetamines and thus caused an overdose — another instance of proving at animals' expense what is already known from human experience.

But to truly unlearn an artificial self and discover a true one, we need to add to the mind's understanding of examples like these by reconnecting with nature in an immediate sensual way. One extraordinary woman who has done just that has made it her life's work to help others find those links, too.

A Magic Glade

Jean Liedloff was born in New York, but as an eight-year-old going to summer camp in Maine, she had a transforming experience. Lagging behind during a nature walk through the woods, she happened on a glade with a fir tree at one side, a knoll covered with luminous green moss at the center, and the afternoon sun lighting the whole scene against a dark forest. It was "a magical or holy place."

"The whole picture had a completeness, an all-there quality of such dense power that it stopped me in my tracks," she wrote later. "I felt the anxiety that colored my life fall away. This, at last, was where things were as they ought to be." She lay down with her cheek against the moss and promised herself that every night for the rest of her life, she would visualize this magical place before she went to sleep.

> I knew, even at eight, that the confusion of values thrust upon me by parents, teachers, other children, nannies, camp counselors, and others would only worsen as I grew up. The years would add complications and steer me into more and more impenetrable tangles of rights and wrongs, desirables and un-

desirables. I had already seen enough to know that. But if I could keep The Glade with me, I thought, I would never get lost.

She kept this memory of "wholeness" and "rightness" for a long time. Then with adolescence, it began to dim.

"By the time I was about fifteen, I realized with a hollow sadness (since I could not remember what I was mourning) that I had lost the meaning of The Glade."

Later, after the death of her grandmother with whom she had been living, she left college and went to Europe. "My thoughts were not very clear during my grief," she explained, "and because turning to my mother always ended in my being hurt, I felt I had to make a giant effort to get on my own feet. Nothing I was expected to want seemed worth having — jobs writing for fashion magazines, a career as a model, or a further education.

"In my cabin on the ship bound for France, I wept for fear I had gambled away everything familiar to me for a hope of something nameless. . . . I wandered about Paris sketching and writing poetry. I was offered a job as a model at Dior, but did not take it. . . . I still could not have said what I was looking for."

When two young Italians invited her to join their expedition to South America, she accepted without knowing why. After a month of difficult travel up a small, unexplored river in Brazil, she, her Italian companions, and two Indian guides made a base camp. Sitting down with a book one day, she

found a seat among the roots of a large tree that overhung the river. I read . . . not daydreaming but following the story with normal attentiveness, when suddenly I was struck with terrific force by a realization. . . . I had lost it, and now in a grown-up Glade, the biggest jungle on earth, it had returned. The mysteries of jungle life, the ways of its animals and plants, its dramatic storms and sunsets, its snakes, its orchids, its fascinating virginity, the hardness of making one's way in it, and the generosity of beauty all made it appear even more actively and profoundly right. It was rightness on a grand scale.

It was The Glade, lost, found, and now recognized, this time forever. Around me, overhead, underfoot, everything was

right, being born, living, dying and being replaced without a
break in the order of it all.

I ran my hands lovingly over the great roots that held me
like an armchair, and began to entertain the idea of staying in
the jungle for the rest of my life.[2]

This rediscovery set her on a very different path from the one
she had been raised to follow. After five expeditions into the South
American jungle and more than two years living with Stone Age
communities there, she wrote a book about her experiences, *The
Continuum Concept: Allowing Human Nature to Work Successfully,* a much-praised and -translated work from which all the quotations above were taken. As part of lecturing, writing, and working
individually with people as a psychotherapist, her personal experience has created her life's mission: helping people bridge a "normal"
distance from nature and arrive at what she sees as the evolutionary
source of human well-being.*

Jean Liedloff's story is only a more dramatic version of one told
by many people who link the loss of a true self to a loss of the natural world. In women, this seems to happen most often at adolescence. Just as boys are growing into *more* freedom, girls are growing into *less:* they are encouraged to put their "center" into other
people. Even dressing and behaving in a "feminine" way create a
barrier with the natural world, for nature and artifice don't mix
well.

As a result, many women who have given away too much of
themselves often talk of recovering their losses by returning to a
particular garden, a tree house, a mountain path, a lake — anything
that was part of their earlier freedom. At Black Lake, Michigan,
during a women's weekend at the United Auto Workers' education
center, for instance, I talked with factory workers who said those
few days in nature allowed them to recover a lost identity in a way

---

* Her message of reintegrating people with nature and infants and children
with adults has spawned an international network of people evolving practical ways
of accomplishing this in modern life. For a network newsletter and list of members
contact: Liedloff Continuum Network, P.O. Box 1634, Sausalito, California 94965.

that just meeting each other in barren rooms never had. As one woman put it, "It's like going back to the days when we skinny-dipped in quarries and never gave a thought to how we looked." Outward Bound and other wilderness groups help both men and women gain self-confidence, but they are often an especially dramatic turning point for women and girls who have been discouraged from such freedom and exploring. There are even special wilderness weekends for women who are recovering from breast cancer and what may feel like body betrayal, or the loss of identity that can come with divorce. There is a reason why these groups are effective in nature.

In industrialized countries, many women are trying to bring nature back into their daily lives by buying land and restoring its natural state, building wilderness cabins, and organizing their own nature expeditions: a little-publicized part of the women's movement. In agricultural countries, women are rebelling on behalf of nature. A case in point is the Chipko movement that began in the Himalayan foothills twenty years ago when women literally hugged local village trees (*chipko* means "to embrace") in order to save them from the ax — and started a contagion of direct action that has spread to many other countries.[3]

This positive use by women of what in the past was used against us — a closeness to nature — has given birth to a new term: *ecofeminism*. There is now a body of theory and groups in almost every country that see the relationship of humans to nature as the paradigm for our relationships to each other, and also equate our view of nature with our view of the inner self.

It will take a long time to undo the hostile relationship that is implicit in everything from pollution to such rites as fraternity hazings that require conquering a symbolic wilderness, or Lyndon Johnson shooting game from the window of an air-conditioned limousine. But there needn't be a trip to Brazil or an ecology demonstration to help us make this connection to nature. The greatest testimony to its power is the strength to be found in its most modest outcroppings available to us all.

Even on my crowded block in New York City, I see clues to the saving grace of nature. In the last month or so I have observed:

- a teacher in the boys' school across the street who nurtures self-esteem in children by giving them boxes of seedlings to care for;
- a garbage man who takes pride in rescuing discarded plants and nursing them back to health;
- a Wall Street banker who leaves his chauffeur-driven car and gets down on well-tailored knees to pluck weeds from around a spindly city tree outside his townhouse;
- a composer and concert pianist who lavishes all the love of gardening she learned from her family in Mexico on the plants that fill her one-room studio;
- a Chinese acupuncturist who will not treat patients without the healing presence of plants and flowers in the room;
- a homeless woman who carries water back and forth in a paper cup to revive shrubs and flowers in front of houses that she will never occupy;
- a call girl who traded in "the life" for a drug-treatment program after she fatally neglected her most constant companion: an orchid plant she had nursed through ten years of blooming cycles.

In fact, many people can vouch for the increased sense of well-being that comes from living around plants — even if it's only a houseplant or two. Invalids, prisoners, and older people have all been found to gain peace of mind, sometimes even lowered blood pressure and better health, from having the opportunity to care for plants in their rooms. And gardeners work to create havens on rooftops and vacant lots in every city. Robin Morgan, poet, international activist, and inveterate creator of urban rooftop gardens, explained to me why she carries pots and dirt up and down her narrow apartment stairs to create the island of green and growing things celebrated in the title of her poetry collection *Upstairs in the Garden.* "Growing anything gives you the most disproportionate pleasure for your efforts. It's the best evidence of life's infinite durability and regeneration — on all counts, the surest source of faith in oneself."

Few modern writers have evoked the life-transforming powers of nature as vividly as Diane Ackerman, a naturalist, explorer, poet, and self-described "earth-ecstatic." In *A Natural History of the Senses,* she describes the "visual opium" of watching the sun go down through a picture window: "Each night the sunset surged with purple pampas-grass plumes, and shot fuchsia rockets into the pink sky, then deepened through folded layers of peacock green to all the blues of India and a black across which clouds sometimes churned like alabaster dolls."[4]

Seeing — really *seeing* — this incredible display also gave her a sense of proportion that comes from an awareness of life's cycles. "When you consider something like death, after which (there being no news flash to the contrary) we may well go out like a candle flame," she wrote,

> then it probably doesn't matter if we try too hard, are awkward sometimes, care for one another too deeply, are excessively curious about nature, are too open to experience, enjoy a nonstop expense of the senses in an effort to know life intimately and lovingly. It probably doesn't matter if, while trying to be modest and eager watchers of life's many spectacles, we sometimes look clumsy or get dirty or ask stupid questions or reveal our ignorance or say the wrong thing or light up with wonder like the children we all are. It probably doesn't matter if . . . a neighbor, fetching her mail, sees us standing in the cold with our own letters in one hand and a seismically red autumn leaf in the other, its color hitting our senses like a blow from a stun gun, as we stand with a huge grin, too paralyzed by the intricately veined gaudiness of the leaf to move.[5]

II *People and Other Animals*

"All things share the same breath — the beast,
the tree, the human. . . . What are people
without the beasts? If all the beasts were gone,
people would die from a great loneliness of
spirit."
CHIEF SEATTLE'S APPEAL TO
PRESIDENT FRANKLIN PIERCE, 1854

By the time he spoke those words, it was too late for
Chief Seattle to save the ancestral homes of the Duwamish, Suquam-
ish, Skagit, and other Indian nations on land that is now called
Washington and Oregon. At least three quarters of the Indians living
on this continent before Europeans arrived had already perished,
and "Indian removal" was isolating the rest on reservations. The
territory governed by his council of nations was sure to be confis-
cated eventually, regardless of whether the council agreed to its
"sale."

Nonetheless, the chief made a leader-to-leader appeal to President Pierce. "How can you buy or sell the sky, the warmth of the
land?" he asked. "If we do not own the freshness of the air and the
sparkle of the water, how can you buy them?"

Only those who respected nature, he said, could claim it:

Every part of this earth is sacred to my people. Every shining
pine needle, every sandy shore, every mist in the dark woods,
every clearing, and humming insect is holy in the memory and
experience of my people. . . . The perfumed flowers are our
sisters; the deer, the horse, the great eagle, these are our brothers. The rocky crests, the juices of the meadows, the body heat
of the pony, and the people — all belong to the same family.
. . . We know that the white man does not understand our
ways. One portion of land is the same to him as the next, for
he is a stranger who comes in the night and takes from the land

whatever he needs. . . . He treats his mother, the earth, and his brother, the sky, as things to be bought, plundered, sold. . . . His appetite will devour the earth and leave behind only a desert.

Yet the chief's request was not for more payment or even for a continuing claim on the land. He knew that was impossible. What he asked for was on behalf of this land's inhabitants, those who could not speak for themselves. "I will make one condition," he said: "The white man must treat the beasts of the land as his brothers. . . . For whatever happens to the beasts soon happens to the man. All things are connected."[6]

This feeling of connection to all creatures, a feeling shared by the most ancient and psychologically sophisticated of cultures, has been lost or suppressed in centuries of religions that demonized nature and created an otherworldly hierarchy. In the fifth century, Saint Augustine declared animals to be outside God's moral universe; in the thirteenth century, Thomas Aquinas maintained that man had unlimited power over animals by virtue of God's gift to Adam of "dominion" over them; and by the seventeenth century, philosopher René Descartes had concluded that animals were soulless machines with no ability to feel pain — an assumption then "proved" by scientists for whom an animal's cries were no more evidence of feeling than a clock's chiming.

Instead of comparing people to animals as an honor, as ancient and indigenous cultures had done, this hierarchical view used such comparisons to keep people in low-status positions. When eighteenth-century activists objected to racial slavery and to women's status as chattel, for instance, they were ridiculed with the argument that, if slaves and women had rights, soon animals would have them, too. Prejudice justified itself by calling people animal names: reducing a man of color to an ape or a monkey, or woman to a bird or a cow. By the nineteenth century, when Charles Darwin postulated evolutionary links between humans and animals, there was shock and rage at the idea that humans might be connected to these despised creatures who existed only to serve us — a rage fed by repressed sexuality, too, since the church and many other structures of patriarchal society were dedicated to the denial of "animalistic" urges, except for purposes of reproduction. It is partly this desire to suppress an "animal" sexual nature that keeps religious fundamentalists fighting against evolutionary teachings even today.

When evolutionism prevailed, it gave a new respectability and clout to those who felt an empathy with other sentient beings. Thanks to the antivivisectionist and prevention-of-cruelty movements of the nineteenth century, and the twentieth-century groups that argue against everything from sadistic methods of trapping wild animals to the testing of medicines and cosmetics on laboratory animals, people in even the most denatured societies have begun to protest against the cruel treatment and extinction of other species. Though such groups are still trivialized, as if only human concerns could be taken seriously, they are gradually forcing us to reexamine our attitudes toward the animal world and to see in them an index of our attitudes toward each other. For some, this reexamination leads to vegetarianism or to using canvas instead of leather. For others, the concern is just to stop the suffering and wanton killing of animals. After all, Native Americans held the buffalo sacred, yet they killed it for food and skins, sparingly, with apologies to the animal's spirit. What they didn't do was take pleasure in pain or killing for no purpose, upset the balance of nature, take more than they needed, or otherwise defile their links to nature and each other. All that changed when hierarchical views of life began to make human beings the most dangerous species on earth.

The eighteenth-century English rationalized everyday sadism by insisting, as Diane Ackerman documents in *A Natural History of the Senses,*

> that torturing an animal made its meat healthier and better tasting. . . . They chopped up live fish, which they claimed made the flesh firmer; they tortured bulls before killing them, because they said the meat would otherwise be unhealthy; they tenderized pigs and calves by whipping them to death with knotted ropes; they hung poultry upside down and slowly bled them to death; they skinned living animals. Recipe openers from the era said such things as: "Take a red cock that is not too old and beat him to death."[7]

In some ways, the only difference between the days of those recipes and the present is that we are now more distant from the killing. But a critical mass of people in most countries seem to be feeling Chief Seattle's "great loneliness of the spirit." Some postindustrial, nonhierarchical sense of linkage with the animal world seems to be forming: a vision that goes beyond evolutionism's picture of Homo sapiens as the peak of the developmental tree and considers each species as an end in itself. As unsentimental a body as the European Parliament is considering an animal-rights act that would outlaw cockfighting, bullfighting, fox hunting, and other time-honored blood sports. In the United States and Canada, both health and animal-rights activists protest the millions of chickens who live out their lives wedged into a space smaller than the pot they will eventually be cooked in, and whose force-fed, hormone-injected flesh may be a long-term health hazard to those who eat it. The U.S. Supreme Court recently upheld an animal-rights argument against the killing of monkeys for experimental purposes by the National Institutes of Health, and many cosmetic and drug companies are bowing to consumer boycotts and also discovering that some alternatives to animal testing are cheaper, quicker, and potentially more accurate. Even Spanish bullfights, the most famous of all sadistic spectacles, are becoming less popular, especially with younger generations. More and more, we have come to recognize that the devaluing of animal life is a kind of training ground for devaluing all life. As one Spanish activist put it, bullfighting is "the root of all the acts of savagery in our country."[8]

Television and films have helped distant and urbanized people to feel an ancient linkage again by showing us intimate glimpses of animals in their natural habitat. We have also become increasingly outraged witnesses to their fate at the whim of humans: gorillas whose hands are cut off for sale as ashtrays, or tropical birds stuffed headfirst into tight cardboard tubes for a Middle Passage to other countries that few survive. In the American Northwest, bears — the animal that Native Americans considered the model of childrearing — are slaughtered so their gallbladders can be sold as aphrodisiacs in Asia. Throughout the country, abandoned or stolen cats and dogs are sold to hospitals where their vocal cords are sometimes cut so their cries won't disturb experimenters. Internationally the tanker spills that suffocate birds and other sea creatures in coats of oil now average one a day. In the Gulf War of 1991, ther image of one lone, staggering seabird dying after Saddam Hussein's vengeful opening of oil pipelines became for many people around the world the symbol of human waste and cruelty; an emblem of all innocent victims who die each time we go into battle with each other.

Because the truth is: We cannot harden our hearts selectively. In *Fire in the Belly,* Sam Keen warns men especially, who have been so historically pushed toward hard-heartedness, "The ability to feel is indivisible. Repress awareness of any one feeling, and all feelings are dulled. . . . The same nerve endings are required for weeping and dancing, fear and ecstasy."[9]

Bonding with animals — or rather, admitting the bond we work so hard to ignore — is óne way of increasing health and strengthening a sense of self. A wide variety of studies have shown that on the average, people who have pets or live close to animals have lower blood pressure, heart rates, stress levels, and incidence of depression, while enjoying longer life expectancies. Anecdotal evidence shows they also have higher levels of responsibility, independence, self-confidence, and optimism. If you haven't experienced the power of this bonding with pets, start a conversation with any group of friends who have them, and watch the faces light up as they tell stories of creatures with whom they share their homes. Even people institutionalized for catatonic withdrawal have responded for the first time when given an affectionate animal to hold, as have the institutionalized elderly so depressed or overmedicated that they would respond to nothing else. In eighteenth-century Germany and England, hospitals and retreats for the insane discovered that cats, dogs, horses, and birds were healing catalysts, as if the animals' freely given energy could pierce a human wall of isolation.

In this country, programs that teach handicapped people to ride horseback have increased their confidence and independence, and others that allow autistic children to swim with dolphins have resulted in unprecedented levels of response and speech. Some observers have insisted that the dolphins seemed to sense the kids' vulnerability and protect them. Among a group of women prisoners in Washington State, recidivism was eliminated when they were given dogs to train and care for. In Ohio, suicide and depression among the criminally insane were reduced by allowing prisoners to care for fish and small animals in their cells.[10]

For skeptics who say this is the power of expectation — that like a placebo, any intervention works if those participating believe it will — there are also plenty of accidental discoveries. In a California hospital, for instance, nurses were asked to care for a patient's Seeing Eye dog by keeping it at their station. To the surprise of everyone, nurses began to report less job stress, and patients became more active and ambulatory. Among people who have animals but become too ill to keep them at home, there is often an unexpected and rapid decline. In major cities hit hard by the AIDS epidemic, pets have had such a clear impact on the self-esteem of homebound patients that volunteer groups now help to maintain them when their owners can no longer cope. Thanks to one such program in New York City called POWARS (Pet Owners With AIDS/ARC Resource Service), volunteers pay daily visits to feed and walk the pets of bedridden patients. "People with AIDS and ARC often feel like pariahs and outcasts," explains Steve Kohn, a cofounder of POWARS, but animals provide the greatest gift: "a feeling that they are unconditionally loved."[11]

In Northern California, the Animal Assisted Therapy Program, a project of the Society for the Prevention of Cruelty to Animals, has selected kittens and roosters, dogs, guinea pigs, and sometimes even a boa constrictor for their sociability and taken them into children's wards and prisons, abuse shelters, and retirement homes — anyplace where people are feeling robbed of affection and identity. "Animals don't care if a person is losing sight or can't walk," as one of the program leaders explained. "All they want is to love you, and that quality brings out therapeutic things in us." There is also another goal: "What we're primarily doing is helping animals by promoting the idea that they are a very valuable part of our lives."[12]

In fact, animals have been found to boost human morale, communication, and self-esteem more reliably and quickly than almost any other kind of therapy. The animals themselves seem to sense their impact and to thrive — unlike their isolated fate in many zoos and other institutions. As a result of the success of such programs, forty-eight states now permit pets in hospitals, all fifty states allow them in nursing homes, and the National Institutes of Health has officially noted "the crucial role pets may play" in physical and mental health — a big change from a decade ago when the presence of any animal was forbidden in health-care facilities.

Perhaps the least expected testimony to our potential for radical empathy is its crossing not just of species lines, but of elements. In addition to dolphins, other underwater creatures respond to human beings — and vice versa — as scuba divers or aquarium lovers can testify. Diana James, a colleague whose pet for twenty-seven years was a medium-sized turtle, found she and he developed a bond. When she had a cold or a migraine, he became sympathetically ill, and when he was wedged under rocks in his aquarium and in danger of drowning, she awoke in another room to rescue him. In an expedition organized by marine explorers Jacques Cousteau and his son Philippe, scuba divers descended into one of the few ocean areas where spear fishermen, ships' motors, and dragnets had never been, and found an underwater life that was curious, friendly, and unafraid. Fish swam close to their human visitors and allowed themselves to be touched and petted. Only because Philippe Cousteau filmed these remarkable scenes were they believed. On the other hand, in ocean areas where humans have brought great danger, sea life seems to learn caution and fear in just one generation.

Clearly, human beings fare better when we feel an empathetic bond with the other passengers on this Spaceship Earth. When we are not being the terrorists on this spaceship, they seem to thrive around us, too.

I often wonder: What would life with animals be like if, as Chief Seattle said, we shared "the same breath"? I've felt that possibility only once, while living in India.

In our student hostel in Delhi, small gray monkeys often left their perch in trees outside our windows and came in to visit. They sat on our desks and watched while we studied. They hid our pencils and jewelry when we were out, watched with amusement as we searched for things they finally "found" for us. They were delightful companions — graceful, funny, mysterious, and never boring. By being so alive in the moment, they made us feel more alive and aware, too.

Later, in a South Indian village where I stayed with a family for a few days, I remember elephants gliding past each morning with their keeper, or *mahout,* on the way to the fields. Often the little boy of the household would give them a treat of plantains, but one morning, he mischievously poked one elephant's trunk with a sharp pin instead. She squealed, but did nothing — until, on the way back from that evening's drink at the river, she raised her trunk over the garden wall and drenched the boy with a trunkful of water she had saved up for the purpose. Then she calmly lumbered on.

As his mother and the *mahout* explained to the little boy, this was *shabash* — very clever — but it was also serious elephant wisdom. Without hurting him, but also without sacrificing one whit of her dignity, the elephant had taught him a lesson in fairness he would never forget.

In a way, animals are professors of self-esteem: unself-conscious, confident, and utterly themselves. I thought again of what humans could learn while reading about Koko, a female gorilla who was taught sign language by Dr. Francine Patterson, a primatologist. Thanks to Koko's ability to understand some spoken language and respond in a vocabulary of 500 signed words, we know some of her thoughts on everything from her favorite foods to using a camera. We know about her dislike for someone she called an "obnoxious nut" and her gentleness and love for a kitten that was given to her as a pet — as well as her sadness and mourning when that kitten was killed by a car.

Here is one of the exchanges Dr. Patterson recorded:

"I turn to Koko: 'Are you an animal or a person?' Koko's instant response: 'Fine animal gorilla.' " [13]

Self-esteem is natural, and only humans create inequality by simply believing in it. By unhardening our hearts to animals, perhaps we open them to ourselves.

III *Religion versus Spirituality*

"Know the Mystery
   that if that which thou seekest
   thou findest not within thee,
   thou will never find it without thee . . ."
WICCEAN (PAGAN) PRAYER

"The Lord of all,
   The knower of all,
   The beginning and end of all —
That Self dwells in every human heart."
UPANISHADS

"The Kingdom of God is within you."
THE NEW TESTAMENT

"Look within, and seek That."
JALALUDDIN RUMI

"i found god in myself
& i loved her / i loved her fiercely"
NTOZAKE SHANGE

Once when I was traveling in the South with Florynce Kennedy and other women in black/white feminist speaking teams — which Flo referred to with a smile as "Little Eva teams, something for everyone" — we spent a weekend with a woman I shall call Ella, the mother of one of the speakers traveling with us, in rural Georgia. Because we arrived on the once-a-month Sunday when the circuit-riding preacher opened the only church in the black area of this small town, we listened to a whole day's singing, testifying, and sermonizing, followed by a big potluck church supper. In this community of houses built on stilts over fresh Georgia clay, there was not a general store or even a gas pump, but people came from miles around to hear this music sung in drawn-out meters with no instruments, in a remembered African style.

While talking over the day's events that night at the kitchen table, my friend and I were both surprised to find that her mother, Ella, a woman who had raised such a strong family and even defied the Klan, still had one regret: she couldn't be a deacon of her church. In addition to the usual duties of singing in the choir, cooking for the congregation, and saving money in a Mason jar to pay the minister's salary, Ella had made cushions for the hard church benches, sewed slipcovers for the preacher's armchair at the altar, and answered all the church correspondence. Indeed, she wrote such effective letters — a by-product of her skill at writing lyrics for her own songs — that she had been made assistant clerk, the highest post ever given to a woman.

But the rules were clear: only men could be deacons. And they were the ones who passed the collection basket, traveled as delegates to church conventions, and made decisions for the whole congregation. When she was young, Ella had accepted this order of things: the deacons had seemed old and wise to her then. But after thirty years, she was only too aware that most of them were less experienced than she was; that some also drank, fathered children "on the side," and were cowardly with local racist employers; and that none had devoted as much time and energy to "the Lord's work" as she had. Yet the church gave them its authority and withheld its trust from her. As she said to us, "It hurts me in my soul."

Listening to my friend and her mother mourning this unfairness, I wondered: How many women have been wounded in their souls by religions that believe God is a man, and thus only men are godly? Her story suddenly seemed thousands of years old — with the difference that she was one of the few with enough independence to know it was unjust and say so. Having had the strength to reject the Bible stories that showed Jesus, a Middle Eastern Jew, as snubnosed and blond, she had acquired the courage to question; yet in her black community, she had support for a rebellion based on race, but not on sex. Her beloved church and preacher, the strongest forces in her life, felt they had the Bible itself behind them when they devalued her as a woman. For every verse she found about women as equal believers, they could find ten preaching female obedience.

As the three of us talked late into the night, we went far beyond deacons. Why were there no black *women* preachers riding from church to church in cars paid for by Mason-jar savings? Why was God so consistently white and male that even Ella found herself picturing a white man when she prayed? She and a few of her women friends sometimes raised these questions among themselves, but they felt blasphemous. Besides, the church was all they had. They didn't want to be thought crazy, divisive, or not "God-fearing women" — an interesting phrase in itself. But if God is white, then whiteness is godly. If God is a man, then man is a god. Any religion in which God looks suspiciously like the ruling class is very different from spirituality that honors the godliness in each of us. It makes us *feel* different. It makes us *act* different.

After we came back to New York, her daughter and I sent Ella a poster. It was Michelangelo's Sistine Chapel ceiling, but with God as a black woman who was giving the gift of life through the touch of her fingertips to a white woman. When Ella called us, she was laughing with shocked delight. Later she showed this poster to her preacher — being careful to explain the poster was just making a point and didn't mean to exclude men — but he only said with disdain that this was obviously a gift from her "Black Panther daughter" (an odd comment, we thought, from a man so separatist that he had refused to shake hands with me, perhaps the only white person ever to stay in this rural settlement). In the end, Ella's rebellion was confined to framing the poster and hanging it on her living room wall as a silent protest for all church visitors to see.

Thanks to Ella, I also began to think about my experiences as the daughter of a Christian-Jewish marriage — two traditions so opposed that both families had objected to the wedding at first; yet to me as a child, they seemed very much alike. Both religions excluded me from their words and imagery, and made me feel a little suspect and unclean, as if I had to behave in a very special way in order to be accepted. Nonetheless, I did turn briefly to religion as an escape from the violence that suddenly seemed everywhere around me as I entered adolescence. Not only were there frightening "Saturday night fights" (the phrase for domestic violence when there was no such phrase) in the apartment downstairs, but the father of a boy in my school had shot his son — and then himself. For many months, I took two buses every Sunday morning to reach the safety of a fundamentalist church on the other side of town. I still remember the poignancy of seeing the Bible held in the big rough hands of a Sunday school teacher, an ex-convict who owned a chicken farm and said he had been saved from a violent life by Jesus. Like countless women before and after me, I looked to religion as the only force strong enough to tame violent men, or at least to protect me if I obeyed. But giving up freedom for safety is a child's bargain, and soon, the safety turned out to be illusory anyway. "Saturday night fights" didn't seem any less frequent among these families than anywhere else, and the congregation itself eventually split between two ministers along class lines over the issue of whether or not to have a neon sign on the church.

That experience helped me understand the appeal of fundamentalism to women. As Andrea Dworkin has so well explained in *Right-wing Women,* the promise *is* safety in return for obedience, respectability in return for self-respect and freedom — a sad bargain. And the impact of that one poster on Ella made me realize the importance of feeling included in whatever form of worship and spirituality we choose. It gave me new respect for all those working to reform organized religion from within, whether they were tracing the Black Madonna of Eastern Europe back to the Great Cosmic Mother of Africa or bringing an ecclesiastical lawsuit in support of the ordination of women as Episcopalian priests. Though still small in comparison to the religious establishments, there were a growing variety of such actions: rewriting Jewish ceremonies, including that infamous prayer in which men thank God for not being born females or slaves; insisting on the right of gay men and lesbians to be both open and part of their faiths; invoking the spirit of Mohammed, a reformer in his day, against literalist and antiwoman interpretation of Islamic law; and supporting a breakaway church of black Catholics. All of them were helping both women and men of all races to see God in themselves. Even the resurgence of Moslem and other nationalist fundamentalisms — anachronisms that justified an internal war against women and an external one against people of other faiths and nations — was better understood as partly a reaction to a European colonial God that had hurt the people of Third World countries "in their souls."

What spoke to me most, however, were the movements that went beyond reforming existing religions and straight to the heart of an immediately experienced, universal spirituality. They were reminding us that *pagan,* a word made to seem negative, really just means "of the country" and originally signified those who believed in the divinity of all living things. By rediscovering prepatriarchal myths and holy places, as well as the still-living pagan beliefs of many indigenous cultures and mystical traditions, spiritual movements were giving us back a universal spirituality — the metademocracy of all living things.

Those were inspiring possibilities — but they were just ideas. It wasn't until 1980, when I took a boat trip down the Nile from near Aswan and the older more Nubian parts of Egypt to Luxor and areas closer to Cairo, that I had any idea what a more universal spirituality might look like — and what emotions it could unearth in me.

We started out with several dozen tourists of varying nationalities in an old boat that looked like a larger version of the *African Queen.* Because of the way my friend, Egyptian feminist and author Laila Abou-Saif, had arranged the trip, we saw the oldest temple and excavations first, so that the millennia seemed to be unfolding as we floated down this river that has been a changeless center of agricultural settlements for at least 10,000 years. It was like watching a gradual shifting from the old pagan, pantheistic world in which all of nature was holy, to the rise of a monotheistic and royal one as if it were happening before our eyes.

In relief on a temple ceiling at Dendera, we saw the goddess Nut, a version of the Great Cosmic Mother worshiped in the rest of Africa. She is a metaphor for creation and the cycles of life; mind and womb inseparable; birth and death in one. Her body, full of stars, forms a living horizon over the earth as she swallows the sun, creates the darkness of night while it travels through her body, and then gives birth again to the sun and a new day. Under her overarching body and nourishing breasts, all living things are sacred and flourishing: male and female, plants and animals, insects and flowers, reptiles and birds, ibises and crocodiles, wild geese and antelope, the fig tree and the papyrus plant — everything in nature's cycle.

For those of us who have been raised in religions that treat sexuality as suspect and women's bodies as symbols of temptation and downfall, the feeling of standing in places that treat both as sacred is like sunlight flooding into a dark room. Looking at the paintings and carvings of goddesses, of wildflowers, of powerful and playful animals, flocks of birds like those still migrating over the Nile — all the scenes of the sanctity of the everyday — created a feeling of peace and empowerment that caught me unaware. It was such a different feeling from standing in huge cathedrals under images of crucifixions that created an awe at one's own insignificance and sinfulness. In Jewish synagogues, where the Torah is locked away from ordinary eyes and images of nature are forbidden as idolatrous, I felt a sense of an intricate and isolated history; and at mosques where there is no imagery of females or nature, and women cannot pray in the same chambers as men, I felt an authority over every part of life.

I thought: *How could we have let body and spirit, sexuality and spirituality, be split apart?*

In later temples and tombs, I noticed divinities in human form that were both male and female; for instance, Hapy, god of the Nile itself, who has breasts but wears a male headdress. Some were both animal and human, like Taweret, the Great Feminine One, goddess of pregnancy, who stands upright and has the body and head of a hippopotamus, the feet of a lion, and often the image of a crocodile down her back. It seemed right that pregnancy in both human and animal form should be worshiped as the symbol of creation the moment when there is the first movement of a new life.

I thought: *Why should we worship a male-only god who makes women feel ungodly, and men feel they must be godlike? Why have we traded the mystery of birth for life created from dust?*

As we continued our journey, I noticed that goddess figures were beginning to give birth only to sons. A little later in historical time, the sons became larger, then larger still as they turned into consorts, and then even larger as they became male rulers seated on the lap of a goddess who had become only a throne.

I thought: *It's beginning; half of humanity is becoming more sacred than the other. Did the mothers rage? Did the daughters mourn?*

Soon, there were male gods and kings who were larger than their female consorts. They were still goddesses, but the Great Cosmic Mother had been shattered into her separate parts: Isis, the Goddess of Wisdom; Maat, the Goddess of Moral Judgment;

Hathor, Goddess of Life; Mehet-weret, Goddess of Death, who wel-comed the dead into the underworld. Meanwhile, as Upper and Lower Egypt became one kingdom through conquest, military scenes began to take on an importance once reserved for the harvesting of crops, the grinding of grain, and other scenes of ordinary life. As if this greater power demanded greater tribute, the first pyramids also began to appear, and pharaohs called themselves Son of Re or Amun-Re, the male god of the sun, as though feeling no need of any mother or goddess-given authority at all. Isis herself was now turned into a throne. There were exceptions among the rulers, the greatest being Hatshepsut, the most prominent of three female pharaohs, who sent trade missions to other countries, restored neglected tem-ples, and ruled largely with diplomacy and in peace. But having as-cended the throne as a widow, she also had to invent lineage from a male god, even wear a false beard as a symbol of authority; and before the death of her nephew and successor, her name and image had been chipped out of the stone of temples, and her name omitted from royal history. But there was no shortage of female figures in these temples and tombs. In addition to queens and royal daughters, paintings and carvings began to show royal harems filled with prin-cesses and ladies-in-waiting of the new kingdom, some brought from as far away as Asia. I wondered: *Did the women of the harem mourn for their native lands?*

By the fourteenth century B.C.E., all religion had been placed in the hands of a male priesthood, and King Akhenaten, often called the "inventor" of monotheism, had declared the Sun God to be not just the most powerful god, but the *only* god. Other god and goddess images were defaced and their temples closed down, including Kar-nak, where Akhenaten's father had worshiped. Paintings and statues commissioned by Akhenaten and his beautiful wife, Nefertiti, en-sured that they and their six daughters would be viewed by posterity as a godlike royal family — improbably fair of skin, as the famous painted bust of Nefertiti shows — and the queen was depicted as a priestess. I wondered: *Had the darker-skinned Nubians of Upper Egypt come to feel excluded by birth? Did women look at Nefertiti and see fair skin or beauty as woman's only power?*

In the centuries that followed, poverty and the increasing alien-ation of the people from royalty and its Sun God religion led to political unrest and even to the ultimate crime of robbing tombs of the riches with which royalty had hoped to enter eternity. Soon, the Egyptian appetite for dynasty and conquest as well as increasing numbers of invasions from the outside world had brought confrontations with Libyan, Nubian, Assyrian, Persian, Greek, and Roman forces, each group leaving behind them the images of gods who looked remarkably like them. The withdrawal of sacredness from all but a few males was now complete, and even for them religion meant worshiping an authority that was not in themselves.

This trip down the Nile was like living through the steps to patriarchy that Joseph Campbell described in *The Masks of God,* his study of Western mythology: a world created by a great goddess, a world created by both a goddess and her consort, a world created by a male from the body of the goddess, and finally, a world created by a male god alone.

But reading James Henry Breasted, the early-twentieth-century scholar of ancient Egypt, I found this process put more simply: "Monotheism is but imperialism in religion."

Before I began that trip down the Nile, I hadn't thought of myself as someone whose life had been limited by religion, and so the freedom I felt while visiting those earliest temples came as a complete surprise. It was the return of a self-esteem and spiritual connectedness I hadn't known was missing — or possible.

In moments of sorrow or joy, too many of us are forced to turn to ceremonies that falsely elevate some and demean others, that separate us from nature, that make us feel ashamed of sacred parts of ourselves. It will take courage, creativity, and community to replace them with inclusive ceremonies that mark life passages; rituals that externalize universal myths and nature's symbols of old and continuing mysteries — and exclude no one. But as the quotations that begin this section show, all religions still have within them some tradition of listening to an inner voice and therefore acknowledging the sacred worth of each individual and of nature. As new archeological discoveries and ways of carbon-dating them show, the last 5,000 to 7,000 years of patriarchy, monotheism, and racism are a brief moment in the vast progression of human history that now seems to have extended for at least three and a half million years. If more than 95 percent of human history existed *before* this period we are taught to think of as history, there can be an even longer *after*.

All we have to remember is this: Seeing holiness only in others — or only in our own group — is the problem. Seeing the sacred in ourselves and in all living things is the solution.

Years later, Ella died without ever becoming a deacon. To the end, no matter what her preacher or neighbors said, she displayed on her living room wall that poster of God as a black woman. She had dared to claim the Hand of God as a symbol of creation. Though the creative power being symbolized lay within her own female body, she was counted a rebel.

As heir to the Great Cosmic Mother, Ella deserved more.

We all do.

IV   *Possibilities*

"When *you* dance,
    the whole universe dances."
JALALUDDIN RUMI

There are two traits that seem to distinguish humans from other life forms, even animals who are our closest evolutionary relatives, and thus are organic to the way we live and feel.

The first is our self-consciousness. Other creatures think and learn, feel and remember, but only humans seem to *reflect:* to think about thinking and learn about learning; to conjure up an imaginary future and memories of a carefully edited past; to shape our emotions and learn from our own dreams. This self-consciousness means we make decisions based on the way we envision ourselves and our links to others. We may weigh our acts for their impact on the seventh generation to come, as Native American leaders are trained to do, or jeopardize our descendants by endangering the ecosystem for our immediate gain. We can choose not to give birth to a child in order to give birth to ourselves, to have children to enhance our sense of self, or to love other people's children as if they were our own. We may enjoy sexual intimacy with those of our own class, race, or gender, or be drawn to difference. We may sweep before we walk lest we tread on one living thing, or build doomsday weapons — and believe in both cases that our actions are necessary to peace. We may feel secure and prosperous with autonomy and simple living, or crave power and possessions. Our range of possibilities is almost infinite.

In the short run, each self-conscious choice affects behavior, our own brain synapses, and sends out ripples of change to those around us. In the very long run, it can affect the environment of our generation, our descendants, our species, the adaptation of their behavior and brains, the recurrence of certain genes, and ultimately, evolution itself.

The second trait that distinguishes us from other living creatures, in degree if not in kind, is our adaptability. Though we can't yet regenerate all our cells like a starfish or hibernate through foodless winters like a bear, our ability to adapt to the demands of our environment, and vice versa, has given us a protean nature. More than any other species, Homo sapiens can be thrust into new environments, adapt, meet different conditions and challenges, adapt again, and thrive — a flexibility that has saved us from extinction and allowed our evolution to continue.

Taken together, these human traits of self-consciousness and adaptability create a spiral of cause and effect, effect and cause, that transform the immediate, polarized, nature-versus-nurture argument into a question only of time frame: Shall we focus on the existing egg or the future chicken? If we pull back from the short-term either/or view and look at a long spiral, we see humans adapting to what exists, imagining new environments, influencing what *will* exist — and then adapting to what they have created out of a unique combination of the actual and the imaginary. The most important difference between biological determinists and cultural determinists is not who is right and who is wrong, but whose prophecy becomes self-fulfilling. We can choose to dampen hopes, thus preserving a current order (if almost everything is determined by biology, why try?), or we can kindle the flames of hope and become agents of change (if anything might be affected by culture, why *not* try?).

The choice is somewhere on the scale between pessimists and optimists. It's also between those who find security in the current order and those who want to change it. As a female human being who dreams of a world in which no one is born into a hierarchy — and as an optimist who looks to areas of research for facts that inspire our vision of *what could be* — I have found two new bodies of knowledge that inspire the most pessimistic imagination.

The first are lessons drawn from tragedy. Suppose, for instance, that after an internal process measurable in milliseconds and based only on your own desire and the needs of the situation at hand, you could:

- change your brain's right- or left-hemisphere dominance to the opposite side — and back again — regardless of your biological sex or cultural gender;
- change handwriting and personal signature for different roles or needs, and also write skillfully and perform other tasks with your nondominant hand;
- raise or lower your pulse rate, blood pressure, temperature, level of oxygen need, and thresholds of pain and pleasure;
- eliminate an allergic reaction to an environmental factor that is healthy or inevitable, or create an allergic reaction to a factor you want to avoid;
- reenter and reexperience your mind's stored memories of the past *as if they were happening in the present;*
- call up your body's somatic memory of everything that has happened to it with such clarity that "ghosts" of past wounds and bruises reappear on your skin in minutes, and then slowly disappear as you leave the memory;
- activate visions of a past or future state of health so powerful that they can speed the healing of current wounds, measurably strengthen the immune system, and give you access at any time to the superhuman abilities usually reserved for emergencies;
- adjust your eyesight to nearsighted, farsighted, or normal, depending on your task, with such physical impact on the eye's curvature that an optometrist examining you would write you an entirely different lens prescription;

- change voice depth and timbre, mannerisms, grammar, accent, facial-muscle patterns, body language, physical style, and even darken the color of your eyes — so totally that an unwitting observer would assume you to be of a different ethnicity, age, race, class, or gender from one moment to the next;
- change your response to medication — or achieve that medication's result without taking it — and thus have all the benefits of a tranquilizer, sleeping pill, "upper," or anesthetic but none of the side-effects;
- heighten or lessen sexual desire, and widen or narrow the range of those people for whom you feel it;
- adjust your body's response to lunar and diurnal cycles;
- become maximally effective and "tuned in" to various challenges — work, parenting, dancing, a back rub, your own creativity, a friend's need, your immediate problem, a future dream — by summoning up that part of yourself that contains exactly the appropriate sensitivities and strengths;
- bring into one true self the strengths of all the selves you have ever been in every setting and situation from infancy to now.

All of these abilities have been demonstrated — and verified through a wide variety of double-blind tests, brain scanning, and other objective techniques — in people who have what is called "multiple personality disorder," or MPD. As is now known, MPD is almost always the result of frequent, sadistic, erratic, and uncontrollable abuse in childhood by someone on whom the child is dependent; abuse so intolerable that children learn to dissociate from it through a form of self-hypnosis and so escape into a "different" person who does not feel the pain. Having once split off from the core personality, this "alter" begins to acquire a separate life history, complete with distinctive mannerisms, behavior, and social relationships, almost as if it were a person born at the moment of "splitting." Once this ability to dissociate has proven to be a valuable way of surviving and dealing with the world, alters continue to be born to meet different needs and demands.

Thus, by adulthood, one person may comprise as many as a

dozen completely different personalities. (When much higher numbers are reported, they probably include "fragments": partial personalities that have specific purposes but not substantial life histories.) And these personalities are so different that they can convince unwitting people of their reality. Since the person suffering from this "splitting" often experiences periods out of his or her host personality as memory loss, this is one of the most frightening examples of a survival mechanism that becomes a terrifying prison.

Obviously, this phenomenon is born of suffering that is literally intolerable. What began as a grim gift renders its victims vulnerable to triggers in the environment over which they have no control. So splintered is the "true self" that there is no overarching consciousness. In fact, the process of treatment *is* the process of integration. It takes great courage on the part of the survivor, empathetic patience from professionals, and an average of three to five years, but the prognosis for integrating and healing is good. That in itself is a testimony to human possibilities.

What we haven't even begun to consider, however, is what would happen if the rest of us could acquire for *positive* reasons the abilities these accidental prophets have learned for *negative* ones. If such extraordinary abilities can be summoned to help survive the worst of human situations, they are also there to create the best. What if we could harness this unbelievable potential of body and mind?

It's quite common, for example, for women to contain one or more personalities who conceive of themselves as male and behave convincingly as males, and for men to have one or several personalities who seem completely female in every way except the biological one. *What if we could each gain access to the full range of human qualities that lie suppressed within us?*

Clearly, the list of human abilities with which this discussion of MPD began is only a hint of the real possibilities. People in different alters can change every body movement, perfect a musical or linguistic talent that is concealed to the host personality, have two or even three menstrual cycles in the same body, and handle social and physical tasks of which they literally do not think themselves capable. We need to face one fact squarely: *What the future could*

*hold, and what each of us could become, is limited mainly by what
we believe.*

The second source of knowledge to fire our imaginations has become
available to us because of all our new abilities to map the living
brain. After centuries of theorizing about brain function from information based on autopsies, the effects of brain tumors and injuries,
or extrapolations from tests on laboratory animals, new technolo-
gies have allowed us to learn more about the workings of our own
minds in these past two decades than in all of previous human history — and we have just begun.

One thing we know is that, whatever the contribution genetics
makes to our mental abilities, the brain we are born with is not the
brain we are destined to have for life: *just 15 percent of brain
growth occurs before birth; 85 percent takes place afterward.* Indeed, its crucial cell-to-cell synaptic connections are so staggering in
their number and variable in their complexity that they couldn't be
dictated by genetic blueprint alone. What takes place after birth, in
response to the stimuli ingested through all five senses, completes
the brain's growth. This long postbirth period of development is
what makes us so uniquely adaptable and flexible, and also vulnerable to our environment.

Unlike other animals who have far shorter periods of early
growth and dependency, a human infant's brain more than doubles
in size during the first year of life, almost doubles again in the next
three years, and continues growing for a decade. Its basic structural
development isn't complete until around the time of puberty. But
even then its limits are not set. Though it was previously assumed
that the brain and nervous system were "hard-wired," their abilities
"programmed" in much the same way that a computer is — with
one group of cells being dedicated to short-term memory, a second
to auditory function, a third to tactile recognition, a fourth to visualization, and so forth — we now know that the brain is full of
backup systems, that brain cells continue throughout our lives to
generate new connections (synapses) between them, and that the
number and complexity of these synapses has an enormous effect on
mental capacity.

In the last dozen years, refined methods of structural measurement and a new ability to measure electrical activity, blood flow, and the metabolism of glucose in the living, working brain, have given us a greater understanding of the workings of the forebrain, that part of the cortex uncommitted to motor and sensory functions and therefore available for such higher mental processes as language and the capacity for future planning. Old, fatalistic assumptions are being cast aside, and new hopes are being born.

Though all development lost to early malnutrition was once thought to be permanent, for instance, recent experiments have shown that some of it is recoverable. It's as if our bodies store up their growth potential, waiting for a chance to make up for losses. In the case of accidents that irreversibly damage one hemisphere of the brain, the other hemisphere may take over its functions, especially if the injury occurs before brain programming has reached its adult stage. In spite of theories of right-brain, left-brain specialization, each hemisphere acts as a potential backup system for the other. The biggest danger of early loss is not the loss itself, but the idea that it is absolute and irreversible. Perhaps it is true that after illness or trauma we never "get back to normal." Instead, we move on to a new and stronger normal. Just as antibodies protect us against getting an infection twice, our body protects itself and may grow even stronger.

In the same way, we may emerge from times of traumatic worthlessness and low self-esteem with an increased immunity to similar assaults, a stronger sense of ourselves, and a better defense against future challenges. It is a law of nature that matter transforms itself: *Nothing is destroyed.* For us as part of nature: *Nothing is wasted.*

We once thought, for example, that the loss of something like 100,000 cells each day made mental deterioration inevitable. But even after the brain has attained its maximal size and structure, signals from the body and the environment are still constantly changing it. While the number of neurons in the adult brain remains fixed, the synapses between them keep proliferating to a greater or lesser extent, depending on the uses to which we put our brains. Groups of existing synapses are strengthened in favor of those made necessary by stimulus. Thus, neurons can become connected and reconnected in an almost infinite number of ways. In enriched environments, even rats at the end of their natural life span have been shown to grow more synapses than those who live in impoverished environments. The number and complexity of brain synapses, these electrically processed interneuronal connections, makes possible mental operations of extraordinary sophistication. The idea that our brains are ever subject to improving, diversifying, and sharpening, if we will only believe in them enough to stimulate them, is good news for everybody.

Perhaps we should have known all this from negative examples. Prisoners kept in dark, isolated cells for long periods have ended up with an impaired eyesight and sense of time. "Brainwashing" and reprogramming have created different beliefs and personality traits, even in adults, by forcing the reinterpretation of memories and beliefs on which our sense of self depends, and also forcing the memorization of large quantities of new information. Compelled by regimentation, fatigue, pain, fear, or any other stress to undertake both tasks at once, the brain's synaptic patterns change and deteriorate. Even a few days in captivity have produced such consistent symptoms in political hostages from different backgrounds that this constellation of traits has come to be called "the Stockholm Syndrome": dependency, passivity, approval-seeking, empathy with captors, sympathy with their cause, and gratitude to those who took them prisoner in the first place and then became their only support. It's a syndrome multiplied in victims of domestic violence who have less sense of alternatives — and over a much longer period of time.

The alternative to the kind of repair and growth we've been talking about is shutting down — a state of disbelief in our abilities that is the negative side of our adaptability. When we are deprived of the ability to stretch our boundaries and capabilities, we can exist in an almost hibernating state, semi-alive, with all but our survivalist abilities on hold, and a feeling of being cold and alone, cut off from nature and the universe. But when our talents are required and rewarded, we can stretch our abilities, use the energy of self-esteem to activate the unique mix of universal human traits we each possess, and uncover a microcosm of the universe within ourselves. Depending on a myriad of choices and circumstances that have been made by us and for us, we voyage somewhere along this vast continuum each day. Thus, self-esteem starts out as a personal blessing, but it becomes nothing less than an evolutionary force.

Even our metaphoric vision of how our minds work changes. When we were exploring other continents, our brain was seen as a phrenology map. With industrialization, our imagery for it became a machine. As technology developed, a telephone system became the prevailing metaphor; with the invention of artificial intelligence, we, too, became a kind of giant celestial computer. Now, we liken the brain to a hologram that, if one part is damaged, retains the entire image in every other part. That, too, is probably limited, but at least it comes closer to the reality of nature in which each leaf contains the genetic reality of the whole plant, and each of our cells contains enough DNA information to replicate our whole body.

What we are gradually relearning is an earlier mystical view that was covered over by reductionist paradigms. We *are* the universe in microcosm: the universe is each of us in macrocosm. If we have respect for one, how can we fail to have respect for the other? Think of the imagery in a parable from *The Flower Garland Sutra:* "In the heaven of Indra, there is said to be a network of pearls, so arranged that if you look at one you see all the others reflected in it. In the same way each object in the world is not merely itself but involves every other object, and in fact *is* every other object."[14]

Just as each cell contains our whole being, so each thought and dream contains our whole self, too. *If our dreams weren't already real within us, we could not even dream them.*

Sometimes when I enter a familiar room or street, I think I see a past self walking toward me. She can't see me in the future, but I can see her very clearly. She runs past me, worried about being late for an appointment she doesn't want to go to. She sits at a restaurant table in tears of anger arguing with the wrong lover. She strides toward me in the jeans and wine-red suede boots she wore for a decade, and I can remember the exact feel of those boots on my feet. She sits in a newspaper boardroom with the sort of powerful men who undermine her confidence the most, trying to persuade them to support a law that women badly need — and fails. She's a ghost in the lobby of an office building that she and all the women of *Ms.*

magazine walked through for so many years. She rushes toward me outside a lecture hall, talking, laughing, full of optimism.

I used to feel impatient with her: Why was she wasting time? Why was she with this man? at that appointment? forgetting to say the most important thing? Why wasn't she wiser, more productive, happier? But lately, I've begun to feel a tenderness, a welling of tears in the back of my throat, when I see her. I think: *She's doing the best she can. She's survived — and she's trying so hard.* Sometimes, I wish I could go back and put my arms around her. Since I've felt that wish, I've also noticed that her different images are coming together. The little girl listening to the radio in an empty room sits next to the woman trying to raise money or begging for ads. The very young woman in a sari with kohl on her eyes looks back from a mirror at a woman in jeans and sunglasses fifteen years later. The worried self in a trench coat outside the Plaza listens to an older self speaking at a rally. A tall and round-faced twelve-year-old walks with me through a sunny street, looking in shop windows, enjoying my ice cream cone, and feeling remarkably happy.

We are so many selves. It's not just the long-ago child within us who needs tenderness and inclusion, but the person we were last year, wanted to be yesterday, tried to become in one job or in one winter, in one love affair or in one house where even now, we can close our eyes and smell the rooms.

What brings together these ever-shifting selves of infinite reactions and returnings is this: There is always one true inner voice.

Trust it.

One Year Later . . . and a Proposal for the Future

I

"A book must be the axe for the frozen sea within us."
FRANZ KAFKA

A book, like a person, is born with the genetic imprint of the past, shaped by parental dreams and society's politics, launched at a certain time in history — and then goes off to lead a life that none of those things could have predicted.

That's certainly true for this one. In the time since it left my bed and board, I've often felt like a parent whose child has grown up and entered mysterious realms. At first, I just missed its intimate presence in my life. As Susan Sontag said after sending off a novel, "It was like taking a beloved person to the airport and returning to an empty house." Then I kept talking to it in my head, wishing I could add this parable or that study, as if only my advice could keep it safe in the world. Finally I realized it was leading a more interesting life than any I could have foreseen, and I began the long parental process of letting go.

From the beginning, it was readers who made me see the folly of prediction. Their responses were so diverse and interesting, so understanding of the book's spirit and yet so surprising in its uses, that I realized each person was bringing a unique reality to her or his half of the conversation. Not only did they supply all the elements I'd been stewing about not including, but they carried the book's thesis into countries I never could have entered or imagined.

In the first weeks of a book tour, for instance, I noticed this offspring was introducing me to an unusually varied group of friends. Though I had thought its acceptance would be limited by its radical thesis — that systems of authority undermine our self-authority to secure obedience, thus self-esteem becomes the root of revolution — readers seemed never to have heard that what is radical can't succeed, and what succeeds can't be radical. If it was empowering in their daily lives, that was enough. In dozens and then hundreds of long informative letters, they shared experiences of self-esteem in response to the book's parables; told what actions they were taking as a result of putting the internal and external together, especially if they hadn't been active before; and described what new self-understanding had arrived, especially if they had been confusing motion with action in the past. They responded on street corners and in supermarkets, at lectures and book signings, in radio call-in shows and women's reading clubs, on a national computer network of male executives and in a local self-help group for women prisoners, in a discussion on the future of democracy and a television forum on the Los Angeles rebellion, at a California convention of librarians and a Washington discussion of foreign policy, even at dinners where old friends told me about their lives in new ways. Whether in letters or in person, they often ended by telling me what friends, spouses, parents, children, co-workers, political leaders, employers, or lovers they were passing the book on to.

I was glad to see it progressing in this trustworthy way, being recommended by one reader to another, because I doubted that critics would praise a book with *self-esteem* in the title; my reporting on the reception of other self-esteem efforts in chapter 1 had convinced me of that. The intellectual establishment seemed to find this subject too soft and intangible to be taken seriously, while a newly influential right wing was clear that it was too subversive of authority to be tolerated.

But at least I had a sense of humor about it. In last year's notes, I scribbled this parody of what a reviewer might say: "*Revolution from Within* has two flaws, both of them fatal. First, it portrays the individual as infinitely redeemable, a romantic notion that flies in the face of history. Second, it describes self-esteem as a birthright that can only be preserved by transforming education and child-rearing; by abandoning patriarchy, racial caste systems, monotheism, and hierarchy as the main form of human organization; indeed, by transforming Western civilization itself."

That would have been tough — but fair. After all, it *is* what this book is saying.

But life and reviews are always a surprise. I certainly hadn't anticipated seeing myself described as "the Ivan Boesky of Nookie" (more about that in a minute), and I'd forgotton that, when the message is unwelcome, the messenger becomes the focus of attention. Though reviewers for less prestigious publications found this

book to be a pioneering blend of the personal and the political —
in fact, the more obscure the review, the more favorable it was —
critics for the most renowned publications here and in England had
three main points:

1. That my interest in internal concerns must mean I had become weaker and/or regretted my earlier years of activism.
2. That including any struggles of my own would disillusion
   female readers, who surely preferred women in public life
   to stay on pedestals; indeed, that my having any struggles
   at all was evidence that feminism had failed.
3. That the pages most deserving of critical attention were the
   three personal ones in chapter 6's romance section: Who
   was my unidentified lover anyway? Why had I included this
   story at all? And why wasn't it longer?

The usually impersonal *New York Times* headlined: "SHE'S
HER WEAKNESS NOW." *Newsweek* described this book as just my
"squishy exercise in feeling better." A network television interview
about the book was edited into such a frivolous "profile" that its
woman producer eventually quit in protest. Journalists on both sides
of the Atlantic theorized that I must have deserted serious political
pursuits to write a self-help book for personal gain. A reporter for
the *Washington Post* misread my romance parable as "falling in love
with someone who treated her badly," added accounts of other feminists' supposedly unacceptable marriages or love affairs (one because her life was too conventionally heterosexual, another because
hers wasn't heterosexual enough), and wrote a nationally syndicated
article headlined "LEADERS' HYPOCRISY KILLED FEMINIST MOVE-
MENT." On the other hand, a reporter for the *New York Post* decided
that it was I who had treated my lover badly, and called this reversal
bad for feminism, too. In support of this theory that I must have
been interested only in his money, a writer for the *New York Observer* described me as "the Ivan Boesky of Nookie."

Okay, some of this is funny now. But at the time, it was painful.
Not only did such trivializing words hurt, but they obscured the
book's content, purpose, and politics. Even the serious disagreement
I had anticipated — and would have welcomed — gave way to
points like those above. For instance, I could find no major review

that noted the book's criticism of traditional childrearing, educational testing, the content of education, gender and race roles, separation from nature, or even monotheism as thieves of self-esteem. There was none that supported, opposed, or even noticed its striving for inclusiveness across lines of sex and race, class, sexuality, and ability; none that mentioned its linking of the social justice and self-realization movements; and no examination, pro or con, of self-esteem as a practical source of revolution. Though reviewers were heavy into the parables from my personal life, none acknowledged the larger points they had been included to make. When I responded to interviewers' inevitably personal questions by explaining that an increased inner awareness had made me *more* effective as an activist — that I felt stronger, not weaker — this, too, was roundly ignored. Certainly, no major publication analyzed this book's feminist world view, or took a look at self-esteem as a serious subject.

I began to wonder if I really had written what I thought I had written. Or if my self-esteem was high enough to survive writing a book about self-esteem.

Then, just as I was gaining comfort from traveling in Canada, where reviewers actually expressed interest in this linking of self-esteem to social change (an "intellectually interesting, well-researched and informative book," said one review, and "revolutionary," said another), *Newsweek* published a cover story: "THE CURSE OF SELF-ESTEEM: What's Wrong with the Feel-Good Movement." Its illustration was a drawing of a small man with a small dog, looking in a mirror to see a tall, handsome man and a large, handsome dog.

By now, I confess, I was talking back to the mainstream media in my head almost as much as I had once talked to my newly departed manuscript.

According to *Newsweek,* self-esteem advocates urged parents to praise children indiscriminately. "Who wants to be bothered waiting for a child to do something right," this report asked rhetorically, "when it's so much simpler just to praise him [*sic*] all the time." (Okay, I thought, there must be a self-esteem expert somewhere who urges that, but in years of research, I've never met one. Indiscriminate anything only shows a child that no one is paying attention, thus she or he must not be worthy of it.) A guest essayist from

England assigned to comment on this odd U.S. interest dispensed with both Plato and me by regretting the good old days when I used to say, "laudably, that 'the examined life is not worth living,' " and then advised this country to "just grow up." In fact, she argued, the world would be a safer place if U.S. self-esteem were *lower*. (That's amusing, I thought, but isn't history full of national inferiority complexes that resulted in hypermilitarism; for instance, Germany between world wars? And what about the U.S. identity crisis over a declining economy that coincided with aggression against such small countries as Grenada and Nicaragua?)

For *Newsweek,* however, the *coup de grace* was clearly a study that showed U.S. schoolchildren to be more self-confident about their math abilities than were their counterparts in Japan, even though the former were far less skilled in math, according to objective tests, than the latter. You could almost feel the writers' triumph.

In fact, the report didn't explain the difference that made sense of the study's results: the distinction between *situational* self-esteem (how we compare ourselves with others) and *core* self-esteem (our sense of intrinsic worth). With that in mind, however, it became understandable that U.S. students might feel more self-confident about their math abilities in schools where math wasn't emphasized and standards were low; while their counterparts in Japanese schools might well feel less self-confidence in schools where math was all-important and standards almost impossibly high. But no matter what the *situational* self-esteem, *core* self-esteem remains crucial. What *Newsweek* failed to note, for example, was that Japan has a far higher suicide rate than the U.S., and so many deaths from overwork that the phenomenon rates a special word in the language. Surely, there is no greater tragedy than lacking the self-esteem to value one's own life.

But the oddest aspect of this cover story was the Gallup poll *Newsweek* commissioned for the occasion, and then buried in a sidebar. Its results showed that Americans were more likely to cite self-esteem as an important motivator than any of the other choices: *Family duty or honor, Responsibility to community, Fear of failure,* or *Status in the eyes of others.* A question even more relevant to the cover story's thesis of the "curse" of the self-esteem movement was: "Is too much time and effort spent on self-esteem?" In spite of phrasing that invited an affirmative answer, and in spite of the sole alternative ("Time and effort could be better spent on work") that made it seem as though work and self-esteem were mutually exclusive, 63 percent of Americans said: "The time and effort spent was worthwhile."

In other words, the results of *Newsweek*'s own poll opposed its cover story's thesis.

This chasm between what authorities believe and what people experience was similar to the distance I'd been encountering between reviewers and readers — sometimes also between intellectual women reviewers and everyday women readers. It was the greatest such distance I'd witnessed in my thirty years as a writer.

So there I was, feeling quite "crazy" and not a little depressed, as if my intentions — and even the reactions of readers — had become invisible. I was doing book readings that had to be moved to movie theaters, churches, school gyms, town libraries, and shopping malls to accommodate those who were interested, and hearing people talk about the book as energizing, activating, a needed unity of the internal and the external — not as a retreat from activism on their part or mine. Yet I was also reading critics and facing interviewers who assumed that I had repudiated my activist past, that I was suddenly attributing women's problems to an individual weakness rather than a woman-hating society, and that my personal stories were the book's sole content.

I confess that most of what I've told you about the quality and quantity of reader response was not what I was feeling then. I remember sitting in a Chicago hotel room, feeling negated by weeks of being told with great authority and publicity that I meant what I didn't mean. Though I understood by then that those blows were hitting a not-quite-healed bruise of childhood neglect that sometimes made me feel less real than other people, they were not imagined. I felt stronger, yet I was being called weaker; I had included many kinds of subjects and people in these pages, yet only a narrow few were treated as visible; I thought I had written a book with serious political implications, yet I was being accused of deserting politics in general and feminism in particular. Though I had been as surprised as reviewers when this book had begun to appear on national best-seller lists a few weeks after publication, even those numbers meant little. When a friend called to congratulate me, for instance, I remember saying, "But you don't understand — that just makes more people who won't like it." He laughed, but I did not.

Fortunately, Susan Faludi's *Backlash,* an important book about the mainstream media's retreat to old values in the face of feminist advances, had been published just a few months before mine. I hadn't read it — I understood its value, but felt that my own years of dealing with the backlash meant I didn't need to learn more — until wise readers explained it had helped them understand why they also felt the media was describing some book other than the one I had written.

Only a few chapters into it, I began to relearn the classic feminist lesson of being rescued and affirmed by other women's experiences. By naming and documenting the political patterns behind common responses, Faludi reminded me (and thousands of other readers) to trust our own perceptions: there *was* a great will to misunderstand out there. I suddenly realized that, if I'd been watching another woman getting media treatment parallel to mine, I would have understood it in a minute and been angry on her behalf; yet it's amazing how being the subject of something painful can keep you wondering what you did to warrant it. Only reading Faludi's well-documented case histories made me realize that I wasn't alone, and so might not be uniquely at fault either.

In example after detailed example, Faludi shows how statistics and studies have been shaped, perhaps unconsciously, to support the message of the backlash: *Feminism is not the cure for women's problems; it's their cause.* Even when the problems being discussed were those that only the women's movement had been trying to solve — violence against women, for instance, or women's double burden of working both in and outside the home — they were still said to stem from the changing of old roles, not from the need to change them even more. Her most famous example, the 1986 study in which researchers from Harvard and Yale statistically minimized women's chances of finding a husband if they delayed marriage, was exaggerated by the media in very big stories, and clarified, if at all, in very small ones. (As *Newsweek* so famously put it, such women became "more likely to be killed by a terrorist" than to marry.) Though Faludi had first exposed the false statistical premises and reporting of this study in an article for *Ms.* magazine, I hadn't thought of bias applied to this book's reception until I read it again *after* my own media experience, and in the context of Faludi's many other examples. The message I'd been getting from mainstream media began to make sense: *If I or other women had self-esteem problems, they were a personal failing at best, and proof of feminism's failure at worst. It was feminism's fault for not solving them, not the fault of an unjust system for creating them.*

No wonder there was such a will to personalize everything, to ask about the examples from my life that made up only a small part of the book, while ignoring the larger points they made. Instead of seeing shared experience as proof of larger political patterns, it was only an admission of individual weakness.

No wonder my inclusion of male readers was mostly ignored. If men came to see male superiority as an impossible goal that undermined their self-esteem, too, they would have an incentive to rebel against it, too. What if a critical mass of men decided to trade in "masculinity" for humanity?

No wonder the media was obsessed with my brief romance story, yet had totally ignored the equally personal but happy love story a few pages later. (Not one single reviewer or interviewer had ever asked me or written about that positive parable — the only personal one they had excluded. Amazing.) The first one supported the backlash belief that feminists can't have good relationships with men. The second did not.

No wonder there was such a will to believe that I had become weak, that examples from my own life would disillusion the readers, and that I would lead women away from activism. The backlash reason was simple: wishful thinking.

Once I got a grip on the political rationale behind otherwise mysterious responses, I stopped talking back to the media in my head and began talking back in reality. I stopped feeling uncertain and started getting angry. In the course of the next few months of book touring, I spoke my mind, as I have in these pages. Getting unsaid words out in the air where they belonged not only helped objectively — after all, "the media" is only composed of people who are also struggling with social mythology, and who can't read our minds — but it made space in my head to hear readers. I began listening, really *listening*. These stories are typical of what I heard: [1]

• In Detroit, a woman with a factory job and three children under eight stayed after a book signing to tell me about her burnout as a single mother. The killing work load hadn't changed, she said, but something almost as basic had: she no longer felt she deserved it.

"I always thought an inner life was for people who went to college," she said, "and meditating was what you did if you were religious. But when I read that getting into burnout is also a form of self-abuse, it really hit home. I realized that I hadn't been making demands or even asking for help because I didn't think I was *worth* helping. Suddenly, a question popped into my head: 'Okay, kiddo, what do *you* want?' I kept hearing it, so just for the hell of it, I started meditating on it. For twenty minutes before the kids got up in the morning, and again during my break from the line, I closed my eyes and let the question drift through my mind. After a few weeks, I found myself shifting from thinking only about what everybody else felt, to thinking about what *I* felt. It wasn't that I found the answer right away, but I did find a place where I knew there would be an answer."

In those months, she had lowered her dangerously high blood pressure, taught her hyperactive son to calm down and improve his basketball game by meditating on shooting a basket, and realized that what she wanted was help with her kids, some real friends, and her supervisor's job. Those were things she never thought she had time for, much less a right to; yet they suddenly seemed like practical goals. "I'd been telling my kids and everybody else that I had no needs by the way I behaved," she explained. "But after I started to treat what I wanted as important, I talked to another woman on the line who was also by herself with two kids. We actually rented a house together. It's made a big difference — we take turns with our kids, and save money with only one washing machine and one TV. We also have each other's company. It was such a relief to talk to another adult that we started inviting four women friends over to play poker once a week. Actually, the poker is kind of an excuse — it's really a family session where we talk about how we feel and what we want, and help each other figure out what to do about it.

"I may or may not get this promotion, but at least I won't have screwed myself by not asking for it. When things don't work now, I get mad instead of depressed — a big change for me. I only slip backwards on the days when I forget to meditate and take time for myself. You won't believe this, but the local zoning board tried to throw us out of our house because we're not a legal family. I got scared again, and I could hear my Mom saying, 'You can't fight city hall.' But then Tuesday rolled around, and a combination of meditating and my girlfriends persuaded me to fight. If we don't win, we'll find another house — and vote the bastards out.

"I thought I couldn't take time for an inner life. The truth is, I can't afford *not* to."

As I listened to that woman's story, the link between self-esteem and action seemed so natural that all the notions of inward exploring as weakness began to lose their sting.

• In Cleveland, a bookstore clerk told me he had been encouraged by chapter 3 to "un-learn" book categories. Instead of putting African-American books only under Black Interest, for instance, he now put additional copies under American History, Politics, and Current Events. "I had to fight the store manager to do it, but he came around when we actually sold a few more copies," he explained. "It's the first self-respecting thing I've done since I marched against South Africa in college."

He also began to notice the way in which his daughter had been absorbing his view of himself and his job. "My daughter used to ask me why I was only a sales clerk, as if she were ashamed of me," he explained. "It felt as angry as when she used to want only white dolls. But a few weeks after I moved the books around and brought her into the store to see what I'd done, she wrote a report for her fifth-grade class, 'Black History Is *All* Our History.' Of course, she didn't tell me about it — her teacher did. But pretty soon, she started reading a children's book from Africa, and the next thing I knew, she wanted to wear her hair in dreadlocks and I noticed she didn't talk so much about envying her white friends. Just last week, she started helping me figure out what books for young readers I should recommend — which ones didn't make anybody feel bad about themselves. She's getting to be proud of the job we do together.

"After my daughter started changing, I realized that before, she'd been repeating my own childhood. I used to feel ashamed of

my father. He was afraid of white people — with good reason —
but I blamed him for this fear; it made me feel ashamed. I realize
now my feelings about myself are just as important to my daughter
as they are to me. Because I hated my job, she did, too. Because I
behaved as if white people would always win, she envied them. And
now that I'm beginning to be proud of myself, so is she. Thanks to
the parallels between race and sexism in your book, I've also started
to think about what my daughter learns from my attitude toward
women. I know she'll need woman-pride, too."

Listening to him was reward enough for including the caste
systems of sex and race as thieves of self-esteem. So was his showing
me where copies of this book were now displayed in his store: under
Black Interest, Women's Interest, Men's Studies, and Current Best
Sellers.

• In Chicago, I met the administrator of a special program for
adolescent boys with dropout or criminal records. He had known
for years, he said, that strengthening self-esteem was the only way
to change self-destructive behavior, but unfortunately, the conventional answers were still discipline, inflexible rules, and other enemies of self-authority. "Self-esteem is seen as self-indulgent," he
explained. "They think we're trying to excuse past behavior when
really, we're just trying to change future behavior. But since your
book wasn't written in educationalese — and since you started out
being a skeptic yourself — I'm giving it to the most hidebound officials I know to try to loosen them up."

For me, that story would have been worth including male readers, even if he had been the only one.

• In Denver, a young woman gave me a slender manuscript in
which she had written her first memories of sadistic sexual abuse by
her father. "When it was going on, I used to feel as if I were watching from outside myself," she explained, "and I pretended it was
happening to somebody with a different name, a bad girl who deserved it. I entered into a world so separate that after a while, I
couldn't remember why my body hurt when it was over. That's how
I grew up to be what's called a multiple personality — and also how
I grew up believing I was a shameful freak.

"I never told anyone — not until I read what you said about
multiple personality in your last chapter. It meant so much that you

included this in a book for 'normal' people, and that you said we who are survivors might be 'prophets of human possibilities.' It's the first time I've seen myself as strong or a survivor, and that I even have something to teach. For the first time, I thought: If I was strong enough to hypnotize myself and 'split' off personalities when I was such a little girl, I must be strong enough to bring them all together now. I've started to tell a few friends instead of hiding all the time, and I'm beginning to get some help from one of the few therapists who understands. We're all encouraged to be false selves by injustice — maybe I'm not so separate after all. Maybe we're all part of a continuum."

The gift she gave me was far greater than mine to her.

But by far the most consistent response came from women who had been active feminists for years before retreating, and from women who'd been turned off by the women's movement. They sounded remarkably alike. Both said feminism had come to seem distant, impersonal, and only for the strong: a way of helping "other" women when they themselves were barely hanging on. Both said the movement had been neglecting the personal and internal half of the personal/political equation.

As one veteran feminist put it: "Looking at self-esteem and the internal strengthening of women makes the movement feel juicy and nourishing again, not just full of necessary, impersonal, dried-up things like legislation and rallies."

As a young waitress said: "I thought I wasn't strong enough to be a feminist — but now I see that feminism is about strengthening women from the inside too."

For myself, I was surprised that both groups expressed relief at discovering that I shared many of the same experiences and problems. If I wasn't immune either, they said in various ways, then perhaps they were not personally at fault, there really was a sexual caste system at work, and together, we could change it. I hadn't realized that I'd ever seemed invulnerable — one more lesson in how public life distances the few in order to disempower the many — but I began to be very glad that I'd heeded the feminist adage of the personal as political (and the political as personal) and included personal parables, no matter how the backlash had used it.

By the time I neared California and the last of this sporadic three-month book tour, reader responses had multiplied. Lines snaked around the block, people introduced themselves and organized in line, and the fact that this book had climbed to number one on the best-seller list and remained there, in spite of opposition, seemed to be viewed as their own triumph. As I moved West to warmer climates, readers began to phone and ask if they could bring sleeping bags to wait in line overnight. I'd never witnessed anything like it. I began to feel there was a new critical mass of people who had learned the hard way, as I had, that activism without introspection and self-discovery turns into imitation at best and burnout at worst; and that introspection without activism leads to isolation and passivity. There seemed to be a community of full-circle consciousness with nowhere to go, no institutions of its own or even places to gather, and so it had assembled around this ad hoc signal.

At Cody's, the largest bookstore in Berkeley, for instance, there were people crowded into an upstairs room and a balcony, sitting on the staircase, and standing downstairs in the aisles around loudspeakers. Susan Faludi, whom I had not met before and who lives in San Francisco, had been invited to introduce me. She explained to the crowd that she was going to read the experience of a twenty-two-year-old college student, written in response to my parables about my mother. I can only characterize that long narrative here, in part because this young woman's violent father has forbidden the printing of her name or any recognizable detail. But it was the story of this student's own mother, "a beautiful and fiercely intelligent woman," who had been ignored or abused for so much of her life that she spent years in an abusive marriage, and eventually tried to commit suicide.

"At the hospital," Susan said, reading this young woman's words, "my mother stayed in a quasi-coma for weeks, not responding to a word or gesture I made. I decided to read to my mother about you and your mother. Even though she was sleeping long and white in a cold room, I knew she could hear me. I read until the nurses started repeating phrases and themes to each other. But my mother didn't respond. Finally, I gave up and just sat there with her, a certain silence and smell filling the room, and started to prepare myself for her death.

"And then suddenly her eyes opened. . . . She often tells me that when she was 'asleep' in the hospital, she was actually thinking about your words, about your mother, about all the songs so many women never get a chance to sing."

The sequence of her recovery after this crisis was like a "rebirth," as her daughter put it. "Now, my mother is a business major in college, raises protest signs with me in pro-choice marches, and is dating as often as she likes with whomever she likes. In her own words: 'The younger the better.' She goes hiking, reads voraciously.

"As for myself, I'm graduating soon with a major in English, am dating one of the few good men on earth, and have embarked on a writing career with a short-story collection dedicated to my mother and to you. I know this sounds hopelessly melodramatic, but I know that if it wasn't for you, both my mother and I would not have survived.

"It is not often that language transforms itself into a true healing device — but it did one morning with a mother and a daughter."

The crowd had been quiet at the beginning of this long story, then laughed with surprise at the mother's unexpected signs of spirit, then grown silent again with a new kind of quiet. Instead of anonymous people filling disparate spaces on two floors, there was now a group whose links to each other brought the spaces together. Instead of the silence of strangers, there was a new willingness to turn toward each other, smile, make room; a new quality in the air.

Stories are medicine for our individual spirits; I could imagine nothing more healing to mine. They are also powerful makers of community.

That was the turning point of my post-book journey. Instead of feeling discouraged and confused, I felt the strength of readers coming back to me. Instead of losing something when this book left home, I understood that I had gained the learning, comfort, and magic of community.

Of course, I wouldn't want to leave you thinking that controversy is ever over. While writing this many months later, I picked up a copy of *Newsweek* and found this book still referred to as "an embarrassment." Even feminist journals published long after mainstream reviews also reflected difference. "It's hard to believe that *Revolution from Within* is going to be good for feminism," said *The*

Women's Review of Books. "[H]er new call to revolution feels like a retreat."[2] On the other hand, *On the Issues* said, "Seven months after its publication, the controversy over Gloria Steinem's *Revolution from Within* can be seen in its proper light: as a national anxiety attack about the fear of hope."[3] Knowing both publications, I can vouch for their equal concern for women's welfare. The first was not indulging in wishful backlash thinking, but worrying about taking time from activism, and the second was using the internal to power that activism.

So what made the difference? I can only put myself in their shoes. After all, a decade ago, I would have been on the skeptical side of internal concerns myself. I can empathize with that feminist naysayer, as well as with intellectual women reviewers writing for mainstream publications, who may have been convinced, as I once was, that sacrificing emotion to intellect, the intangible to the tangible, was necessary to have an impact in the male world. To them, I may have seemed to be doing the feminist equivalent of "eating watermelon" when I chose the "feminine," mysterious, internal, whole-body subject of self-esteem.

Or perhaps the problem was the linear one of assuming that childhood and inner conflicts are something one resolves first; as if inner exploring achieves "normalcy" and then stops. Since I had been functioning quite well, looking inward must have seemed a mystifying regression. In fact, it is a continuing, never-ending source of rebellion, not just a way of changing old patterns — but that was a long way from viewing it as therapy.

Or perhaps I'd succumbed to the linear view myself. Having started out so far on the external, activist side, I may have taken it for granted and overemphasized what was newer to me. Was there an imbalance in these pages? If so, I welcome this chance to set it right, and to ask you to unlearn again (think of chapter 3) the infallibility of those of us who happen to appear in print.

In some ways, however, this difference was a rerun of the seventies division between "politicos" and "cultural" or "spiritual" feminists. I had been on the political side in those days, but even then it seemed to me there was room for both — if only for the tactical reason that leaving out big chunks of women's experience left it with nowhere but patriarchal places to go. By the 1980s when

I was thinking about writing this book, I'd come to agree with what feminist theologian Mary Daly had predicted: that the internal would grow out of the external. As she wrote more than twenty years ago, "Women should be sensitive to the fact that the movement itself is a deeply spiritual event which has the potential to awaken a new and post-patriarchal spiritual consciousness."[4]

I confess, however, that I still have a harder time empathizing with those male intellectuals who seem to believe a serious political message can't be conveyed in a personal, accessible way, and who treat self-esteem as "selfish," especially when sought by groups on whose self-sacrifice they have been depending. Nonetheless, I can see that anyone schooled in *either/or* might think I was just beginning a new hierarchy in which the internal was on top. They might mistake my *synthesis* for an *antithesis* of their *thesis,* if you see what I mean.

Whatever the reason for differences in perception, we're where our experience has put us. Thus, a critical mass of us may have to experience the full circle — internal exploring as a continuing source of energy, not just as emergency therapy — before we can ditch either/or thinking, and before a full-circle approach no longer needs explaining. Like modern theories of fish schooling or birds flocking that posit a critical mass acting together as an energy field in which "emergent properties have nothing to do with the original rules,"[5] we may have to wait until a paradigm change is pervasive enough to transform the centers of culture and education.

If so, there's a collective reward as well as an individual one. Even if we are not among those who trigger the critical mass, each one of us is still helping to create it. Perhaps those worried about the impact of this book will have to wait and see its long-term results — as will I.

For those who still mistrust inner exploring and "the examined life" as detracting from activism, as I once did, however, perhaps the responses of readers are comforting. Their stories are a kind of quilt in which each one is a special stitch, color, or pattern, but all together, they create a design.

I tell you all this about these experiences of the past year because you, too, may be finding resistance from those around you or within yourself; a similar fear that looking inward will negate what it actually nourishes.

I also offer differing responses because I've come to the conclusion that each reader will have to be the authority on whether I was clear enough about self-esteem as a source of positive action — not a substitute for it — and about positive action as a source of self-esteem, for it is this never-ending spiral that I meant and still mean, with all my heart.

As for getting clear and getting angry, I offer my post-publication experience as proof that a book is also a process that never ends. I'm thinking in particular of a reviewer who said I had "forgotten to get angry" about sexism. I don't agree: this book is about the step after getting angry, which is finding a center of power within ourselves to change an unjust system; but if you also missed anger in these pages, you should know that it arrived later in the postpartum process and became the energy for another turn of the spiral.

And if you find that you, too, are talking back to disembodied critics in your head, I hope you will consider getting your words out in the air. That silent dialogue only allows someone else to be the prime mover, but once you speak, you become a force on your own. More important, getting the words out leaves room in your head to hear understanding voices around you, and your own inner voice.

In my case, a reward was, is, and continues to be learning from readers (and now that this book is being translated into fifteen languages by publishers in other countries, including some in Asia, Latin America, and the Middle East, I'm looking forward to learning much more from readers; as a writer, I promise to keep giving it back). Gradually even now, however, the quality and quantity of responses have changed a few firmly made-up minds in the media.

Because our books had turned into such unexpected best sellers, for instance, Susan Faludi and I were interviewed after that session at Cody's by two women editors from *Time* magazine, whose reviewers had originally been skeptical of Faludi's thesis and found mine not personal enough. As it turned out, I think it was less what we said than the depth of interest they heard from readers that impressed them.

When our joint interview became part of a cover story analyzing the popularity of our two feminist books, Susan and I found ourselves looking out together from the cover of *Time*. It was a pairing that made sense — her book was documenting what was wrong; mine was exploring ways to make it right — but the heart of *Time*'s cover story came straight from listening to readers. For instance:

"Something must have happened in the climate of relations between men and women for these books to have such an impact. . . . Faludi's book has set off firecrackers across the political battlefield. . . . She has inspired men and women to take a new look at the messages they absorb, messages that act as barriers to understanding or to justice."

"Many reviewers . . . virtually ignored the political implications of [Steinem's] thesis in order to elaborate on the minimal amount of personal details she chooses to divulge. . . . But with ordinary readers, Steinem's message has broken through. They don't ask her about the personal much. They want to know about the self and how to gain and trust their own. It is a fine triumph for this woman . . . to succeed in holding the feminist course while expanding its horizons to include everyone."[6]

What more could any writer ask?

II *Revolutionary Groups*

Books have a built-in limitation: reading is solitary. I learned from the intensity of interest in groups described in these pages — the Royal Knights of Spanish Harlem in chapter 1, for instance, or the Confidence Clinic and other examples in "Creating Psychic Families" in chapter 4 — how much we long for extended-family-size circles of people who are committed to each other's welfare, both internal and external; in other words, for community.

It's as if the two great movements of our time, those for social justice and for self-realization, were halves of a whole just waiting to come together into truly revolutionary groups.

Women are far more likely to express the need for communities of our own than men are — and with good reason. Females of all races, classes, ages, ethnicities, sexualities, and abilities are still the only oppressed group that doesn't have a nation, a neighborhood, or usually even a bar. In our own homes, we may be sabotaged in our deepest sense of self, used as servants, or treated with violence. Though feminism often sprang from small, free-form groups that forged the link between the personal and the political — the ones called "consciousness-raising," "rap," or just "women's" groups — current organizations have become larger and more specialized than those small extended families of women where patterns of shared experience were the source of learning. That growth is a sign of energy and success, yet larger groups rarely offer the same depth of personal/political support and transformation.

On the other hand, many men are missing each other's community, too, though in different ways. Male turf and chances for mutual support are common, but they usually come with a penalty for speaking intimately, expressing emotion, confessing uncertainty, and doing other "unmasculine" things that are necessary to the acceptance of a whole self — and thus to self-esteem. Without an effort to change gender politics, men tend to police roles by punishing the weak member of their group (just as women punish the strong one), and to bond only around power (just as it's easier for women to bond around pain). That's why men are missing a special kind of men's group that consciously confronts gender and helps to free its members to develop the full circle of human qualities.

As I've seen over and over again in the past year, the prison of "masculinity" *is* being questioned by more and more men. They are looking for places to explore such things as how much they missed having nurturing fathers (thus growing up to think they couldn't nurture their own children), and also missed having achieving mothers (thus growing up to think they couldn't be close to achieving women). Those drum-beating, "warrior" groups of the pseudo men's movement symbolized by Robert Bly's *Iron John* appeal to this need, too, but their regressive efforts to restore "masculinity" turn off many and leave a hunger for talking, thinking, feeling groups that go beyond it.

Of course, there are many reasons why all of us, women and

men, are also missing small, diverse groups together. The nuclear family, a new and cruel event in human history, has replaced the extended family that once sustained us. (Think of the contrast, for instance, between the isolation of the two-parent household and the wisdom of "It takes a whole village to raise a child.") When we do manage to create a chosen family from among our neighbors, friends, and colleagues, modern mobility means we'll probably have to remake it several times. The old town-meeting way of getting information and making decisions has narrowed to the isolation of a living room or polling booth. People with the time and resources may seek out group therapy as a form of intimate community, but it rarely includes group action or is seen as a normal and continuing part of life. (Indeed, therapists themselves often tell me that they're burning out without a community of peers.) In the parent-teacher and religious organizations that are the only community groups to which most people belong, purpose is limited, and women especially are more likely to be the source of support than the ones supported. As for twelve-step and other recovery groups, they also have spread in part because of our longing for community — they are free and available, and offer the healing power of personal stories — but their model of permanent, individualized illness doesn't encourage action against its social causes, and their philosophy of admitting power-lessness over addiction and accepting the existence of a higher power may actually discourage it.

On the other hand, the small, full-circle, personal/political groups we're yearning for are neither small in importance nor rare in history. They've been the major means of sustaining daily life in older cultures and of personal/political transformation in modern ones. It was the "testifying" meetings in black churches in the South, for instance, that allowed personal experiences to be shared and become a common source of insight and action. They gave birth to the civil rights movement. The Chinese revolution against centuries of despotism was nurtured in small groups where people were finally allowed to "speak bitterness to recall bitterness," and to begin digging out the deep roots of self-defeating tradition, including that of male dominance and female subservience. In the late sixties and early seventies, women's consciousness-raising groups that were inspired by both those examples, especially by the civil rights one, spread into a national honeycomb of small groups. Women told the stories of their lives, analyzed their shared patterns, gave names to injustices once just called "life," and turned them into public issues through speak-outs and political action. In many ways, it was those early c-r groups that gave feminism its heart, depth, and most lasting legacies.

I remember meetings about which we never said, "I can't believe I have to go to another meeting," because they were the highlights of our week. We brought our problems and experiences, from what to do about a racist/sexist boss to tensions with mothers and lovers; we went around the room with serious personal themes and also with outrageous jokes; we talked about sex with an honesty I'd never heard before; we listened, really *listened* to each other for clues to our mutual welfare; and we uncarthed archeological fragments of our lives that were parts of larger political patterns. The result was a personal exhilaration, and an amazing political impact.

In the last dozen years especially, however, the very success of the feminist movement has created a backlash, and the resulting necessity of fighting hard to hang on to external gains has often caused us to neglect internal ones. Over and over in this year, I've heard women wish for more time, space, and energy for themselves, and more links to other women for support, community, and growth. Yet I've also heard the women's movement described as admirable but remote, valuable but inaccessible, more concerned with protecting legislative gains than with the everyday stuff of women's lives — and the same is true for other hard-pressed social justice movements. Recovery and self-realization movements have spread partly in response to this hunger; yet they lack an activist side.

As a result, we seem to have come into a time of polarization, with self-explorers refusing to vote and activists refusing to restore themselves; with New Agers who put off action for so long that, like women restricted to the house who develop agoraphobia, they've come to fear it; and with activists who criticize self-realization or recovery movements without ever asking what they are offering that social justice movements are not.

Fortunately, many people are now figuring out that the internal half of the circle doesn't work for long without the external. Groups and movements that are *only* external are realizing that imitation or exhaustion are their fates. That's part of the yearning to put both together in small groups that can truly be communities.

Perhaps our first job is to envision a full-circle, extended-family-size group and know we have a *right* to it. Otherwise, we will go right on turning to big organizations, narrow interest groups, and nuclear family units that can't take the pressure of all our hopes and needs. Look at it this way: if each cell within our bodies is a whole and indivisible version of those bodies, and each of us is a whole and indivisible cell of the body politic, then each of us has an organic need to be part of a group in which we can be our whole and indivisible selves.

So, as a result of what I've learned from readers of this book, here is a suggestion for a goal by the year 2000: *A national honeycomb of diverse, small, personal/political groups that are committed to each member's welfare through both inner and outer change, self-realization and social justice.* It doesn't matter whether we call them testifying or soul sessions as in the civil rights movement; consciousness-raising or rap groups as in early feminism; covens, quilting bees, or women's circles as in women's history; or revolutionary cells, men's groups, councils of grandmothers, or "speaking bitterness" groups as in various movements and cultures. Perhaps they will have an entirely new name, since combining the elements of diverse communities will make them different from all of them. I think of them just as "revolutionary groups," for a revolution is also a full circle. The important thing is that they are free, diverse, no bigger than an extended family — and everywhere.

This isn't as large an order as it sounds. If two white male alcoholics could start a national network of meetings that are free, leaderless, and accessible, so can we.

If early consciousness-raising groups could analyze the politics of women's daily lives at a time when biology, God, and Freud were still thought to be immutable, we can deepen and widen that personal/political process to encompass our own childhoods and those of our parents, links with our counterparts in other countries, divisions and diversity among women, the politics of everything from eating disorders to religion, the relationship of self to nature — and much more.

If the self-realization and healing movements can tap powers through meditation, visualization, and other internal techniques, these full-circle groups can explore those powers, too.

If political movements have taught us the necessity of turning out our vote, block by block, and technology has given us electronic networking, these local groups can use such decentralized tactics very well.

A nationwide network of full-circle groups doesn't have to start from scratch. There are already bits and pieces of relevant experience lying around the landscape waiting to be gathered up. Some women have had versions of such groups in their lives for years, for instance, and are walking testimonials to how important they are in growing personally and staying effective politically. A few men have had this experience, too; for instance, members of the Oakland Men's Project who define "men's work" as combating male violence and have evolved a rare, multiracial, gay-and-straight community of men who work with adolescent boys. (Perhaps *Iron John* groups will also help children to have the experience of fathering whose lack they mourn by, say, lobbying for parental leave, or becoming workers in childcare centers and kindergartens.) There are also women's reading clubs that are consciousness-raising groups in disguise (though with less activism), and women's professional networks that are centers of activism (though they're often too big to be personal). Carol Kleiman, the author of *Women's Networks,* estimates there are now 5,000 such networks in the country. As for recovery programs, there are feminist writers like Kay Leigh Hagan and psychologist Charlotte Kasl who have critiqued or revised the twelve steps to be more empowering for women. And there are also a wide variety of parallel efforts, from groups of male ex-convicts helping each other to stay straight and reform prisons at the same time, to single mothers helping each other to stay sane and also to lobby for childcare. Most recently, women's self-esteem circles have begun to form in such disparate places as women's prisons and "Self-Esteem for Women" weekend retreats in the country where diverse women gather. In fact, crossing barriers is so personally enriching and politically crucial that some groups now take this as their organizing principle and call themselves "bridge groups" or "diversity groups."

If such group making still seems like a luxury only some people can afford, I think the hundreds of stories I've read and listened to as a result of this book would convince you otherwise. In Minneapolis, a young farmer told me he would still be a part-time handyman and full-time alcoholic if he hadn't found a group of men who were helping each other to stay clean, figure out what inner emptiness they had been trying to fill with drugs or alcohol in the first place, and use their experience to help keep school kids off drugs. In rural Oklahoma, a school official said that only meeting with other women, and seeing the price they were paying for the violence inflicted on them in childhood, helped her confront religious groups trying to retain corporal punishment in the schools. Neither the farmer nor the public school administrator sounded much different from the well-to-do therapist I met in the rarefied air of Aspen, who told me that meeting regularly with a group of women as equals had helped her take care of herself, and take on the politics of her profession.

Do these groups still seem more useful personally than politically? The 1992 Women's Voices Project, the biggest, most diverse nationwide poll on women's attitudes about their lives ever conducted, says otherwise. It concluded that "strategically, the women's movement needs to organize locally where women live their lives, and where women see themselves most likely to want to be active."[7]

And if women especially have just begun to realize how deeply our self-esteem has been undermined by centuries of woman-hating cultures, then the constant presence in our lives of a woman-loving group can help us believe in our authentic selves.

In fact, females of all ages and groups need this kind of personal/political community to increase our self-authority, and our ability to take on unjust authority. In this last year alone, for example, I've talked to hundreds of women with one of the country's most common problems — a full-time job inside the home and another outside it — yet they lack the sense of entitlement to ask men to be equal parents or even to pick up their own socks, much less to demand a national system of childcare. I've also met smart and brave women in an all-black housing project of a Midwestern city, single mothers trying to survive on welfare, who see their neighbors as sister victims, not as potential supporters, because they believe the women's movement is for any woman but them. I've met equally smart and brave young white mothers in Southern suburbs who go to the shopping mall with their babies and sit on benches for hours because it's their only chance to see other adults. In city offices, I've met women executives who feel so dependent on their bosses' approval, and have so little experience of female support, that they don't share information with their women co-workers, and are fearful even of being seen having lunch together. There are also a lot of activists who are constantly on the edge of burnout, with no system of personal support or political renewal, and a lot of women and men in recovery groups who are ready to take on an addiction-producing society.

For all social justice movements and other efforts to make self-respecting change, these new-and-improved small groups could be a crucial bridge between organizations and the people they're designed to help; between personal experience and its political cause; between the present and the future. And from what I've seen, they're not that hard to create. Unlike many other ways we try to confront sexism, racism, and other thieves of self-esteem — ways that would be fueled by such groups anyway — this one doesn't require those in decision-making positions to change their minds, give us permission, vote for us, provide funding, or even say hello. We can do it by ourselves.

But it's only such groups that let us know a movement isn't just for "other people" who are somehow stronger, smarter, and better equipped to act. And it's only such groups that allow us to share life experiences, understand we are not alone, see similarities, gain community, create a shared basis for action, and evolve organic politics that can change us *and* change the world.

This need for small full-circle communities has become so clear over this year of listening that I've come to mourn the price we've paid for neglecting it in the past.

In a landmark new book, *Trauma and Recovery*, Judith Herman, a professor of psychiatry at Harvard Medical School, documented the links between the "political" suffering of men in wars and the "personal" suffering of women and children in domestic wars. Not only were the two kinds of personal experiences parallel, she found, but cruelty at the hands of those loved ones resulted in more severe trauma than cruelty at the hands of enemies. In both cases, the acceptance of the reality of posttraumatic stress came only when people who had experienced it shared their stories and organized politically to force its recognition: in the case of war veterans, after Vietnam survivors challenged the old assumption that shell-shocked soldiers must be cowardly or weak, and in the case of women and children survivors of domestic wars, after the women's movement allowed sharing and speaking out about everyday violence.

In other words, even the deepest personal insight will not be accepted unless there is a grass-roots movement of experience to force its recognition. As Judith Herman says, "In the absence of strong political movements for human rights, the active process of bearing witness inevitably gives way to the active process of forgetting."

It doesn't matter on which side we begin this personal/political, internal/external journey, but it matters desperately that we complete the circle. It doesn't matter whether we begin with the individual or the group, for we need both.

If a small group of people devoted to their own and each other's welfare appeals to you, then you have already begun.

Guidelines for Groups
THE BASICS

When I asked people with experience of long-term groups that worked both internally and externally if there were practices they considered basic, a body of shared wisdom began to appear. Some recommendations could rejuvenate any small group, even boards and other conventional task-oriented bodies; for instance, going around the room to speak personally as a prelude to any meeting, thus guarding against impersonality and burnout. Others suggested measures for specific groups; for instance, sharing babysitting expenses in groups where some have children and others do not, thus starting out in an equal and committed way. In general, it seemed that the more of the following guidelines that were honored, the more likely the group was to be satisfying and effective.

However, these are not rules. They are organic practices that help produce desired results by being desirable in themselves. The ends *are* the means.

• *Speaking from the "I."* The point is to tell our own stories:

to focus on what we ourselves have experienced. We may offer first-person experiences in response to those of others or ask questions for clarity (unlike the twelve-step rule against "crosstalk"), but judgments, criticism, the advice of experts and others not in the room, and sentences beginning "You should . . ." begin to divide up the senses. Try to stick with those things you've experienced with all five.

• *Equality.* There is no leader. Part of the purpose is to challenge habits of passivity, dominance, hierarchy, and the need for outside instruction. Each person deserves to become her or his own leader, and that means being listened to carefully, with no interruptions other than questions for clarity, and with the right to as much time as any other member. If one or more people are monopolizing or holding back, it's up to each one to name what's going on and restore a balance. If tasks have to be done, rotation or drawing lots is a good idea, so that no one dictates by skill or resource, or ends up feeling put-upon. Sitting in a circle — on the same level, so that each member can see the face of every other — makes equality concrete.

• *Confidentiality and honesty.* Both are the prerequisites of trust. Stories and experiences shared in the group are kept within it, unless otherwise indicated by the speaker, and all members try to be as honest about their real feelings, thoughts, and experiences as they know how to be. Speakers need to know that their words will stay within the group, and listeners need to know that words being spoken are honest ones.

• *Going around the room.* At least once early in the meeting, each member addresses the question at hand, says what she or he hopes will come out of this meeting, what has happened since the last go-round — whatever. Hearing each person's voice breaks the spell of silence, bonds the group, and keeps it from breaking into speakers and listeners. The number of times a group can go around the room depends on the time and the topic, but any subject *not* addressed by everyone will feel incomplete. This needn't be uniform every time. No one is forced to speak. But it is a goal of such groups to create an encouraging atmosphere in which everyone feels comfortable speaking.

• *Analyzing and making connections.* After everyone has spoken personally for at least one round and responded to each other,

patterns and connections often emerge. Going around again to identify patterns is an important time of naming and analyzing.

• *Self-respecting action.* Each person commits herself or himself to an action before the next meeting. This may be an individual
action, a shared action with this group, or an action taken with
others outside the group. The important thing is that energy and
understanding have an activist place to go, and that each member
uses the group as a witness to his or her resolve.

• *A time of looking inward.* One of the differences between
current groups and the early c-r ones is the number of people who
have discovered meditation, visualization, and other paths to inner
strength. At a minimum, a few minutes of shared silence at the beginning of each meeting deepens whatever experience is to come. A
few minutes of silence at the end deepens whatever has been learned.
Both help to keep the inner part of the circle alive, as well as aiding
the group in bonding together.

More focused kinds of inward journeying are undertaken by
groups looking at childhood patterns (for instance, the politics of
patterns still being acted out); suppressed memories (for instance,
veterans dealing with the trauma of battle, or women dealing with
the trauma of domestic abuse); or addiction and health-related concerns (for instance, meditation as a way of filling the inner void that
invites addiction, or visualization as a way of strengthening the immune system). See Appendix I for guided meditations.

• *Mutual empathy.* Some groups meet to celebrate and mourn
each other's life occasions like a chosen family. Still others arrive at
a telephone "buddy system" so members may call each other at regular times, or when a reminder of resolve is needed. In any case,
most remarked on the growth of empathy over the long term, no
matter how different members had felt at the start. Many groups
had focused their group support from time to time on a member
who was going through some crisis of health, relationship, or activism — yet that didn't unbalance the group. As one teacher said to
me, "We created an equality among ourselves, and that helped to
make up for outside circumstances that treated us *un*equally. It was
emotional insurance: I might not need the group's support at that
moment, but I knew it was there if I *did* need it."

• *Bridging difference.* Especially when groups set out to bridge barriers between and among members, it's important that each member feel permitted to say what she or he feels, regardless of whether it's "acceptable" or not. Thus, an early exercise might be: "Go to the person in the group you feel is the most different from you, and ask the question you're most afraid to ask." But the most apparently similar group will soon reveal difference. Our heads may have been filled with biases and stereotypes that lurk just beneath the surface of our thoughts, even though we know intellectually that they're wrong. They will remain powerful barriers until we get them out in the air, discover the equally odd biases others have toward us, and become unique individuals to others and to ourselves.

VARIABLES

• *Affinity versus difference.* It doesn't seem to matter in the long run whether people gather around a common experience or challenge (for instance, work, parenting, or aging) or around difference (for instance, African American and Latina women together, gay and heterosexual men together, youth and age together): shared experience eventually reveals diversity, and diversity reveals shared experience. The most important qualification is that each person wants such a group in their life.

• *Size and frequency.* The number is usually from five to thirteen (though it's good to start out with more than five to allow for dropouts). Fewer than five doesn't provide enough diversity, and more than thirteen makes it difficult for everyone to speak and be heard. Meeting once a week seems to be the minimum for personal/political change (though some groups stop for a period of each year due to school or work patterns). Long-running groups report that once a month works for "family" maintenance plus some shared action.

• *Duration.* From two to four hours is the average meeting time, depending on size. Many groups try to have an occasional open-ended retreat. Some groups have a life that continues for many years, but the minimum duration for meaningful change seems to be about six months.

• *Location.* Privacy and freedom from interruptions are the most essential ingredients for a meeting place, but it's also important that meetings don't put an unequal burden on any one member.

Either rotating meetings at each other's homes or finding a neutral community space is the most frequent choice, but meeting places of groups whose experience contributed to these guidelines varied from a large booth in the back of a roadhouse (East Texas), to a bookstore after closing (New Hampshire), and a barrio church basement (California). The idea is to create free space in which no person feels more responsible than any other. The same goes for food and drink, so bring your own, or take turns supplying the group — but keep it simple.

• *How to find a group.* Group members have come together in a variety of ways. Some local women's centers or YWCAs help women's groups to form, and the National Organization for Women does the same, both for members and nonmembers, as well as offering consciousness-raising guidelines by mail (see Resources at the end of this chapter). In some communities, there are men's movements that help men's groups to form specifically for the purpose of getting free of controlling behavior, violence, or other parts of the "masculine" role, and community organizations may offer groups for everyone from new fathers to workers facing retirement. Mixed groups of women and men occur less frequently, but they do form around addiction or some other shared problem — for instance, the death of a spouse or surviving cancer. The most important requirement is wanting a full-circle, continuing group as a part of one's life.

If you want to begin a group, here are some ideas:

- Ask people you see at work, school, or in your neighborhood if they are interested.
- Put an ad in a community newspaper, or post a notice on a gym, PTA, or other community bulletin board.
- Ask members of any issue-oriented or interest groups you may belong to if they feel the need of a more personal connection.
- Check with an existing small group or with former members of one to see if they have room for a newcomer or advice on starting a group.
- Call people with whom you already have some shared experience, problem, or hope.
- Ask people you admire, you feel you can learn from, or who seem supportive.

- Look for differences you would like to bridge, whether it's age, race, gender, sexuality, ability, or class, or a group of mothers and daughters, fathers and sons. Such "bridge" or "diversity" groups are among the most important and rewarding.

SUBJECTS FOR DISCUSSION

Some groups allow the themes to emerge from the experiences of the members. Others set a theme for the next meeting at the close of each preceding one, so that members will have time to see what resonance it has in their lives. Some set a year's worth of general themes that represent a growth or progression; for instance, from childhood experiences through adulthood to feelings about aging. Others progress in concentric circles, as this book does, from childhood to education, unlearning, relationships, nature, and spirituality. Still others start with a shared issue and take it from private to public; for instance, equalizing male/female parenting at home, then in school texts, advertising imagery, and parental leave and other legislation. Simply starting with the question "What do you hope will change because of this group?" will reveal themes. See chapter 3 for more suggestions.

As a general rule, progress lies in the direction we haven't been. Thus, for a talkative person to learn to listen is progress — and vice versa. For a group of men to stop repressing weakness or emotion is progress, just as it's progress for women to stop punishing strength.

Simple physical tactics can help. The man who has a hard time listening and empathizing may be helped by something as small as focusing on the speaker's face and trying to guess emotion. The woman who is too good at listening and empathizing might try closing her eyes when others speak, as if she were listening to music, to focus on the impact of the speaker's words *on her.*

Many people said there were differences between these full-circle groups and consciousness-raising or therapy ones. As usual, one example is worth a hundred generalities. Here are two:

"Back then, my life was being controlled by my radical boyfriend," said one veteran of an early consciousness-raising group.

"Nothing I did politically was serious enough for him. He blamed me because he was poor and I had a middle-class background. Sometimes he even hit me, and I felt guilty enough to take it. Without my c-r group, I wouldn't have realized that male dominance is a political system, and that I wasn't alone in this experience. Those women literally saved my life. The only trouble was that I *kept on* being attracted to controlling men, no matter how I fought it. Since I knew better this time, I *really* blamed myself. Only getting into a group twenty years later — one that looked at our childhoods as well as our current lives — made me see that my violent father and stepfather had caused me to grow up believing that you couldn't get love *without* violence and control. Now that I've recognized where the feelings came from, I can work against male dominance in the outside world *and* in my own life."

"I never stopped looking 'in control' to my friends," said a man who had spent four years in a therapy group, "but I knew that I was addicted to a kind of 'high' I got from being in physical danger. I drove too fast, I got in fistfights, and I got a kick out of danger — even gambling and losing money. I got help from a therapy group. I realized I couldn't allow myself to feel vulnerable — the football coach I'd worshiped had taught me that — so I'd put all my need for emotion into taking risks. That therapy group helped me dig out the reasons, but I still felt like I'd wasted years of my life, and I was still having depressions. It wasn't until I got into a new kind of men's group at the YMHA that I saw I could help kids who were as hooked on danger as I was. For the last two years, I've been working with boys who steal cars just to joyride, and also boys in a juvenile home. For the first time, I feel as if my experiences are useful to somebody else. It wasn't all for nothing. I've got something to give."

Whatever form your own group takes, committing yourself to your own welfare and self-authority — and to the welfare and self-authority of others — will nurture personal and political revolution.

As Judith Herman writes, "Commonality with other people carries with it all the meanings of the word *common*. It means belonging to a society, having a public role, being part of that which is universal. . . . The survivor who has achieved commonality with others can rest from her labors. Her recovery is accomplished; all that remains before her is her life."[8]

Since there can be no revolution without poetry, I'll leave you
with these lines by Marge Piercy.

Alone, you can fight,
you can refuse, you can
take what revenge you can
but they roll over you.

But two people fighting
back to back can cut through
a mob, a snake-dancing file
can break a cordon, an army
can meet an army.

Two people can keep each other
sane, can give support, conviction,
love, massage, hope, sex.
Three people are a delegation,
a committee, a wedge. With four
you can play bridge and start
an organization. With six
you can rent a whole house,
eat pie for dinner with no
seconds, and hold a fund raising party.
A dozen make a demonstration.
A hundred fill a hall.
A thousand have solidarity and your own newsletter;
ten thousand, power and your own paper;
a hundred thousand, your own media;
ten million, your own country.

It goes on one at a time,
It starts when you care
to act, it starts when you do
it again after they said no,
it starts when you say *We*
and know who you mean, and each
day you mean one more.[9]

RESOURCES

As with other listings in Bibliotherapy that may also be helpful in creating groups, not all of the books listed below are in print and may take a trip to the library.

Allen, Pamela. "Free Space," 1970, *Notes from the Third Year.* Reprinted in *Radical Feminism,* Anne Koedt, Ellen Levine, and Anita Rapone, editors. New York: Quadrangle/New York Times Book Co., 1973, pp. 271–279. Philosophy and goals of consciousness-raising.

Evans, Sara. *Personal Politics: The Roots of Women's Liberation in the Civil Rights Movement and the New Left.* New York: Knopf, 1979. The birth of small-group feminism.

Hagan, Kay Leigh. "Co-dependency and the Myth of Recovery," "The Habit of Freedom," *Fugitive Information: Essays from a Feminist Hothead.* San Francisco: Harper, 1993. Two essays: a feminist critique of co-dependency groups, and the necessity of women sharing experience as an escape from the colonized mind.

Kasl, Charlotte. *Many Paths, One Journey.* San Francisco: HarperCollins, 1992. A feminist psychologist replaces "recovery" with "discovery" of the self, and adapts the twelve steps to women.

Kimmel, Michael S., and Thomas Mosmiller, editors. *Against the Tide: "Pro-Feminist Men" in the United States: 1776–1990, A Documentary History.* Boston: Beacon Press, 1992.

Kivel, Paul. *Men's Work: How to Stop the Violence That Tears Our Lives Apart.* Center City, Minnesota: Hazelden, 1992. A personal journey, with exercises and group topics at the end of each chapter, by a co-founder of the Oakland Men's Project.

Kleiman, Carol. *Women's Networks.* New York: Lippencott & Crowell, 1980. The gamut of women's support, self-help, and networking groups.

"NOW Guidelines for Feminist Consciousness-Raising," 1982, National Organization for Women, 1000 16th Street N.W., Suite 700, Washington, D.C. 20036, (202)331-0066. Process and topics used by NOW in groups with leaders, of eight to ten weeks duration. Many chapters offer these groups for anyone, not just NOW members. Join one — or order this $10.00, 93-page guide to help start your own.

Pennebaker, James W. *Opening Up: The Healing Power of Confiding in Others.* New York: Avon, 1991.

Sarachild, Kathie. "A Program for Feminist Consciousness-raising." *Notes from the Second Year.* 1968. Reprinted in *Women Together,* Judith Papachristou, editor. New York: Knopf, 1976. Outline of subjects and process as presented to early women's liberation conference by a pioneer.

Self-Esteem for Women, 1079 West Morse Boulevard, Suite A, Winter Park, Florida 32789. (800) 531-2208. Three-day weekends, twenty-five women each, in various parts of the country, for a fee, scholarships available. Also help with creating continuing groups.

Stambler, Sookie, editor. *Women's Liberation.* New York: Ace Books, 1970. Although out of print, this book is worth tracking down at a library for its essays by June Arnold and Susan Brownmiller on their experiences with consciousness-raising groups. Also of interest are excerpts from an essay by Patricia M. Robinson, "A Historical and Critical Essay for Black Women of the Cities," which explores connections between race and sex, women and nature.

Stettbacher, J. Konrad. *Making Sense of Suffering: The Healing Confrontation with Your Own Past,* with Foreword and Afterword by Alice Miller. New York: Dutton, 1991. A four-step program — usable by groups or individuals — for confronting and interrupting cycles of childhood trauma.

Appendix I: Meditation Guide

Read this text all the way through first. You may then decide to improvise your own induction, use the instructions printed here *in italics* as a general guide, tape-record yourself reading them (with appropriate pauses to stretch them out to about twenty minutes) so that you can be guided through each meditation by your own voice; or go on this journey with a trusted partner who will read the induction aloud to you, then ask you questions afterward to strengthen what your conscious mind has learned — and then reverse roles. Find the way — and the words — that suit you.

The induction that follows serves as a signal to your deeper, unconscious, back-of-the-mind self that it is to be your guide. Your conscious, front-of-the-mind self will be only a passenger on this journey, but because you are doing something new, that conscious self may be skeptical at first:

• Do you feel that you simply don't have time to meditate? Remember all the ways it will more than pay back the time by helping you work more efficiently and benefiting your health, as well as taking you on an inward journey. (I've listed some books that go into these results in more detail.)

• Do you fear that you can't concentrate? Don't try to shut out distractions; just let any thoughts come into your mind, observe them as they float through — and then let them go.

• Do you feel you become less real if you are not acting, responding, or being responded to? Remember that as you sit quietly, you are an active part of the universe. "Unlikely as it seems," as Edward Lorenz, a meteorologist at the Massachusetts Institute of Technology, explained, "the tiny air currents that a butterfly creates travel across thousands of miles, jostling other breezes as they go and eventually changing the weather." Like the air moved by a butterfly, even your breath travels miles and links you to all things, large and small.

• Are you afraid of what you may discover if you turn inward? Your unconscious self can be trusted to take care of you. It is the part that always protects you, even when you are asleep. As it sends up feelings and images, the conscious and observing mind will become more interested — and trusting.

• Do you feel skeptical about this process, or about whether it's right for you? Then just proceed *as if* you believed.

Have a notebook with you in which to jot down your impressions after each of these voyages, even if they are only in phrases and fragments. Later, your conscious self will discover associations, patterns, and insights that may help you to understand events in the past, how they are shaping your present, and how you would like them to shape the future.

Entering Inner Space

In the early morning or other quiet time, take a half hour for yourself, find a comfortable chair that supports your back, and turn off the phone and other distractions. If this is impossible where you live, find a public library, religious space, or other quiet place for you (or for you and your partner) to absorb instructions like these:

Sit with your back supported, feet flat on the floor, hands resting on your lap with palms upward.

Now bring your consciousness to one part of your body at a time, tensing each area as hard as you can, then just letting go. Feel the heaviness in each part of your body as you let it go — completely. Start with your toes . . . feet . . . calves . . . thighs . . . then the muscles of your torso . . . shoulders . . . arms . . . hands . . . then your face. Tensing each area — then letting go. Now feel your head balancing easily over your shoulders. Let your body center itself.

Inhale deeply and slowly. Feel your ribs expand and your belly push out as you slowly inhale — then exhale the air more slowly than you breathed it. Do this six times — with consciousness. Feel the cool air as you breathe it in, and the warmer air as you breathe it out. Feel your body become larger with each inward breath and smaller with each outward breath.

Now forget about your breath completely and just feel the balance as you slowly close your eyes. Relax your eyelids, your forehead, relax your jaw. Let your mind "settle." If thoughts float up to the surface, don't resist them or pursue them. Just observe each one as it arrives — and then let it go.

Ask the back-of-your-mind to imagine a safe place. It may be a room you once knew or a place you once cherished. It may be a place you've never seen before except in this imagination of it — a beach, a mountaintop, a sunny room. As images come, trust them. If they don't come right away, just relax and wait. If they still don't come, imagine what a safe place would be like if you could imagine it.

Look around at this special place. What colors do you see? Run a hand over a surface near you: How does it feel? Are there special smells in this place? Are there tastes that seem part of this place? Can you feel the sun, the air, a breeze? What sounds do you hear? Notice which of your senses is the clearest or comes most quickly. Those are the strongest bridges to this safe place. You will be able to recall those feelings in everyday life when you need to feel safe. When you visit this place again, you may want to spend more time imagining with other senses and strengthening them, too.

Now just relax and be in this place. Nothing can happen here except what you wish to happen. If anything unwelcome appears, you will imagine it away. Only good things can happen to you here. Your unconscious is taking care of you. It has brought you to this special place of peace, restfulness, safety, and discovery.

Do you notice feelings? What is it about this place that makes you feel safe? Are there absences of things that give you that feeling? What other images, feelings, and associations do you notice? Let your conscious mind observe the gifts your unconscious is bringing you.

When your thoughts slip out of this place or you simply feel enough time has elapsed, you are ready to return. When you are back in your daily life, you will know that this place of peace and well-being exists within you. It will always be there whenever you need it. You will awaken feeling refreshed, centered, strong, and peaceful.

Inhale deeply and slowly as you count to six. Then exhale as you count to three. Do this several times — and feel the energy returning to your body. On the last count of three, open your eyes slowly. You have visited the home of your true self.

Your Child of the Past

After you have done the first exercise for a few days — or whenever your curiosity signals that it's time — go through the steps of the induction above, but this time, you're going to ask your inner child of the past to join you. Read through this additional stage of induction below, and record, remember, or share it — and then add it to the first stage.

Take a moment or two to be aware of your feelings about today's adventure. Are you fearful of this meeting? Or eager for its discoveries? Is this child a familiar part of you, or someone you've tried to forget? The emotion is less important than your ability to feel it.

Allow an image of your inner child to float to the surface from that back-of-the-mind. Trust whatever comes: a shadowy figure, an image from an old photograph, a version of the child you've never seen before, an infant, a teenager, a little child who runs to you, one who ignores you or turns away.

Before you reach out to this child, ask yourself what emotions she or he evokes in you. Do you feel happy or ashamed? Angry or impatient? Indifferent or affectionate? Awkward or at ease? Judgmental or accepting? Once you have sensed this, ask another question: "Am I feeling this way toward my inner child because my mother, father, or other caretaker felt this way toward me?" If so, take some time to understand that you did not invent this feeling, it was given to you. It isn't yours. It can be changed. Stay with these thoughts for this first meditation or come back to them for as long as you need.

Invite the child to be with you — but respect the child's response. If she or he isn't ready yet, that's fine. Explain that this is a special place where you do only what you wish. Your inner child may have been forced to pretend in the past, and it's important that this doesn't happen here. Try waiting until the child speaks to you — and if the child isn't ready yet, just stay there quietly and observe this child of the past. There will be a next time. There's plenty of time.

After the child does talk or come to you, see if he or she would like to be hugged or to sit on your lap. Feel the warmth and weight of the child's body, its contrast in size with yours, a small hand in your hand, the texture of skin and hair. Take a moment to be aware of the emotions this evokes in you — and in the child.

If the child comes to you easily and is open and happy, you might say: "I am your friend from the future. I'm here because I love you. I want to learn from you."

If the child is shy, unhappy, or afraid, you might say: "I've come from the future to help you and love you. I will protect you. Just tell me what you want and need."

At any point along the way, one of you may sense that you've come as far as you want to for today. That's fine. Assure the child that this special place will always be here. Whenever you need it. If the child is troubled or lonely, you might leave a part of yourself to comfort the child — and tell him or her that you are doing this. If the child has a spontaneity or other qualities you feel you have lost, you might ask a part of the child to stay with you after you return.

As your time together ends, remember that whatever you have thought, learned, or felt here is now part of you. The child is also part of you. You will come to know, trust, and help each other.

Take some energizing breaths, inhaling more slowly than you exhale. Count to six as you breathe in, count to three as you breathe out. On the last count, open your eyes. Look at your hands and imagine that a child's hands are inside them. You are one and the same person — but different. You can protect and care for your inner child.

Don't forget to make notes of your thoughts, impressions, associations, and feelings.

Meeting one's inner child is an experience both common and unique. Instructions like the ones above will change spontaneously when you are with your child, but some ritual does help. So does meeting regularly. If you find that you resist — for instance, if you fear that revisiting the past will imprison you there forever, or if you feel weaker than your inner child — follow the additional suggestions in the next exercise. Or just wait. Curiosity will tell you when you are ready.

Your child may appear in the safe place you've imagined, or in rooms the child knows that your conscious mind had forgotten. Eventually, you will bring your child into the present and show her or him where you live now: an important step in bringing the parts of your life together. You will recognize feelings (or absences of feelings) that protected you in childhood but aren't necessary anymore.

Even without this meditative trance state, you will be able to comfort the child, to reexperience feelings, or perhaps to experience them now as you couldn't then, and to know that painful past events were not your fault. You deserve to be loved and cared for — and you always did.

Reentering the past as your own protective parent doesn't change it, but it *can* change your emotional response to past events. The traditional benefit of hypnosis is *remembering* what the conscious mind has repressed. Self-hypnosis offers that — and also the activist benefit of self-empowerment and intervention.

After all, no one — not therapist or friend or even parent — knows the experiences, feelings, and needs of your inner child. Only you do.

Your Future Self

In meditation, you have met your child — your inner children, really, since they will come to you at different times and ages. Whenever you need the creativity and spontaneity of childhood — or a childhood self needs your comfort and protection — you can find them within.

But your present self also travels toward the future. That is a place not only of safety, but also of hope, dreams, and the greatest strength of your true self. If you let it, that true self will lead you. For this, you no longer need to visit rooms of the past. Instead, you will sense all the powers of nature within you. Thus, once you have gone through the first step of the induction as usual, you will add the passage below — or whatever version of it you prefer. Read through it first to see if you would like to make changes. You will be conjuring up your own magic place in nature.

Ask that back-of-the-mind part of you to imagine a beautiful natural scene that you would like to be part of: the ocean's edge, a pine woods, a mountain view, a river at sunrise, a moonlit field — whatever images arrive. There is a path or a road on which you have been traveling. It stretches out in front of you farther than the eye can see: it is your life's journey. Take a moment to use your senses and feel this place: breeze, ocean spray, sun, starlight, the scent of flowers, the sound of water — whatever comes to you with pleasure.

Now imagine there is a figure on the path ahead of you, walking where you have not walked, seeing what you have yet to see. It is your future self: wiser, more evolved, more productive, stronger, at peace — whatever you would like to be. This is your best self, your guide, who is leading you on life's path.

Pause to observe everything you can about this person. How does she or he look? What is her manner? What emotions does she elicit in you? What bond do you feel with her? How is he or she different from the self you are now? or the same? How does this future self feel toward the child in you? How does the child in you feel about this future self?

Now imagine that you are that future self, and you are looking back at yourself as you are now. As the future guide, how do you feel about this present self? Do you want to help him or her? What do you want her to know? What important things must she do or understand before becoming this best and future self?

Pause and think about the self-wisdom your future self is giving you. Let the conscious part of your mind take note of this gift from the unconscious. If it's too much to absorb now, ask your unconscious to store it up and give it to you at exactly the right time.

As your current self, say: "I will become you."

As your future self, say: "I'll always be inside you."

Leave a part of yourself to stay on this path, walking into the future, becoming more and more what you wish to be.

Let the scene fade from your imagination, breathe deep and energizing breaths, as before, and slowly open your eyes.

Note in your journal what seemed most important, surprising, wise. Make a new section for this future self. You will be visiting each other often.

There are many ways of meeting your future self. Imagining a figure ahead of you on life's path is one way. You might also think about a desired future event and imagine your future self within it. Or imagine a protecting future self who advises you in hard times, celebrates in good ones, and is always there for you to ask: What would my guide say?

The remarkable thing is that contemplating this best self will bring out those qualities in you and enable you to do seemingly impossible feats. For instance: If you have been stopped from visiting your inner child by a screen of fear — if you simply cannot go back as your present self — try asking your future self to visit that child. You will send back all your strengths, and your future self may be able to comfort that child of the past in a way you cannot yet do in the present.

Imagining yourself being led by both is the balance of past and future. Your child self brings you spontaneity and creativity. Your future self brings you wisdom and strength. Many people call on one or the other for help with a problem at hand — or remember both each morning as a guide to the day.

FOR FURTHER READING

Herbert Benson with Marion Z. Klipper. *The Relaxation Response.* New York: Avon Books, 1976. Eastern meditative techniques combined with Western scientific proof of effectiveness by a professor of medicine at Harvard Medical School: a simple how-to book with both graphs and poetry.

Joan Borysenko and Larry Rothstein. *Minding the Body, Mending the Mind.* New York: Simon and Schuster, 1988. Meditation as part of emotional and physical self-healing by a cofounder of Harvard's Mind/Body Clinic: her self-rescue plus experience with clinic cases from AIDS to allergies.

Diane Mariechild. *Mother Wit.* Freedom, California: The Crossing Press, 1988. Guided meditations and rituals for women, from relaxation to dream-recall and wicca ceremonies. A chapter of meditative exercises for children.

Nancy J. Napier. *Recreating Your Self.* New York: W. W. Norton, 1990. Theory and practice of self-hypnosis as a path to the inner child, changing family myths, healing traumatic events, and developing one's authentic self. (See chapter 4.)

Dr. Dean Ornish's Program for Reversing Heart Disease. New York: Random House, 1990. Meditation as a stress-reduction technique when combined with exercise, diet, and group support.

If you sense pain in your past or for any reason feel the need of a more long-term and orderly process, consider the four well-designed steps of self-therapy in *Making Sense of Suffering: The Healing Confrontation with Your Own Past* by J. Konrad Stettbacher, with foreword and afterword by Alice Miller, New York: Dutton, 1991. It also provides sensitive guidelines for selecting a group or therapist.

Appendix II: Bibliotherapy

I know we all learn in different ways, and books are no substitute for all-five-senses experience. But in case you are as helped as I am by what my friend Ginny Corsi, a New York activist in the financial world, calls "bibliotherapy," I wanted to leave you with some heartfelt suggestions. These are all books that I've found mind-opening myself or that I've witnessed as rescuing for others. All offer the self-confirmation of seeing shared experience on the page, some provide literal help with self-therapy and rescue, others contain facts and authoritative opinions we may need to stand up for what we think and feel, some open windows on new worlds and possibilities — and many do all of that and more. Not all are inclusive in their pronouns and vision of a reader's identity, but all offer ideas and information that are inclusive.

I haven't divided them up by constituency, partly because there was no room to be truly representative, but more important, because these are books we all should read. Usually, the less powerful know more about the powerful than vice versa — women know more about men, people of color know more about white people, lesbians and gay men know more about the heterosexual world, and so on. It's an imbalance that diminishes visibility for the first group and human possibilities for the second. According to a 1990 study conducted by the National Commission on Working Women, for instance, there are as many extraterrestrial aliens on television as there are Hispanic and Asian women and men. Several books here will show just how culturally deprived that makes everybody else. On other fronts, men may discover the self-rescuing and history-changing possibilities of raising children when they read *The Mermaid and the Minotaur*, and many readers may find they're reinventing wheels that have existed in our backyards for centuries when they read books by and about Native Americans. I've also included childrearing books, in this case less for parents than to help us become nurturing parents and advocates for our own child within: to understand what we missed, and to restore it.

Finally, I haven't confined myself to books currently in stores, so some of these may have to be ordered or found in libraries — perhaps your interest will bring them back into print, as they deserve — and I've only added a phrase of description when the title doesn't fully explain why it was included. And remember, this listing of nonfiction is a diverse and tantalizing sampler. Each book will lead you to many more.

Healing Childhood and Other Wounds
(See also Meditation Guide)

Alyson, Sasha, editor. *Young, Gay and Proud.* Boston: Alyson Publications, 1985. (A basic guide: coming out, health care, finding support groups.)

Bass, Ellen, and Laura Davis. *The Courage to Heal: A Guide for Women Survivors of Child Sexual Abuse.* New York: Perennial Library/Harper & Row, 1988. (An analysis and a personal workbook.)

Brightman, Alan. *Ordinary Moments.* Syracuse, New York: Human Policy Press, 1985. (Eight personal stories of women and men living full lives with physical handicaps.)

Brownmiller, Susan. *Against Our Will: Men, Women, and Rape.* New York: Bantam Books, 1975.

Chernin, Kim. *The Obsession: Reflections on the Tyranny of Slenderness.* New York: Harper Colophon, 1982.

Crewdson, John. *By Silence Betrayed: Sexual Abuse of Children in America.* Boston: Little, Brown, 1988. (A journalist's overview of the abuse of male and female children, with chapters on legal recourse, therapy, and prevention.)

Davis, Laura. *Allies in Healing: When the Person You Love Was Sexually Abused as a Child.* New York: Harper Perennial, 1991.

Dworkin, Andrea. *Woman Hating.* New York: E. P. Dutton, 1974. (From footbinding to pornography, the lethal results of negating the "feminine." Also see anything else by this author.)

Finlayson, Judith. *Season of Renewal: A Journal for Women Moving Beyond the Loss of Love.* New York: Crown, 1993. (A journal-keeping workbook for ending a love relationship.)

Forward, Susan. *Toxic Parents: Overcoming Their Hurtful Legacy and Reclaiming Your Life.* New York: Bantam Books, 1989.

Gilligan, Carol, Nona P. Lyons, and Trudy J. Hanmer. *Making Connections: The Relational Worlds of Adolescent Girls at Emma Willard School.* Cambridge, Massachusetts: Harvard University Press, 1990. (Female strengths "going underground" with adolescence — and what to do about it.)

Hemphill, Essex, editor. *Brother to Brother.* Boston: Alyson Publications, 1991. (Self-affirming writings by gay African-American men.)

Hochschild, Arlie. *The Second Shift.* New York: Avon Books, 1989. (A study of two-career couples that lets women know it's impossible to "do it all.")

Jack, Dana Crowley. *Silencing the Self: Women and Depression.* Cambridge, Massachusetts: Harvard University Press, 1991.

Jones, Ann, and Susan Schechter. *When Love Goes Wrong: What to Do When You Can't Do Anything Right.* New York: HarperCollins, 1992. (Self-rescue during and after a controlling relationship.)

Kasl, Charlotte Davis. *Women, Sex, and Addiction: A Search for Love and Power.* New York: Ticknor & Fields, 1989.

Kunjufu, Jawanza. *Developing Positive Images and Discipline in Black Children.* Chicago: African American Images, 1984.

Liedloff, Jean. *The Continuum Concept: Allowing Human Nature to Work Successfully.* Reading, Massachusetts: Addison-Wesley, 1991. (Modern childrearing and alienation from nature as a source of violence and pandemic pathology, and how to return to ancient, natural ways.)

Madhubuti, Haki. *Black Men: Obsolete, Single, Dangerous?* Chicago: Third World Press, 1990. (Healing the wounds of racism and strengthening the bonds between African-American women, men, and children.)

Martin, Del. *Battered Wives.* San Francisco: Volcano Press, 1981, revised edition. (The pioneering book on this issue.)

Masterson, James F. *The Search for the Real Self: Unmasking*

Personality Disorders of Our Age. New York: Free Press/Macmillan, 1988. (Narcissism as the false and inflated self, from adolescence through adulthood, with therapeutic suggestions.)

Miller, Alice. *For Your Own Good: Hidden Cruelty in Childrearing and the Roots of Violence,* with a new preface by the author. New York: Farrar, Straus and Giroux, 1990. (And any other books by this author.)

Missildine, W. Hugh. *Your Inner Child of the Past.* New York: Pocket Books, 1963. (Common excesses of childrearing, the patterns that result in adulthood, and simple self-therapies.)

Napier, Nancy. *Getting Through the Day: Strategies for Adults Hurt as Children.* New York: W. W. Norton, 1992. (A practical guide that explains dissociation and other discoveries.)

NiCarthy, Genny. *Getting Free.* Seattle, Washington: Seal Press, 1986. (A practical and inspirational guide for victims of domestic violence.)

Olsen, Tillie. *Silences.* New York: A Laurel/Seymour Lawrence Book, 1978. (Moving, classic expression of creative working-class women without time or resources to create.)

Orbach, Susie. *Fat Is a Feminist Issue: A Self-Help Guide for Compulsive Eaters.* New York: Berkley Books, 1990. (A classic on the politics of women's overeating.)

Pharr, Suzanne. *Homophobia: A Weapon of Sexism.* Little Rock, Arkansas: Chardon Press, 1988. (Everyday and far-reaching effects of falsifying one's true sexuality, and strategies for eliminating homophobia.)

Pogrebin, Letty Cottin. *Deborah, Golda, and Me: Being Female and Jewish in America.* New York: Crown, 1991.

Sanford, Linda T., and Mary Ellen Donovan. *Women & Self-Esteem: Understanding and Improving the Way We Think and Feel About Ourselves.* New York: Anchor/Doubleday, 1984. (An overview of women's self-esteem problems, with remedial exercises.)

Saxton, Marsha, and Florence Howe, editors. *With Wings: An Anthology of Literature By and About Women with Disabilities.* New York: The Feminist Press, 1987.

Schaef, Anne Wilson. *Co-dependence: Misunderstood — Mistreated.*

San Francisco: Harper & Row, 1986. (Expands the definition: a co-dependent as a well-socialized woman.)

Snodgrass, Jon, editor. *For Men Against Sexism: A Book of Readings*. Albion, California: Times Change Press, 1977. (A pioneering anthology.)

Stallibrass, Alison. *The Self-Respecting Child*. New York: Warner Books, 1979. (Especially good about early need to explore physical abilities.)

Wisechild, Louise M., editor. *She Who Was Lost Is Remembered: Healing from Incest Through Creativity*. Seattle: The Seal Press, 1991.

History As If Everybody Mattered — and Other Clues to a Remedial Education

Asian Women. Berkeley, California: Berkeley Asian American Studies, 1973. (A now-classic anthology by contemporary women.)

Chesler, Phyllis. *Women and Madness*. New York: Harvest/HBJ, 1989. (A basic critique of gender-bound definitions of sanity and madness, with an updated introduction by the author.)

Debo, Angie. *And Still the Waters Run: The Betrayal of the Five Civilized Tribes*. Princeton, New Jersey: Princeton University Press, 1991. (A 1940s history records the U.S. campaign against indigenous cultures.)

Dworkin, Andrea. *Right-Wing Women*. New York: Coward-McCann, 1983. (Why women may choose safety over self-respect.)

Ehrenreich, Barbara, and Deirdre English. *For Her Own Good: 150 Years of the Experts' Advice to Women*. New York: Anchor/Doubleday, 1978.

Faderman, Lillian. *Surpassing the Love of Men: Romantic Friendship and Love Between Women from the Renaissance to the Present*. New York: William Morrow, 1981. Also see her *Odd Girls and Twilight Lovers*. New York: Columbia University Press, 1991.

Faludi, Susan. *Backlash: The Undeclared War Against American*

Women. New York: Crown, 1991. (Documents the current media bias. Imagine the problems for future historians.)

Feig, Konnilyn G. *Hitler's Death Camps: The Sanity of Madness.* New York: Holmes and Meier, 1981. (The facts of genocide—including Ravensbruck, a women-only camp where medical "experimenting" was most common.)

French, Marilyn. *The War Against Women.* New York: Summit Books, 1992. (By the author of *The Women's Room,* a short book that summarizes what's wrong for the female half of the world.)

Geok-lin Lim, Shirley, and Mayumi Tsutakawa, editors. *The Forbidden Stitch: An Asian American Women's Anthology.* Corvallis, Oregon: Calyx Books, 1988.

Grahn, Judy. *Another Mother Tongue: Gay Words, Gay Worlds.* Boston: Beacon Press, 1984.

Greven, Philip. *Spare the Child: The Religious Roots of Punishment and the Psychological Impact of Physical Abuse.* New York: Knopf, 1991. (Distortions of American history and character by four centuries of punished children.)

Harding, Sandra. *Whose Science? Whose Knowledge?: Thinking from Women's Lives.* Ithaca, New York: Cornell University Press, 1991. (Rethinking the premises of knowledge itself.)

Jacobs, Harriet A. *Incidents in the Life of a Slave Girl.* Jean Fagin Yellin, editor. Cambridge, Massachusetts: Harvard University Press, 1987.

Katz, William Loren. *Black Indians: A Hidden Heritage.* New York: Atheneum, 1986.

Katz, William Loren. *Breaking the Chains: African-American Slave Resistance.* New York: Atheneum, 1990.

Lerner, Gerda. *The Creation of Patriarchy.* New York: Oxford University Press, 1986. (The changeover from "prehistory" — that is, prepatriarchy.)

Leghorn, Lisa, and Katherine Parker. *Women's Worth: Sexual Economics and the World of Women.* Boston: Routledge & Kegan Paul, 1981.

McAllister, Pam. *This River of Courage: Generations of Women's Resistance and Action.* Philadelphia: New Society Publishers,

1991. (Women's nonviolent actions, from Egypt of 1300 B.C.E. to the present.)

Mernissi, Fatima. *The Veil and the Male Elite: A Feminist Interpretation of Women's Rights in Islam*. Reading, Massachusetts: Addison-Wesley, 1991.

Miller, Jean Baker. *Toward a New Psychology of Women*. Boston: Beacon Press, 1986.

Minnich, Elizabeth Kamarck. *Transforming Knowledge*. Philadelphia: Temple University Press, 1990. (The biased assumptions underlying traditional scholarship.)

Moraga, Cherrie, and Gloria Anzaldua. *This Bridge Called My Back: Writings by Radical Women of Color*. New York: Kitchen Table/Women of Color Press, 1983. (Poems, essays, personal fragments: politics from the heart.)

Morgan, Robin, editor. *Sisterhood Is Global: The International Women's Movement Anthology*. New York: Anchor/Doubleday, 1984. (Essays by and on the female half of sixty-seven countries, plus herstory, mythography, and statistics. Invaluable.)

Plaskow, Judith. *Standing Again at Sinai*. New York: Harper & Row, 1990. (Fills in the silences of women in Judaic tradition.)

Rich, Adrienne. *Of Woman Born: Motherhood as Experience and Institution*. New York: Bantam Books, 1986.

Riley, Glenda. *Divorce: An American Tradition*. New York: Oxford University Press, 1991. (Divorce since the Puritans.)

Rodney, Walter. *How Europe Under-developed Africa*. Washington, D.C.: Howard University Press, 1982.

Rothschild, Joan, editor. *Machina ex Dea: Feminist Perspectives on Technology*. New York: Pergamon Press, Athene Series, 1983.

Rush, Florence. *The Best-Kept Secret: Sexual Abuse of Children*. New York: McGraw-Hill, 1980.

Salmonson, Jessica Amanda. *The Encyclopedia of Amazons*. New York: Paragon House, 1991. (A cross-cultural reference on women warriors from antiquity to modern times.)

Schiebinger, Londa. *The Mind Has No Sex? Women in the Origins of Modern Science*. Cambridge, Massachusetts: Harvard University Press, 1991.

Sjoo, Monica, and Barbara Mor. *The Great Cosmic Mother: Rediscovering the Religion of the Earth.* San Francisco: Harper & Row, 1987. (One of the few books on prepatriarchal religions that includes their African origins.)

Smith, Barbara, editor. *Home Girls: A Black Feminist Anthology.* New York: Kitchen Table/Women of Color Press, 1983. (A now-classic anthology, with many diverse personal voices, and "The Combahee River Collective Statement" on the origins and beliefs of contemporary black feminism.)

Spender, Dale. *Men's Studies Modified: The Impact of Feminism on the Academic Disciplines.* New York: Pergamon Press, Athene Series, 1987. (An introduction to changed premises in many fields.)

Swirski, Barbara, and Marilyn P. Safir. *Calling the Equality Bluff: Women in Israel.* New York: Macmillan, 1991. (Wide-ranging essays on life in Israel focused on secular Jewish women, including religious, Arab, and Oriental women.)

Takaki, Ronald. *Strangers from a Different Shore: A History of Asian Americans.* Boston: Little, Brown, 1989. (The full sweep of Asian immigration — with a human face.)

Thompson, Robert Farris. *Flash of the Spirit: African and Afro-American Art and Philosophy.* New York: Vintage Books, 1984.

Todorov, Tzvetan. *The Conquest of America.* New York: Harper & Row, 1984. (A history of the Latin invasion of America.)

Washington, Mary Helen. *Invented Lives: Narratives of Black Women 1860–1960.* New York: Anchor/Doubleday, 1987.

Weatherford, Jack. *Indian Givers: How the Indians of the Americas Transformed the World.* New York: Fawcett Columbine, 1988. (From the origins of the U.S. Constitution in the Iroquois League to old wisdom for new ecology.)

Williams, Patricia J. *The Alchemy of Race and Rights.* Cambridge, Massachusetts: Harvard University Press, 1991. (How racial and sexual bias has been encoded in U.S. laws and values.)

Zinn, Howard. *A People's History of the United States.* New York: Perennial Library/Harper & Row, 1980.

Zuckermen, Harriet, Jonathan R. Cole, and John T. Bruer, editors. *The Outer Circle: Women in the Scientific Community.* New York: W. W. Norton, 1991.

New Possibilities, New Paradigms

Allen, Paula Gunn. *Grandmothers of the Light: A Medicine Woman's Sourcebook*. Boston: Beacon Press, 1991. (Stories of many civilizations.)

Allen, Robert L., and Herb Boyd, editors. *Brotherman: An Anthology of Writings by and about Black Men*. New York: Ballantine, 1993.

Anderson, Sherry Ruth, and Patricia Hopkins. *The Feminine Face of God: The Unfolding of the Sacred in Women*. New York: Bantam Books, 1991. (Spirituality from the true self unmediated by religion, as experienced by diverse contemporary women.)

Anzaldua, Gloria, editor. *Borderland/La Frontera: The New Meztiza*. San Francisco: Aunt Lute Press, 1991. (Essays, fiction, and poetry by a range of Latina women, anthologized by one of the creators of *This Bridge Called My Back* — and a worthy successor.)

Asian Women United of California. *Making Waves*. Boston: Beacon Press, 1989. (An anthology of new voices and future directions.)

A Basic Call to Consciousness. Rooseveltown, New York: Akwesasne Notes/ Mohawk Nation, 1978. (A pamphlet of position papers addressed to the Western world and presented by the Iroquois Confederacy to United Nations in 1977: part of an international movement among indigenous cultures.)

Bracey, Hyler, Jack Rosenblum, Aubrey Sanford, Roy Trueblood. *Managing from the Heart*. New York: Delacorte Press, 1990. (A step-by-step parable of how an insecure, dictatorial manager became a nurturing and productive one: for anyone who is, or has, a boss.)

Brown, Melanie. *Attaining Personal Greatness: One Book for Life*. New York: William Morrow, 1987. (Inspiring personal stories, new connections on a we-can-do-anything theme.)

Buzan, Tony. *Use Both Sides of Your Brain*. New York: Dutton, 1983. (A workbook.)

Calyx Editorial Collective. *Women and Aging: An Anthology by*

Women. Corvallis, Oregon: Calyx Books, 1986. (Diverse voices, with vision and humor.)

Capra, Fritjof. *The Tao of Physics: An Exploration of the Parallels Between Modern Physics and Eastern Mysticism.* New York: Bantam Books, revised edition, 1984.

Cousins, Norman. *Head First: The Biology of Hope.* New York: Dutton, 1989.

Dinnerstein, Dorothy. *The Mermaid and the Minotaur: Sexual Arrangements and Human Malaise.* New York: Harper & Row, 1976. (How men raising children as much as women do could change inequality, the inevitability of war, and human nature.)

Edwards, Audrey, and Dr. Craig K. Polite. *Children of the Dreams: The Psychology of Black Success.* New York: Doubleday, 1992. (Interviews with forty-one successful African-American women and men on their empowerment through positive racial identity.)

Eisler, Riane. *The Chalice and the Blade: Our History, Our Future.* San Francisco: Harper & Row, 1988. (Using a prepatriarchal past to create a partnership future.)

Estes, Clarissa Pinkola. *Women Who Run with the Wolves.* New York: Ballantine Books, 1992. (Multicultural myths and stories to evoke a true self "civilized" into an endangered species.)

Feuerstein, Georg. *Sacred Sexuality: Living the Vision of the Erotic Spirit.* Los Angeles: Jeremy P. Tarcher, 1992.

Finlayson, Judith. *A Book of One's Own: A Journal for Women in Search of Themselves.* New York: Crown, 1993. (A journal-keeping workbook to help in finding one's authentic voice.)

Gilligan, Carol. *In a Different Voice.* Cambridge, Massachusetts: Harvard University Press, 1983. (Women's culturally different standards of ethics.)

Goldberg, Natalie. *Writing Down the Bones: Freeing the Writer Within.* Boston: Shambhala, 1986.

Hagan, Kay Leigh. *Internal Affairs: A Journal-keeping Workbook for Self-Intimacy.* San Francisco: Harper & Row, 1990. For *Fugitive Information,* her quarterly essays on such subjects as a feminist critique of co-dependency (and for a good example of self-publishing), write to Escapadia Press, P.O. Box 5298, Atlanta, Georgia 30307.

Haraway, Donna. *Primate Visions: Gender, Race, and Nature in the World of Modern Science.* New York: Routledge, 1989.

Heilbrun, Carolyn G. *Toward a Recognition of Androgyny.* New York: W. W. Norton, 1973. (Possibilities of wholeness.)

Herman, Judith Lewis. *Trauma and Recovery: The Aftermath of Violence — from Domestic Abuse to Political Terror.* New York: Basic Books, 1992. (A new understanding of links between the trauma men suffer in public wars and the trauma suffered by women in private ones gives new hope for recovery to both.)

Imber-Black, Evan, and Janine Roberts. *Rituals for Our Times: Celebrating, Healing, and Changing Our Lives and Our Relationships.* New York: HarperCollins, 1992. (Restoring meaning in old traditions, and creating new ones that fit our lives and families.)

Kivel, Paul. *Men's Work: How to Stop the Violence That Tears Our Lives Apart.* Center City, Minnesota: Hazelden Educational Materials, 1992. (Personal, commonsense guide, with group discussion subjects, by cofounder of Oakland Men's Project.)

Klepfisz, Irena. *Dreams of an Insomniac: Jewish Feminist Essays, Speeches, and Diatribes.* Portland, Oregon: Eighth Mountain Press, 1990. (A rabbinical love of ideas in a lesbian feminist head.)

Kohn, Alfie. *No Contest: The Case Against Competition.* Boston: Houghton Mifflin, 1986.

Lippard, Lucy R. *Mixed Blessings: New Art in a Multicultural America.* New York: Pantheon Books, 1990. (Out of museums and into everyday life: art as a way of expressing complex identities.)

London, Peter. *No More Secondhand Art: Awakening the Artist Within.* Boston: Shambhala, 1989.

McGaa, Ed, Eagle Man. *Mother Earth Spirituality: Native American Paths to Healing Ourselves and Our World.* San Francisco: Harper & Row, 1990. (A primer of spiritual and communal concepts and practices.)

MacKinnon, Catharine A. *Toward a Feminist Theory of the State.* Cambridge, Massachusetts: Harvard University Press, 1989.

Miedzian, Myriam. *Boys Will Be Boys: Breaking the Link Between Masculinity and Violence.* New York: Doubleday, 1991. (Societal origins of a mystique that punishes both men and women — and how to change.)

Morgan, Robin. *Anatomy of Freedom: Feminism, Physics, and Global Politics.* New York: Anchor/Doubleday, 1984.

Ostrander, Sheila, and Lynn Schroeder. *Super-Learning.* New York: Delacorte/Confucian Press, 1979.

Pifer, Alan, and Lydia Bronte, editors. *Our Aging Society: Paradox and Promise.* New York: W. W. Norton, 1986.

Rico, Gabrielle Lusser. *Writing the Natural Way: Using Right Brain Techniques to Release Your Expressive Powers.* Los Angeles: J. P. Tarcher/Houghton Mifflin, 1986.

Schechter, Susan. *Women and Male Violence.* Boston: South End Press, 1982. (History and resources of the antiviolence movement, but also analysis and agenda for the future.)

Shepard, Paul. *Nature and Madness.* San Francisco: Sierra Club Books, 1982. (Failed self-development as a cause of destructiveness toward nature.)

Shuman, Sandra G. *Source Imagery: Releasing the Power of Your Creativity.* New York: Doubleday, 1989. (Art-making to find our unique image — with a brief section on writing.)

Slater, Philip. *A Dream Deferred: America's Discontent and the Search for a Democratic Ideal.* Boston: Beacon Press, 1991. (Taking on the authoritarianism mindset.)

Stoltenberg, John. *Refusing to Be a Man.* New York: Penguin USA/Meredian, 1990. (A visionary view that leaves masculinity behind.)

Tompkins, Peter, and Christopher Bird. *The Secret Life of Plants.* New York: Harper & Row, 1989. (An amazing compendium of studies on the intelligence of plant life.)

Walker, Alice. *In Search of Our Mother's Gardens.* New York: Harcourt, Brace, Jovanovich, 1983. (You'll be a better person when you finish these womanist essays — or anything else by this author.)

Walker, Barbara G. *The Crone: Women of Age, Wisdom, and Power.* San Francisco: Harper & Row, 1985.

Waring, Marilyn. *If Women Counted: A New Feminist Economics.* San Francisco: Harper & Row, 1988. (An international, practical, visionary plan for attributing value to women's unpaid labor and to the environment.)

Notes

A PERSONAL PREFACE

1. Dr. Joseph Murphy, *The Power of Your Subconscious Mind,* New York: Bantam Books, 1982, pp. 9–10.

2. Judith Briles, *The Confidence Factor: How Self-Esteem Can Change Your Life,* New York: MasterMedia Limited, 1990, p. 199. A compilation of a nationwide survey completed in 1988.

3. *The Current Digest of the Soviet Press,* volume XLI, number 8, 1989, pp. 5 and 24.

4. "Estonia," produced by William McClure, *60 Minutes,* New York: CBS News, August 6, 1989, p. 11.

5. Speech by Gabriela Bocec, vice president of the newly formed Family Planning Association of Romania, for Voters for Choice, Los Angeles, August 7, 1990.

6. For instance, when college students were divided into two groups labeled "alphas" and "betas," individuals with high self-esteem rated the other group *and* their own more highly than low self-esteem participants, who had a negative view of both. For a report on this experiment by Jennifer Crocker from the State University of New York at Buffalo, and Ian Schwartz, a student at Northwestern University, see "Effects of Self-Esteem on Prejudice and Ingroup Favoritism in a Minimal Intergroup Situation," *Personality and Social Psychology Bulletin,* volume XI, number 4, 1985.

ONE: WHAT IS SELF-ESTEEM?

1. The 1971–72 Virginia Slims Poll, the first national survey of women's opinions on women's issues. Designed by Carolyn Setlow, Louis Harris and Associates, 630 Fifth Avenue, New York, New York.

2. Ryszard Kapuscinski, "Revolution," translated from the Polish by William R. Brand and Katarzyna Mcoczkowska-Brand, *The New Yorker,* March 4 and March 11, 1985.

3. For a summary of Task Force research, see *The Social Importance of Self-Esteem,* Andrew M. Mecca, Neil J. Smelser, and John Vasconcellos, editors, Berkeley, California: University of California Press, 1989.

For ongoing activities and conferences nationwide, contact the private group that took over from the Task Force: National Council for Self-Esteem, P.O. Box 277877, Sacramento, California, 95827-7877, (916) 455-6273.

4. This quote, and those from the Upanishads, are from *A Source Book in Indian Philosophy,* Sarvepalli Radhakrishnan and Charles A. Moore, editors, Princeton, New Jersey: Princeton University Press, 1957, pp. 38 and 45.

5. Gloria Steinem, *Marilyn: Norma Jeane,* New York: Henry Holt, 1986.

6. W. Hugh Missildine, *Your Inner Child of the Past,* New York: Simon and Schuster, 1963, pp. 222 and 224.

7. Elizabeth Kamarck Minnich, *Transforming Knowledge,* Philadelphia: Temple University Press, 1990, pp. 37–38.

8. Marilyn Murphy, *Are You Girls Travelling Alone?,* Los Angeles: Clothespin Fever Press, 1991, p. 20. For her current columns, write to *The Lesbian News,* P.O. Box 1430, Twenty-nine Palms, California 92277.

9. For Gandhi's quotations and descriptions of his life though 1921, see *An Autobiography or The Story of My Experiments with Truth* by M. K. Gandhi, translated from the Gujarati by Mahadev Desai, Ahmedabad, India: Navajivan Publishing House, 1982.

For later references, see *Gandhi the Man* by Eknath Easwaran, Petaluma, California: Nilgiri Press, 1983; and *Gandhi: His Life and Message for the World* by Louis Fischer, New York: A Signet Key Book/New American Library, 1954.

References to the Indian Women's Movement are from interviews with Devaki Jain, Indian Council of Social Science Research, New Delhi, India, March 1978.

10. For a full story of SEWA, see *Where Women Are Leaders: The SEWA Movement in India,* Kalima Rose, Beverly Hills, New Delhi, London: Sage Publications, 1991.

For information on women's economic empowerment projects in the United States, contact the Ms. Foundation for Women, 141 Fifth Avenue, New York, New York 10010.

11. Alan Watts, *The Book: On the Taboo Against Knowing Who You Are,* New York: Random House, 1989, p. 124.

TWO: IT'S NEVER TOO LATE FOR A HAPPY CHILDHOOD

1. Those usually pointed to are tribal and indigenous cultures. For instance, Paul Shepard points out in *Nature and Madness*, "There have been and are societies in which a demonstrable affection for children is manifest in loving concern and a benign strategy of appropriate, age-grade care that fosters growth toward maturity and the capacity for wisdom and mentorship. Some examples are the Manus of New Guinea, the Crow and Comanche of North America, the Aranda of Australia, and the !Kung San of Africa." (San Francisco: Sierra Club Books, 1982, p. xii.) But of course, there are also many such examples within modern industrial societies; they are just not yet strong or numerous enough to be the mainstream.

2. Narcissism is generally defined as an inability to know one's own emotions or to empathize with those of others, grandiosity, an equation of oneself with the world and vice versa, intense ambition, conscious or unconscious exploitation of others, and an excessive need to be admired — all covers for an inner emptiness and terror of abandonment due to the underdevelopment of a true self. The narcissist greets losses with anger instead of sadness, for anger puts one in the right, and sadness or depression would be an admission of vulnerability. Because such behavior is culturally more masculine, it's assumed that this personality disorder is more common among men, though the reluctance of the narcissist to seek or remain in treatment means there are no reliable statistics. For a general discussion, see James F. Masterson, *The Search for the Real Self*, New York: The Free Press/Macmillan, 1988. For its societal expression, see Christopher Lasch, *The Culture of Narcissism*, New York: W. W. Norton, 1979. For its historical construction as male dominance, see Marilyn French, *Beyond Power: On Women, Men, and Morals*, chapter 2, New York: Summit Books, 1985.

3. In the United States and in most Western societies, twice as many women as men report major depressive symptoms and are diagnosed with depression. See studies and analysis in *Silencing the Self: Women and Depression* by Dana Crowley Jack, Cambridge, Massachusetts: Harvard University Press, 1991.

4. D. W. Winnicott, "Ego Integration in Child Development," *The Maturational Processes and the Facilitating Environment*, New York: International Universities Press, 1962, pp. 56–63.

5. Quoted in *The Self-Respecting Child* by Alison Stallibrass, London: Thames and Hudson, 1977, p. 201.

6. Linda T. Sanford, *Strong at the Broken Places*, New York: Random House, 1990, p. 14.

7. For the first in-depth study of randomly selected women, see Diana E. H. Russell, *The Secret Trauma: Incest in the Lives of Girls and Women,* New York: Basic Books, 1986.

8. Alice Miller, *For Your Own Good: Hidden Cruelty in Childrearing and the Roots of Violence,* New York: The Noonday Press, Farrar, Straus and Giroux, 1990, pp. 59–60.

9. Gloria Steinem, "If Hitler Were Alive, Whose Side Would He Be On?" *Outrageous Acts and Everyday Rebellions,* New York: Holt, Rinehart and Winston, pp. 305–326.

10. Miller, *For Your Own Good,* p. 142.

11. Ibid., pp. 160–161.

12. Ibid., p. 168.

13. Ibid., p. 156.

14. Peter Z. Malkin and Harry Stein, *Eichmann in My Hands,* New York: Warner Books, 1990, pp. 206–207.

15. For two studies showing children's charges to be fabricated in less than 2 and 4 percent of cases, see *By Silence Betrayed: Sexual Abuse of Children in America,* by John Crewdson, Boston: Little, Brown, 1988, p. 169. For an analysis of specific child abuse cases, see "Child Sexual Abuse: An Analysis of Case Processing," March 27, 1987, Criminal Justice Section, American Bar Association, 1800 M Street N.W., Washington, D.C. 20036.

16. Sylvia Fraser, *My Father's House: A Memoir of Incest and of Healing,* New York: Perennial Library, 1987, p. 12.

17. W. Hugh Missildine, M. D., *Your Inner Child of the Past,* New York: Pocket Books, p. 67.

18. Sanford, *Strong at the Broken Places,* pp. 9–10.

19. Carol Gilligan, Nona P. Lyons, and Trudy J. Hanmer, editors, *Making Connections: The Relational Worlds of Adolescent Girls at Emma Willard School,* Cambridge, Massachusetts: Harvard University Press, 1990, pp. 2–5. For information on programs based on the insights of Gilligan's research and aimed at strengthening healthy rebellion in little girls, contact the National Girls Initiative, Ms. Foundation for Women, 141 Fifth Avenue, New York, New York 10010.

20. Carolyn Heilbrun, *Writing a Woman's Life,* New York: Ballantine Books, 1989, p. 130.

21. Bryan E. Robinson, *Work Addiction,* Deerfield Beach, Florida: Health Communications, 1989, pp. 1–21.

22. Carol Burnett, *A Memoir: One More Time,* New York: Avon Books, 1987.

23. National Foundation for the Children of Alcoholics, 555 Madison Avenue, New York, New York 10022.

24. For the problems of families and family policy in the United States — and what to do about them — see *Family Politics: Love and Power on an Intimate Frontier* by Letty Cottin Pogrebin, New York: McGraw-Hill, 1983.

25. For more information, write Cherokee Nations Communications, P.O. Box 948, Tahlequah, Oklahoma 74465.

26. Alice Miller, *Pictures of a Childhood: Sixty-six Watercolors and an Essay*, New York: Farrar, Straus and Giroux, 1986, pp. 4–5.

27. Ibid., p. 11.

28. Ibid., p. 5.

29. Alice Miller, *Breaking Down the Wall of Silence: The Liberating Experience of Facing Painful Truth*, New York: Dutton, 1991, pp. 9–12.

30. J. Konrad Stettbacher, *Making Sense of Suffering: The Healing Confrontation with Your Own Past*, New York: Dutton, 1991.

31. Alice Miller, *The Drama of the Gifted Child*, New York: Basic Books, 1987, new preface, pp. vii–viii.

THREE: THE IMPORTANCE OF UN-LEARNING

1. An interview with Joan Erikson, wife of the psychologist Erik Erikson, *New York Times*, June 14, 1988. If her name is not as familiar as his, that's part of the problem of education. For more than forty years, she has been coauthor and editor of his many books on psychology and the human life cycle. Wisdom, she explained, is "not what comes from reading great books. When it comes to understanding life, experiential learning is the only worthwhile kind; everything else is hearsay."

2. "College Reunion," *Outrageous Acts and Everyday Rebellions*, New York: Holt, Rinehart and Winston, 1983, pp. 119–128.

3. Reported in "If Only We Had Learned Differently: The Impact of Formal Schooling," Linda T. Sanford and Mary Ellen Donovan, *Women and Self-Esteem*, New York: Anchor/Doubleday, 1984, pp. 177–196.

4. Reported by Sharon E. Epperson, "Studies Link Subtle Sex Bias in Schools With Women's Behavior in the Workplace," *Wall Street Journal*, September 16, 1988, p. 19.

5. Myra Pollack Sadker and David Miller Sadker, *Beyond Pictures and Pronouns: Sexism in Teacher Education Textbooks*, U.S. Dept. of Health, Education and Welfare, Office of Education, Women's Educational Equity Act Program, 1980, p. 25.

6. Sadker and Sadker, "Sexism in the Schoolroom of the 80's," *Psychology Today,* March 1985, p. 54.

7. United Press International, "Study of Black Females Cites Role of Praise," *New York Times,* June 25, 1985.

8. "Short-changing Girls, Short-changing America," American Association of University Women, 1111 16th Street, N.W., Washington, D.C. 20036.

9. Herbert Kohl, *I Won't Learn from You! The Role of Assent in Learning,* Minneapolis: Milkweed Editions, Thistle Series, 1991, p. 25.

10. Carol Gilligan, Nona P. Lyons, and Trudy J. Hanmer, *Making Connections: The Relational Worlds of Adolescent Girls at Emma Willard School,* Cambridge, Massachusetts: Harvard University Press, 1990.

11. From press release for AAUW's "Short-changing Girls, Short-changing America."

12. Marcia C. Linn, Tina De Benedictis, Kevin Delucchi, Abigail Harris, and Elizabeth Stage, "Gender Differences in National Assessment of Educational Progress Science Items: What Does 'I Don't Know' Really Mean?" Lawrence Hall of Science, University of California, *Journal of Research in Science Teaching,* vol. 24, no. 3, 1987, pp. 267–278.

13. John D. Miller and Robert Suchner, "Longitudinal Study of American Youth," cited in *The SAT Gender Gap: Identifying the Causes* by Phyllis Rosser, Washington, D.C.: Center for Women Policy Studies, April 1989, p. 64.

14. Bernice Sandler, "The Classroom Climate: A Chilly One for Women?," a 1982 report of the Project on the Status and Education of Women, Association of American Colleges, 1818 R Street N.W., Washington, D.C. 20009. To receive "About Women on Campus," a newsletter by Bernice Sandler begun in the fall of 1991 to cover issues of higher education for women, contact Bernice Sandler, Center for Women Policy Studies, 2000 P Street N.W., Washington, D.C. 20036.

15. Alexander W. Astin, *Four Critical Years,* San Francisco: Jossey-Bass, 1988, pp. 232–233.

For additional studies, contact the Women's College Coalition, 1090 Vermont Avenue, N.W., Washington, D.C. 20005.

16. Mary Conroy, "Where Have All the Smart Girls Gone?" *Psychology Today,* April 1989, p. 20.

17. Astin, *Four Critical Years,* p. 216. See also pp. 213–233.

18. Karen D. Arnold, "Values and Vocations: The Career Aspirations of Academically Gifted Females in the First Five Years After High School," College of Education, University of Illinois at Urbana-Champaign, 1987, p. 5.

19. Karen D. Arnold and Terry Denny, "The Lives of Academic Achievers," Bureau of Educational Research, College of Education, University of Illinois at Urbana-Champaign, 1985, p. 16.

20. Arnold, "Values and Vocations," pp. 94–95.

21. Gerda Lerner, *The Creation of Patriarchy,* New York and Oxford: Oxford University Press, 1986, p. 225. This is volume I of a two-volume history of Western Civilization.

22. Carter G. Woodson, *Miseducation of the Negro,* Washington D.C.: Associated Publishers, 1933, pp. xiii, 5, 38. The use of *man* may have been Carter's own unconscious evidence of miseducation, since many African cultures and languages are more inclusive of women than are European ones.

23. E. Franklin Frazier, *Black Bourgeoisie,* New York: Collier Books, 1962, p. 112.

24. Lerner, *Creation,* p. 3.

25. Reported by Jawanza Kunjufu, *Developing Positive Self-Images and Discipline in Black Children,* Chicago: African-American Images, 1984, p. 9.

26. Quoted by Carol Steinberg, "How 'Magic Circles' Build Self-Esteem," *New York Times,* February 18, 1990.

27. L. Perry Curtis, Jr., *Apes and Angels,* Washington, D.C.: Smithsonian Institution, 1971. (With thanks to its editor, my cousin Louise Heskett.)

28. Sigmund Freud, "Some Psychical Consequences of the Anatomical Distinction Between the Sexes" (1925), *Standard Edition of the Complete Psychological Works,* James Strachey, translator and editor, London: Hogarth Press, 1961, XIX, pp. 257–258.

29. See Margaret Murray, *God of the Witches,* London: Oxford University Press, 1970; Margaret Murray, *Witch Cults in Western Europe,* London: Oxford University Press, 1962; C. L'Estrange Ewan, *Witch Hunting and Witch Trials,* London: Kegan Paul, 1929; Heinrich Kramer and James Sprenger, *Malleus Malificarum,* New York: Dover, 1971. Also see works by Gerald Gardner, Pennthorne Hughes, Robin Morgan.

30. Ruth Bleier, *Science and Gender,* New York: Pergamon Press, 1984, pp. 48–50.

31. Ibid., p. 49.

32. Stephen Jay Gould, *The Mismeasure of Man,* New York: W. W. Norton, 1981, p. 104.

33. Elizabeth Fee, "Nineteenth-Century Craniology: The Study of the Female Skull," *Bulletin of the History of Medicine,* The American Association for the History of Medicine, Johns Hopkins Institute for the

History of Medicine, volume 53, number 3, Fall 1979, pp. 430–431. Fee's careful analysis and research of quotes from the day make clear that these scientists were often well aware of and responding to arguments for equality.

34. Tom Wicker, "An Elusive Dream," *New York Times,* November 10, 1989.

35. "Stalin's Brain," *New York Times,* September 16, 1991.

36. Gould, *Mismeasure of Man,* p. 28.

37. Quoted by Stephanie A. Shields, "The Variability Hypothesis: The History of a Biological Model of Sex Differences in Intelligence," *Sex and Scientific Inquiry,* Sandra Harding and Jean F. Barr, editors, Chicago: University of Chicago Press, 1987, p. 191.

38. C. A. Dwyer, "The Role of Tests and Their Construction in Producing Apparent Sex-Related Differences," *Sex-Related Differences in Cognitive Functioning,* Wittig and Petersen, editors, New York: Academic Press, 1971, p. 342.

39. Marilyn French, *Beyond Power,* New York: Summit Books, 1985, p. 385.

40. Gould, *Mismeasure of Man,* p. 233.

41. *New York Times,* February 4, 1989. See Rosser (note 13) appendix I, for the complete court ruling.

42. For one state's experiment, see Karen De Witt, "Vermont Gauges Learning by What's in Portfolio," *New York Times,* April 24, 1991.

43. Rosser, *SAT Gender Gap,* p. 36.

44. Interview, David White, September 9, 1991.

45. Robert Williams, *Black Pride, Academic Relevance and Individual Achievement,* St. Louis: Robert Williams and Associates, undated, pp. 2–3.

46. Richard Dawkins, *The Selfish Gene,* New York: Oxford University Press, 1976, p. 158; Edward O. Wilson, *On Human Nature,* Cambridge, Massachusetts: Harvard University Press, 1978, p. 125; W. D. Hamilton, *Biosocial Anthropology,* New York: John Wiley, 1975, p. 134; Lionel Tiger and Robin Fox, *The Imperial Animal,* New York: Holt, 1989, p. 21.

47. Natalie Angier, "The Biology of What It Means to Be Gay," *New York Times,* September 7, 1991.

48. Rita Arditti, "Feminism and Science," *Science and Liberation,* Rita Arditti, Pat Brennan, and Steve Caviak, editors, Boston: South End Press, 1979, pp. 366–367.

FOUR: RE-LEARNING

1. See the findings of the Pioneer Health Center in Peckham, England, a family research group that became internationally known in the 1930s and '40s, and personal observations from two decades of running an experimental playgroup, by Alison Stallibrass, in *The Self-Respecting Child*, New York: Warner Books, 1979.

2. Marilyn French, *Beyond Power*, New York: Summit Books, 1985, p. 498.

3. René Dubos, *The Dreams of Reason: Science and Utopias*, New York: Columbia University Press, 1961, p. 116.

4. Alix Kates Shulman, *Red Emma Speaks: Selected Writings and Speeches of Emma Goldman*, New York: Random House, 1972, p. 133.

5. Michael Murphy and Steven Donovan, *The Physical and Physiological Effects of Meditation*, Big Sur, California: The Esalen Institute, 1989. Their massive survey is skewed toward "beginner's experiences," since they are more often studied. As Murphy says, it "maps the foothills of meditation, with a few glances at the peaks."

6. Nancy J. Napier, *Recreating Your Self: Help for Adult Children of Dysfunctional Families*, New York: W. W. Norton, 1990, p. 139.

7. John Bradshaw, an "adult child" of an alcoholic father, developed these techniques in his own life and now teaches them widely. His television series for the Public Broadcast System are available by writing Bradshaw Cassettes, P.O. Box 980547, Houston, Texas 77098. It is also in book form as *Bradshaw On: The Family, A Revolutionary Way of Self-Discovery*, Deerfield Beach, Florida: Health Communications, 1988. Also see John Bradshaw, *Homecoming: Reclaiming and Championing Your Inner Child*, New York: Bantam Books, 1990.

8. Louise De Salvo, *Virginia Woolf: The Impact of Sexual Abuse on Her Life and Work*, New York: Ballantine Books, 1989.

9. From interviews with Judy Collins, June 1991. For one of her watercolors, see the cover of her album "Sanity and Grace," Gold Castle Records, 1987.

10. See *African Canvas: The Art of West African Women*, photographs and text by Margaret Courtney-Clarke, foreword by Maya Angelou, New York: Rizzoli, 1990.

11. Lucy R. Lippard, *Mixed Blessings: New Art in Multicultural America*, New York: Pantheon Books, 1990.

12. David Feinstein and Peg Elliott Mayo, *Rituals for Living and Dying: How We Can Turn Loss and the Fear of Death into an Affirmation of Life*, San Francisco: HarperCollins, 1990.

13. Robert Farris Thompson, *Flash of the Spirit: African & African-American Art & Philosophy,* New York: Random House, 1983; Vintage Books, 1984.

14. For an overview of such studies and his experiences, see Norman Cousins, *Head First: The Biology of Hope,* New York: Dutton, 1989.

15. For information, write Paul Winter, Earth Music, P.O. Box 68, Litchfield, Connecticut 06759.

16. For information, send a $5 mailing fee to: UCAN Confidence Clinic, 308 S.E. Jackson Street, Roseburg, Oregon 97470. The clinic also needs funds for programs that government funds will not support. Contributions are tax deductible.

17. As a result of visiting the Cherokee Nation in 1885, Senator Henry Dawes of Massachusetts wrote: "There was not a pauper in that nation, and the nation did not owe a dollar . . . the defect of their system was apparent. They have got as far as they can go, because they own their land in common . . . there is no enterprise to make your home any better than your neighbors. There is no selfishness, which is at the bottom of civilization." (Quoted in *Mankiller: An Autobiography* by Wilma P. Mankiller with Robert J. Conley, unpublished manuscript.) For the Cherokee Nation's path back to the autonomy Dawes described, see "Leaders as Guides of Return" in chapter 2.

18. Letty Cottin Pogrebin, "Anti-Semitism in the Women's Movement," *Ms.,* June 1982. Reprinted in *Deborah, Golda, and Me* by Letty Cottin Pogrebin, New York: Crown Publishers, 1991, pp. 208–209.

19. To value the work of production, human maintenance, and reproduction done by women, and to value the environment, see a recommendation on restructuring the National System of Accounts in Marilyn Waring, *If Women Counted,* New York: Harper & Row, 1989.

20. Alfie Kohn, *No Contest: The Case Against Competition,* Boston: Houghton Mifflin, 1986, pp. 46–47, 99.

FIVE: BODIES OF KNOWLEDGE

1. Dean Ornish, M.D., *Program for Reversing Heart Disease,* New York: Random House, 1990.

2. Norman Cousins, *Anatomy of an Illness,* New York: Bantam Books, 1981, pp. 49–69; also *Head First: The Biology of Hope,* New York: Dutton, 1989, pp. 229–242. The force of physical response unleashed by belief is so strong that, even when a real medication is given, its logical effect can be reversed; for instance, a nausea-inducing drug can cure nausea.

3. Deepak Chopra, *Quantum Healing: Exploring the Frontiers of Mind/Body Medicine,* New York: Bantam Books, 1989, p. 33.

4. "Survey: Sex and Self-Esteem," *Medical Aspects of Human Sexuality,* vol. 17, no. 5, May 1983, pp. 202–203. The key is choice: the survey also noted that some people are "intentionally and happily celibate."

5. Laura Lederer, editor, *Take Back the Night: Women on Pornography,* New York: William Morrow, 1980.

For a compendium of studies on the impact of pornography, also see Franklin Mark Osanka and Sara Lee Johann, editors, *Sourcebook on Pornography,* Lexington, Massachusetts: Lexington Books, 1989.

6. Susan Saegert and Roger Hart, "The Development of Environmental Competence in Girls and Boys," Michael A. Salter, editor, *Play: Anthropological Perspectives,* West Point, New York: Leisure Press, 1977, pp. 157–175.

7. Alison Stallibrass, *The Self-Respecting Child,* New York: Warner Books, 1979, p. 206.

8. Study by D. Laura Ann Petitto, McGill University, Montreal, Canada, reported by Natalie Angier, *New York Times,* March 22, 1991.

9. For the origin of this insight — and the sort of book women give each other as an inspiring gift — see *Writing a Woman's Life* by Carolyn Heilbrun, New York: W. W. Norton, 1988.

10. " 'They respected what I said on the same level that they talked to their friends,' said one gifted girl. 'My parents always talked to me as if I were an adult,' said another." From a study of gifted children reported by Phyllis Rosser, "How to Help Your Gifted Daughter," *Gifted Children Newsletter,* September 1990, p. 14. Also see Teresa M. Amabile, *Growing Up Creative: Nurturing a Lifetime of Creativity,* New York: Crown, 1989.

11. Jane Howard, *Margaret Mead: A Life,* New York: Simon and Schuster, 1984, p. 22.

12. Jean Houston, "The Mind of Margaret Mead," *Quest,* July/August 1977, p. 25.

13. Houston, "Consider the Stradivarius . . . ," *Dromenon,* 1977, p. 40.

14. Houston, "The Mind of Margaret Mead," p. 24.

15. Ibid., p. 26.

16. Houston, "Consider the Stradivarius . . . ," p. 41.

17. In 1947, psychologists Kenneth B. and Mamie Clark conducted a classic study of black children ages three to seven in Massachusetts and Arkansas. Two thirds of them picked white dolls when given a choice of four, two black and two white. It was such poignant evidence of low

self-esteem among black children that it was cited in the 1954 Supreme Court decision mandating school desegregation. Forty years later, however, a Connecticut study using Cabbage Patch dolls, identical except for color, produced the same sad result — 65 percent of black children chose white dolls — as did another study in Trinidad. As one of these two later studies found, only when self-esteem was bolstered by praising children who selected the black doll was the preference for the white dolls reversed. See proceedings of the American Psychological Association meeting, New York City, 1987. Also reported in *Time,* September 14, 1987, p. 74.

18. Study in *Pediatrics* as reported in *New York Times,* February 11, 1988.

19. Cathy Meredig, a Minneapolis engineer, has created the Happy To Be Me doll, with realistic measurements, as an alternative fantasy/fashion doll. "I want to offer girls a healthier body image," as she explained in August 1991 about her Self-Esteem Toy Corporation. At this writing, it's too soon to know whether her entry can compete with the giant Mattel Corporation, which manufactures Barbie.

20. This insight is developed by Naomi Wolf in *The Beauty Myth: How Images of Beauty Are Used Against Women,* New York, William Morrow, 1991, p. 17.

21. Joan Jacobs Brumberg, *Fasting Girls: The Emergence of Anorexia Nervosa as a Modern Disease,* Cambridge, Massachusetts: Harvard University Press, 1988, p. 3.

22. Wolf, *The Beauty Myth,* p. 182. Wolf's anger at the ignoring of this problem that is destroying some of the most talented women of her generation has produced an effective chapter, "Hunger," that anyone who doubts the seriousness of eating disorders should read; pp. 179–217.

23. Dr. Elizabeth Morgan, the Washington, D.C., plastic surgeon best known for having gone to jail rather than disclose her daughter's whereabouts to a sexually abusing father, had previously done research showing that women addicted to multiple plastic surgeries were also often trying to punish their bodies for "attracting" incestuous abuse.

24. Gloria Steinem, "Men and Women Talking," *Outrageous Acts and Everyday Rebellions,* New York: Holt, Rinehart and Winston, 1983, pp. 176–190.

25. For one account of the life of Stephen Biko and the messages of the Black Consciousness Movement, see *Biko* by Donald Woods, New York: Henry Holt, 1987.

26. Clitoridectomies and often infibulation — the removal of the entire clitoris and the labia, plus joining the scraped sides of the vulva so they grow together in a chastity belt of flesh that must be ripped open and

resewn for every insemination and birth — are practiced in large areas of the Middle East, Africa, and some other parts of the world by some groups of Moslems, Coptic Christians, indigenous tribal religions, Catholics and Protestants, and Fellasha, an Ethiopian Jewish sect. In England and in the United States, clitoridectomies were sometimes performed as treatment for masturbation, sexual "deviance," or prostitution. Robin Morgan and Gloria Steinem, "The International Crime of Genital Mutilation," *Outrageous Acts and Everyday Rebellions,* pp. 292–300.

27. R. Harding, "Gay Youth Six Times More Likely to Commit Suicide," *The Washington Blade,* May 16, 1986, p. 1. For information on gay adolescents, both problems and helpful programs, contact The Hetrick-Martin Institute, 401 West Street, New York, New York 10014.

28. The highest medical estimate of males who need circumcision due to the tightness of the foreskin is 10 percent. No increased cleanliness has been proved, and there is considerable testimony that circumcision toughens the tip of the penis and reduces sexual pleasure. It seems to be largely a symbolic testimony of allegiance to a patriarchal god.

29. Blanche Wiesen Cook, *Eleanor Roosevelt,* New York: Viking Press, 1992. The first of two volumes.

30. Vincent Bozzi, "The Body in Question," *Psychology Today,* February 1988, p. 10. (For the entire study, see the *International Journal of Eating Disorders,* vol. 6.)

31. Rita Freedman, *Bodylove: Learning to Like Our Looks — and Ourselves,* New York: Harper & Row, 1988, pp. 21–25.

32. Wolf, *The Beauty Myth,* p. 94.

33. Ibid., pp. 49 and 95.

34. Linda Tschirhart Sanford and Mary Ellen Donovan, *Women and Self-Esteem,* New York: Anchor/Doubleday, 1984, pp. 370 and 369.

35. Freedman, *Bodylove,* pp. 168–169 and 241.

36. Elaine Hatfield and Susan Sprecher, *Mirror, Mirror,* New York: State University of New York Press, 1988.

37. "Self-Esteem," *The Lancet,* October 22, 1988, p. 943.

38. Freedman, *Bodylove,* pp. 28–29.

39. *Vogue,* August 1988, p. 250.

40. Freedman, *Bodylove,* p. 82; Wolf, *The Beauty Myth,* pp. 185–187.

41. With thanks to Carolyn Heilbrun who used this Márquez line in a more positive way when told she looked young: "No, not young, I am an older woman with pizazz, which is not the same thing." "Naming a New Rite of Passage," *Smith Alumnae Quarterly,* Summer 1991, p. 28.

42. Thomas D. Rees, M.D., *Aesthetic Plastic Surgery*, vol. II, Philadelphia: W. B. Saunders, 1980, pp. 19–39.

43. Wolf, *The Beauty Myth*, p. 290.

44. John B. McKinlay and Sonja M. McKinlay, "Depression in Middle-Aged Women: Social Circumstances versus Estrogen Deficiency," *The Psychology of Women*, Mary Walsh, editor, New Haven: Yale University Press, 1987, pp. 158–159.

45. Bettyann Kevles, "Hot Flash," *Moxie*, April 1990, pp. 26 and 118.

For Yewoubdar Beyenne's research, see *Menarche to Menopause: Reproductive Lives in Peasant Women of Two Cultures*, New York: State University of New York Press, 1989.

46. Study conducted by James Pennebaker at Southern Methodist University, as reported in *New Age Journal*, July/August 1990, p. 32.

47. Robin Morgan, "Network of the Imaginary Mother," *Upstairs in the Garden*, New York: W. W. Norton, 1990, p. 93.

SIX: ROMANCE VERSUS LOVE

1. G. D. Klingopulos, "The Novel as Dramatic Poem," quoted in Emily Brontë, *Wuthering Heights*, New York: Random House, Modern Library Edition, 1978, p. xvii.

2. Royal A. Gettmann, "Introduction," *Wuthering Heights*, p. ix.

3. Charlotte Brontë, "Biographical Notice of Ellis and Acton Bell," *Wuthering Heights*, pp. xxv–xxvi.

4. Ibid., pp. xxv, xx, and xxiv–xxv.

5. Adrienne Rich, "Jane Eyre: The Temptations of a Motherless Woman," *On Lies, Secrets, and Silence*, New York: W. W. Norton, 1979, p. 90.

6. "Survey: Sex and Self-Esteem," *Medical Aspects of Human Sexuality*, volume 17, number 5, May 1983, pp. 197–211.

7. Helen Handley, editor, *The Lovers' Quotation Book*, Wainscott, New York: Pushcart Press, 1986, p. 63.

8. Linda Sanford and Mary Ellen Donovan, *Women and Self-Esteem*, New York: Anchor/Doubleday, 1984, p. 123.

9. Virginia Goldner, Peggy Penn, Marcia Sheinberg, Gillian Walker, "Love and Violence: Gender Paradoxes in Volatile Attachments," *Family Process*, December 1990, volume 20, number 4, p. 343.

10. Handley, *Lovers' Quotation Book*, p. 45.

11. Charlotte Davis Kasl, *Women, Sex, and Addiction: A Search for Love and Power*, New York: Ticknor & Fields, 1989, p. 130.

12. Frank Pittman, *Private Lies,* New York: W. W. Norton, 1989, p. 183.

13. Q. D. Leavis, "Introduction," Charlotte Brontë, *Jane Eyre,* London and New York: Penguin Books, 1966, p. 11.

14. Rich, "Jane Eyre," p. 96.

15. Ibid.

16. For a critical look at measures of masculinity and androgyny, see Joseph Pleck, *The Myth of Masculinity,* Cambridge, Massachusetts: MIT Press, 1983.

17. For conditions of creativity in our children and ourselves, see Teresa M. Amabile, *Growing Up Creative: Nurturing a Lifetime of Creativity,* New York: Crown, 1989.

18. For more about the case for and tradition of androgyny, see Carolyn G. Heilbrun, *Toward a Recognition of Androgyny,* New York: Harper Colophon Books, Harper & Row, 1974.

19. Barbara Risman, "Intimate Relationships from a Microstructural Perspective: Men Who Mother," *Gender and Society,* vol. I, 1987, pp. 6–32.

20. Marilyn French, "Self-respect: A Female Perspective," *The Humanist,* November/December 1986, p. 22.

21. Alice Walker, *Revolutionary Petunias and Other Poems,* New York: Harcourt Brace Jovanovich, 1973, p. 66.

SEVEN: A UNIVERSAL "I"

1. Marilyn French, *Beyond Power,* New York: Summit Books, 1985, p. 458.

2. Jean Liedloff, *The Continuum Concept: Allowing Human Nature to Work Successfully,* Reading, Massachusetts: Addison-Wesley, 1991, pp. 4–8.

3. Interview with Vandana Shiva by Ann Spanel, "Indian Women and the Chipko Movement," *Woman of Power,* Spring 1988, pp. 26–31. For direct information, write to: Chipko Information Center, P.O. Silyara via Ghansali, Tehri Garwhal, U.O. India 249 155.

4. Diane Ackerman, *A Natural History of the Senses,* New York: Random House, 1990, p. 255.

5. Ibid., p. 256.

6. From an 1854 speech given in Duwamish by Chief Seattle (also known as Chief Sealth) at an assembly of tribal nations in the Pacific Northwest and translated by Dr. Henry Smith in the style of the day. Writer Ted Perry reconstructed it from Smith's notes in 1970, and it has been used

with some modifications by Native American and environmental groups since then. For the original Smith notes, see W. C. Vanderwerth, *Indian Oratory: Famous Speeches by Noted Indian Chieftains,* New York: Ballantine Books, circa 1887, pp. 97–102. For Perry's version, see John Seed et al., *Thinking Like a Mountain,* Philadelphia: New Society Publishers, 1988, pp. 68–73.

7. Ackerman, *Natural History,* p. 147.

8. Paul Delaney, "El Toro Fights Go On, But 'Oles!' Are Fewer," *New York Times,* August 6, 1988.

9. Sam Keen, *Fire in the Belly: On Being a Man,* New York: Bantam Books, 1991, p. 139.

10. Beth W. McLeod, "Someone to Care For," *Christian Science Monitor,* February 13, 1989.

11. "Loving Paws, Helping Hands," *New York Times,* May 16, 1991.

12. McLeod, "Someone to Care For."

13. Francine Patterson, "Conversations with a Gorilla," *National Geographic,* October 1978, 154:438–65. To become a member of the Gorilla Foundation dedicated to the protection, preservation, and propagation of threatened and endangered gorillas and great apes, send $25 to the Gorilla Foundation, P.O. Box 620-530, Woodside, California 94062.

14. Quoted by John P. Briggs and F. David Peat, *Looking Glass Universe: The Emerging Science of Wholeness,* New York: A Touchstone Book, Simon and Schuster, 1984, p. 276.

AFTERWORD

1. Some of the details in the following stories are disguised, since I did not ask permission to publish them while they were being told.

2. Carol Sternhell, "Sic transit Gloria," *The Women's Review of Books,* volume 9, number 9, June 1992.

3. Lead-in text for Naomi Wolf, "Fear & Loathing Deconstructed: A Long View of Gloria Steinem's New Book," *On the Issues,* fall 1992.

4. Mary Daly, "The Spiritual Dimension of Women's Liberation," *Radical Feminism,* Koedt, Levine, and Rapone, editors, New York: Quadrangle/New York Times Books, 1973, p. 259. (This 1971 article first appeared in *Notes from the Third Year.*)

5. James Gleick, "New Appreciation of the Complexity in a Flock of Birds," *New York Times,* November 24, 1987.

6. Nancy Gibbs, "The War Against Feminism," Joelle Attinger, "Stei-

nem: Tying Politics to the Personal," *Time,* March 9, 1992, pp. 50, 51, and 55.

7. Commissioned by the Ms. Foundation for Women and the Center for Policy Alternatives. For information, write Women's Voices, Ms. Foundation for Women, 141 Fifth Avenue, New York, New York 10010.

8. Judith Lewis Herman, M.D., *Trauma and Recovery,* New York: Basic Books, 1992, pp. 235–236.

9. Marge Piercy, "The low road," *The Moon Is Always Female,* New York: Alfred A. Knopf, 1980. Reprinted in *Cries of the Spirit: A Celebration of Women's Spirituality,* Marilyn Sewell, editor, Boston: Beacon Press, 1991, pp. 170–171.

Acknowledgments

You have met some of this book's family in its pages, but not all. Joanne Edgar, a sister founder of *Ms.* magazine, encouraged me to do it long before I had time to write a letter, and Letty Cottin Pogrebin spent many days going around to publishers with me as its agent, and then gave what would have been an agent's fee to the Ms. Foundation for Women. Robert Levine spent lawyerly and friendly time guiding it to a home with Little, Brown in Boston, where Jennifer Josephy, who had been my editor on *Outrageous Acts and Everyday Rebellions*, became the caring parent she is to all her books, and as you can guess from the preface, gave an extra measure of understanding here. If there were a Medal of Honor for editors, Jennifer would deserve it. When I was making a place to work after so many years of not-writing, Kristina Kiehl gave new meaning to friendship by doing everything from moving stacks of cardboard boxes to helping me get healthy, and Filippa Naess contributed her special magic to my first real home — which, I realized belatedly, is a symbol of the self. Many people kept this book in mind and sent ideas, especially Ann Marie Karl and Edith Van Horn, and others gave me access to new worlds that enriched it, especially Dr. Bennett Braun, creator of the pioneering Dissociative Disorders Program at Rush Presbyterian Hospital in Chicago. Journalist Mary Beth Guyther searched out books and checked facts, and friends brought their sensitivities to reading and commenting: Suzanne Braun Levine, Robin Morgan, Donna Jenson, Frank Thomas, Rebecca Adamson, Robert Allen, and Alice Walker especially, plus Egyptologist James Romano, and one young woman in the middle of a disastrous romance who field-tested chapter 6. There are also people who took on more work because I was around less: Ruth Bower and Robin Morgan at *Ms.* magazine, Marie Wilson at the Ms. Foundation for Women, and Kristina Kiehl and Julie Burton at

Voters for Choice; groups from Canada to Japan who let me cancel or rearrange events; and Irwin Winkler, Alice Mayhew, and Carolyn Heilbrun, who generously allowed delays in major projects. Beth Rashbaum, my New York editor for the last two years — without whose invaluable advice and deadline-setting I probably would still be writing — also spent many late nights in the last months, as did Diana James, my assistant and a sister Ohioan who has lived through all of this book's gestation. My former *Ms.* partner Patricia Carbine sent supportive health food, and copyeditor Peggy Freudenthal gave up her weekends to my manuscript and galleys. I owe special gratitude to Suzanne Braun Levine, a member of my chosen family, who has been part of all of the above. Most personally of all, I thank Kitty LaPerriere, a wise woman and family therapist whose work in depth and in private helps me and many others write the book of our own lives.

Index